The London Sketch Club

David Cuppleditch

ALAN SUTTON PUBLISHING LIMITED

First published in the United Kingdom in 1994 by
Alan Sutton Publishing Ltd
Phoenix Mill · Far Thrupp · Stroud · Gloucestershire

First published in the United States of America in 1994 by
Alan Sutton Publishing Inc
83 Washington Street · Dover · NH 03820

British Library Cataloguing in Publication Data
A catalogue record of this book is available from the British Library.

ISBN 0 7509 0696 0

Library of Congress Cataloguing in Publication Data applied for

Front cover illustration:
Detail taken from a design by Lee Hankey to a London Sketch Club smoker of 27 March 1903
at the Continental Gallery, 157 New Bond Street.

Typeset in 10/11 pt Sabon
Typesetting by
Alacrity Phototypesetters, Banwell Castle, Avon.
Printed in Great Britain by
Redwood Books, Trowbridge.

Contents

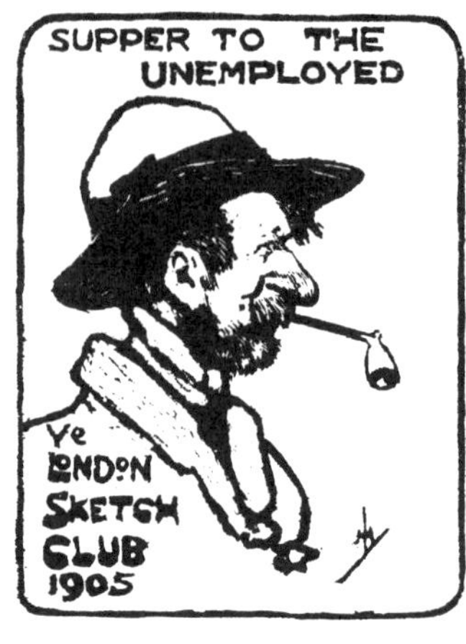

Foreword

In the late 'fifties I remember looking through some back numbers of *Punch*, stored away in my old school library, which were full of wonderful cartoons. These cartoons were, to say the least, mini works of art. Little did I realise then that, some fifteen years later, I was to discover the haunt where many of these artists met to discuss their work, a little known art club called The London Sketch Club. I then started researching this subject but it has taken some twenty years to resolve my researches. In the meantime I assembled my notes together in book form in 1978 in *The London Sketch Club*, which has since become something of a collectors' item (a recent volume offered for sale was at £55.00, ten times the original price of £5.50). I should be flattered that the book has been plundered by a variety of people currently interested in the subject. In putting this volume together I am extremely grateful to John Newman of Grantham who patiently typed the manuscript, Jean of Alacrity Phototypesetters who put everything together and last but not least Simon Thraves formerly of Alan Sutton Publishing who agreed to publish it. There are so many people to whom I am indebted for information that it is difficult to know where to begin. In particular I am grateful to the late Arnold Beauvais for his correspondence and wit; Ern Shaw, a cartoonist of Cottingham, Hull, who in his nineties could still crack a joke (Ern Shaw was a pupil of Percy Bradshaw's Press Art School); Derek Van Abbe (son of Solomon Van Abbe) who became a TV presenter and journalist in Australia; the late Joan Hassall who retired to the pretty village of Malham in Yorkshire and with whom I went to stay; Joan was extremely kind and, despite her considerable reputation as an engraver, also very modest (she lived frugally but still cooked me a concoction of scrambled and curled eggs, the only meal her father John Hassall was known to have cooked for himself); Roy Heron, author of *Cecil Aldin – Story of a Sporting Artist*, whose suggestions have been invaluable; Roy Carne of Helston in Cornwall; David Langdon; Phil May (son of Fred May, long time caricaturist on the *Tatler*; Michael Felmingham, author of *The Illustrated Gift Book 1880-1930*; Clifford Fisher (present archivist of the LSC); Geoffrey Johnson of Saltford nr Bristol; and indeed anyone else whom I have not had space to mention.

David Cuppleditch
1994

CHAPTER 1

Formation of the London Sketch Club

In the nineteenth century an Englishman's club was of great importance. The order of daily life forced groups of people with a common interest to gather together and face the world collectively. The range of clubs from the You-be-quiet Club to Whites or Pratts and the Constitutional was enormous.

The story behind the London Sketch Club started with the Langham Sketching Club founded in 1838, which, in turn, was an off-shoot of the Artists Society founded eight years earlier in 1830. The Langham met every Friday evening during the winter months to complete a two hour sketch from one or two given subjects. The sketches were then fixed around the walls and "received much criticism", after which supper was served. This was followed by entertainment.

All the leading black and white artists were members of the Langham at some time or another including Fred Walker, George Pinwell, Sir John Tenniel and Charles Keene to name but a few. Probably the most significant book illustrator was Arthur Rackham. During the Victorian era the illustrated book was the delight of every middle class household and there was always plenty of work for up and coming illustrators. Once or twice during the season, members' friends were admitted to the Langham where in crowded, smoke-laden rooms they were "regaled with the best bread and cheese, and beer that man could desire". After this they were entertained by professional and amateur artists alike.

The century culminated in "the glorious nineties" or "naughty nineties" when Edward VII, then Prince of Wales, was the darling of the realm. Conversaziones and smoking parties were commonplace, with music hall humour topping the bill. It was an age where the Bohemian and the aristocrat could rub shoulders in the bars of the Ritz or the Cafe Royale. Much has been written about the nineties and even more was recorded at the time in the dozens of weekly, monthly and quarterly periodicals such as the *Yellow Book* or *The Savoy*.

Against this background of frivolity the London Sketch Club was formed in 1898 by a few members of the Langham. The argument was over hot or cold suppers! It might seem laughable now but then after a hard day's work and a couple of hours sketching, a substantial meal was paramount. The breakaway group were sick of bread and·cheese and wanted a more adventurous menu. However the debacle included a number of underlying differences. Some older members of the Langham felt that these young "upstarts" were too big for their boots and their high spirited humour was hard to stomach so that when they left to form their own club it came as no surprise.

The prime movers were Dudley Hardy, Walter Fowler, Frank Jackson, Lance Thackeray, Robert Sauber, Tom Browne and Cecil Aldin. These, with Walter Churcher and Phil May, formed the first council and George Haite was asked if he would be president (an honour he couldn't refuse). So as far as talent was concerned, the new club had just as much artistic ability as the Langham, and the new society was inaugurated by a dinner at the Florence Restaurant on 1 April 1898 (April Fool's Day!)

Just as the Langham met on Friday nights at seven o'clock from October to May and completed a two hour sketch, so did the London Sketch Club. This method of working tested the artists' retentive powers, especially if there was no model present. It also improved the artists' imagination, examples of which came out in the illustrations of Arthur Rackham and Edmund Dulac (the former of the Langham Sketch Club and the latter of the London Sketch Club).

At nine o'clock lay members and visitors were admitted to the London Sketch Club and the evening's work was set up around the walls for criticism. Although the quality varied considerably from week to week, most of the work was of a very high standard and possessed a quality of freedom and spontaneity. At nine-thirty after a plain *"hot"* supper, the rest of the evening was given over to entertainment. Generally some professional singers or entertainers would turn up "giving generously of their best to such an appreciative audience". But if no professional entertainers were available, members improvised and entertained themselves with an equally amusing, if less conventional, programme. Light-hearted fooling and good natured leg-pulling were features of the Club. The only people not well received were "the self-opinionated bumptious snobs infatuated with their own self importance." Such people were roughly handled.

The hero of the Sketch Club was undoubtedly Phil May who in 1898 was already famous and an alcoholic. Although he never worked at the Club and only made one or two visits at supper time he regularly sent in contributions to the exhibitions. He was very much the figure head of the Club and has been nicknamed "the grandfather of English illustration". His one and only sculpture entitled "If I ever reach ninety" used to hang in the Sketch Club but sadly in recent times has disappeared.

Phil May's exploits around London's clubland are legendary. A delightful example regarding Phil May and Frank Brangwyn had occurred only three years earlier in 1895, when the artists went on holiday to Picardy with their wives. Lillian May who was concerned about her husband's drinking habits appealed to Brangwyn to encourage her wayward husband to do some serious painting. "You know, Brangwyn", May is reputed to have said, "I really do want to paint".

They arrived at the village of Longpré, near Amiens, and put up at a pension. Phil May was enthusiastic and after breakfast the two artists set off to find a suitable spot to paint. En route Phil May said he was so hot that he needed a drink. Brangwyn's protestations fell on deaf ears as Phil May insisted he only wanted one drink. The pair soon found a nearby cafe where Phil May insisted on buying drinks all round and sketched one or two of the customers. Every time Brangwyn suggested they leave, Phil May would insist on "just one for the road", and promptly bought another round.

By lunch time the two artists tottered back to the pension. The following day Phil May apologised for his disgraceful behaviour but insisted on just one drink before the day's work. By now rumours of a generous Englishman buying drinks had gone round the village and there were hoards of people to greet the two artists as they

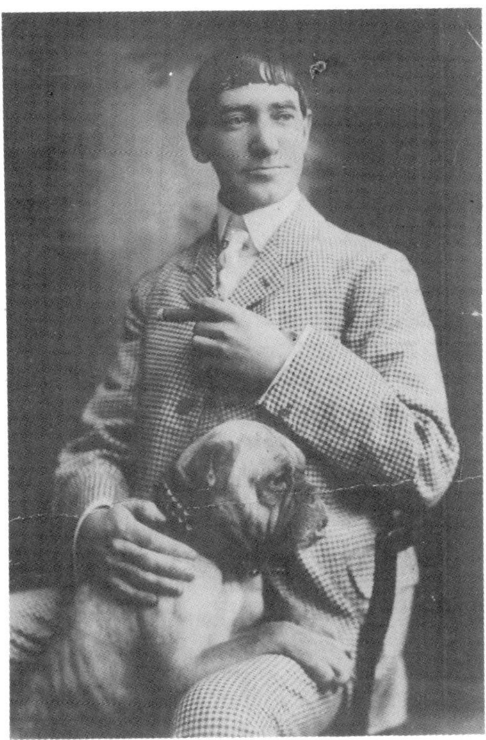

Phil May, RI (1864-1903). In this photograph of Phil May, with his dog Mr Blathers, we can see he was a snappy dresser. At one of his soirées he is reported to have said "Come into the next room and listen to my suit sing!" The London Sketch Club was comprised mostly of Phil May fans and his influence on cartoonists of the 20th Century cannot be underestimated.

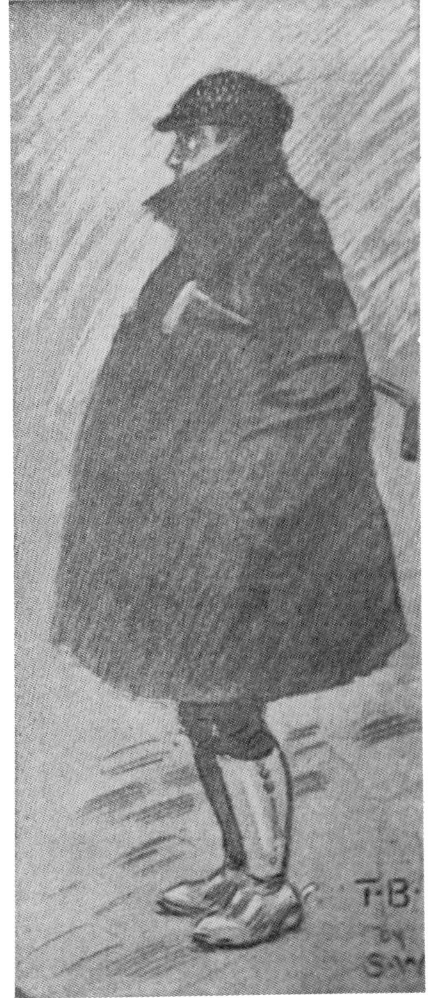

Tom Browne, RI (1872-1910). Caricature by Starr Wood. Tom Browne was a confirmed traveller, whether by horse, bicycle or cart. He was even referred to as the "cycle artist" because of his posters for the firm of Raleigh and journals such as *Cycling*, *The Wheel* and *Cycle Magazine*. He travelled extensively in the Far East (including China and Korea), on the Continent (notably Holland and Spain) and to the U.S.A. in 1904 and 1906. On the first of these American visits he drew a series of cartoons entitled "Boston Types" for the *Commercial Tribune*.

arrived at the cafe. Phil May was in his element chatting to everyone including the convivial patron.

This went on for a week and each day Phil May would thwart Brangwyn's attempt to entice the two artists into the countryside to paint. Brangwyn's failure led Lillian May to suggest that they start touring. But at every village where they stayed Phil May would always find a cafe. When at last they reached Paris Brangwyn left Phil May and his wife. He was annoyed that he had done no work and feared that if he remained in May's company for much longer he too might become alcoholic.

Phil May was an excellent horseman and he frequently rode from home to the office. He was determined not to make the same mistake as his father who died in a riding accident when Phil May was only nine years old. However someone remarked about his riding gear, with the inference that he gambled. "By the way, I believe that some people imagine that I am a dare devil sporting man. I don't so much mind the application of the first part of the phrase but I am not a betting man, and have never been to a race meeting in my life, except on one or two occasions when I went on behalf of a paper", Phil May replied.

Phil May had never had a drawing lesson in his life, but he was to surpass all the other Victorian giants, Tenniel, Du Maurier and Sambourne, in his influence on modern day cartoonists. Even Lord Leighton wanted to see him elected to the Royal Academy. Unhappily the benign President's death in 1896 put an end to any such proposal and instead May had to be content with the accolade of his brother artists. As G. R. Halkett, a contemporary from the *St Stephen's Review* and the *Pall Mall Gazette* said, "If the admiration and the love of his fellows be any warrant for an artist's immortality, Phil May is assured already of his seat with the immortals". He rose above his contemporaries with amazing verve and dexterity. And if one were to look at his drawings as a type of handwriting then his cartoons tell his auto-biography.

He was born in Leeds on 22 April 1864, the son of a failed engineer who had been an apprentice under the famous George Stephenson. His mother came from a theatrical family and nurtured her son's hankering for the stage. He was educated at St George's School, Leeds and subsequently joined the Grand Theatre in Briggate as a part time actor and assistant scenery artist. He was described by Augustus Moore (the brother of George Moore) as a "delicate, sensitive little fellow, whose father died when Phil was only nine". Despite this he faced life with true Yorkshire grit and determination.

In 1881 he left Leeds for London where he eventually obtained commissions from *Society* and the *St Stephen's Review* through the intervention of Lionel Brough, the celebrated Victorian actor. After his appointment to the staff of the *St Stephen's Review* in 1883 he married Lilian Farrer, whom he had first met when he was working at the Grand Theatre, Leeds. The turning point in his career came about when he was offered a three year contract with the *Sydney Bulletin*. A certain Mr William Traill, managing director of the *Bulletin*, had come over to London from Australia and managed to tempt Phil away.

The three years in Sydney were happy ones. It was here that he learnt how to eliminate the unnecessary lines in his drawing: "perhaps I should say that the printing machines of the *Bulletin* were my real master", he once confessed. The *Bulletin* was known as the "Bushman's Bible" and touted admirers from Alice Springs to Perth. Through Phil May's influence, according to David Low, "The

Bulletin grew a team of social and political artists it would have been hard to beat anywhere in the world. In the matter of style and ability it was good: in the matter of satirical approach and content it was better."

On his return to Europe he studied for a time in Rome and Paris before rejoining the *St Stephen's Review* in 1890. His joint series "The Parson and the Painter", which William Allison wrote and he illustrated, was to set the seal on his fame. It was the demise of the *St Stephen's Review* that forced Phil May to work for *Pick-me-up* and the *Daily Graphic*, although he contributed to nearly all of the important magazines and journals of the 1880-1900 period.

His advice to younger artists was to draw from life and keep on drawing from life. Observation was the key-note and in this context he collected masses of material for his characters and types. Filling literally hundreds of sketch pads and notebooks with his doodles and delicate drawings, he would turn them into cartoons at a later date. Unfortunately he was a kindly soul and often gave his work away. Moreover there was always "open house" at the Mays' which attracted many scroungers as well as admirers. No doubt this was due to the barrel of whisky which often had to be refilled at many of May's impromptu soirées. Eventually his wife had to put a stop to his generosity because not only were the "leeches" drinking his whisky but they were stealing his work as well. She forced Phil to sign his drawings with "Not to be taken away, the property of Lilie May".

This same generosity was extended to practically every bar in London where Phil May was known for his "drinks all round" attitude. If he ran out of money he would simply dash off a sketch, hawk it around Fleet Street, where he had an arrangement with one or two of the editors, and draw the money. A five pound note was always made available with the hall porter in case Mr May needed some ready cash.

On one occasion Phil May and a journalist named Grew were sent by the *Daily Graphic* to cover the Chicago World's Fair. The journey was a glorious binge and although May said that America did not agree with him the two came back via a westerly route and made it a round-the-world cruise. When the pair landed in London, having done nothing in Chicago, they expected an editorial reproof. But there were flags, banners and bunting embroidered with "G" and "M". "Look George", said Phil, tugging at his friend's sleeve. "Welcome to Grew and May. They're pleased to see us back again." They soon found out that the festivities were not for them but to celebrate the engagement of Prince George and Princess Mary.

When he was eventually asked to join the famous *Punch* table in 1895 — the same year as the famous Oscar Wilde trials — he carefully carved his initials next to those of that other great *Punch* cartoonist, Charles Keene. On that day in February 1895 Phil May was slightly nervous, a bit shy and overawed by the traditions of such a distinguished group. He sat at the deal table, roughly shaped like a running track, and listened to the discussion about the week's business. Eventually it was time to talk of next week's political cartoon and the editor F. C. Burnand, with his customary aplomb, rose to his feet. "Gentlemen, the cartoon!" he ordered. The first few minutes after a generous meal was not necessarily the best time to discuss weighty matters and although Phil May stayed unusually sober on this occasion he was reputed to have slid under the table at future *Punch* dinners.

The magazine *Punch* was a national institution but it is difficult to believe that it was started as early as 1840, when Mark Lemon, the first editor, eventually called it *Punch* rather than the initial *London Charivari*. As a magazine it had been

Robert Sauber, RBA. (1868-1936). Although he was principally a "fine" artist, Sauber was not averse to designing a few advertisements, notably for Hinde's Hair Curlers.

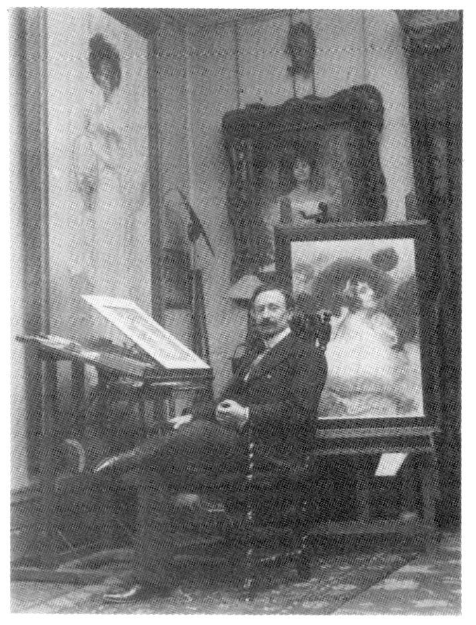

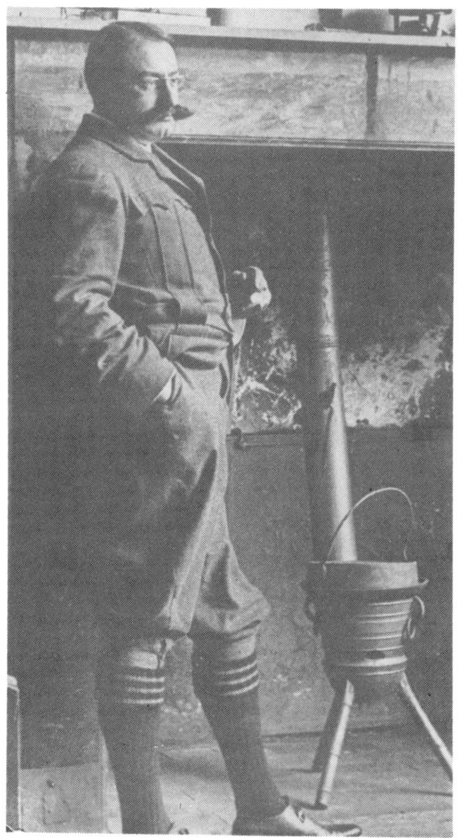

Dudley Hardy, RI (1867-1922) was responsible for reintroducing the poster craze which swept through Britain in the 1890s. Together with John Hassall their posters were bright, eye-catching and popular. Some of Hardy's posters for Sir Augustus Harris's theatrical ventures and the "Gaiety Girl" are still remembered to this day. But the most effective design was "The Yellow Girl" designed for Jerome K. Jerome's monthly magazine *To-day*, which took London by storm. Dudley Hardy had a way of shocking folk into attention in much the same way that French contemporaries made similar use of the poster.

responsible for giving the word "cartoon" its present meaning, and through it artists such as Richard Doyle, John Leech and John Tenniel achieved enormous popularity. Perhaps it was John Leech who did the most to upgrade the status of the British cartoon, even more than Rowlandson and Gillray, but his drawing lacked a certain bite. He mixed well in society and was a popular figure with the hunting set. He tended to ridicule the working classes whereas Phil May was sympathetic to the costers and tramps of Victorian low life.

Francis Burnand was wary of the amiable newcomer Phil May, whose appointment was unusual amongst the staid illustrators of Bouverie Street. May gave Burnand some hair-raising moments. Once he sent in a sketch of "A page drawing" which should have been a full page drawing, not the tiny thumbnail sketch of an hotel page drawing a cork from a bottle. Nor was this an isolated incident. On another occasion when Phil May had "gone to ground" in Margate, leaving Burnand waiting for his illustrations for a Christmas issue, in desperation he sent a sandwich-board man to parade the streets of Margate with a special message for Phil May: "Remember the Christmas Issue".

Like a tiresome schoolboy Phil May was frequently hauled into the editorial sanctum for some outrage or other. Possibly the best example of Phil May's humour arose when one day he was given half an hour to think of an excuse. Hansoms were available at the office door and any number of theatrical costumiers were within a few minutes' drive. With this knowledge Phil made good use of his time. He left the *Punch* offices and returned within the half hour. After tapping timidly at the editor's door he made his entrance. Burnand, furious, turned around to find the penitent artist transformed into a forlorn Little Lord Fauntleroy. In his pathetic costume of black velvet with lace collar and white socks, once again Phil May had turned an editorial reproof into a roar of laughter.

In a sense he continued the grand tradition of John Leech who often kept Mark Lemon waiting for illustrations. As Edmund Yates recorded: "Half of Mark Lemon's time was spent in hansom cabs bowling away to Notting Hill, Brunswick or Kensington, chasing up his weekly cartoon". Although Phil May lived a rakish bohemian life and squandered his money on his friends, M. H. Spielman constantly championed his work and wrote:

> *Punch* was long in discovering him, but found him at last. Indeed, *Punch* could not afford to do without him, for Mr May, though barely more than thirty years of age, was already in the foremost rank of humorous draughtsmen of the day.

M. H. Spielman also wrote the monumental *History of Punch*, and described the famous *Punch* room in *The Magazine of Art* in 1894: the table was an oblong piece of deal with a water jug and two distinctly unbeautiful bohemian goblets standing on it. There was a tobacco box, "hardly less ugly", a snuff box and several long clay pipes. The portraits of *Punch*'s four editors, Mark Lemon, Shirley Brooks, Tom Taylor and Francis Burnand, hung amongst a plethora of cartoons on the walls. The original of John Leech's celebrated "Mr Punch's Fancy Ball" took pride of place amongst several coloured prints of hunting sketches. And there was a caricature of Mr Furniss by Mr Sambourne, another of Mr Sambourne by Mr Furniss, and a third of Mr Sambourne by himself.

The tradition that everyone who joined the *Punch* table carved his initials with a pen-knife on the famous piece of deal had started nearly forty years earlier. It began with Thackeray and John Leech who had both gone to Charterhouse: it was perhaps a throwback to their public school days. Another feature of the *Punch* room was a pair of statuettes in plaster of John Leech and Thackeray by Sir Edgar Boehm. Phil May frequently treated the weekly *Punch* dinner with irreverence, and although the legend that he was so drunk that he signed his initials under the table is totally unfounded, he was often absent. On these occasions Bernard Partridge would supply him with a menu card "to take back to Lil as evidence".

It seems fitting that Phil May called his horse Punch, and he frequently lost it. The first time was when he visited Romano's, the fashionable meeting place of the 'nineties for bohemian artists and journalists. Phil returned home by hansom cab after a riotous evening. The next morning he went back to Romano's to find that Punch had been stabled overnight. For a long time afterwards whenever Phil showed his face in the bar at Romano's, the cry rose, "Where's the horse, Phil?"

He repeated this piece of absentmindedness at the Savage Club on more than one occasion when he had imbibed too freely, and his famous comment derived from one of those incidents: "Most extraordinary thing. Lost my horse. Had it a few days ago, but I can't for the life of me remember where I've left it". Numerous friends tried to "see Phil May home", usually unsuccesfully, and a score of amusing tales sprang from these intoxicated evenings.

May's style was the reverse of Aubrey Beardsley's. He threw out the decorative accoutrements and used economy of line to effect. If Beardsley was the dandy of Piccadilly, Phil May was the dandy of the racecourse. His peculiar features, fringe and loud suits were as individual as they were "sporting". Like the cigar which dangled from his lips he was as original as his slogan: "Have a whisky and soda! Have a cigar! Have a drawing!" Indeed this lifestyle was taken advantage of to such an extent that Phil May remained as poor as a churchmouse to the end of his days. He died on 5 August 1903 of cirrhosis of the liver, at the age of 39. Sir Henry Lucy (Toby of *Punch*) said: "With all his faults he was too good a fellow to go anywhere but heaven, although it will be a disappointment to the other place. The first thing he would have done was to stand drinks all round."

Phil May burnt the candle at both ends and towards the close of his life lived almost entirely off whisky and cigars. He was only five stone when he died and although he was referred to as an irresponsible genius the caption on his memorial plaque read, "A fellow of infinite jest". Phil May's London was strewn with pitfalls of every description: the Silver Grill, the Cheshire Cheese, Romano's, the Coal Hole and, last but not least, the Savage Club itself. Each served as an open door to the weary or thirsty traveller and Phil May took advantage of them all. Wherever he went he was easily recognisable and in every lounge he reigned supreme. As G. R. Halkett said,

> May's humour and his pathos were, alike, primitive and elemental. Laughter and tears were equally at his command. His fun was youthful and rarely tainted by cynicism, his pathos was instinctive and unsentimental. He was not the poet of low-life only; his was the pervading spirit that envelops every class and breed of men.

It is difficult to assess just how much Phil May influenced twentieth-century illustrators and cartoonists. A melange of followers sprang up after his death and acknowledged his wit and genius. Perhaps the most unusual of these was Bert Thomas, another *Punch* draughtsman. He brushed his hair forward in the same style

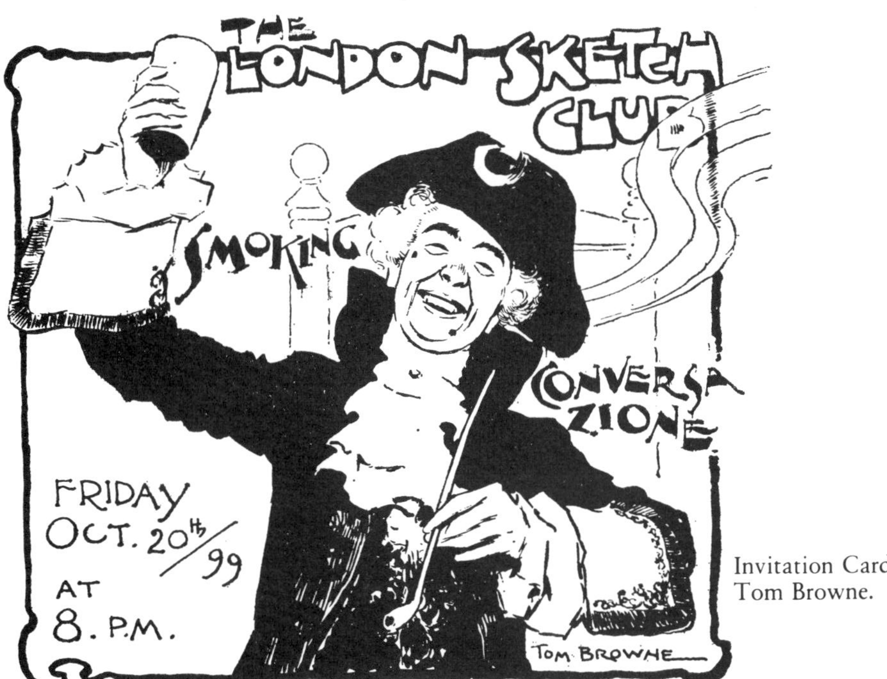

Invitation Card by Tom Browne.

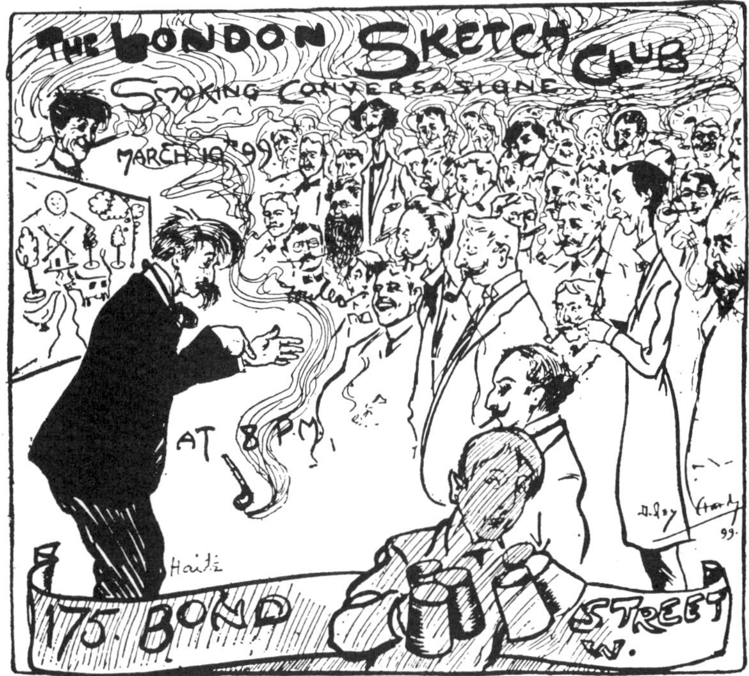

Invitation Card by Dudley Hardy.

as May and even asked to be buried next to his idol in Kensal Rise Cemetery. This was a Roman Catholic Cemetery. Phil May was buried there because not long before his death he had been converted to Catholicism by Francis Burnand. Like Beardsley he had been plagued by illness throughout his life, but unlike Beardsley he wrote his own epitaph a few days before he died:

Here lies poor old Phil.
While he lived he lied his fill.
And, now he's dead,
He's lying still.

Phil May's death marked the end of an era but heralded another. He was one of many graphic artists who died before they reached forty. Others included Houghton, Caldecott, Pinwell and Walker. Nevertheless the final word must rest with Charles Dana Gibson — of "Gibson Girl" fame, who said: "If a man's bad, I can tell you why he's bad; but when he's good as Phil May I can't tell you why he's good, because if I could I would do exactly the same."

One of Phil's closest friends was the actor, E. J. Odell. "Old Odell" was a member of the Langham, Savage and the London Sketch Club. He would often recite in his swallow-tailed beard and black sombrero, which gave him the mysterious air which seemed to surround his lifestyle. A good description of him came from Sidney Dark in his autobiography *Not such a Bad Life* (published in 1941 by Eyre & Spottiswoode):

> With his slouch hat and long white beard, he was a dignified and impressive figure; but he really was a thorough-paced old humbug, who for many years had managed comfortably to exist without any income and without doing a stroke of work. Odell had once been an actor, but it was so many years before that not even the next oldest inhabitant had ever seen him on the stage.

Thanks to the good offices of the late Lord Alverstone, Odell was elected a Brother of the Charterhouse and was a considerable nuisance to the authorities. One evening the Master took him by the arm and asked if he would be good enough carefully to read the rules and regulations hung on one of the walls. The old man polished his glasses, read the list carefully and slowly, and then, putting his glasses back into his pocket, remarked, "Thank God, I've broken every one of them."

One night when he had been drinking with Phil May at the Savage, Phil had fallen asleep. "Old Odell", taking pity on Phil, decided to take him home. He summoned a cab and took his drowsy charge to Maida Vale where Phil had a flat. He gently took Phil's latch key from his pocket and dumped him on a couch without disturbing Mrs May. Then he let himself out, carefully closing the door behind him. Unfortunately, he did not have enough cash by this time to charter a cab for the return journey so he walked all the way back to the Savage Club. Still he felt that he rendered a service to an old friend and so was comforted by this in his weary walk back. But when he returned, there was the figure of Phil May at the bar, glass in hand. Phil had woken from his sleep and returned to the club ahead of Odell in a smart hansom. Thus they finished the evening in style with drinks and more drinks.

After Phil May's death in 1903 a critic of the time is quoted as saying, "Tom Browne fills the gap that is left so tragically by Phil May." Like Phil May, Browne was phenominally successful at an early age and died before the age of forty. But,

14

unlike him, he had a very good business head and ran a prosperous printing business in Nottingham which produced his poster designs and show cards. Also their styles are so completely different: you could never mistake a Tom Browne for a Phil May, or vice versa.

Tom Browne had a struggle to reach fame and fortune. He was born in Nottingham and first attended St Mary's National School. He had to leave school at the tender age of eleven because, as he put it, he had become "a realisable family asset". He started as an errand boy, first with a milliner and then in the lace market. After a couple of years he changed his job and entered a lithographic firm of printers as an apprentice. He drew no pay but gained a lot of experience. He served his year's apprenticeship and then received the princely sum of one shilling a week. In his spare time he started designing labels for cigar boxes and any other work he could find. When he reached the age of seventeen he discovered the possibilities of cartoons.

Up to this point he had done drawings to amuse his friends and he regarded them as "an idle occupation". Then a friend suggested that he send some to one or two editors. The editor of a comic called *Scraps* was very interested and paid for them. (He paid 30 shillings for them, which represented three months wages!) Browne spent the next two years in Nottingham preparing to go to the great metropolis, and when he felt ready that's what he did.

Once down in London his first big success came when he was asked to produce the front page of a comic: he invented two characters, Weary Willie and Tired Tim. Halfpenny comic papers had come into their own and were tremendously popular. Weary Willie and Tired Tim, along with Ally Sloper, were an instant success. One paper recorded weekly sales of 600,000 due to these whimsical characters. Tom Browne had the market at his mercy and he cashed in on it.

He quickly established his reputation as a humorous artist. Not long after arriving in London he joined the Langham, being proposed by Dudley Hardy. He worked assiduously at the Friday evening meetings and his first picture was hung in the Royal Academy in 1897. Tom Browne managed to bridge the gap between fine art and illustration. Very few artists have ever been able to achieve one or the other, let alone both.

Stories similar to those surrounding Phil May seemed to surround Tom Browne. He travelled extensively in the Far East, including China and Korea, and on the Continent. He also visited the United States of America in 1904, where he drew a series of characters for the *Commercial Tribune* entitled "Boston Types", and revisited America in 1906. On one of his trips to Spain Tom Browne confessed that he did not know anything of the language. He used his pencil to convey his message to an innkeeper. To indicate that he would like some soup he drew a rough sketch of a soup tureen. Much to his dismay the innkeeper returned with the largest chamber pot the establishment possessed!

The Spanish trip was reported in the *Poster* magazine of October 1899:

Mr Browne had some great adventures in Spain and in the most savage districts positively took his life in his hands (and a revolver in his knapsack!). He actually undertook a tandem ride from Paris to Gibraltar, ploughing through hot weathers, snow and five days' continuous rain. He rides a Gee-gee, is fond of athletics, likes boxing and keeps a stout pair of single-sticks ready for interviewers. He says "I was in Paris during the recent troubles at the Grand Prix. There were four of us, we felt jolly and sang 'John Brown's Knapsack' as

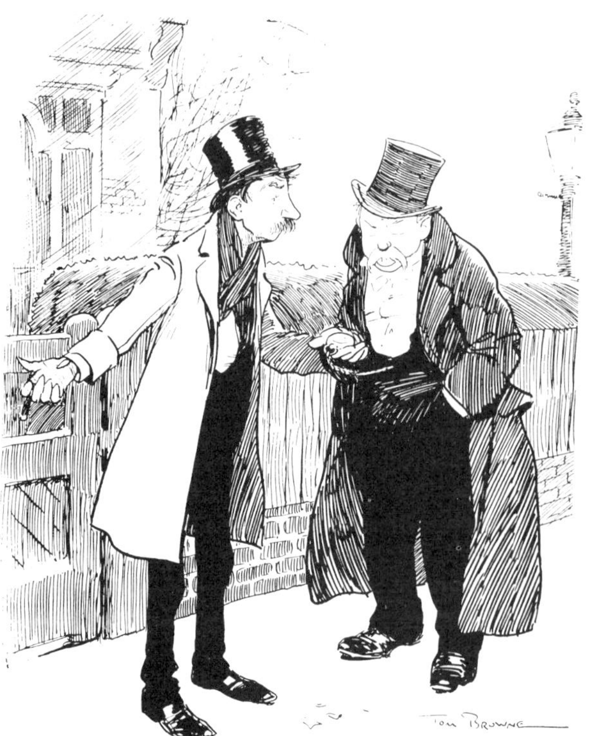

Cartoon by Tom Browne
After the Annual Dinner.

TUBBS: "Come inshide an' have a final, ole man."
TOOTLE: "Don shink sho, Rara late (looking at his
            watch) howsh the enemy?"
TUBBS: "Oh, thash allright, she's in bed."

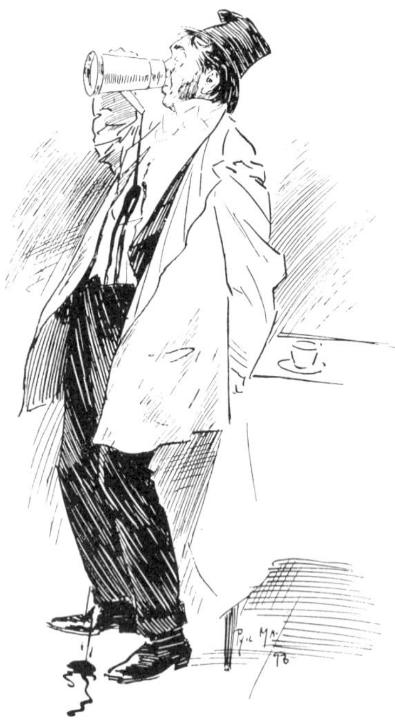

Cartoon by Phil May
"Mos' 'strornary thing! a'most
shertain th'was shome coffee in
it."

The Night Watchman by W.W. Jacobs
played an important role in the Sketch Club
annals. This version of Bill the Night
Watchman was by Joseph Simpson, RBA
(1879-1939), a prolific illustrator and designer of bookplates. W.W. Jacobs was
himself "a sad gloomy man", like Pett
Ridge, yet they were both humorous writers.

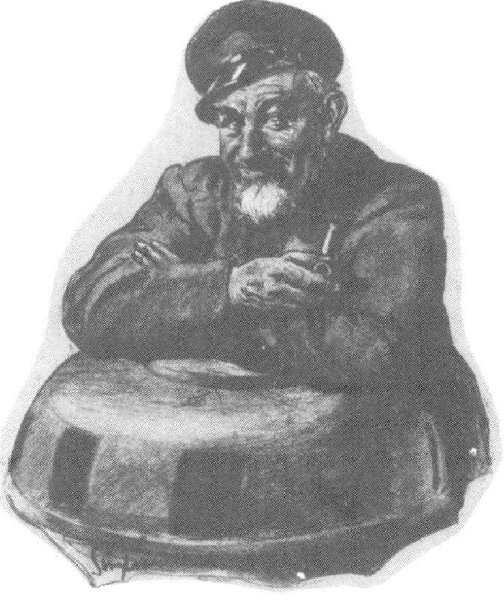

we strolled along. Suddenly we were surrounded by fierce gendarmes and arrested!''

If Tom Browne was one of the most popular members of this group, it was Dudley Hardy who was the ringleader of the rebels. Dudley Hardy was the son of T. B. Hardy, the marine painter and spent his early childhood pottering about his father's studio. As someone said, "he was born with a paintbrush in his mouth". At the age of fifteen he was sent to the Academy in Dusseldorf, where he rebelled and soon left. He remained in Dusseldorf, working on his own before being re-admitted to the Academy. Finding the conditions still stifling, he left after three months, returning to England to work first in his father's studio and then under A. A. Calderon. Eventually he went to Antwerp to study under Verlat before going on to Paris where he spent two years working under Raphael Collin and Carl Rossi. It was this nomadic art training that gave him a wide range of talents and knowledge.

Hardy, who had been an enthusiastic member of the Langham, now proceeded to knit together the various eccentric bodies of the London Sketch Club. He had worked in the Sudan as a war artist, had gone on a working holiday with Brangwyn to Morocco and had drunk with Phil May in France. He was well connected in the arts world, was something of an opera buff, and was also a very accomplished actor. It was his influence and drive that set the Club in motion.

Only three years earlier, in 1895, Dudley Hardy had been wining and dining the art correspondent from *The Sketch*. His report published on 6 March shows Hardy as one of the mainstays of the Langham, but that he had been thinking of an alternative art club for some time.

> One of the few really Bohemian institutions that I know is the Langham Sketching Club. Of course, there are sketching clubs all over the world, but in none is good fellowship in art so perfectly realised. As I went on its annual show the other night with Dudley Hardy, he was speaking warmly of its Friday evenings, most of which he has attended for years past. "We tried an imitation of it," he said. "Paris, in an upper room at Robinet's — of course, you know Robinet's, almost opposite the Gare Montparnasse. First night twelve of us came and worked, next week four men arrived, and then one turned up with a girl — he called her a 'lady student' — she didn't work. The following week five men came and four girls, and we danced. After that we gave it up. No; I just love the two hours' work at the given subject, and some stunning work is done that way; and I've sold a heap of my sketches there."

Also mentioned in the article were Claude Shepperson, D. Green, George Haite (who was President of the Langham in 1895) and Robert Sauber. All these members defected to the new London Sketch Club when it was formed in 1898. Behind them they left members of the Langham to cope with cold beer, whisky, bread, cheese, celery and tobacco.

Out of this group probably the best known in the 1890s was Robert Sauber, RBA (1868-1936). His studio was at 22 West Kensington Gardens and, apart from a brief spell later in life in Northampton, he lived most of his life in London. His work was described as piquant and graceful and he started his career as a lithographic artist. At the age of seventeen he won first prize at a lithographic exhibition held in Berlin and on his return he joined the Langham Sketching Club in 1887. He worked at the Langham every evening for about two years before setting off for Paris, where he studied at the Academy Julian under M. Benjamin Constant and Lefevre. A critic writing of his work in 1897 said, "Mr Sauber's success may be mainly attributed to his types of female beauty and his intimate knowledge of figure composition."

Sauber had a vast wardrobe of period costumes and was knowledgeable "with regard to the photographic value of colour in reproduction", which made him one of the most sought after illustrators of his day. He worked on Bristol board, which had a very smooth surface, and his drawings did not need much alteration before going to press. Sauber's style, a cross between that of Watteau and Franz Hals, caught the mood of the Edwardian era well. He even started his own School of Art, operating from "the old studio" in Phillimore Gardens, in 1897. Helping Sauber to run the school Mr Alyn Williams (then President of the Society of Miniature Painters whilst Sauber was Vice-President) gave lectures on miniatures. Sadly Sauber's school never rivalled Heatherley's and Sauber eventually retired to Hartwell near Northampton in 1925.

Sauber remained a member of the London Sketch Club during its formative years but resigned in 1903 after Haite was asked to step down as President. Meanwhile those early weekly suppers were held at various venus and restaurants, including Shelley's and The Goat, until they found suitable premises for their first working meetings: the Modern Gallery at 175 Bond Street.

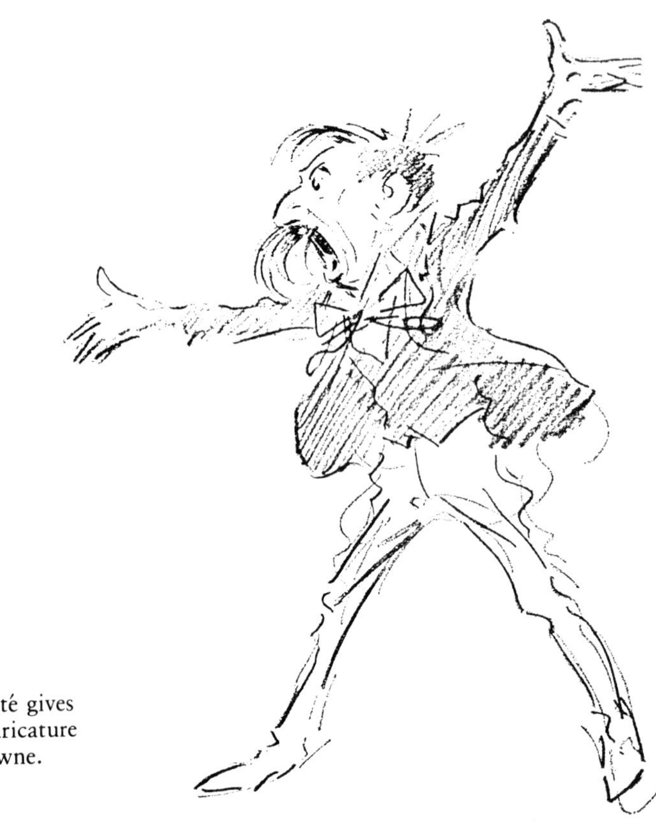

"George Haité gives advice", a caricature by Tom Browne.

CHAPTER 2

Sketchy Beginnings in the Modern Gallery

Only a year after the Sketch Club was formed, England found itself in the depths of the Boer War (1899-1902). Everything went badly to begin with and English troops suffered a great many defeats. They were also constantly locked up. First there was Kimberley and then Ladysmith, which were released only to be besieged once more; but it was Mafeking that was to affect the Club.

Robert Baden-Powell had put his name forward for membership when fellow artists, mostly with *Graphic* connections, were looking to swell their numbers. Baden-Powell admired the work of fellow clubman Conan Doyle and this could have tipped the balance: his decision to join the London Sketch Club was to lead to a lifelong commitment. Although he appears to have paid only one visit to the Club prior to the season's close in 1899, he became a regular sketcher at their weekly suppers after 1903. When Baden-Powell joined the Club, his only distinction was that he was the youngest Colonel in the British Army. However this was to change after Mafeking.

When news of the relief reached the Sketch Club towards the end of the 1900 season, President Haité proposed that members of the Club should march to the War Office in columns of four — although no one knew precisely why. England, at this time, was gripped by a great patriotic fever and Baden-Powell's photograph appeared in newsagents' windows, with Union Jacks, throughout Britain. Mafeking was not the only part of the world relieved: England was also highly relieved!

An enormous crowd gathered at Piccadilly Circus in London after hearing this joyous news. Everyone went mad and made as much noise as possible. Cabs and buses were covered with men and women clinging precariously to their perches or to one another. Elderly city men, normally very respectable and staid gentlemen, danced the cancan and kissed girls in the street. One distinguished looking gent even took off his top hat and deliberately jumped on it. The police, realising the hopelessness of the situation, just smiled and remained passive.

Baden-Powell had become a hero overnight. Not that he was the only member of the London Sketch Club reporting events in the Boer War. When Baden-Powell sent his sketches to the *Daily Graphic* his name had to be omitted from the drawings for security reasons. Not so René Bull, who was working for the magazine *Black and White*. Bull's combined skills of draughtsmanship, photography and literacy made him an excellent reporter. The other *Black and White* artist was the American Charles M. Sheldon. Born in Indiana in 1866, he had first worked in his father's publishing business before accepting the post of special correspondent for the

American Press Association. In 1890 he visited Paris and worked briefly under Lefevre whilst, at the same time, sending sketches of Parisian low life to the *Pall Mall Budget*. Then he became a war correspondent in the Sudan where he met Dudley Hardy, and covered the Boer War in conjunction with Bull for *Black and White*.

Skilful draughtsmanship and the ability to produce a quick, accurate sketch was essential to these artist-reporters. Things were to change in the 1914-18 War when photography took over, but at the turn of the century there was a major role for the artist in journalism. Often Baden-Powell's sketches were weak and he had to rely on artist friends "to pep them up a bit", especially if they were to be used for publication. His election to the Club as a working member was something of an oddity. The rules of the Club insisted that working artist members should rely on income from their art, whereas Baden-Powell only used his artistic skill to supplement his Army pay.

His admiration for Conan Doyle was justified by the Sherlock Holmes stories. What impressed Baden-Powell were Holmes's great powers of deduction. In his *Scouting for Boys* Baden-Powell frequently referred to Sherlock Holmes and in one case to Dr Joseph Bell, the Edinburgh professor upon whom Conan Doyle based his character. Conan Doyle had introduced Sherlock Holmes in 1890; then he compiled a *History of the Boer War*. In 1902 he returned to fiction with "The Hound of the Baskervilles" and several other stories, and the play *The Fires of Fate*, after which he devoted much of his life to spiritualism.

Conan Doyle was born in Edinburgh in 1859, the son of Charles Doyle, the humorist and fairy illustrator. Three of his uncles were artists, including the famous Richard Doyle of *Punch* fame, and his grandfather was the political caricaturist John Doyle who for over thirty years concealed his identity behind the initials "HB". It was natural that Conan Doyle should feel at home among artists, and in particular secondary or graphic artists. He travelled widely and enjoyed sport. Although he played football and golf, his main sport was cricket and it was through his interest that the annual LSC cricket match was instigated.

To begin with it was "The Married Men versus The Single Men" and these matches continued up to the First World War. Other enthusiasts who joined the teams included James Thorpe (who wrote *A Cricket Bag*), Frank Reynolds, Tom Browne and John Hassall. Artists do not necessarily make good cricketers and in one match Joseph Harker, the scenic painter, was roped in to make up the team. It was a hot day and Harker decided that he would do his fielding in a deck chair, with a bottle and soda syphon, shared generously with the spectators. Nor was Tom Browne an expert, arriving as he did in ordinary clothes (no whites!) and batting with only one pad. If anyone had a good eye it was Frank Reynolds, who was capable of scoring a good few runs and was no mean bowler.

Conan Doyle also played for the MCC and in one match against the Artists' Cricket Club James Thorpe had the pleasure of shying down Conan Doyle's wicket from deep mid-off. It was A. P. Herbert (a later member of the Sketch Club) who confessed that, although he was no cricketer himself, he liked the game because so many pleasant people played it.

In those early days of the London Sketch Club the literary-artistic mix could not have been better. On the literary side, in addition to Conan Doyle, there was that other leading literary figure from *The Strand*, Frankfort Moore. There was also A. M. Binstead, better known as "Pitcher" of the *Sporting Times* (author of *More*

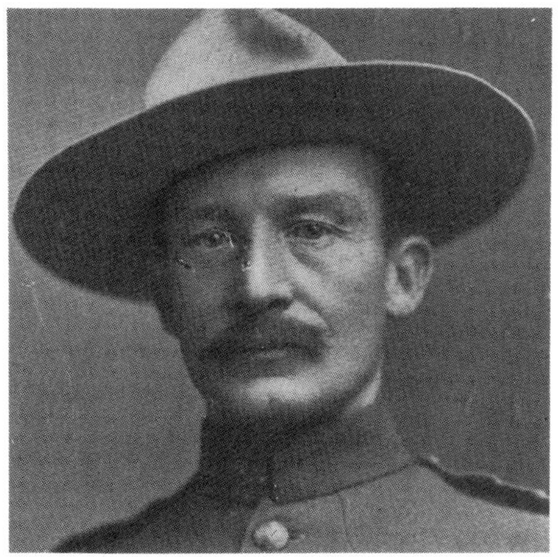

Robert Stephenson Smyth Baden-Powell

Born in London on February 22nd, 1851, the son of Rev. Prof. Baden-Powell and Henrietta Grace Smyth, he entered Charterhouse and later went into the army, where he remained until 1910. He enjoyed a distinguished career, being chiefly remembered for holding Mafeking during the Boer War, and for his Boy Scout Movement started in 1908. He showed artistic talent from an early age, being an ambidextrous sketcher, and later in life illustrated his books with his own drawings and watercolours and supplemented his meagre army pay by sending drawings to illustrated journals, notably the *Graphic*. He designed varius play-bills for amateur theatricals which he organised during his career and his "Are You in this?" war poster appeared in the 1914-18 war. He died in 1941.

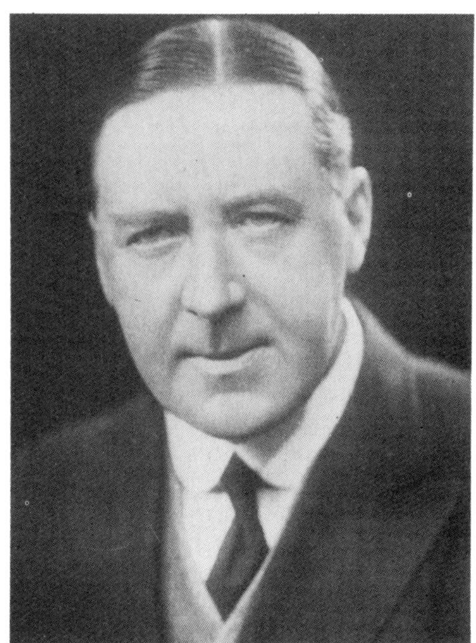

Keble Bell

Although Keble Bell wrote profusely under the pseudonym of Keble Howard, he will probably be best remembered today for introducing radio into hospitals. Over the years many patients listening quietly to the radio were probably unaware that this modest writer was responsible for aiding their plight back in 1925.

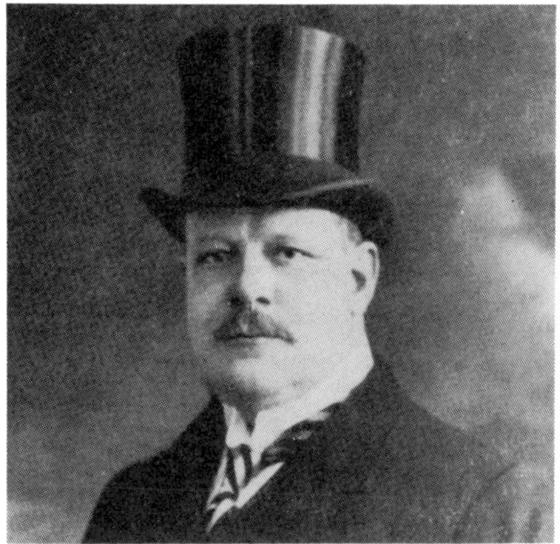

A.M. Binstead

Better known as "Pitcher" of the *Sporting Times*, Binstead was a crony of Phil May. He would sometimes illustrate his stories or features whilst receiving tips from Phil May and Caton Woodville on how to improve his drawing.

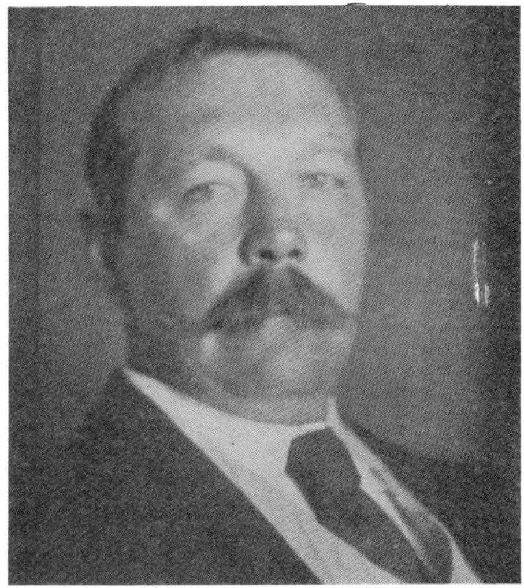

Sir Arthur Conan Doyle, 1859-1930

Conan Doyle was plagued by his supersleuth Sherlock Holmes throughout his life, although some critics have rated his historical romances above those by Haggard.

Gals' Gossip and *Houndsditch Day by Day*). And there was Aaron Watson who wrote the definitive history of the Savage Club (with a chapter by Mark Twain), published in 1907 by T. Fisher Unwin. There were also Keble Bell, who edited *The Sketch*, and his brother R. S. Warren Bell, who edited *The Captain*. Last but not least there was P. G. Konody, the art critic who in later life wrote an excellent biography of Orpen in conjunction with Sidney Dark. It was Konody who reviewed the London Sketch Club's first exhibition in *Table Talk*, dated 5 November 1898:

> If the autumn exhibitions have little to commend them to the interested public, there is at least one smaller picture show, which will be found eminently satisfactory, which is not built up according to a stereotyped model, which differs in many respects from all kindred exhibitions. I am referring to the Inaugural Exhibitions of the London Sketch Club, held at the Modern Gallery in New Bond Street. The London Sketch Club is a newly-formed association of artists who meet once a week at the Modern Gallery for the purpose of doing "Time-Sketches". A subject is given and every member has to give his rendering of the theme — the choice of medium is left to his discretion — within the strictly limited space of two hours.
>
> The present exhibition is not confined to these "two-hour sketches", although they are well represented, but includes other work by the members. The liberty left to the contributors has been productive of a very creditable result.
>
> The work is, throughout, original and fresh, and as varied in style as in medium. Everybody can find something to his taste. Excellent landscapes by the President, George G. Haité; richly-coloured time sketches by Dudley Hardy, the Vice-President; pencil drawings by Phil May; a charming series of watercolour drawings treated in flat tints by Cecil Aldin and Hassall, most of which are illustrating English Nursery Rhymes; quaint Japanesque designs by Newton Shepard; and, last but not least, a delightfully humorous series of posters, designed by some prominent members, a selection of which we are publishing in the present issue. The new enterprise ought to be a financial as well as an artistic success, as the low prices set forth in the catalogue ought to be a strong inducement for would-be purchasers.

The Inaugural Exhibition was not the only write-up that the Sketch Club received from the press that year: The *Morning Leader* recorded the antics of the Club on 29 October, under the heading "Artists at Play".

> Everyone by this time has heard of the London Sketch Club, the members of which meet once a week, and after dashing off a *chef d'oeuvre* in a couple of hours, adjourn across the road to a beefsteak and onions and intellectual fare of the sort that the soul of the Bohemian loveth.
>
> Within the last few days the inaugural exhibition of sketches has been opened at the Club's headquarters, the Modern Gallery, 175 Bond Street, and last night was held the first invitation *conversazione* — which being translated from the Italian was a smoking concert of very superior quality. Before the vocalists got to work, however, there was some ceremony to be got through. Artists receive their guests as they do everything else, artistically. This explains why Mr George Haité donned his presidential robes, having for train bearer Mr Robert Sauber's celebrated Ethiopian *maître d'hôtel*, while Mr Claude

22

Shepperson assumed the airs and functions of an usher, and honoured announcements of Messrs Dudley Hardy and Tomlin.

But before the distinguished foreign members could gain the audience chamber, had they not to have their passports vized by that eminent member of the police force, Mr J. Hassall [his favourite fancy dress costume before the War].

Truly splendid in their multicoloured robes were the artistic notables who played their part in the merry burlesque. Then when the masque was over the solid business of the evening began. The entertainment was in the hands of that inimitable dumb orator Mr Walter Churcher, himself an artist of no mean tensions, as two sketches upon the walls of the gallery testify.

The company which he had gathered together was worthy of the occasion. Signor Arbos, who ranks second to none but Sarasate as a violinist, contributed two delightful solos. Mr William Nicholl sang deliciously, and the vocal quartets of the "Amplil of Glee" men brought down the house.

Other much appreciated items were the imitations of Mr George Robins, Mr Mel B. Spurr's humorous sketch, Mr Henry Thomson's guitar song and the Stavordale's Banjo Quartet, while Mr Arthur Hilton's stump speech concerning the elephant that used its india rubber trunk to rub out its footprints went with a bang.

Mr Churcher's own share in the programme was, as usual, excellent. Many of the party learnt more than they had ever heard before of the early history of the Garden of Eden. They had an opportunity later on of improving their acquaintance with London when Mr Churcher presided at a screen on which were projected by lantern a series of nocturne photographs taken by himself. These were followed by a number of portraits of members of the club, most of which were recognisable, though one distinguished artist was for the moment mistaken for an enlargement of a drop of East London water.

Wild was the banter that rattled through the darkness as these amusing views were displayed.

The reference to George Haité's attire is interesting. There is no doubt that Haité made an impressive chairman. He had after all been Chairman of the Langham from 1883 to 1887, and it is probable that he had intentions of playing a similar role in the London Sketch Club. Sadly Haite had one fault: he would persist in making speeches, sometimes for no reason at all. If there was one thing the Sketch Club crew *hated* it was speeches.

An article in *The Art Record* dated 11 May 1901 stated that "one prominent member has so great a propensity for speech making that the others, upon a certain occasion, rose as one man, to violently discourage the orator. A number of cards and canvasses etc were prepared with appropriate legends lettered thereon, so that when the speechist rose to his feet at the first provocation, there was a sudden movement all over the room, and upon the ends of sticks, and grasped in upheld hands, the afore mentioned notices were thrust out so that there was nothing to be seen but such boldly lettered exclamations as 'Oh Chuck it!', 'Rats!', 'Do Crop it!', 'Dry Up!', 'Give us a charnse' and other encouraging remarks. The remedy was efficacious."

The prominent member was, of course, Haité, whom the Club loved as a man — but not his habits! George Haité (1855-1924) had had a difficult life. The son of an

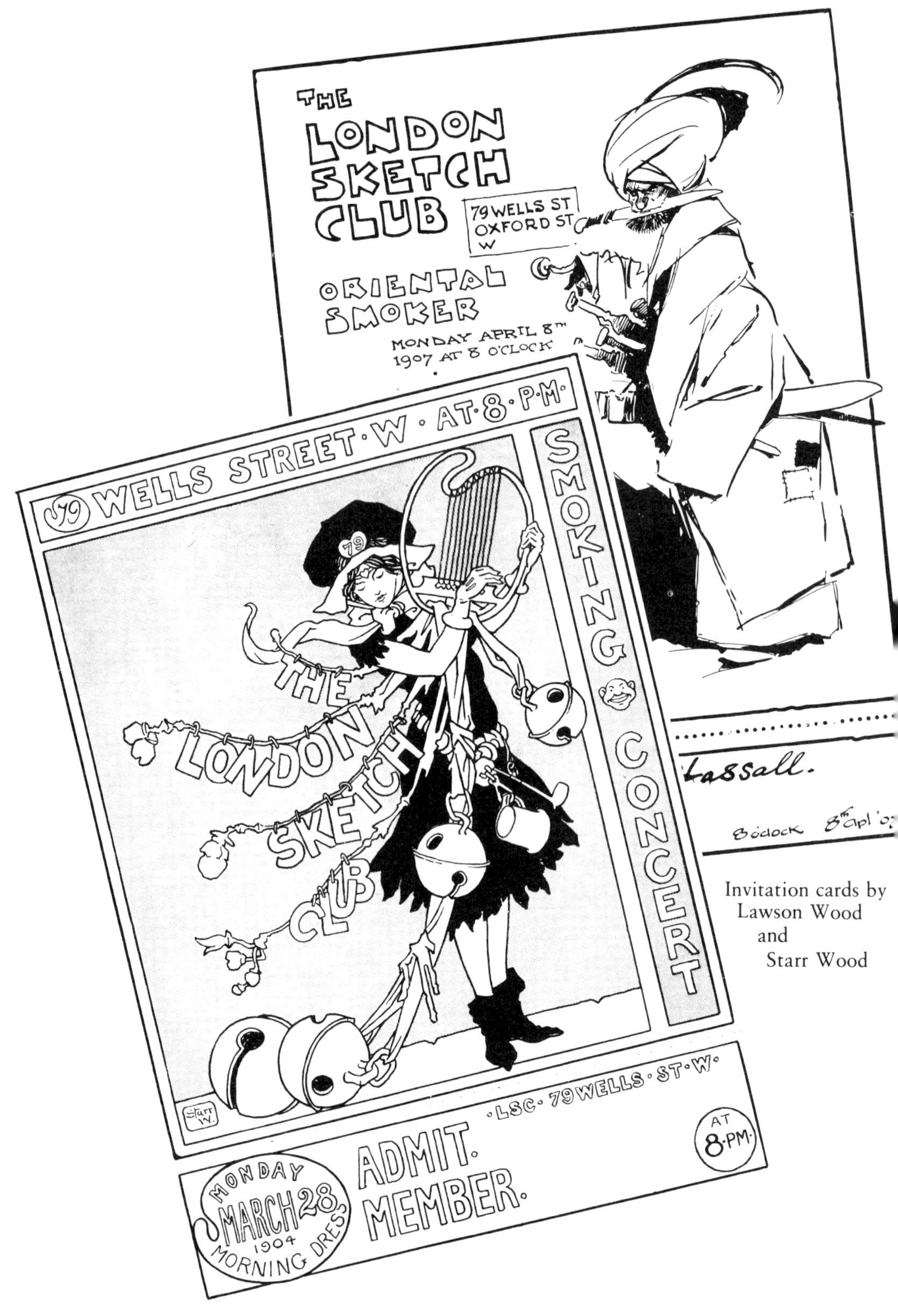

Invitation cards by
Lawson Wood
and
Starr Wood

artist with the same name, young George Haité had had little encouragement from his father. He was self-taught and, by the sound of it, self-made. He was probably the most able of the London Sketch Club members in their dash for the perfect two-hour sketch. Lionel Edwards said "he was the most facile two-hour sketcher I ever saw" and James Thorpe described him as "perhaps the greatest of the two-hour sketchers".

Haité was a kind man, and sympathetic to any youngster who needed advice. He was also in his element when welcoming visitors to the Club, his greatest ally being Robert Sauber. Sadly he seemed to have only one stock phrase: "Art holds no nationality." This got on everyone's nerves and in the subsequent ribbing that Haite was subjected to he did well to keep his composure.

Just as Dudley Hardy had good connections in the art world so did Haité. He exhibited at the Royal Academy from 1883 onwards; in 1892 he was elected to the RBA, to be followed by the RMS in 1900, the RI in 1901 and, finally, the ROI in 1907. During his lifetime he exhibited a total of 212 paintings at the RBA, a colossal amount for one artist. He also designed the once familiar cover for *Strand Magazine*, illustrated numerous books and articles and even found time to write. After Haité's resignation from the London Sketch Club in 1903, Dudley Hardy took over. Since then there has been a different President every year.

Meanwhile George Haité rejoined the Langham and became its President once more in 1908. His studio was in Bedford Park. He typified the spirit of every young aspiring art student of his day, having risen from the ranks of wallpaper, stained glass and metalwork designer. Did it go to his head? A story of 1901 recounts:

There was once a very famous reception held at the Bond Street premises [the Modern Gallery]. A huge stolid policeman guarded the top of the stairs. Someone recognised the features of John Hassall in the guardian of the peace and, greeting him heartily, was only met with the gruff reply, "Cloakroom upstairs, please."

"Ripping", exclaimed the newcomer at this, "You do the part beautifully Jack." [Jack was John Hassall's nickname.]

"Cloakroom upstairs, please," replied the policeman, still more gruffly.

"That's all right. Shake hands, anyhow."

"Cloakroom upstairs, please."

"Oh! hang the cloakroom."

"Cloakroom upstairs, please."

The constable's eyes glared, and his voice had grown into a growl. The other, wondering if he had made a mistake, went up to deposit his hat and coat, while others tried to greet the policeman similarly, to be met with the impeturbable reply, " Cloakroom upstairs, please."

It was, of course, Hassall all the time. As soon as the members had divested themselves of their outer garments, reaching the room where the reception was being held, a gorgeous sight was at once revealed. Upon a resplendent throne at the end of the room sat Haité in regal dignity, with a robe about him and all the adjuncts of royal magnificence displayed about him. Dudley Hardy stood by, similarly attired, with a gold mace that forgot to give out a metallic sound when it was dropped — and Newton Shepard, in a medieval costume fished out from somewhere, acted as usher and attendant.

The members, as they arrived, were escorted by the usher to be presented to

King Haité the First, where they were knobbled on the head by a sword as they knelt, and bidden rise with such fitting honours as His Majesty thought fit to lay his tongue to. Then the presented member, with his blushing honours thick upon him, would join the others previously presented, who formed a long lane from the door to the throne, down which the victims walked, and provided the hoorays necessary as each newcomer was led up.

The costumes at the reception were strange and varied. Charles Sheldon was robed in a Dervish jellaba and other trimmings that he had brought with him from the Soudan. Starr Wood had the blue bags and blouse of a French peasant. There were monks and Volendamers, fishing women and Spanish peasants and all the motley collection of a score of studio costume chests.

One feature of the London Sketch Club was that members frequently caricatured each other purely for amusement. James Thorpe and Starr Wood kept their caricatures within the confines of the Club, but the adventurous Tom Browne, according to the *Art Record* made "base use of members' countenances in his *published* drawings, often placing them in most undignified positions and circumstances". It went on to say, "He will probably be shot on sight for this some day!"

Another original Sketch Club idea was making sopped bread models, an early kind of "Fluck and Law". A report which mentioned Sauber as being particularly adept in this medium, described it thus:

The bread-crumb is wetted, and then squeezed to a paté between the fingers, and then the model is built generally upon some foundation such as a bottle, or if a bas-relief, upon a plate which has been previously tinted over with smoke black from a match. A week or two ago Sauber turned out a really good model of Dudley Hardy. The slightly upturned moustache of a reddish hue [Dudley Hardy was ginger] was supplied by a strand or two of finely-cut tobacco, and this medium also supplied the hair.

In these early days members of the London Sketch Club were allowed to use The Modern Gallery in Bond Street largely through the benevolence of Edward Freeman, the gallery owner, while using Longs Hotel, just opposite, for their dinners. It was a dangerous favour, as Keble Bell remembered:

One night there was a special supper party, with Dudley Hardy in the chair. At a certain moment in the evening, Hassall rose and begged leave to make a statement. He said that no man had worked harder for the Club than Dudley Hardy and that the members had decided to offer him a testimonial in recognition of these services. They hoped that he would always treasure it in memory of innumerable friends and innumerable merry evenings. Two uniformed hotel porters then entered, bearing a handsome marble clock, which they placed in front of Dudley amid a hurricane of applause.

The uniformed porters were Starr Wood and Keble Bell and they had borrowed the clock from the mantleshelf in the hall of Longs Hotel!

Starr Wood was a great 'nineties clubman. He bridged the gap between art, wit and literacy in his own very individual way. When attending the London Sketch Club he usually donned a cap, scarf and white working man's suit. In his later days at the Savage Club he often wore a bow-tie and was known as a great raconteur. If anyone could have written the inside story of 'nineties "Men Only" clubs it would

Starr Wood (1870-1944)
produced his own Christmas
card every year, which he sent
out to fellow clubmen and
friends. This practice was
later continued by Harry
May Hemsley and Harry
Riley, RI.

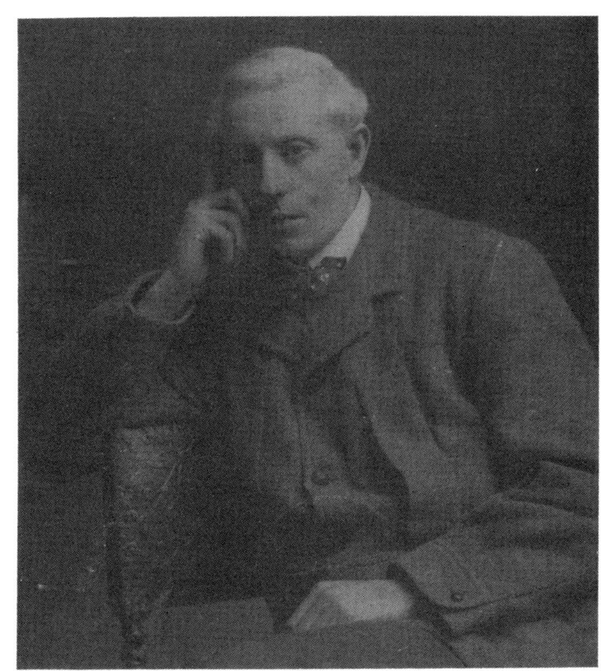

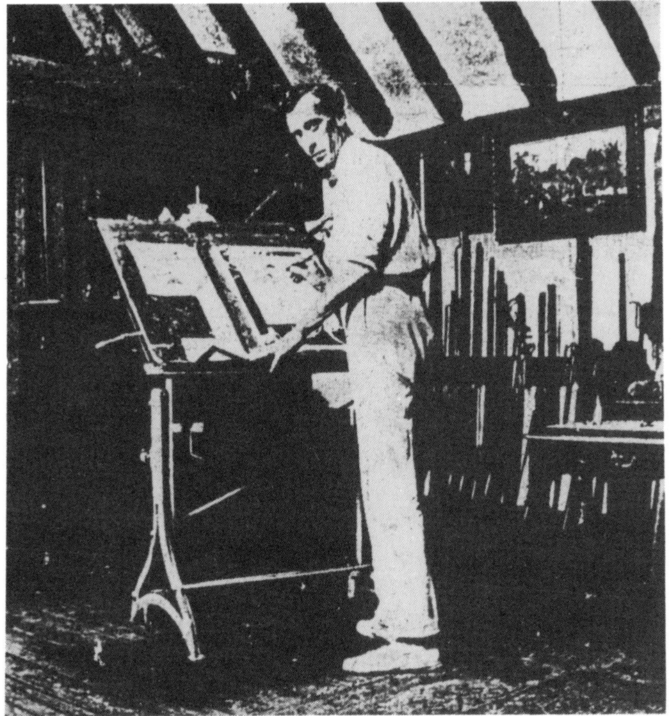

The young Lawson
Wood at work in
his studio at Court
Lodge, where most
of his famous
watercolour
drawings were
produced. His love
of oak, antiques,
guns and an olde
worlde atmo-
sphere is apparent.

have been Starr Wood. Unhappily he never put pen to paper, although there was an informative article about him in the *Sunday Despatch* in 1939.

As his niece said, "He was always a very generous man and full of fun." Starr Wood had been born in London on 1 February 1870. His father was a civil servant in HM Customs and his grandfather, Captain Starr Wood, was King's Pilot. The young Starr Wood received no formal art training; after leaving school his family "tried to make an accountant out of him", but he was always doodling and sketching when he should have been totting up figures. Starr Wood remained in chartered accountancy for five years, three of which were spent as a dogsbody debt collector. Many of his debtors had no money, as he recalled in a small anecdote:

> I was sent to collect eighteen shillings rent from a muffin baker with five children in a slum off Holloway Road. After telling me that they had had nothing to eat but stale crumpets for the last week, he took me to an upper room and asked me if I thought he could realise anything on the remnants of an umbrella that was fixed in the roof to keep the rain out!

Starr Wood was obviously dumbfounded and did not press for the eighteen shillings.

Before finishing his apprenticeship, Starr Wood persuaded his father to keep him for a year to "see how things went" in his new career in art. Before the year (1892) was up, Wood's first published drawing appeared in that most brilliant of comic papers, *Ariel*, edited by Israel Zangwill. Soon he was contributing to *Fun, Judy, Moonshine* and the *Sketch*. Zangwill's opinion had been that he "had the humorous instinct, but had better learn to draw!"

Starr Wood had an excellent head of hair, which at the age of twenty-seven turned white overnight. Apropos of this personal oddity, he recalled: "I had an old woman — whom I discovered in the street — sitting to me as a model for a sketch I was making, and, much to my inconvenience, she kept turning her head and looking at me curiously while I was endeavouring to draw her profile. At length she blurted out, "Excuse me, sir, but are you what they call an albumen?""

In 1893 Starr Wood contributed to *Punch* and from 1898 onwards regularly sent cartoons. Also that year he became editor of *The Windmill*, a high class literary and artistic quarterly. This lasted only a few issues, but he had more success with the *Snarks Annual* (sometimes referred to as Starr Wood's Magazine) a few years later.

In his bachelor days Starr Wood enjoyed walking holidays and golf. However, on the death of his father, his mother engaged the services of a companion, Winifred Humpherson, the eldest daughter of William Humpherson of Cliffords Mesne in Gloucestershire. She and Starr Wood were married in 1904 and had one son. After a few years in London (mostly at various addresses in Fulham and Putney), the couple moved to an old Georgian house in West Street, Hertford in 1910. One of their visitors was James Thorpe, who remembered their "delightful secluded garden".

Hertford in those days retained all the charm of a quiet country town, despite being only twenty miles from London. After the 1914-18 war the Starr Woods bought a holiday cottage at Barton-on-Sea, Hampshire where they spent their summers. He illustrated a few books including *Rhymes of the Regiments* (1898), a clever book of caricatures and limericks, and *Cocktail Time* (1933), a collection of saucy drawings described as "a picture-book for grown-ups". Nearly all of Starr Wood's drawings were done in pen and ink or two-tone sepia because he was colour blind. On the rare occasions he used colour, it was generally red. His subjects were mostly in the field of marital contretemps or other domestic incongruities. He was

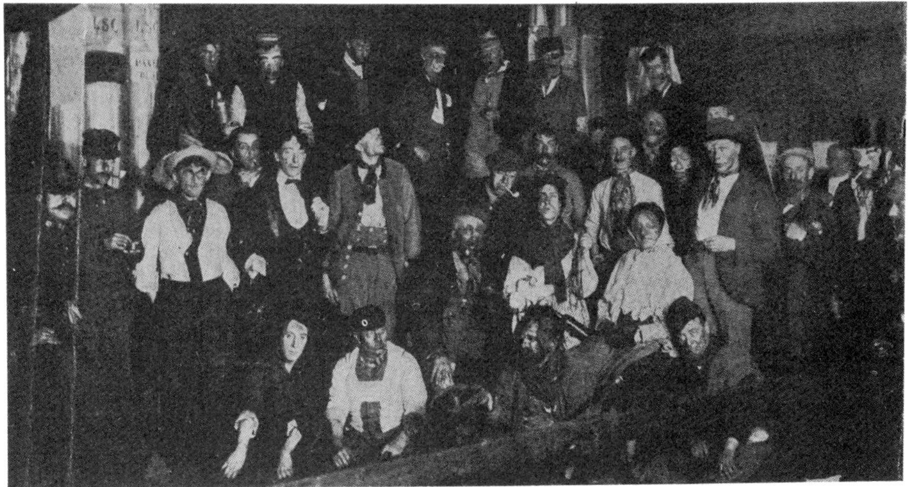

"Artistic Weary Willies and Tired Tims": Members of the London Sketch Club
at their recent 'unemployed' dinner.

Left to right, from the back: de la Bere, Harold Goldthwaite, Lawson Wood, Champion Jones,
W. S. Parkyn (back row); H. May Hemsley, Starr Wood (next to the gentleman in 'evening-dress'),
P. Wadham, Cecil Aldin, Edkins Clarke, Lee Hankey, Edgar L. Patterson, J. W. Gilmer, E. A.
Norbury, John Harker, Walter Churcher, W. P. Ritchie (second row from the front); John Hassall
(the policeman), Broughton Black, J. Protheroe, H. Sandham, and Lance Thackeray.

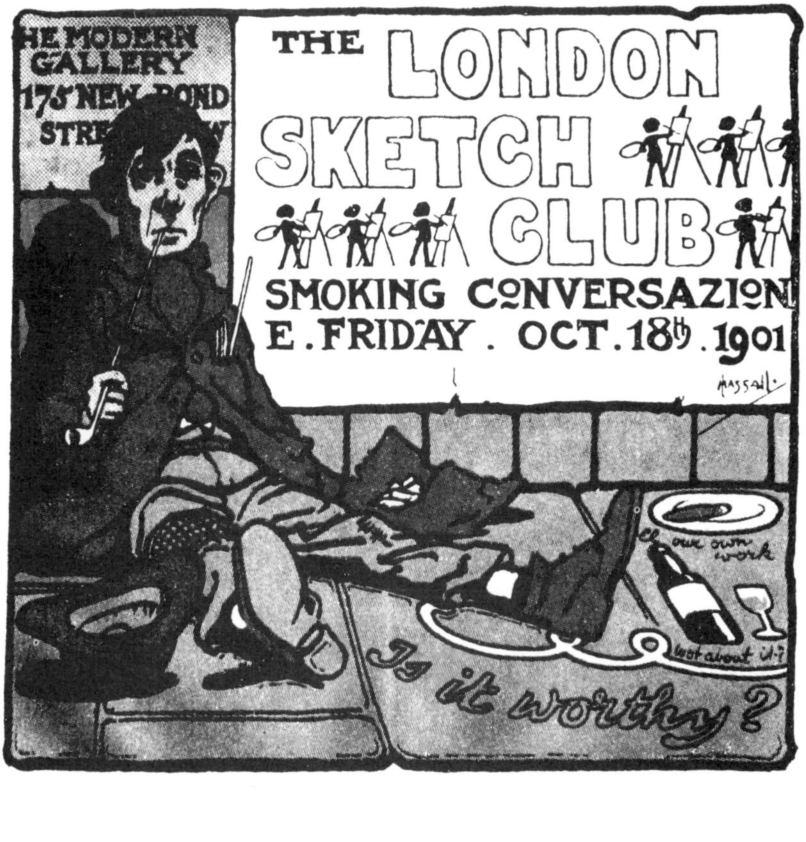

Invitation card by John Hassall

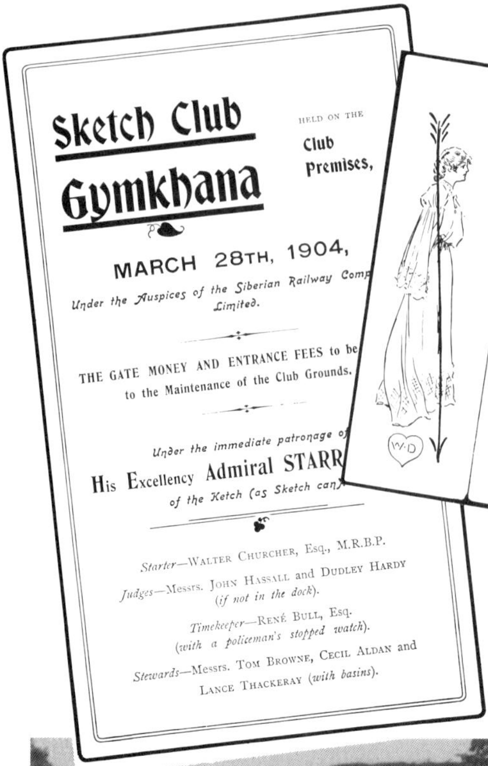

Sketch Club Gymkhana

HELD ON THE
Club Premises,

MARCH 28TH, 1904,

*Under the Auspices of the Siberian Railway Comp
Limited.*

THE GATE MONEY AND ENTRANCE FEES to be
to the Maintenance of the Club Grounds,

Under the immediate patronage of

His Excellency Admiral STARR
of the Ketch (as Sketch can)

Starter—WALTER CHURCHER, Esq., M.R.B.P.
Judges—Messrs. JOHN HASSALL and DUDLEY HARDY
(if not in the dock).
Timekeeper—RENÉ BULL, Esq.
(with a policeman's stopped watch).
Stewards—Messrs. TOM BROWNE, CECIL ALDAN and
LANCE THACKERAY *(with basins).*

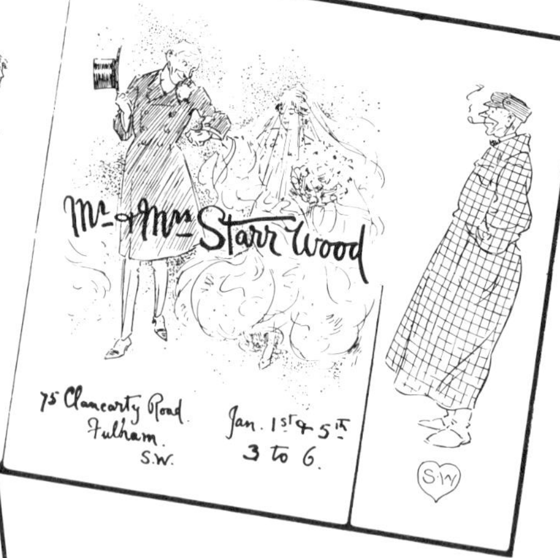

Invitation to the wedding of
Mr & Mrs Starr Wood

The Sketch Club Gymkhana, 1904
This may have seemed like organised tom-
foolery — which of course is exactly what it
was.

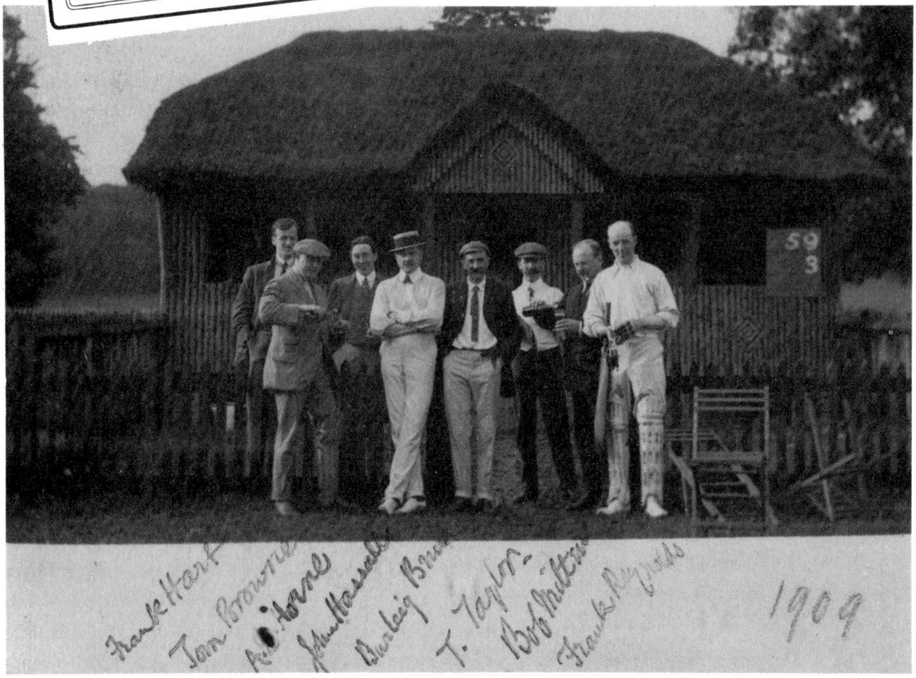

The Cricket Match, 1909

one of the contributors to *Printer's Pie*, along with other London Sketch Club
members including Thackeray, Studdy, Hassall, Hardy, Reynolds, Bull, Rountree,
Sarg and Earnshaw. He was also a popular member of the Savage Club where Lee-
Hankey's portrait of him now hangs.

In his reminiscences James Thorpe described Starr Wood as "a delightfully
friendly person with a humorous outlook on life peculiarly his own." He reinforced
this statement with two examples:

> He was quite irresponsible and reckless in his enjoyment of playing the fool.
> On one of our trips to Belgium we were dozing in the sun in one of the most
> fashionable parks in Brussels. Gradually I began to notice a small amused
> crowd collecting in front of our park bench, and turning round found Starr
> Wood inverted perpendicularly on his hands. "Must do something to make
> the beggars laugh!" was his only explanation.

The second story concerned James Thorpe and Frank Reynolds who used to meet at
Starr Wood's studio to draw from the model once a week. Starr Wood frequently
went out into the street to persuade someone to model for him,

> . . . a policeman, flower-girl, newspaper-boy or char-woman — anyone he had
> happened to meet. Once he approached an interesting old reprobate holding a
> horse's head. "I want you to come round to my studio just to make a few
> drawings", he said.
> "Lord luv yer gov'nor," was the astonished reply "I can't draw!"

Starr Wood died in 1944 and his obituary appeared in *The Times*. He should not
be confused with the other Wood who was also a member of the Sketch Club at this
time, namely Lawson Wood. Both men were tall and thin, and in their youth had a
boyish enthusiasm for life, but whereas in later life Starr wood retreated to the
confines of the Savage Club, Lawson Wood became a semi-recluse, rarely venturing
outside his front door.

Lawson Wood (christened Clarence Lawson Wood) (1878-1957) was born in
Highgate, London. His father Pinhorn Wood was a water-colourist, as indeed was
his grandfather Lewis John Wood (1813-1901), a painter of landscape and
architectural subjects who exhibited at the Royal Academy. Lawson Wood's skill
was inherent rather than taught, although he studied at the Slade, Heatherley's and
Frank Calderon's School of Animal Painting. As a small boy he spent many hours in
the farmyard at the back of his father's house in Highgate sketching animals from
life.

His father's friend and publisher Arthur Pearson, later Sir Arthur, spotted the
boy's talent when he paid an unexpected visit for tea and predicted that "if the boy
goes through art school he will have a good job — with me". Pearson was as good as
his word. After his art schooling Wood emerged as head artist on the staff of
C. Arthur Pearson Ltd. It was here that he met his future wife, Charlotte Forge, then
employed as a fashion artist. The married and had twins, a boy and a girl, who are
both still alive, and another son who died in Australia. Wood, rebelling against the
name Clarence, gave them all the second name Lawson, even his daughter.

After his marriage at Chiswick in 1902, Lawson Wood had settled at Bexhill, but
on holiday at Udimore, near Tye in Sussex, he had spotted a row of 13th-century
tumbledown cottages which he was able to buy from the Church of England, though
they refused to sell the site. So, with the help of horse-drawn wagons and a couple of

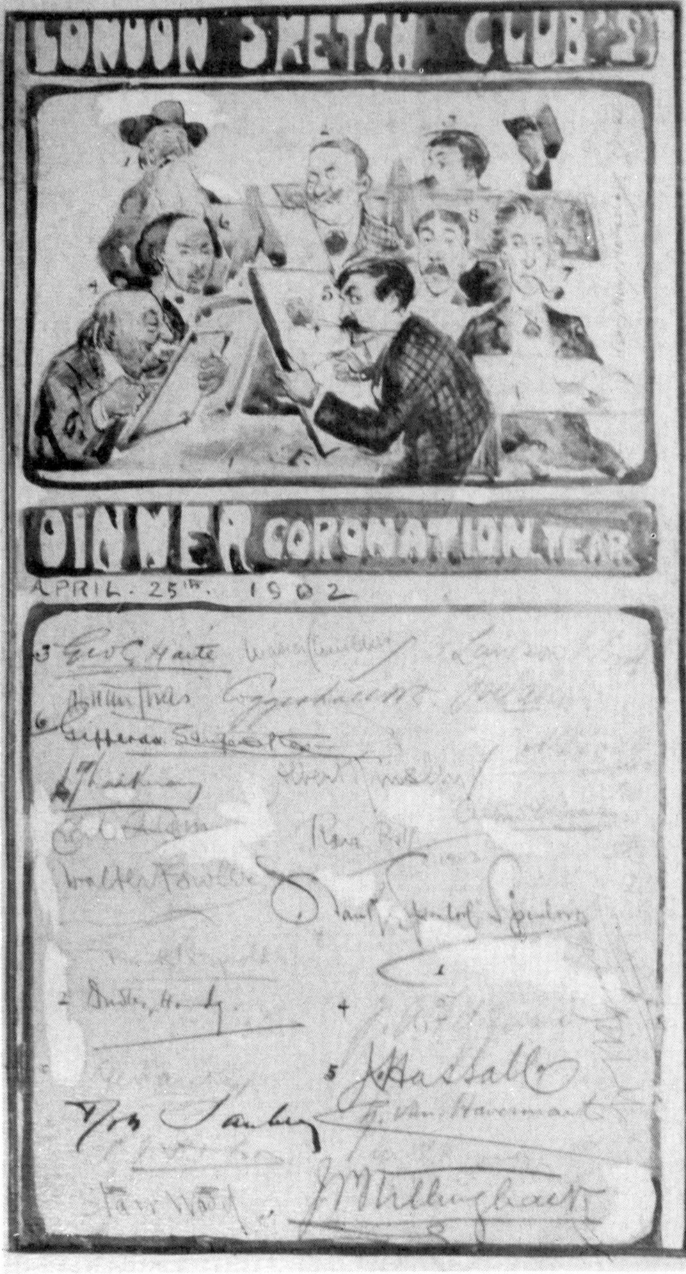

The London Sketch Club's Coronation Dinner, 1902

The signatures to this dinner include, pictured:
F. Spenlove, RBA,
Dudley Hardy,
George Haite,
J. A. Fitzgerald,
John Hassall,
Giffard Lenfestey,
Lawson Wood,
Lee Hankey
and others,
Lance Thackeray,
Cecil Aldin,
Walter Fowler,
Frank Reynolds,
Rob Sauber,
Cecil Hobson, RI,
Starr Wood,
Walter Churcher,
Coggeshall,
Albert Kinsley, RI,
Rene Bull,
Charles van Havermaet,
A. Diosy,
H. M. Hemsley,
Alfred E. Craven

steamrollers, he moved the buildings piece by piece to their present site overlooking Groombridge near Tunbridge Wells in Kent, where they now form one of Britain's most picturesque country houses. He called it Court Lodge, retaining the historic name and preserving the original appearance. It was since proved that those derelict cottages, dilapidated and used only by hop-pickers in season when he had bought them, had royal connections and had been a complete house when Edward I was reputed to have stayed there!

Lawson Wood did some of his best work in the studio of Court Lodge surrounded by oak, old guns and antique furniture. Curiously, for such a prolific artist, there have been only two major exhibitions of his work, one during his lifetime, the other posthumously. Reproductions of his work regularly appeared in print form and on postcards but Wood retained the copyright on all his work — an astute move.

Lawson Wood's most famous creation was a chimpanzee called "Grand Pop", who decorated cards, calendars and posters for almost half a century. He never appeared in annual form like the *Bonzo Annual*, but the plethora of books which included Grand Pop, such as *Meddlesome Monkies, Mischief Makers* or *Lawson Wood's Merry Monkeys* did come out as annuals.

During his lifetime Lawson Wood was considered a commercial artist, but he was more than that. It was a label that stuck to too many English artists: Russell Flint was another. In retrospect it is difficult to see how the art establishment could have considered either of these artists to be "commercial", though their mastery of watercolour was fluent and possibly a bit slick. Perhaps someone was envious of their talents and managed to repress their reputations. This may have been a reason why Lawson Wood became reclusive in the latter part of his life.

Basically the London Sketch Club comprised an extraordinary bunch of illustrators, caricaturists and secondary artists, with a sprinkling of writers, actors and entertainers thrown in for good measure. Illustrators such as Alick Ritchie, who contributed to *The Ludgate Monthly, Pall Mall Budget* and *Vanity Fair*, or Frank Richards (not to be confused with the author of Billy Bunter), who contributed to *The Graphic, Pick-Me-Up* and *Sketch*, have largely been forgotten, but they were very talented. Even the two most prominent artists of those early Sketch Club days, E. J. Gregory, RA and Alfred (later Sir Alfred) East have fallen from high esteen but their standing in Edwardian times was unprecedented. Fortunately there has been a revival of interest in the work of early Sketch Club members which has led to a boost in saleroom prices for their work. The most notable increases have been for the work of Claude Shepperson, Hugh Thomson and Clarles Dana Gibson (the last certainly attended the London Sketch Club but I have found no evidence of his having been a member).

Shepperson, best known for his "Shepperson Girl", was intended for the law but like Dulac switched to fine art and illustration. He shared a flat with fellow London Sketch Club member Giffard Lenfestey and achieved a lasting reputation in the pages of *Punch*. Claude Allin Shepperson (1867-1921) was born in Beckenham, Kent and went on to study at Heatherleys and in Paris. His fellow literary *Punch* contributor E. V. Lucas always reckoned Shepperson to be the finest illustrator of his day. Percy Bradshaw, who founded the Press Art School where Shepperson worked briefly as a tutor, agreed with Lucas, adding "in whatever medium Shepperson worked — pencil, pen, chalk or watercolour, there was an elegance". Latterly Shepperson left his flat at 18 Kensington Court Place and took a studio in Mulberry Walk, Chelsea, where he died. He was a refined gentleman who possessed a

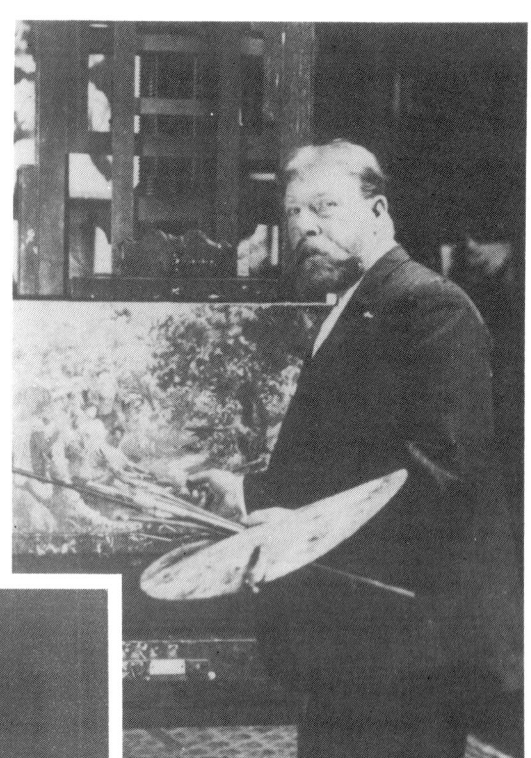

(*Right*) E. J. Gregory, RA.

(*Below*) Alfred East, RA,
(1849-1913).

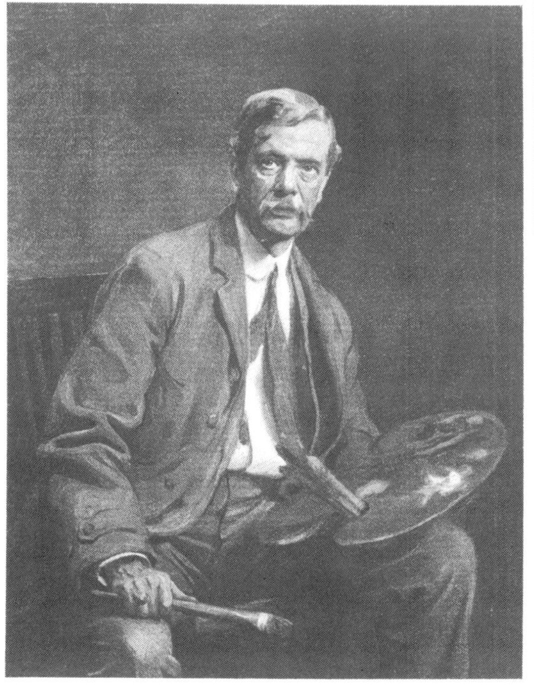

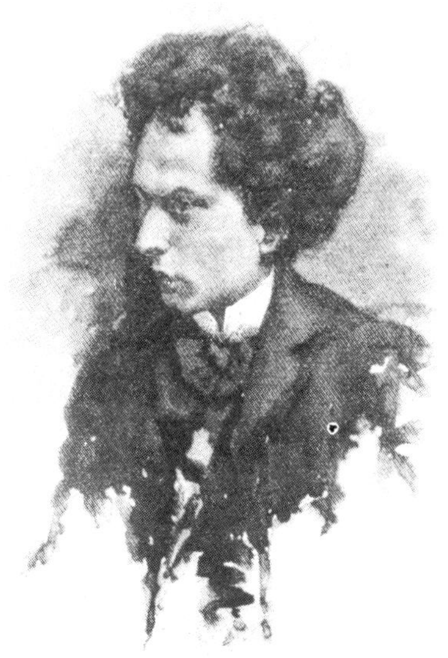

(*Right*) Giffard Hocart Lenfestey, RBA, from a
sketch by Edward Ertz of Paris. Lenfestey trained
at the Royal College of Art under Raphael Collin,
and in Paris.

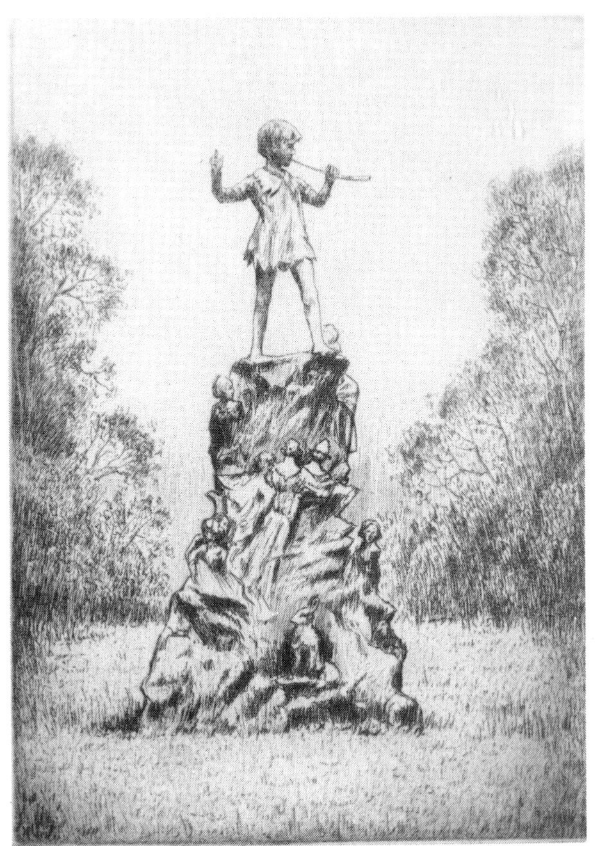

(*Left*) George James Frampton, RA (1860-1928), later Sir George, studied at Lambeth School of Art and the RA Schools. He is famous as the creator of the Peter Pan statue in Kensington Gardens. Other works include the Dr Barnado Memorial, Barkingside and his monument to Canon Major Lester in Liverpool.

(*Below*) Invitation card by Claude Shepperson.

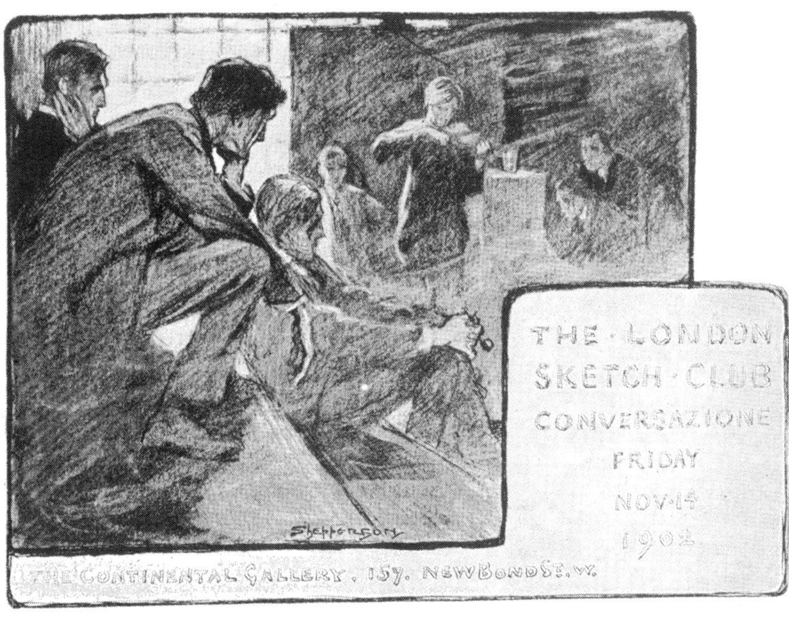

charming personality which resulted in the nickname of "the aristocrat who sketched".

Shepperson's ex-flatmate Giffard Lenfestey started one of the many schools which were to originate from the London Sketch Club. Others were started by Robert Sauber, John Hassall, F. Spendlove, Lee Hankey and Percy Bradshaw. Lenfestey's technical art correspondence college founded in 1897 was unquestionably the first. It was a brave venture for the twenty-five-year-old artist but like so many of these ventures was short-lived. It gave Lenfestey a lot of unnecessary work; in later life he withdrew from society altogether, only bothering to send in a few paintings to exhibitions.

E.J. Gregory was another artist who sat uneasily in company, yet, despite suffering from a stammer, he felt quite at home within the confines of the Sketch Club. Edward John Gregory (1850-1909) had been born in Southampton, the grandson of John Gregory, an engineer with Sir John Franklin's expedition. His masterpiece was "Boulter's Lock, Sunday Afternoon 1898": it was this painting which saw Gregory elected to the RA (it now hangs in the Lady Lever Art Gallery, Port Sunlight). Gregory was a simple but sincere man who swung between commercial and fine art most of his life. Fortunately the coin eventually flipped down on the side of fine art despite his early start in the P & O Company's drawing office, where he worked with Hubert von Herkomer, and then on *The Graphic*. Gregory was a bulky man, bearded in his Sketch Club silhouette, who worked slowly and deliberately. His paintings were never repetitious as were so many from Edwardian artists who churned out pot-boilers on closely related themes.

It was much the same with Alfred East whose talent so enchanted the Edwardians. East (who was knighted in 1910) hailed from Kettering and attended Glasgow School of Art before going on to Paris where he worked under Bouguereau (a name which keeps cropping up) and was strongly influenced by the Barbizon School. Despite the honours bestowed on him, East remained a bohemian all his days. In 1911 he decided to give back something to the town of his birth and approached the then Urban District Council with the offer of a collection of his paintings to go on permanent display. The offer was accepted and a gallery was built, but, alas, when Lord Spencer went to open the exhibition, East was not present: he lay on his deathbed, dying three months later.

There was always a flow of members either resigning from or joining the Club. For example Cecil Hobson, RI, Hans Trier, RBA, F. Hamilton Jackson, RBA, Nico Jungman, George Haite and J. Alsop, RBA all resigned in 1902. Their replacements included Jo Harker, Charles Dixon, Terrick Williams, Percy Wood, Henry Sandham and F. Hobden, RBA in 1903. It is notable that all this chopping and changing eventually left the Club with more or less the number of members today as it had at its conception.

Sketch Club membership was not confined to illustrators, cartoonists, fine artists, writers, actors and entertainers: there were also sculptors, of which George Frampton was one. Frampton (who was later knighted) was Professor of Sculpture at the Slade. Albert Toft was another (he was also knighted) who joined a few years later. Then there was Captain Adrian Jones. If Frampton was to be remembered for Peter Pan in Kensington Gardens and Adrian Jones for his Quadriga, it only needed Alfred Gilbert, who designed Eros in Piccadilly, to complete the trio. Sadly, however, Gilbert was not a member, though his nephew Adrian Bury was to join the Club many years later.

CHAPTER 3

A Permanent Home in Wells Street

The Club continued to use the Modern Gallery at 175 Bond Street until 1902, during which time Bouza's Band made its first appearance. The spoof band, the name of which combined "Boozer" and Souza (the famous American bandmaster) included artist members of the Club. They made their first triumphal appearance with elaborate instruments of gilt cardboard from which weird and unearthly sounds were emitted. Their efforts were much appreciated and so well received by their audience that "a return visit was immediately booked by the management".

It must have made a welcome change for the professional entertainers to be entertained by the artist members (immortalised by Lance Thackeray). Everyone who saw Bouza's Band was highly impressed: the gathering *looked* like a professional band, especially with Dudley Hardy as conductor. But the illusion must have vanished when they actually had to play something. Then, with a succession of peculiar noises, the audience realised the truth!

After 1902 the Club used the Continental Gallery at 157 New Bond Street for a year until a rented room became available at 79 Wells Street, just off Oxford Street. The room which the Sketch Club used for a short time was below a riotous institution known as the Punch Bowl.

The Punch Bowl Club was one of many institutions founded and run by Percy Wood. Wood was a tall, sturdily built man with black hair brushed smoothly back, and dressed always in a snuff-coloured Georgian suit. He was a good raconteur, a fine judge of food, and an excellent cook. He ran the club entirely on his own and rumour had it that he never left the premises! Theirs was a very interesting room and the entertainment, apart from excellent food, consisted solely of conversation, which was generally of a high level. When the Sketch Club occupied the first floor, groups of its members would disappear up to the Punch Bowl once their own meetings were over, where they would talk until the early hours of the morning.

There is a story about Phil May and Percy Wood concerning £50 which Percy Wood tried to borrow from Phil May. Both men's finances were uncertain and this amount was beyond Phil's resources. However, he did manage to raise £25 which he handed over with his usual generosity and sincere apologies. A few weeks later someone asked Phil why he didn't come to the Club as often as before. "Well, I can't very well. You see, I still owe Percy twenty-five pounds," was his reply.

It was after Wood's death and the consequent dissolution of the Punch Bowl that the Sketch Club went aloft. To quote an early member: "We were certainly happier and less restricted in our own home; here the wildest and happiest evenings were

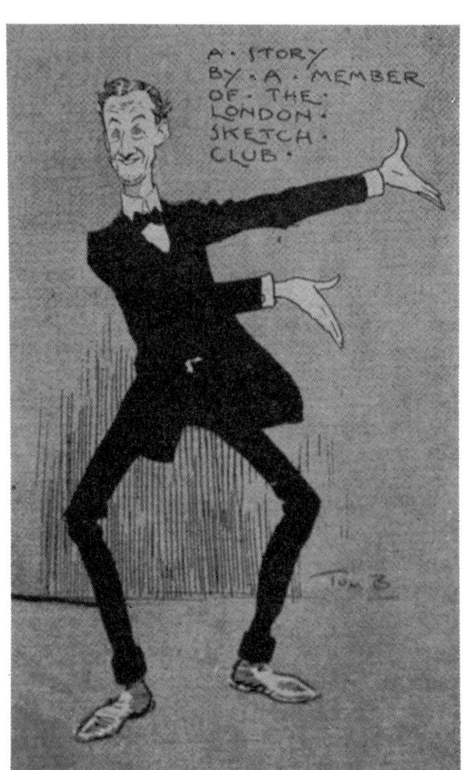

"Walter Churcher obliges with a yarn."
Caricature by Tom Browne.

(*Below*) Invitation card by
Walter Churcher.

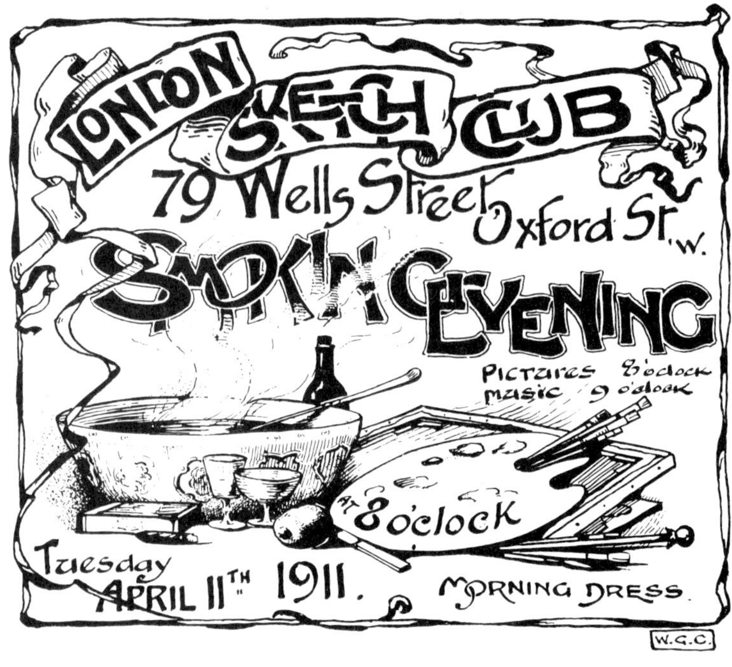

spent." The members furnished and decorated the big room and a kitchen was equipped for the weekly suppers. A piano was installed; Jo Harker painted an excellent curtain for the stage; costumes, properties, curios and sketches were freely contributed, and the place became one of the best-known haunts of professional and Bohemian life in London.

By now Walter Churcher had relieved Rene Bull as Honorary Secretary. Churcher had two great assets: diplomacy and enthusiasm. It was his drive and determination that put some sort of discipline into the Club. Although his own graphic work is largely forgotten now, a good tribute to him comes from another up-and-coming illustrator who later worked for *Punch,* namely James Thorpe:

> One of the earliest and most determined men who took an interest in my work was Walter Churcher, that excellent reciter and raconteur, who will be remembered with joy by concert-goers between 1890 and 1920. Some of my childish efforts to decorate the programmes attracted his attention and he persistently encouraged me to continue. Many delightful Sundays I spent at his charming house at Bedford Park where he very kindly introduced me to the local Art Colony. Here I met George Haite, the designer of everything that could be made beautiful, and Cecil Aldin, that cheery soul and great artist who still continues to draw dogs better than anyone else has ever drawn them. Churcher also gave me introductions to people who were good enough to pay me for my immature work to encourage me to do more. In gratitude for his kindness I did a number of drawings of his best known characters. These were more excellent in intention than in execution, but he had them reproduced as a booklet and circulated copies amongst his friends and acquaintances.

When the lease for the Punch Bowl Club needed signing by all the council members, Churcher had difficulty in obtaining Phil May's signature. It was the year that Phil May died and Churcher's patience was put to the test, as he recalled:

> On one occasion it was necessary to obtain the signature of Phil May to an important document, as a member of the Club Committee. Phil was in his most elusive mood but at last one Sunday morning I ran him to earth at a member's studio [Dudley Hardy's] outside which I found a cabman who requested me to inform "the gent inside with a fringe" that he had been waiting an hour. I advised him not to worry, but wait. The elusive Phil, when faced with a demand for his signature, "stone-walled", but finally agreed to attach his autograph to the deed on condition that the thing was done in style. An historic tableau was therefore duly arranged: Phil impersonated "King John signing Magna Carta", Cecil Aldin was a baron knelt with the pen and document, while Hardy, as another noble armed with a fearsome weapon, threatened violence in case of further reticence in the autograph department. Thus the deed was done "in style". I have reason to think that after our drive homeward the cabby was able to congratulate himself on accepting my advice to wait for the gent with the fringe. Phil was generous.

Churcher was greatly relieved that now not only did the Club have a firm financial footing, but also a permanent home. The transient meetings and alarums of the last five years were a thing of the past. It was this leasehold that enabled the Club to survive the twentieth century.

In those halcyon days before the First World War the relationship between Aldin,

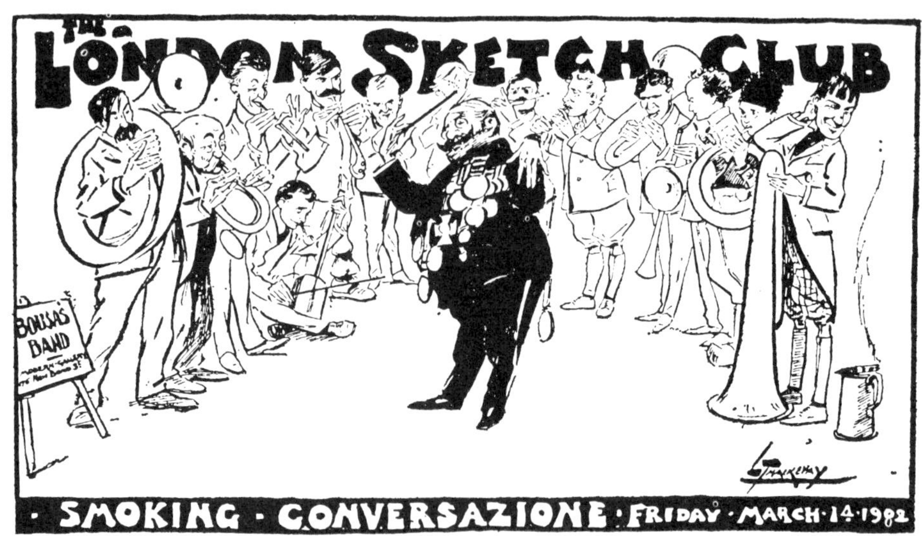

(*Above*) Invitation
card by Lance
Thackeray.

"Dudley Hardy does
a cake walk."
Caricature by
Lance Thackeray.

Hardy and Hassall could easily have come tripping out of the pages of Jerome K. Jerome's *Three Men in a Boat*. Aldin lived in the artistic quarter of Bedford Park (at 47 Priory Road), Hassall in Notting Hill Gate (at 88 Kensington Park Road) and Hardy in South Kensington (at Clareville Grove Studios). They all held bohemian parties in their studios and their attitude to life could best be described as "happy-go-lucky".

No white shirtfront was safe when the Sketch Club crowd were about. Edwardian clubgoers paid much attention to their dress and in particular their starched collars and boiled crisp shirtfronts. One evening at the Sketch Club a guest arrived in just such attire and proceeded to enjoy the Club fare. As the evening wore on, and after much imbibing, the stout gentleman dozed off. He awoke to find nearly all the other guests had sketches drawn over their sparkling shirtfronts and pleaded for the same treatment.

To placate the man, Dudley Hardy drew a goddess in chalk, working in the shirt studs as part of the design. Hassall steadied the man as other Sketch Club members added nymphs and unctuous female bodies to the dicky. The portly gent insisted that each member should sign his masterpiece and was told the subjects consisted of harmless doodles such as landscapes, still lifes and seascapes. Since the Sketch Club had no mirrors the guest had to believe them, and besides by that time he was past caring. When he arrived home in the early hours of the morning, he awoke his wife with an erotic scene of scantily clad females. It must be said that the guest was a pillar of his local community, a church warden and choral singer to boot, who had never mixed in bohemian company before. After this event it was likely that he would never repeat the exercise again.

According to the *Art Record* this practice of drawing on shirtfronts was the origin of the phrase "Our artist at the front!" However, if the artists' lifestyle seemed frivolous, their attitude to work was deadly serious, even though they tried to make light of it, as described in an anecdote by Cecil Aldin:

> One still winter's evening between eight-thirty and nine o'clock, twenty industrious artists were seated according to Sketch Club custom in the large room, trying to produce masterpieces in the space of two hours. Not a sound had been heard for a quarter of an hour except the deep breathing of the London Sketch Club workers, the suck of luscious pipes, the splash of full watercolour brushes as they flung paint on to already over-saturated paper, or the scrape of the palatte-knife on canvas. No talking was permitted. Suddenly, to the indignation of the older members, a loud clink of china water-bowl against china water-bowl reverberated through the still room, and in the intensified silence that followed, the sepulchral voice of Jack Hassall came from the still shadows at the far corner: "Push it under the bed!"

It was in this atmosphere of hard work and tom-foolery that the London Sketch Club Style originated. As Anthony Anderson, the biographer of H. M. Bateman, noticed: "Often groups or pairs of artists admired and inspired one another. There was almost a sense of a Sketch Club Style." In fact there were two distinctive styles. The first appeared in advertising and book illustration, with bold black lines heavily separating subjects from background. Followers of this school included Dudley Hardy, John Hassall, Will True, Cecil Aldin, Will Owen, Tom Browne, James Pryde, Frank Reynolds and, latterly, Alfred Leete. The standard they set was to influence advertising for the next fifty years.

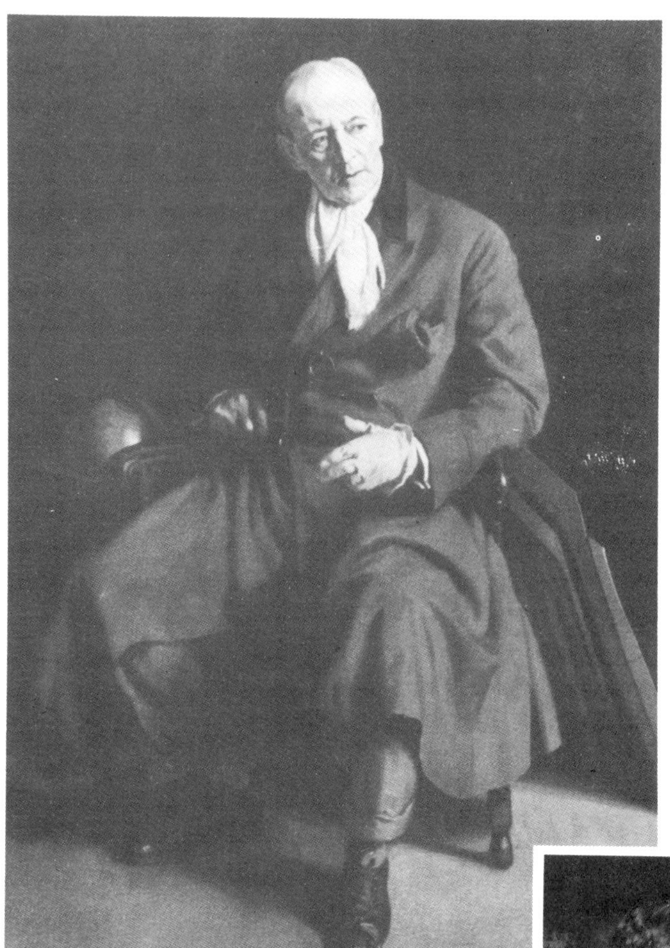

Portrait of James Pryde (1866-1941) by Sir James
Gunn, RA (1893-1964), born and educated in
Glasgow, who studied at Glasgow School of Art,
Edinburgh College of Art and at Julian's in Paris.
During the First World War he joined the Artists'
Rifles and later received a commission in the 10th
Scottish Rifles (the Cameronians). After the War he
turned to portrait painting: his "Conversation
Piece", an informal portrait group of Hilaire Belloc,
G.K. Chesterton and Maurice Baring, was the out-
standing picture at the Royal Academy Summer
Show of 1932. He also painted Delius's portrait,
shown at the RA in 1933. Gunn always looked for
the applause of fellow artists, which he never got.
In addition to this portrait of Pryde, Gunn's por-
trait of John Hassall is reproduced on page 78.

Charles Chaplin

The other school was the Fairy School, which chiefly appeared in book illustration. The inspiration for this school lay with the elderly J. A. Fitzgerald, and followers included Claude Shepperson, Edmund Dulac, George Sheringham, Harry Rountree, Charles Robinson, Willy Pogany and Stephen Baghot de la Bere. There were exceptions such as Lawson Wood or Heath Robinson who could not easily be placed in either category. Also a few artists were clever enough to roam from one camp to the other, notably Harry Rountree and Stephen Baghot de la Bere.

Such was the camaraderie between Club members that they often collaborated on projects, accepting commissions on a fifty/fifty basis. Aldin and Hassall illustrated Harry A. Spurr's *A Cockney in Arcadia* and *Two Well Worn Shoes* (a nursery rhyme book). Similarly Reynolds and Hassall shared the illustration of *By the Way Ballads* by W. Sapte and numerous articles for the now defunct *Playgoer* magazine. Hardy and Hassall even shared the design of invitation cards by drawing on each side of the card.

Recalling his youth, Frank Reynolds confessed:

> It was very good experience to have to sit down in this crowded room, full of competent artists, and plunge into a two-hour sketch, for that was the time allotted, and turn out something which would bear inspection, and I can't tell you how nervous I felt on my first attempt, for it was on this that you were elected or 'chucked'. I had the misfortune to sit next to Robert Sauber — not that he was hostile in any way. No, it was the bewildering way he went about a subject full of Georgian figures drinking a toast. 'The Toast', I think, was the subject that night. He squeezed bright oil colours straight from the tube on to a board and smeared them about with his fingers, and then transformed them into the velvet coats of the period. It was an amazing sketch when finished, with all the dash that a good sketch should have. Glancing at this out of the corner of my eye now and then was no help to my poor effort, but I managed to get elected.

The older element of the Sketch Club clearly inspired the younger members. Take for example J. Fitzgerald, who in his youth had contributed to *The Illustrated London News* along with Myles Birket Foster, or E. J. Gregory, RA who had worked for *The Graphic* before being accepted along the Royal Academy Walls. James Linton (now Sir James Dromgole Linton, PRI), who had also worked for *The Graphic*, also gave the younger element of the Club something to look up to. The likes of H. M. Bateman, Lionel Edwards, Tom Webster and Frank Hart (all young men) respected their older counterparts.

In his student days James Linton (1841-1916) had been a typical bohemian in appearance. Harry Furniss said of him: "His hair hung down over his shoulders, he favoured a Titian-shaped beard and moustache, a salmon-coloured tie, and brown velvet coat; his eyes were intelligent, his face refined, and he smoked good cigars, which he handed round in a liberal fashion." Nearing the end of his life he tidied up his appearance, had his hair cut and donned smart clothes. The result looked not dissimilar to Edward VII.

Another great bohemian was the much maligned Jimmy Pryde. More often than not he would arrive immaculately dressed in "the most exquisite evening dress" and then proceed to look around and select the most likely member from whom to borrow the cab fare. After dinner, with the simple aid of a napkin draped over his

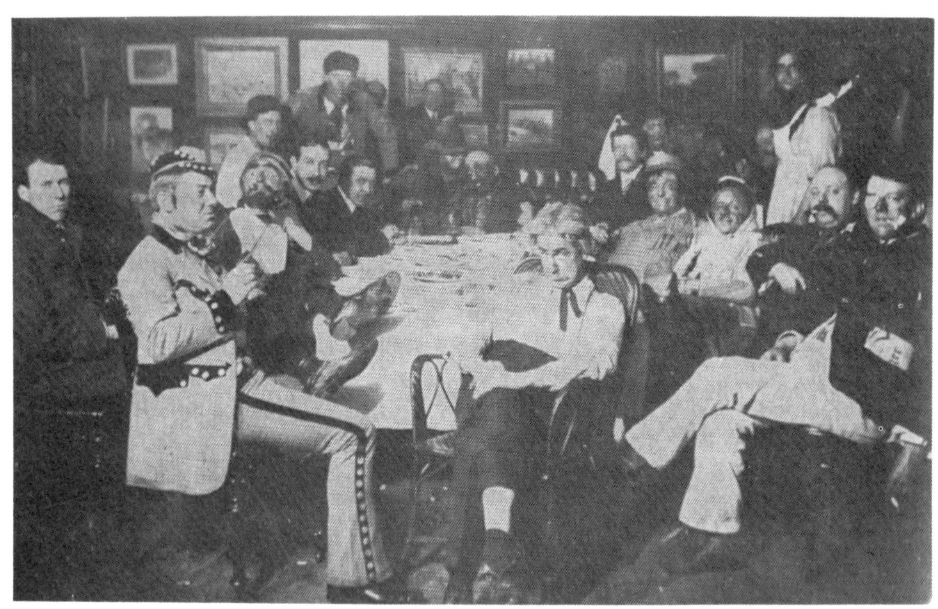

Early London Sketch Club Smoker in the Wells Street Studio.
Cecil Aldin (third from left) with pipe and hat; Starr Wood (sixth from left) with pipe and cap); Tom Browne (seventh from left) seated; Sandham and Harker, the two tramps (seated centre); behind them, Conan Doyle (standing); Montague Smyth, ROI (eighth from right, with moustache); behind him, Lee Hankey and Sir James Linton (seated); and, in the foreground, a coster (the model), with Walter Churcher seated centre.

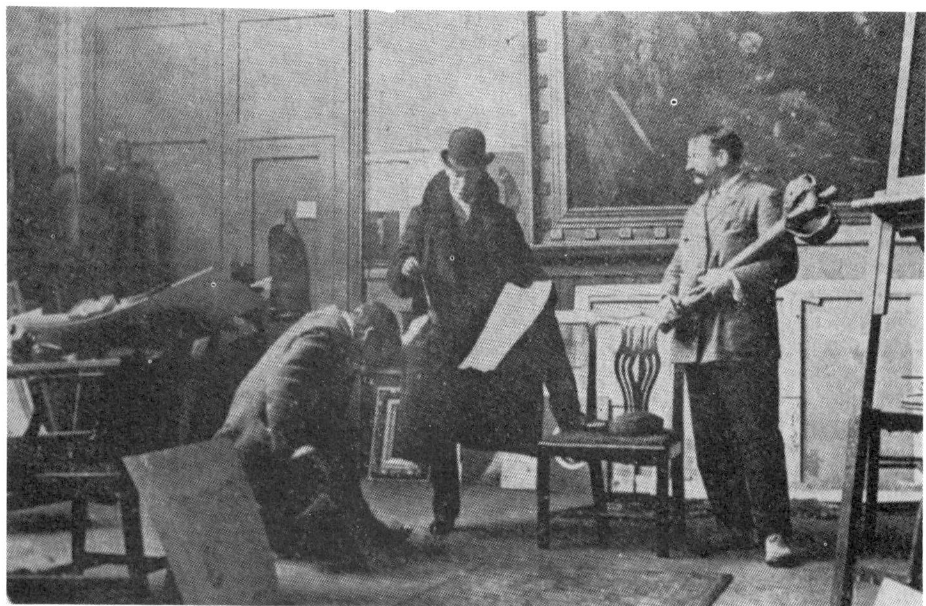

Signing the Wells Street Studio lease: Cecil Aldin, Phil May and Dudley Hardy.

head surmounted by the lid of a pepper pot, he would give a lifelike impersonation of Queen Victoria.

Jimmy Pryde was born in Edinburgh, the son of Dr David Pryde, a lecturer in English Literature. He became a student at the Royal Scottish Academy Schools before he went to Paris, where, like John Hassall, he studied under Bouguereau. On his return he came to London where his sister Mabel had persuaded her parents, when she was about seventeen, to let her study art at Hubert von Herkomer's School in Bushey. Max Beerbohm thought she looked like the result of an intrigue between Milton and the Mona Lisa, and she attracted William Nicholson, the youngest of the boy students at Herkomers. After her first term there they became engaged.

James Pryde shared lodgings with his sister at Bushey and naturally came to know Nicholson well. Not a student at Herkomers himself, Pryde was a subversive outside influence, making clear his contempt for the dingy academicism taught in the school. In 1890 he exhibited a pastel of his landlady's daughter, Miss Mutton, under the more romantic title "The Little Girl in Black", at the Grosvenor Gallery. It was favourably noticed by the critics. Nicholson, who was given the drawing, was by this time strongly influenced by Pryde: for a similar "piece of Whistlerian impudence" he was expelled by Herkomer. In 1893 Mabel Pryde married Nicholson and a year later their eldest son Ben, who was to become the famous abstract painter, was born.

The two brothers-in-law James Pryde and William Nicholson were to team up as "the Beggarstaff Brothers" (the name Beggarstaff came from a sack of corn stacked in a corner which they saw one day whilst out sketching) who were to revolutionise advertising. In later years, however, Nicholson and Pryde grew apart and there was some bad feeling between them, perhaps caused by Pryde's jealousy of Nicholson's establishment success and eventual knighthood. Max Beerbohm, in one of his series of cartoons, "The Old and Young Selves", maliciously showed the two of them looking back at a sort of Siamese twin formed of both of them. Jimmy Pryde, talented though he was, did not possess the business acumen of William Nicholson and, after the success of the J. and W. Beggarstaff team in the 1890s, he turned his hand to acting. He toured Scotland in 1895 with Gordon Craig and produced little work after about 1925. He died a disillusioned man. After the enormous success of the Beggarstaff Brothers it was sad that the relationship between William and Jimmy should have developed this rift: when they worked together their combined talent was brilliant.

Probably the best description of Pryde came from his wife's reminiscences, *Some Years of My Life*:

> Tall, handsome, amusing as he was, and entirely unpractical in wordly affairs, Pryde was one of those men who are attractive to women without making any great exertions to be so ... It is probably true to say that he was always a bachelor at heart.

Pryde fitted easily into the Sketch Club format, being an amateur thespian and bohemian to the end of his days. He greatly influenced Orpen and Brangwyn and was admired among his contemporaries. In an article from *John O'London's Weekly* dated 27 January 1923, two eminent portrait painters discussed who was the greatest living British artist in 1923. The conversation took place in a Paris café and the conclusion they came to was: "James Pryde, a painter who only exhibits three or

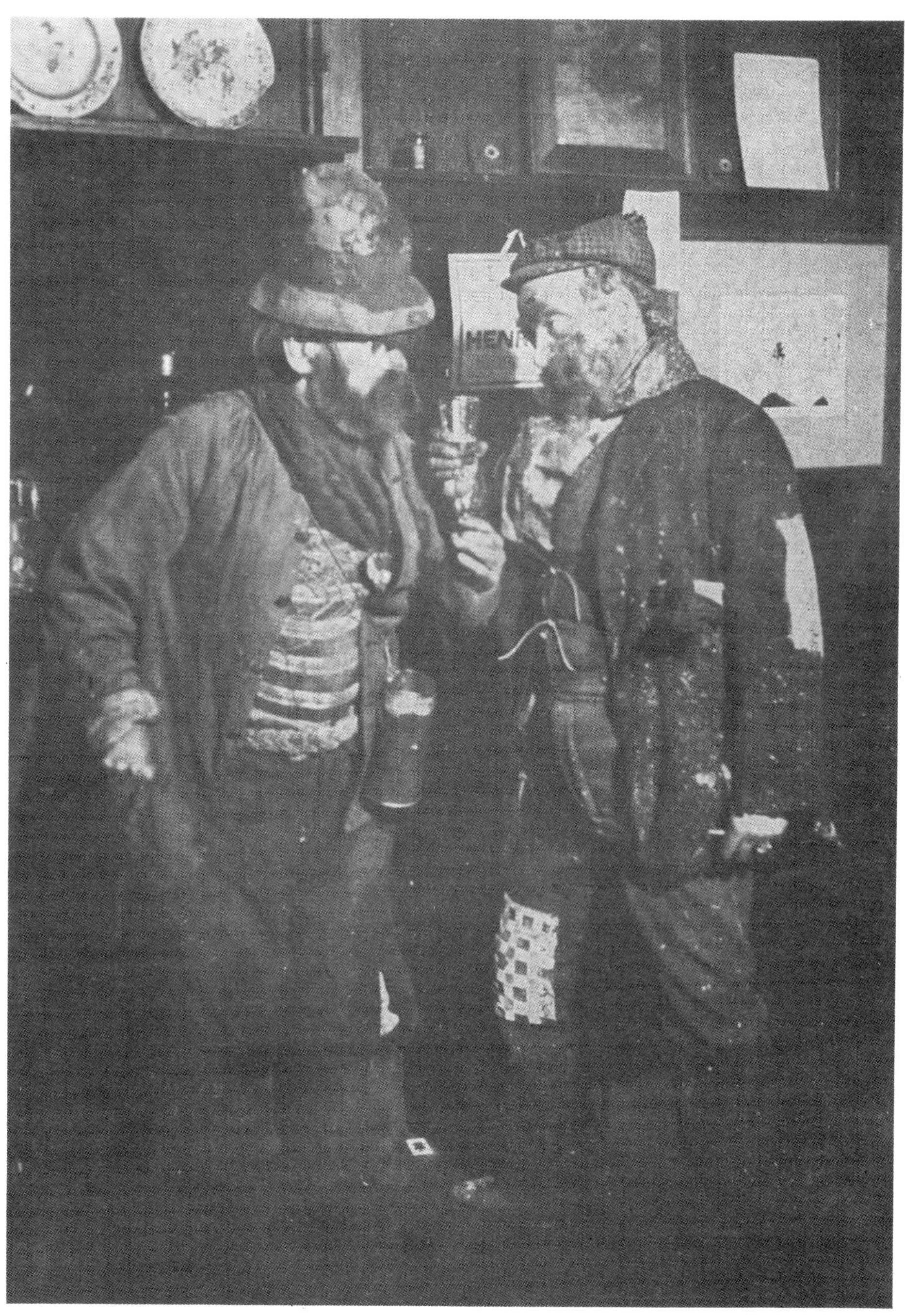

Henry Sandham and Jo Harker go through their paces at the London Sketch Club
as two tramps.

46

four new pictures a year, who never sends to the Academy, and who never courts any kind of publicity.''

The problem with Pryde was that he spent more than he earned, and when he was ''in the money'' he would stand drinks all round. However, his borrowing tendency did not diminish and he eventually came, for some of his friends, to seem less amusing than of old. His reputation was not enhanced by remarks such as: ''Jimmy Pryde came to stay the night — two years later he left!'' (as Hassall often remarked).

In complete contrast to Pryde was that other great friend of John Hassall, René Bull. Born in Dublin of an English father and French mother, René was self-disciplined. He was ''an inexhaustible reconteur, a musician, and wizard of leger-de-main — especially with cards!'' He had no great aspirations to become a fine artist, unlike Pryde: he was content with ''commercial art''. He worked first for the Magazine *Pick-Me-Up*, which was then just starting, and latterly as a regular contributor to *Black and White*.

> His connection with *Black and White* led to some hairy experiences as a war artist and correspondent. In that field his expeditions include the Armenian Massacres, the Chitral and Tirah Campaigns in India, the Indian Plague and Famine, the Atbara Campaign, the Greco-Turkish War and Kitchener's Sudan Campaign. Finally, he went to South Africa at the outbreak of hostilities, and was one of the lucky passengers of the very last train which crept out of Ladysmith the night before the siege was completed. He recalled that famous journey as one of the most thrilling of his experiences; how the lightless train crept slowly with its precious and frightened freight of women and children through the hills, on the summits of which they could see the Boer camp fires.

René Bull was a great admirer of the Frenchman Caran d'Ache, whom he had met in Paris. If anything, he adapted the Caran d'Ache principle to illustration in England. His line was sure, his subjects bold and he was a first rate illustrator.

René Bull had a nephew with an entomological turn, and as a correspondent during the Greco-Turkish War, he was expected to take advantage of his frequent foreign trips to add to the boy's collection of beetles and ''other fearsome beasts''.

> One day he was cycling along a hilly road in Greece during hostilities when he observed a flicking movement in the grass of the hillside; scenting new ideas in grasshoppers for his nephew, he dismounted and commenced to prospect for specimens, but in spite of the continued flicking, he had no luck, and if Bennet Burleigh had not appeared, another and a worst kind of ill-luck would have befallen him. Seeing René Bull, Burleigh asked, with obvious surprise, what he might be doing, and upon being informed the older correspondent advised him to give up his search and take shelter, for what he took to be the flicking of grasshoppers was the flicking of shots from Turkish rifles!''

Like Caran d'Ache, who took up toymaking as a hobby, Bull became a model engineering enthusiast with a particular interest in model railways (he bought his first model train for 6½d). As he said:

> One fine day, I bought an O-gauge clockwork locomotive in Dublin for 4/- or 5/-. Then I bought a ''Don'' electric motor and wondered how I could fit the engine in it. I lived in Kew Gardens then, and my voltage was 200 continuous. With difficulties I fixed the ''Don'' into the shell of my clockwork engine, and

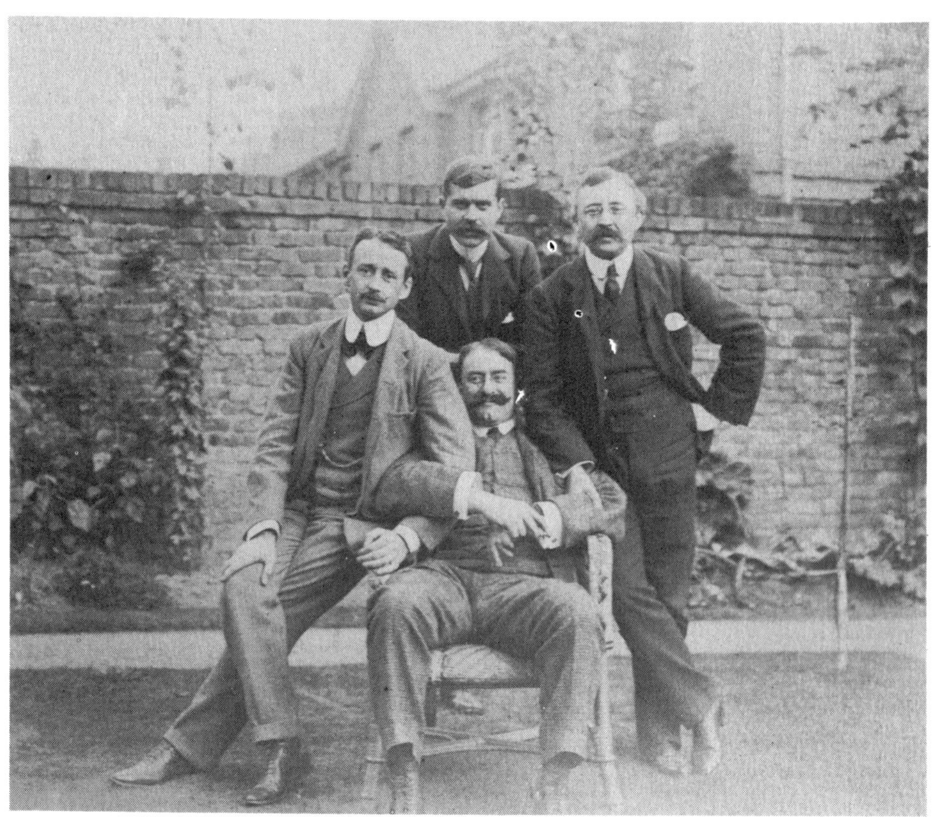

René Bull, John Hassall, Dudley Hardy (seated) and Walter Fowler.

put the full current from my wall plug on. The line was laid on my dining-room table; the engine flew at 100 miles an hour down a straight, then it met a curve and went clean through the window.

In 1907 John Hassall held a spoof entertainment in his studio at 88 Kensington Park Road. René Bull helped with a great many parts: the item "The Brothers Honey and Mudd" saw Hassall and Bull dressed as two eccentric musicians giving performances that "would drive the audience crazy". (Fortunately their pathetic ballads were limited to two and it was stated that no encores were allowed.) In a further skit involving Monsieur le Dompteur (played by Bull) and his famous ostrich Leslie (played by Hassall) it was requested that "the audience would not feed the bird!" The programme ended with the scourings of the Orient by Mahmond Ben Hassa (Hassall) and Abdulla Ahmed (Bull) in their world famous act "The Mongoose Tree and the Mango Fight!"

Such lighthearted entertainments were part of the Edwardian age. Edward VII had relaxed the tight corsets of Victorian repression and it spilled out in gaiety and fun. Hassall's studio party of 1907 echoed memories of "The London Sketch Club Walk to Brighton and Back" held on 1 April 1904, the year Hassall was President of the Sketch Club (1904-1905). First prize was "a slightly soiled Season Ticket for Earls Court dated 1900"; second prize was "the island of Crete"; third prize a piece of plate, bearing the arms of the Holborn Restaurant, presented by Mr Cadbury. The judges consisted of Messrs. C. B. Fry, Chirgwin, Winston Churchill, G. R. Sims, Billington, Mornington Cannon, Bassano, Jamrach, Haddon Chambers and Sunny Jim, whilst the referee was Herr Julius Seeth and official timekeepers were Messrs. Swan and Edgar. The competitors were asked to assemble at 6.30 pm in Leicester Square and then proceed via The Strand, Chigford, Wells Street, New Barnet, Gloucester Road, Shadwell, Wilton Crescent, Derby, Bix Hill, Hemel Hempstead, Lower Thames Street, Ipswich, Baker Street and Wakefield to Brighton, touch wood and return via Willesden.

The assembled crowd met in the bar to discuss the route, but after some hours, when they finally decided which was the best and easiest route to take, it was too dark for any such undertaking. In the interests of safety they all went home and abandoned the project.

At this time there was a great deal of spoofing. At the first of the evening conversaziones, held in 1899, John Hassall (or P.C. Hassall) organised seating arrangements and controlled traffic generally (it was usually to the bar), whilst Newton Shepard acted as Court Chamberlain announcing everybody more or less incorrectly.

Hassall's love of spoof was shared by Starr Wood; they were both members of the Savage, too. Starr Wood had an extremely realistic tank act. He was the intrepid diver who remained below the surface of the water for a full ten minutes, during which time he engaged in hand-to-hand combat with a marine monster. Eventually he emerged triumphant and breathless, the contents of a soda-syphon dripping from his brow and holding at arm's length an enormous lobster, made by John Hassall (who "in the cause of realism had spared no expense of orange vermilion").

Over the years the Wells Street studio took on a mellow look. Niccotine-stained plates and crockery lined the walls and the fire was generally lit; there was a sprinkling of coal dust and embers. During working sessions a haze of smoke from members' pipes curled around the old gas lamps: the atmosphere was like a music-hall tap-room. There were no licensing laws prior to the 1914-18 War though, strangely enough, in the nineteenth century you needed a licence for singing! Presumably the government had given up on the "dreaded alc", realising that everyone drank; but it was a different matter to sing.

Most of the dissenters who formed the original London Sketch Club came from the Langham and these included J. A. Fitzgerald and Sir James Linton. However, two members who were not part of the Langham but who made up the original Council of the London Sketch Club were Phil May and Cecil Aldin. Aldin, whose work is now highly collectable, seems to have been the odd one out. It was he who designed the original chimney-corner for the "Punch Bowlers" which the London Sketch Club inherited.

Aldin, like Walter Churcher, had a deep desire to recreate a Britain of yesteryear. His was the dream of a "Pickwickian" club where the individual was important. In real life he was a Master of Foxhounds, and he once surprised everyone by coming to the Club in full hunting gear. Hassall always said he would go to the dogs and indeed much of Aldin's popularity came through his wonderful canine creations.

The other hunting artist who preceded Aldin was John Leech but one always gets the impression that Leech's cartoons served only to pay for his hunting expeditions.

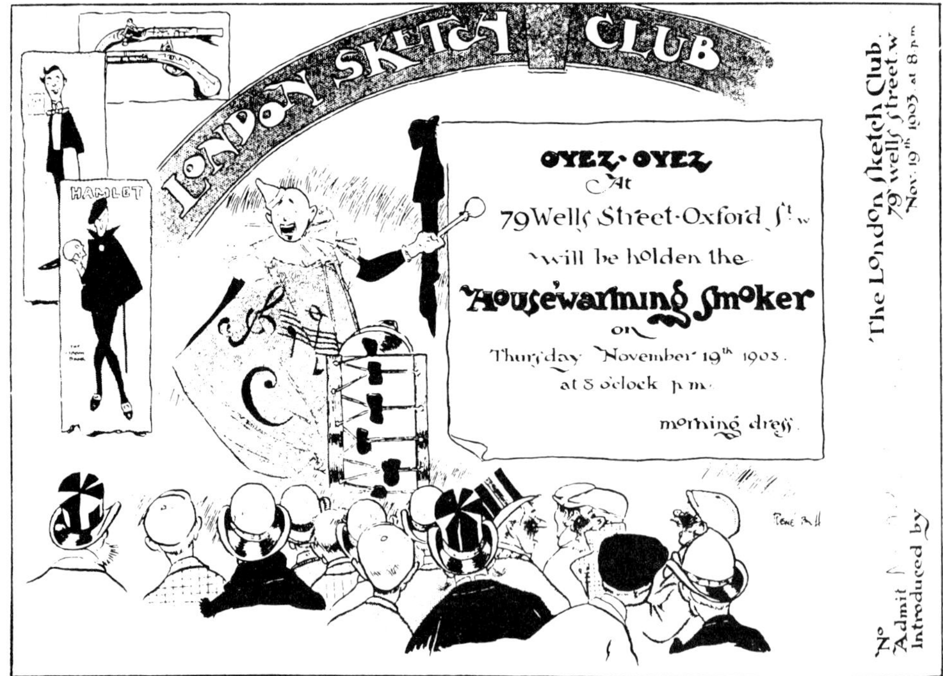

Invitation card by René Bull.

With Aldin there is somehow more sincerity. Aldin, like Hassall and Lawson Wood, loved "olde worldy" things, clay pipes, waistcoats, punch ladles, oak furniture and the like. A streak of such sentiment was a common trait of London Sketch Club members. They looked back to the good ol' days, yet little did they realise they were probably living in the most unconstrained and uninhibited time of their lives. The First World War was fast approaching and the world as they knew it was about to be revolutionised.

Two important guests visited the London Sketch Club during its time in Wells Street. The first was the imposing G. K. Chesterton (1874-1936), novelist, poet and humorist. Chesterton, whose catchphrase was "If a thing's worth doing, its worth doing badly," was a genuine wit, and members were still talking about his visit sixty years later.

The second was a shy, rather insignificant young lad who had just toured the provinces in a play called *Sherlock Holmes*, written by William Gillette. He was a seventeen-year-old unknown actor called Charles Chaplin, who was to achieve fame and fortune after leaving Britain for the States in 1910.

The professional entertainers at the Club during this time included Charles Pond, a great comedian specialising in monologues of pub life, Alfred Lester, who later became famous in *The Arcadians*, Willie Nicholl, who with a still small voice could hold silent the noisiest crowd to listen to old Scottish ballads, Whitworth Mitton, who could sing tenor songs with great sweetness, and not forgetting Mel Spurr with his face of India rubber who sang at the piano, and of course the one and only Walter Churcher.

50

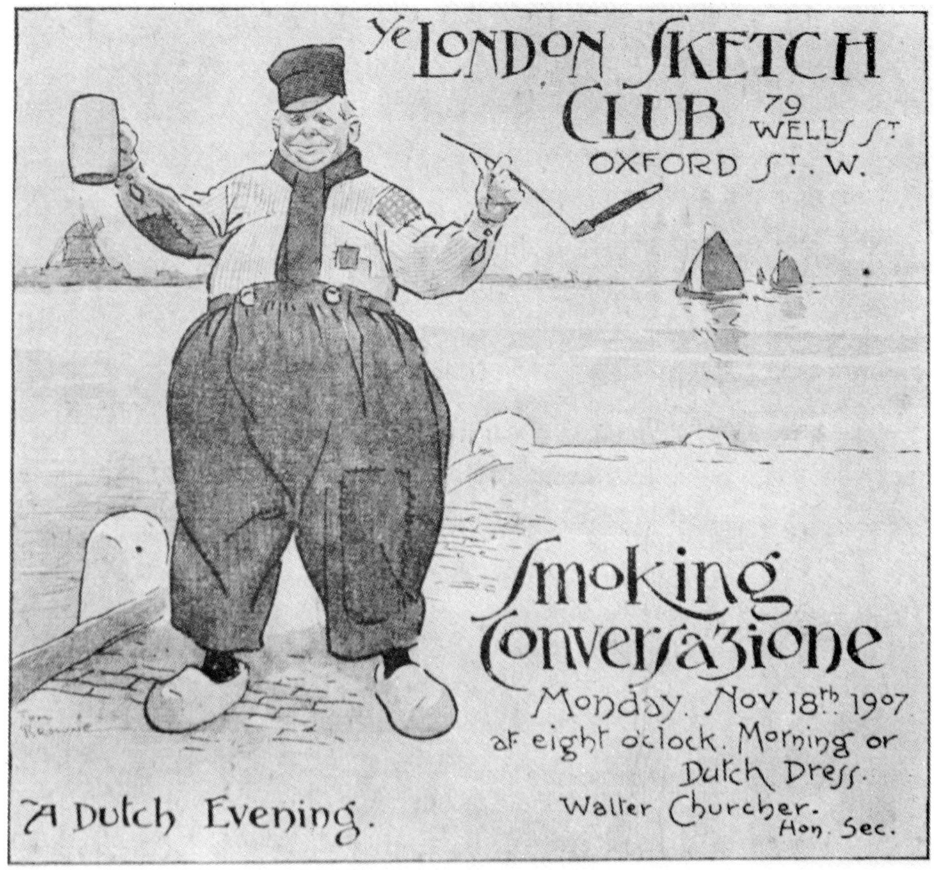

Invitation card by Tom Browne.

Tom Browne died in 1910 from cancer. At his funeral in Shooter's Hill Cemetery, Blackheath, he was buried with full military honours. His coffin was laid on a gun carriage and his sword, belt and helmet were placed on it. The 18th Company (ASC Kensington Barracks) fired a volley over his grave. Among the principal mourners were John Hassall, Dudley Hardy, René Bull, Walter Churcher, Frank Reynolds and Frank Jackson. Wreaths were sent by General R. S. S. Baden-Powell, and Major and Mrs Tennent (the editor of *Printers Pie*).

Tom Browne had always been one of the most popular members of the Sketch Club: his mercurial humour was infectious. On special nights when "he foresaw that they were likely to be more than convivial, he used to make arrangements for friends to see him home". This was when he lived at Westcombe Park and, to quote a friend who was one of those who would often see him home, "it involved spending the night as his guest — or what was left of it, and the next morning, after more talks and drinks, I could then go home." Although Tom Browne was a lighthearted, boisterous person, he would often talk about spiritualism and the survival of friendships in the afterlife. Apparently he was quite "earnest in his search for

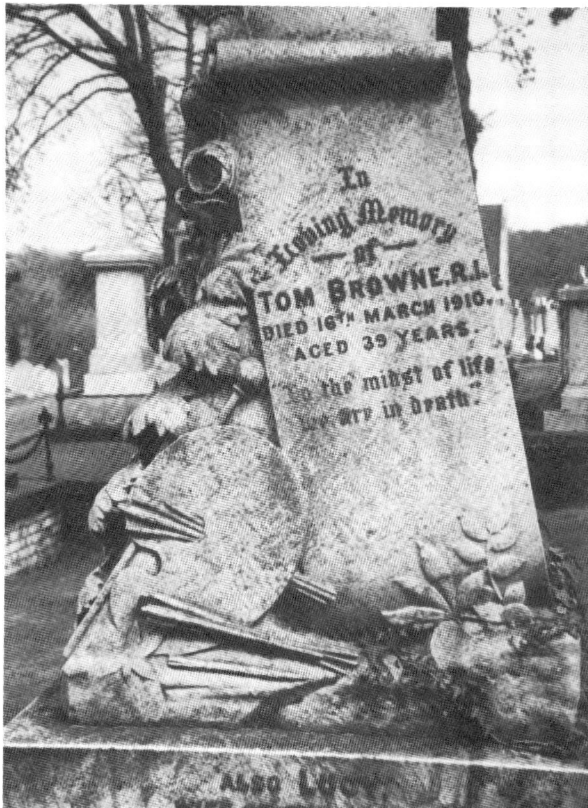

Tom Browne's grave.

knowledge on this subject, although one could do little to help except listen with sympathetic ear, which is probably all he wanted.

To commemorate the respect in which the London Sketch Club held Browne, an exhibition of his work was held on 19 January 1914. A total of 161 works, including paintings and unfinished studies, were shown. While the exhibition was in progress a man stopped in front of a drawing entitled "The Sick Child". Tears were rolling down his face, and when the Secretary asked him what was amiss, he replied that years ago he had sat for Tom as a model. During the session the man mentioned he was from Nottingham: Tom gave him half-a-crown instead of the usual shilling. He wept at the memory. This illustrates the effect that Browne had on people: he was a very intense man, and very generous too. Reading one or two accounts of people who met him, it seems he was the sort of person you were not likely to forget. He died of throat cancer at the age of thirty-eight and, oddly enough, so did his son who used to be a car salesman. His old studio in Blackheath was made into a museum by John Bratby who bought the studio and filled it with Tom Browne relics, including a photograph of Browne on his favourite horse over the mantlepiece. Sadly the house has been left to deteriorate and these days is in need of some repair.

Of course there were other deaths before the Great War, such as Phil May, Alfred East, Walter Fowler and J. A. Fitzgerald, but none affected the Sketch Club more than Tom Browne's sudden demise.

CHAPTER 4

Artists and Bohemians

Membership of the London Sketch Club was at its most prestigious in the years leading up to the 1914-18 War. Only a certain number of artists were admitted to this select group and a set of rules were laid down. (Curiously the rule book still applied some seventy years later, with few alterations.) As Lionel Edwards remarked, "Most of the prominent artists (outside the RA circle) were then members of the London Sketch Club." Edwards was lucky to be elected whilst still a student; he saw the Club at its best. He was highly impressed by George Haite's talent, was introduced to Phil May, met Cecil Aldin and became a great friend of Lance Thackeray, often working in Thackeray's studio at 42 Linden Gardens, Bayswater.

One summer Lionel Edwards and Lance Thackeray went to stay at Edward's mother's house in Wales. They stayed for a month painting every day. However the house was reputed to be haunted and at breakfast one morning "Thack" appeared very quiet, white and silent — most unlike his usual boisterous self. He stated that he had had a wire from London and had to return at once. "Thack" never admitted to seeing an apparition although he later conceded the wire was an invention. Edwards and Thackeray often collaborated on projects which were completed in Sketch Club style.

Thackeray was a talented and quick witted character with an immense knowledge of Egypt. He was also a generous and sometimes self-effacing individual. When Gilbert Frankau, the novelist, wrote a short satire entitled *The XYZ of Bridge*, the publishers thought it worth publishing if illustrated. Lance Thackeray was recommended and after dining with Frankau undertook the commission. As Frankau said later, "Thackeray did a marvellous job for a ridiculously small fee!"

The trio of Thackeray, Browne and Hassall were prolific in the postcard field and left a plethora of cards which are highly sought after. All three would frequently meet in the Savage or Eccentric Club as well as at the London Sketch Club. Both Browne and Thackeray had an impish sense of humour and one of them (possibly both) put some schoolgirls up to a prank against their mate John Hassall.

Hassall's famous poster for the British Vacuum Cleaner Company Ltd had just been placed on the hoardings. It depicted a parlour maid being chased by a vicious looking vacuum cleaner, in the style of John Wyndham's triffids, with the caption "Help!". Soon after its appearance Hassall received a note from a young lady — a complete stranger — addressed from a house in South Kensington, begging for a thumbnail sketch of the poster which she hoped to put in her postcard collection. Being a gallant gentleman, "Jack" Hassall made a sketch on a card and posted it. Two days later the lady wrote again, hoping that her request had not seemed presumptuous, but adding wistfully that she would *so* value the sketch. Hassall,

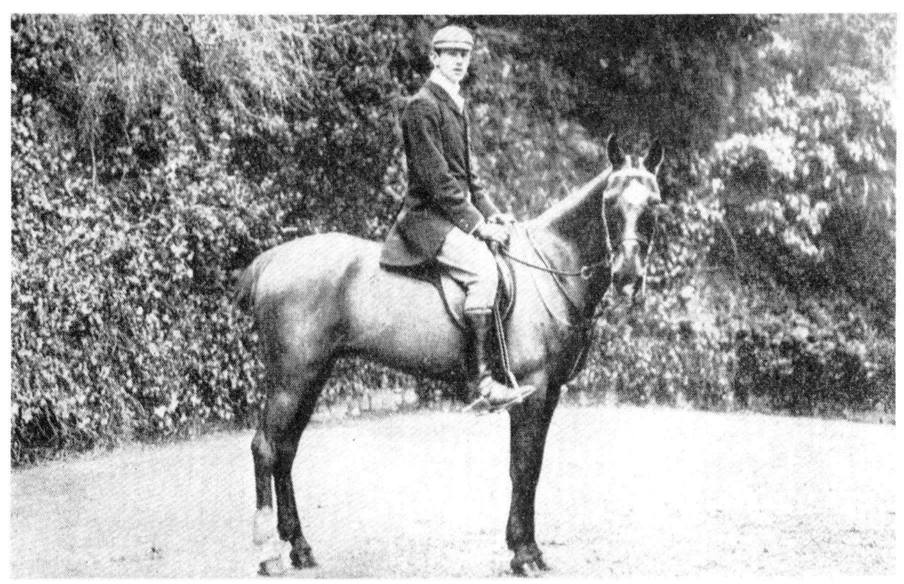

Lionel Edwards (aged nineteen) on his first horse. Two years later Lionel Dalhousie Robertson Edwards (1878-1966) joined the London Sketch Club.

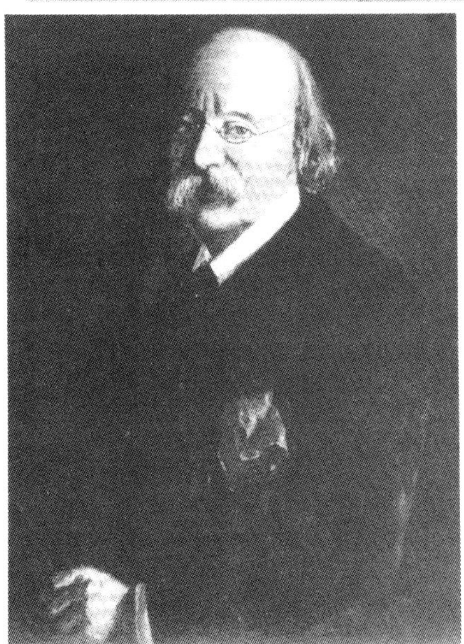

"Fairy" Fitzgerald's last wish was to die in the Savage Club. As Aaron Watson remarked, "It was a weird idea; but in his latter days he came to the club every Saturday expecting to die and only missed his expectation by three or four days." John Anster Fitzgerald (1819-1906) was given the extraordinary favour of a pension by the Royal Academy. (Could this have been the Artists Benevolent Fund?)

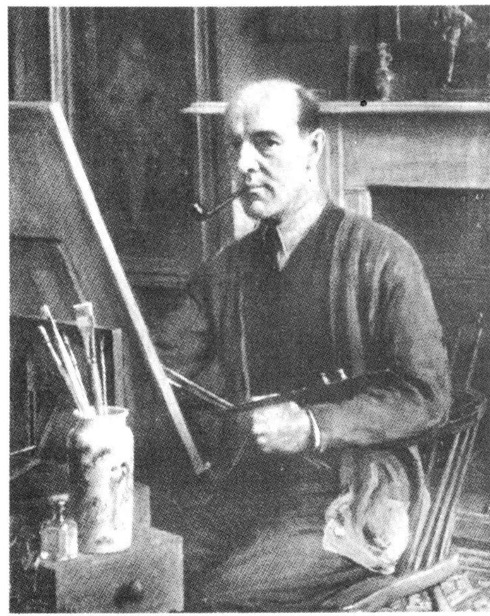

Frank Reynolds, RI (1876-1953) was a confirmed bibliophile all his life, a trait inherited by his daughter who runs a secondhand and antiquarian bookshop in Cumbria. This self portrait was exhibited at the Royal Academy in 1941.

wondering how the first card had gone astray, posted a second. After a few days a third letter arrived with an abject apology from the lady who by now was plunged into dejection. She explained that she understood the total unreasonableness of her request on such a busy and famous artist . . . but if he would excuse her persistence, etc, etc. Hassall made a third sketch and posted it, this time registering the envelope at the Post Office.

As Hassall was leaving the Post Office he felt troubled by the vagaries of a service which hitherto had been extremely reliable. He looked up the lady's address in the Post Office Directory, only to discover his leg was being vigorously pulled by the pupils of Miss Euphemia Orkin Trooler's select Establishment for the Daughters of the Aristocracy and Gentry!

Thackeray, Hassall, Hardy and Browne were a boozy lot. But Frank Reynolds, James Thorpe, H. M. Bateman and Lionel Edwards wre all moderate in their drinking habits. To keep fit, Reynolds and Thorpe would go on winter rambles after the cricket season had finished. One year they walked around Devon, the following year in Wiltshire, Dorset and so on. These were the days when motor traffic was light and country life ran at a peaceful pace.

Reynolds had a difficult time early in his career, as is borne out by the following anecdote related in *Humorous Drawings for the Press*, published in 1947:

It was at about this time (I was terribly hard up) that a friend of mine told me of a paper that paid cash down over the counter for humorous drawings. It was a most successful venture, in spite of its gruesome title — *Sketchy Bits*. I duly made up a portfolio of drawings and set out to call on the Editor. This turned out to be something of an ordeal. On arriving at the office, which was in a court off Fleet Street, I was faced with a crowd of artists — not an orderly queue, but just a throng who grinned and nudged each other at the sight of a new hand. Suddenly the doors were thrown open and the whole mass of us fought our way up the crazy stairs and into the editorial presence. Here we were ranged on one side of the room, facing the desk. The Editor, who wore a top hat on the back of his head and smoked a cigar, was supported by his brother, who did the paying out. There he was, complete with cheque-book and pen poised. The Editor, a shrewd but formidable-looking man, would, with an imperious gesture, beckon to one of us to step forward and display his wares. When he selected something, the fortunate artist passed on to the brother, who wrote the cheque (a flat rate of thirty bob a time), and the happy warrior departed down the stairs, two at a time! In due course the great man beckoned to me — at least I thought so, and, stepping gaily forward, was ordered away. "Get back, you!" This was said with such vigour that the top hat fell on the floor. Yes, dear reader, I was doing nicely — nice going, you'll admit, and I was made to wait until the last had been dealt with before he turned to me with, "Now then, cheeky!" By this time I had recovered my wind and for two pins would have knocked the top hat off again, but all went well and he bought about half a dozen of the subjects, one of which showed some figures in evening dress. "Ah!" he said. "That's the stuff! I can do with plenty of that! Society people! See?" And "see" I did, for later I plied him with these subjects good and plenty. We became very good friends and the top hat remained in position. I appeared on the front page for some time, and had the usual privilege of being allowed to send my contribution through the post.

It was all very comfortable and jolly. I had a good time and played an awful lot of cricket, but I wasn't learning much, and it was a good thing for me when Cecil Aldin put me up for the London Sketch Club.

Reynolds soon found refuge in the Sketch Club and in later life advised, "I strongly recommend any young artist to become a member of a Sketch Club. It is a great stimulant." Reynolds was a staunch admirer of Claude Shepperson. His life was one of constant work with little reward. Some of his best work can be found in back copies of *Punch*. Reynolds was invited to join the *Punch* Table in 1919 and in 1921 took over as Art Editor from Frederick Townsend, a post he held until 1931.

Reynolds had worked on *The Sketch* under the editorship of Keble Bell and went on to illustrate three of Keble Bell's books (written under the pseudonym Keble Howard), *Smiths of Surbiton, The God in the Garden* and *Love in June*. In 1904, when Keble Bell was editor of *The Sketch*, Reynolds was sent to Paris to complete a commission on behalf of the paper. He took James Thorpe and Starr Wood as escorts, as Thorpe recalled:

On the cross-channel part of the journey I had donned a pair of stout walking boots in case of rough weather, and the French customs authorities were so convulsed with laughter — "veritables bateaux" was their comment — at this fresh example of the Englishman's traditional madness that they declined to make any inspection of our baggage. An American lent us his studio which, with its glass roof in a real Parisian Heatwave, used to reach the temperature of an oven. Much of our time was spent lying full length and gasping for air, and work was only possible in the lightest of garb or even less. In spite of all this, Reynolds seized his opportunity wholeheartedly and did some of the best drawings he has ever done — true individual character studies of real Parisian characters. The articles which accompanied the drawings were written by John N. Raphael, the well-known correspondent for many English papers, and under his competent guidance we saw much of the heart of Paris life which is unknown to the casual visitor. Particularly do I remember the almost rural charm of Montmartre in those days and the wide views of the great city. The excellent series of articles and drawings which resulted were published in book form in 1908.

Few artists from the younger element of the London Sketch Club had much money. They mostly came from working class or middle class families who violently disapproved of their careers as artists, leaving them to eke out what little they could from their chosen vocation. Hence the "Bohemian" tag; but the London Sketch Club had a bohemian atmosphere anyway. Even the older element of the Club, the likes of Hugh Thomson, J.A. Fitzgerald and E.J. Gregory, had had a similar grounding and were sympathetic. Nevertheless, when the occasion arose they all managed to find dress suits or dinner jackets. Take Edmund Dulac for example: there is hardly one photograph of him in existence in which he is not looking more like a city stockbroker than a bohemian book illustrator — but a bohemian he was. It was the same with René Bull and John Hassall. Even Cecil Aldin as a young struggling artist was always smartly turned out.

The lifestyle London Sketch Club members adopted was one of intense mental concentration followed by relaxation. It was a bit like the spring of a watch being slowly tightened and then left to unwind. This was how the Sketch Club crew

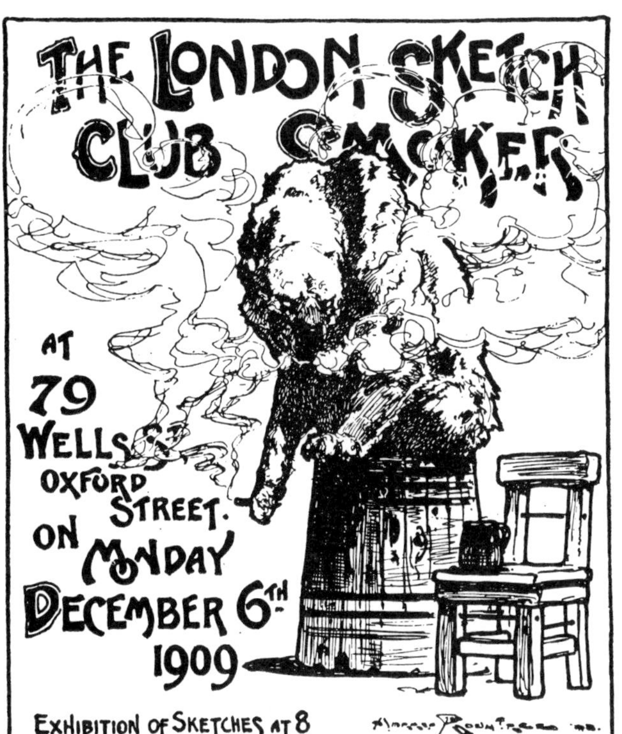

Invitation card by
Harry Rountree.

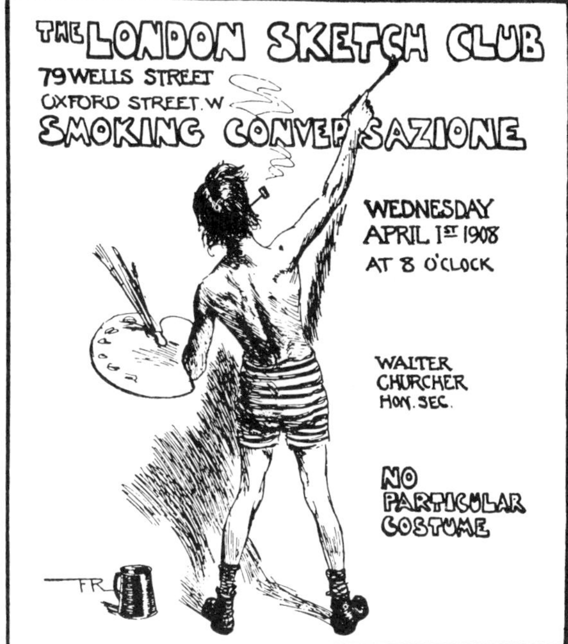

Invitation card by
Frank Reynolds.

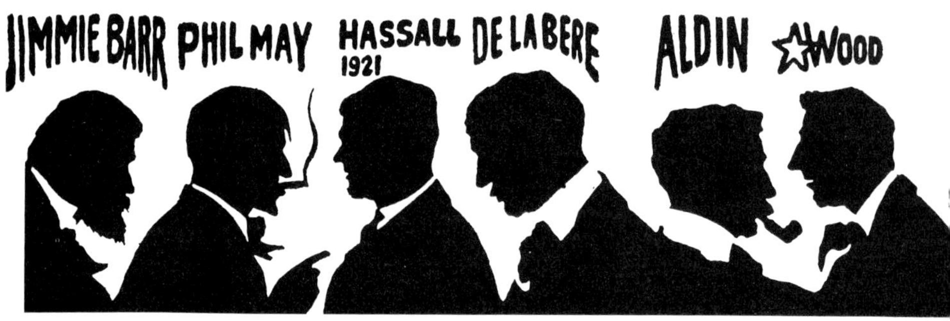

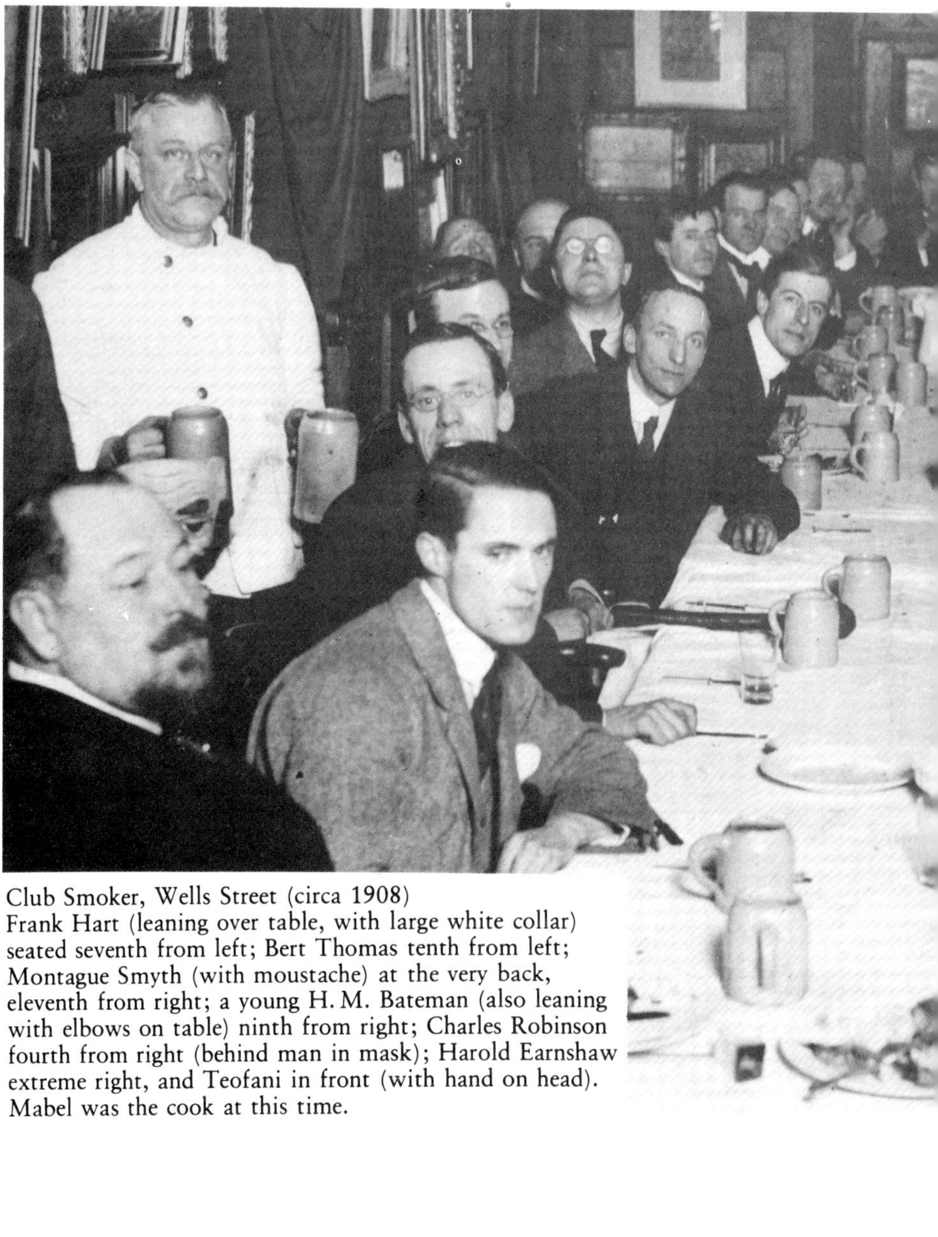

Club Smoker, Wells Street (circa 1908)
Frank Hart (leaning over table, with large white collar)
seated seventh from left; Bert Thomas tenth from left;
Montague Smyth (with moustache) at the very back,
eleventh from right; a young H. M. Bateman (also leaning
with elbows on table) ninth from right; Charles Robinson
fourth from right (behind man in mask); Harold Earnshaw
extreme right, and Teofani in front (with hand on head).
Mabel was the cook at this time.

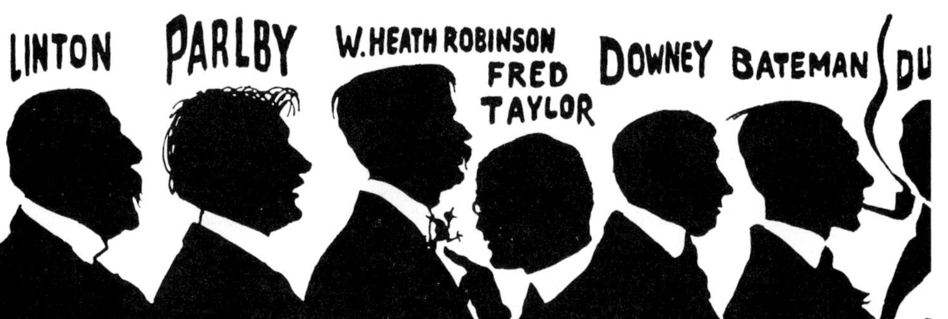

LINTON
PARLBY
W. HEATH ROBINSON
FRED TAYLOR
DOWNEY
BATEMAN
DU

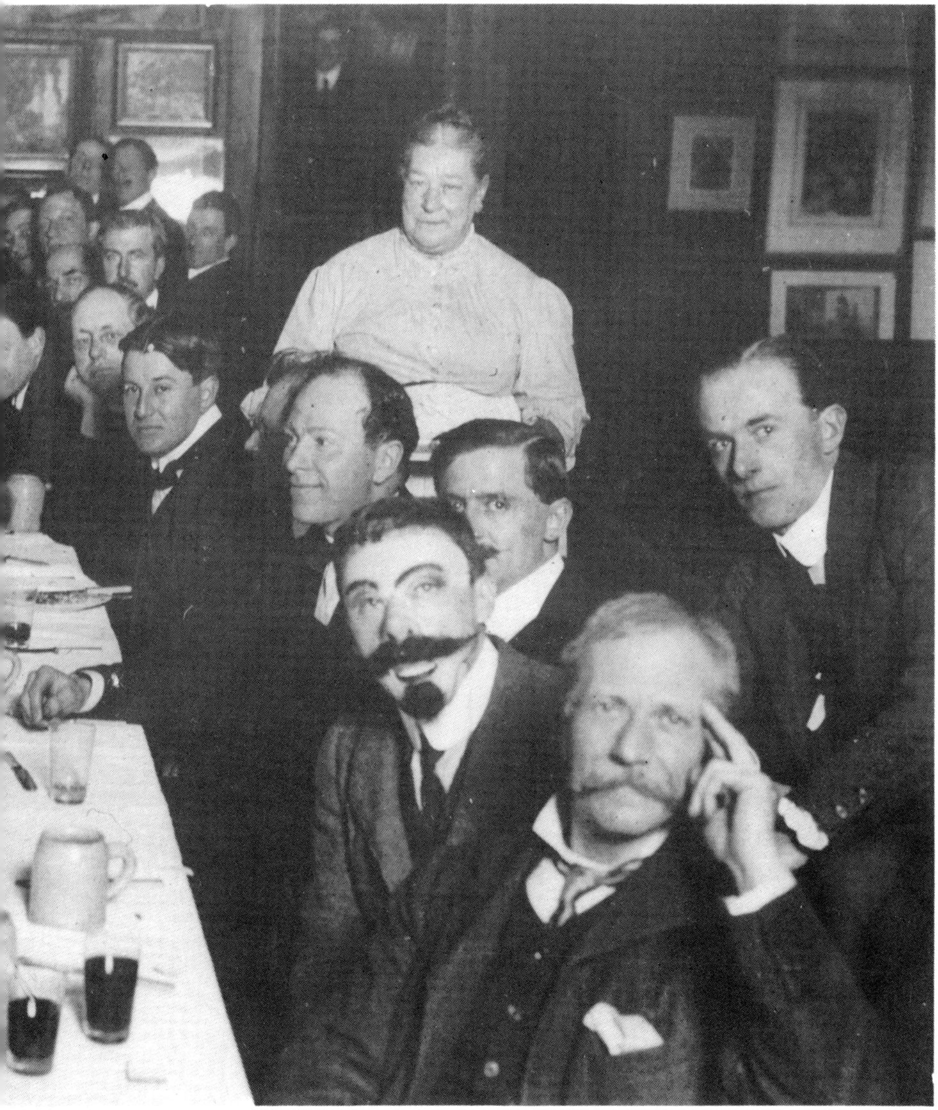

survived. Theirs was a totally different lifestyle from that of the bureaucrat who filled his time with obscure trifles and clockwatching. With the Sketch Club mob every work was a race against time: they created their own pressure, which was heightened if the painting did not go well. The range of subjects varied. Members were given cards of subjects for the season, one figure the other landscape. There is a story of two old members of the rival Langham Sketch Club (which operated the same system) saying, "I see the subjects for tonight are 'Old Age' and 'Wind'!"

The most successful exponent of the Fairy School was Edmund Dulac. He was born in Toulouse and studied law at Toulouse University. However, after attending local art classes, he abandoned law for art. He arrived in London in 1905. Fascinated by the Englishness of Hardy, Aldin, Hassall and Thackeray, he soon joined the London Sketch Club. No other artist benefited quite so much from the two-hour sketch discipline. By nature a perfectionist, this method of working allowed him to make mistakes. Dulac soon learned from these mistakes and, with Rackham, became a doyen of book illustration. His caricatures did not reach the same standard as his book illustration but Dulac was a craftsman in every medium. He designed costumes for the theatre, stamps, banknotes, book plates and medals; he even played the nose flute, which came in useful for after dinner turns at the London Sketch Club.

Many London Sketch Club members were associated with particular newspapers or periodicals. Dulac's name will always be linked to a weekly newspaper *The Outlook*. René Bull and Charles Sheldon had worked for *Black & White*; there were also the *Graphic* and *Strand* illustrators. Harry Rountree, another great benefactor of the two-hour sketch, will always be associated with *Little Folks*, edited by S. H. Hamer. Rountree, like Dulac, was an immigré, having arrived in London from New Zealand. He was the first of many London Sketch Club members to use anthropomorphic themes in his work. Hassall drew his mongrel dog in many cartoons and posters, purely as a mascot; Aldin was well-known for his canine studies; Rountree encompassed the whole animal kingdom in his repertoire: turtles, mice, owls, fishes . . . He began his professional life designing jampot labels in New Zealand, arriving in London in 1901, and he joined the London Sketch Club circa 1904/5. The Club's sense of humour appealed to him but he took his work very seriously. Often described as mercurial, Rountree fitted into the Sketch Club format like a hand into a glove. Next to Dulac he was the most talented of book illustrators, but it is only in recent times that galleries have taken an interest in his work. Rountree is one of that group of artists, like Charles Robinson and Harold Earnshaw, who has suddenly come into vogue.

For a time he was one of Percy Bradshaw's tutors in the Press Art School, and Bradshaw said of him:

> He brought to this enterprise all his breezy enthusiasm, all the knowledge he had gained in his years of experience as a designer of posters, playing cards, showcards and calendars, as an illustrator of animal stories and travel books, and an outstanding humorous artist. Like most humorists he takes his work very seriously. Behind the lightest and most vivacious of his water-colours is — *knowledge*; and he confesses that his studio is a nightmare to his housemaid — with its bones and horns, hooves and skeletons. He has studied animal anatomy, but he insists on the student expressing his own individuality.

For relaxation Rountree enjoyed golf as a scratch player — when he was not

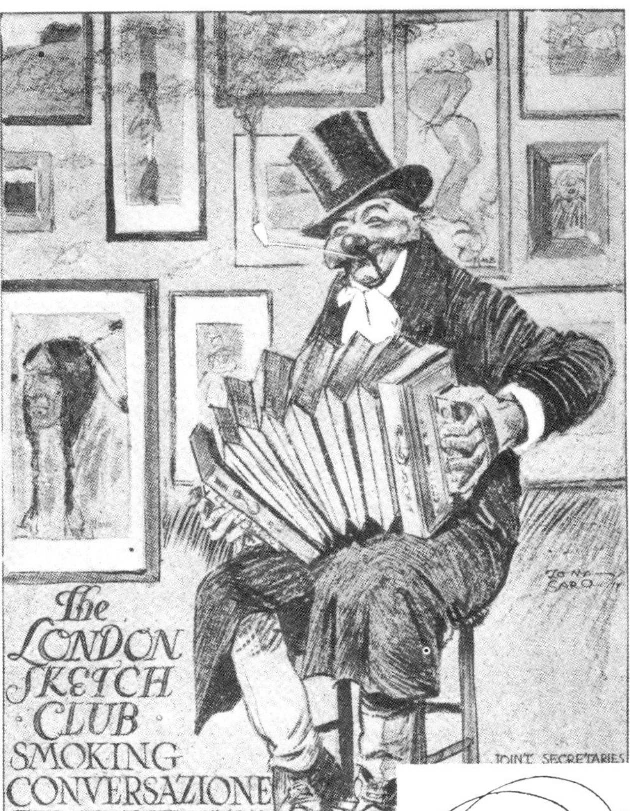

Invitation card by
Tony Sarg.

Invitation card by
Edmund Dulac.

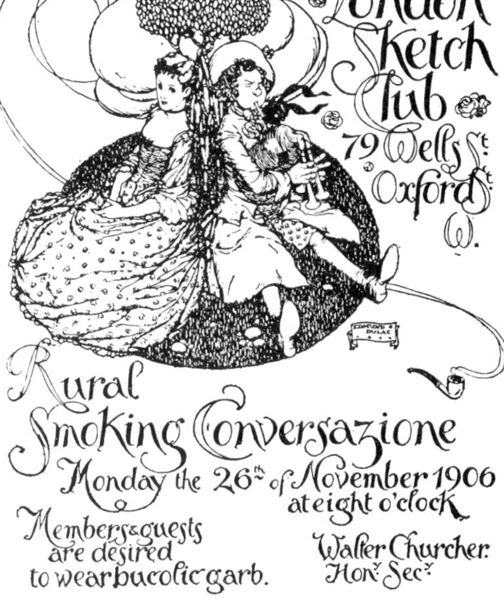

61

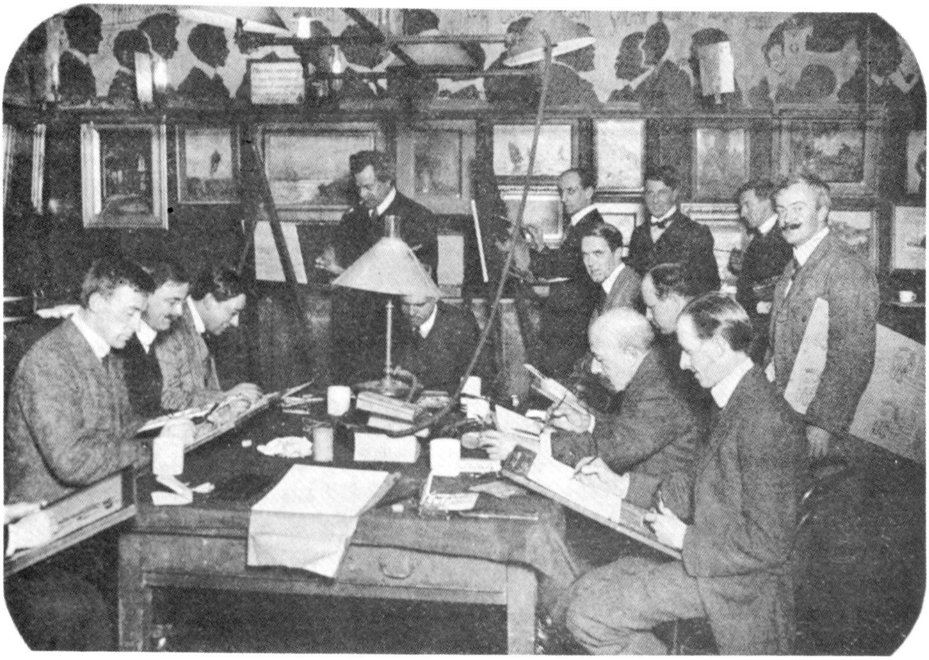

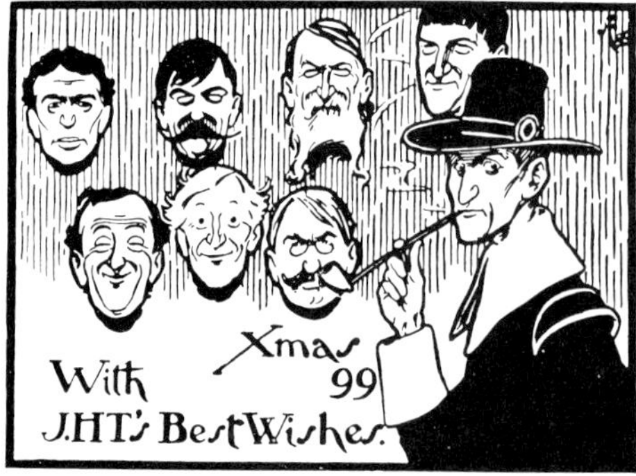

A group of sketchers
(from left to right): Ernest Moore, Charles Robinson, unknown, Dudley Hardy (standing at easel), John Hassall, Edgar Pattison, two more unknown faces, J. A. Fitzgerald (the old man), Pat Earnshaw (seated right foreground). The three at the back are Keble Bell, Will True and (extreme right) Harry Rountree.

Christmas card by James Thorpe.
Members depicted, left to right, top row:
René Bull, John Hassall, E. J. Odell and
Phil May; bottom row: Walter Churcher,
Starr Wood, Dudley Hardy and James
Thorpe (with clay pipe).

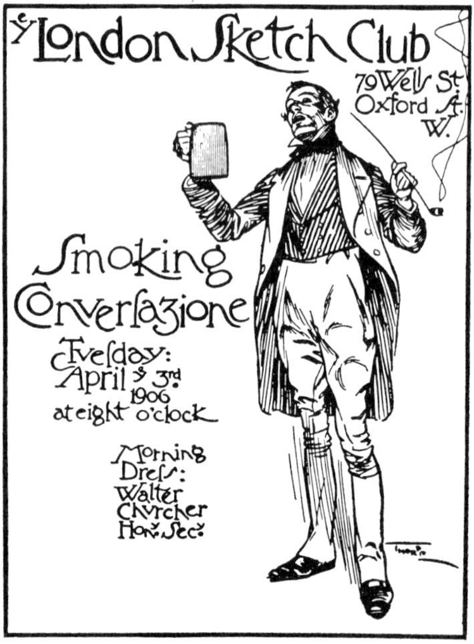

James Thorpe invitation card.

ensconced in his "cosy Bohemian den", the studio in which he spent many hours crouched over his drawing board. One turn which was remembered in the Sketch Club was "The Walk from York": the progress of the competitors was relayed throughout the evening by a succession of telegraph boys until at last the winner appeared at the door, battered and bloodstained, with clods of turf sticking to his feet. It was none other than Harry Rountree, who did admit he had spent most of the evening in the cloak room "making-up"!

When he retired to St Ives in Cornwall, Rountree spent many pleasant evenings at the Sloop Inn, amusing fishermen and locals with his tales and humour, a special type of humour peculiarly his own. The locals thought enough of him to subscribe to a memorial plaque which was placed on the quay after his death.

Two other artists who benefited from the fairy school were Charles Robinson and George Sheringham. Charles Robinson, brother of Tom and W. Heath Robinson, was apprenticed to the lithographers Waterlow & Son. He gained a place at the Royal Academy Schools but insufficient funds prevented him from continuing his course. Instead he attended evening classes at the West London Art school and at Heatherley's.

Charles Robinson was basically a self-trained illustrator although, as the son of Thomas Robinson the magazine illustrator and wood-engraver, his talent was inherent. I have always maintained that Charles Robinson is one of the finest talents in both book illustration and fine art of the twentieth century. The fluidity of his water-colours and the fairy-like dream world of his later compositions was brilliant. Just prior to his death he was elected to the RI in 1932. He died, as so many illustrators did, in difficult financial straits.

Always cheerful and ever diligent, Charles Robinson took over the task of painting the silhouettes of past and present members around the Sketch Club walls, an onerous task started by Henry Sandham. Robinson was one of the chief instigators of the London Sketch Club life class, started about 1923. Held on a different night to the sketching evenings, it is continued to this day.

In his youth Charles Robinson looked more like a cashier than an artist, with his waxed moustache, starched collar and suit; but during the 'twenties he began to put on weight. His brother W. Heath Robinson recorded:

> On 13 March, 1937, my brother Charles died. It was unbelievable. He was always so alive with an irrepressible vitality, it seemed impossible it could cease. His life had been one of work and some hardship. It had been a brave and successful struggle to be an artist and at the same time to bring up a large family. Yet there was always something of youth and of being on holiday about Charles. I went into his studio a few days before he died; besides unfinished pictures, there was the incomplete model of a Spanish galleon. It was already taking shape. Painted here and there with brilliant colour it gave promise of the proud and beautiful thing it was to have been. Although unfinished, it was a triumph of the spirit over the years and the many vicissitudes of life that had at last laid him low.

George Sheringham (1884-1937) achieved an enormous reputation during his lifetime and rivalled Edmund Dulac. Sheringham was, like Dulac, influenced by Eastern culture and its customs. He was one of the first artists to rebel against the rectangular frame, often painting in a lunette shape or fan. Sheringham loved music, was knowledgeable about Eastern philosophy and appreciated the English language.

This depth, combined with a glorious sense of colour and unusual sense of the ridiculous, made him stand out from other artists. It was Geoffrey Holme who said:

> It should not be forgotten that George could talk and write as beautifully as he could draw, but never considered words to be his 'métier' and it was with the greatest difficulty and upon rare occasions that he could be induced to put his thoughts into writing. The privileged few who would gather round his bedside towards his last days heard, between the intervals of rolling cigarettes, with which he exercised his long thin fingers, and the paroxysms of coughing which was also characteristic, a very profound philosophy of life and painting. And so, suffering intense pain with the greatest fortitude, passed at last, in November 1937, one of the most attractive personalities I have ever known.

Sheringham's work was in part a cross between that of Dulac and Pryde, but he carved out an individual niche which has not been filled since. The only other artist possibly in this category was Rex Whistler. Sherringham's wife, who painted under the name of Sibyl Meugens, was also no mean talent with the brush.

The last two artists of the fairy school were Willy Pogany and Stephen Baghot de la Bere. Willy Pogany (1882-1955) was born in Hungary and, after studying at the Budapest Academy and in Munich and Paris, had intended to emigrate to America after a brief stop-over in London. The stop-over lasted ten years, during which time he joined the London Sketch Club. In 1915 Pogany finally arrived in New York and in the 'thirties became an art director for Warner's studios. Through his friendship with Dulac, Pogany was lastingly influenced by oriental art. Stephen Baghot de la Bere (1877-1927), however, started his career under the influence of John Hassall and the Sketch Club style of illustration and poster design. Later he developed a more atmospheric use of water-colour. Dulac always thought that de la Bere prefigured the work of the Swiss painter Paul Klee. His illustrations for *The Adventures of Don Quixote*, published in 1905 by Adam & Charles Black, certainly smack of the London Sketch Club style, but with Dulac's encouragement he developed as a fine artist. He was elected to the RI in 1907.

The other school within the London Sketch Club was the poster school — very down to earth but serving a highly lucrative market. Followers included Cecil Aldin, Tom Browne, Lance Thackeray, James Thorpe, Will True, Will Owen, Fred Taylor, Tony Sarg, S. T. C. Weeks, Bert Thomas, Maurice Greiffenhagen and Alfred Leete. The leading lights of this fashionable trend were Dudley Hardy and John Hassall.

The style of the London Sketch Club poster school was highly distinctive. Bold black lines emphasised the subject matter, which was often dealt with humorously. Cecil Aldin's posters for Cadbury's Cocoa or Colman's Blue echoed the Beggarstaff brothers, and Will Owen's "Ah! Bisto!" and theatrical posters were treated in the same way. Cecil Aldin was born in Slough on 28 April 1870. He was educated at Eastbourne College and Solihull Grammar School before studying animal painting under Frank W. Calderon. Like John Hassall, Cecil Aldin's first published drawing had appeared in *The Graphic* in 1891, and the two artists were the mainstay of the "Happy Animal". As an illustrator, Aldin was prolific. He illustrated Kipling's jungle stories for the *Pall Mall Budget* in 1894 although it is his illustrated books (now collectors' items) which capture the best facets of his work. *Dogs of Character* (published 1927), *The Romance of the Road* (1928) and *An Artist's Models* (1930) were three excellent books. In real life Aldin was a Master of Foxhounds and helped to pave the way for fellow London Sketch Club member Lionel Edwards with the

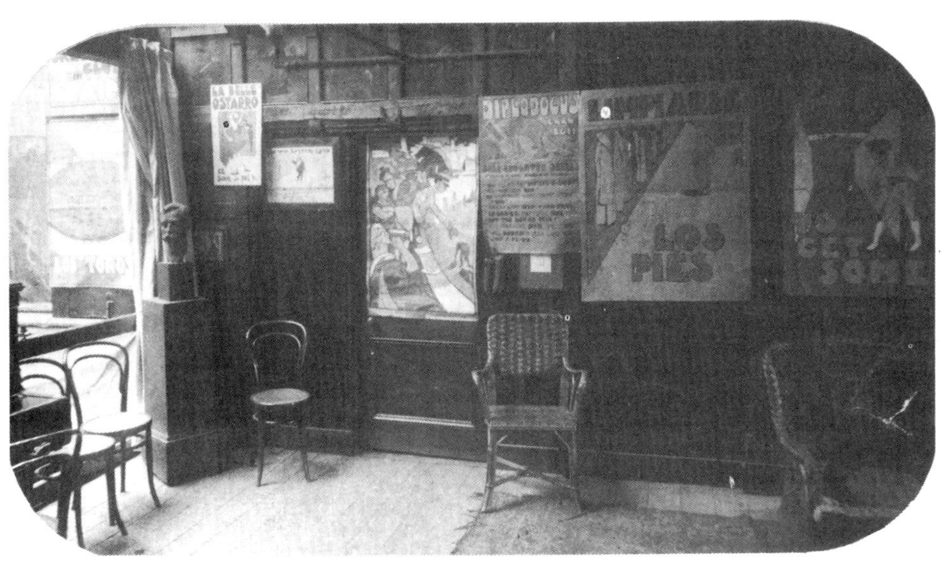

Interior of the London Sketch Club.
(*Above*) A plethora of posters around the walls.
(*Below*) Behind the closed hatch was the bar. Edmund Dulac painted the panels of this bar but they have since disappeared.

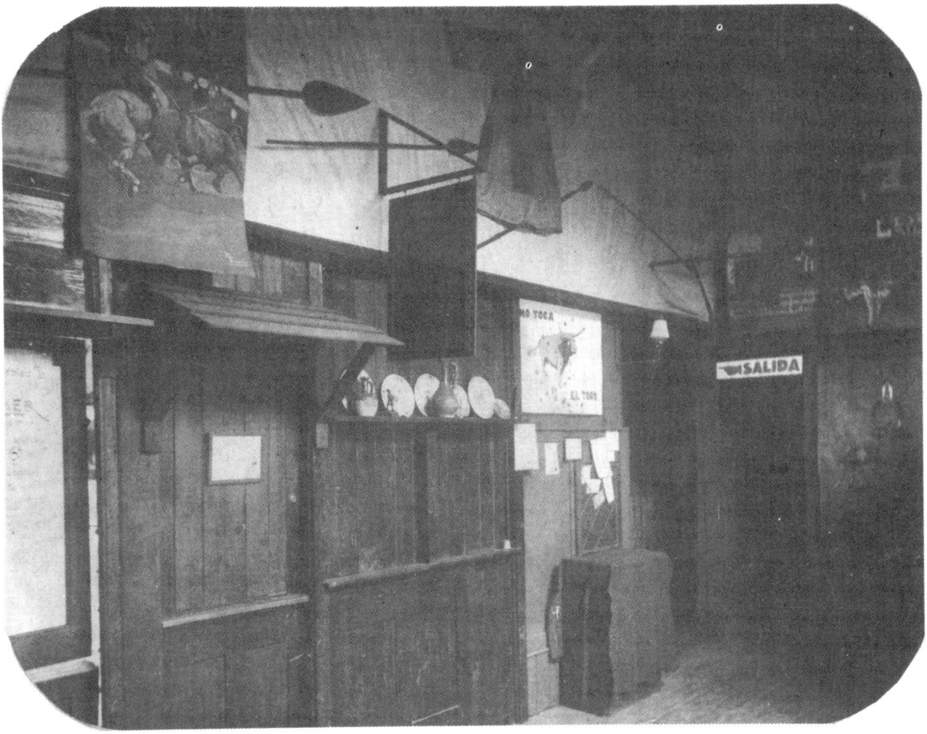

"sportin' and huntin'" set. Towards the end of his life he moved to Majorca where he designed his own house, before returning to England, where he died in 1935.

The other poster artist Will Owen has long fascinated me. He was born in Malta in 1869 and, like Hassall, was the son of a naval officer. After studying at Lambeth School of Art he joined the London Sketch Club and was clearly influenced by this Bohemian band of artists. His chief claim to fame was his collaboration with W. W. Jacobs, Owen illustrating many of Jacobs' stories. In later life Will Owen turned to writing and often illustrated his own books, such as *Old London Town* (published 1921) in which he described The Cheshire Cheese in Fleet Street:

> Had the old tavern relied solely upon its historical associations it would probably have disappeared long since, but it has always been famous for its catering. "The Cheshire Cheese" pudding has a world-wide reputation, both for size and quality, and contains many things — steak and kidney, lark and oysters are but some of them. It is like the pudding mother used to make — only better. As might be expected in so Bohemian a survival as "The Cheese" there are many things of interest scattered through the house — Johnson relics, sketches by famous artists, and so on. If you love old passages and narrow winding stairways, low-ceilinged, panelled rooms, and a sawdusted floor, take my advice and try "The Cheese".

It was a good advertisement for a place Will Owen knew only too well: he had dined there often enough.

Despite his encouraging start, Owen turned his back on art and chose journalism, finishing his days working on the *East Kent Mercury*. He died in 1957. A footnote: it is likely that John Hassall collaborated with Will Owen on his "Ah! Bisto!" poster, as was common Sketch Club practice, which accounts for Hassall's being credited with it in *The Times'* obituary of 1948.

The other great poster artist from this group was Fred Taylor (1875-1963) who did much work for London Transport. Born in London, the son of William Taylor, Fred studied art for a short time at Goldsmiths, where he won a gold medal for his posters and a travelling scholarship to Italy for decoration. On his return he found a steady flow of commissions from shipping and railway companies, particularly the North Eastern railway. He decorated the ceiling of the Underwriting Room at Lloyd's and completed murals for Austin Reed's Red Lacquer Room in 1930. He married Florence Sarg, the sister of his great friend Tony Sarg, and they had one son and one daughter.

Tony Sarg, an American, was born in Guatemala in 1880. He executed murals in several New York hotels before coming to Britain in about 1908. He worked with fellow London Sketch Club members for *Printer's Pie* and, like Fred Taylor, was one of Frank Pick's army of poster artist's for the London Underground. Sarg often worked in pastel as well as water-colour or pen and wash and his work has a haunting charm. He relied heavily on Phil May's East End terminology (such as "'Appy 'Ampstead" or "Lorst yer Luggidge?" in the captions to his cartoons but the drawings hold up well.

Sarg was fascinated by Cockney slang and James Thorpe was also only too well aware of it. Thorpe, born in Homerton, North London in 1876 and educated at Bancrofts school, lived for part of his early life in Walthamstow. He studied at Lambeth School of Art and Heatherleys and served with the Artists' Rifles in the First World War. Along with Frank Reynolds, Starr Wood and H. M. Bateman,

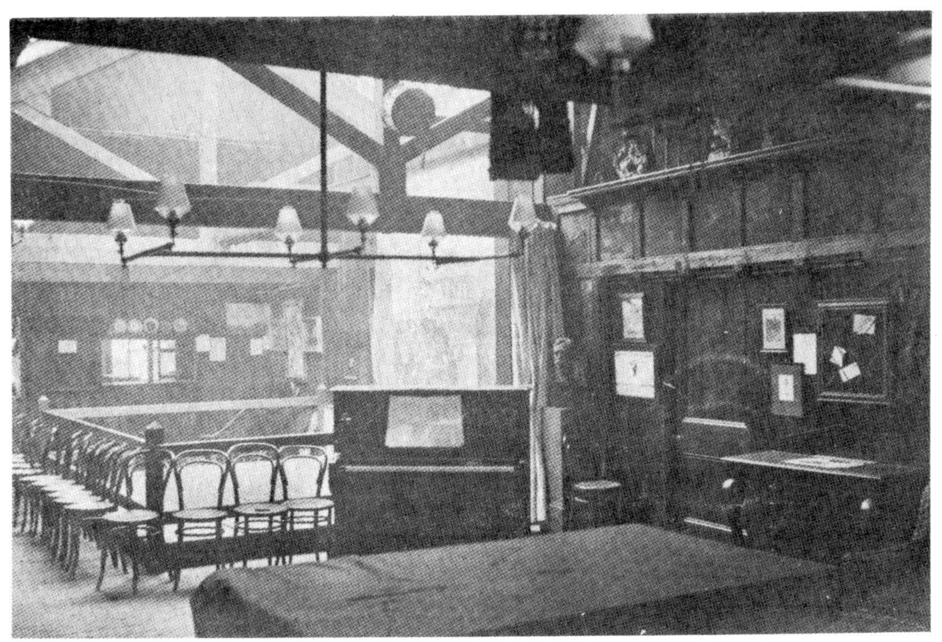

(*Above*) The stage in the Wells Street studio where artistes performed their "turns".
(*Below*) The Club Chimney corner at Wells Street.

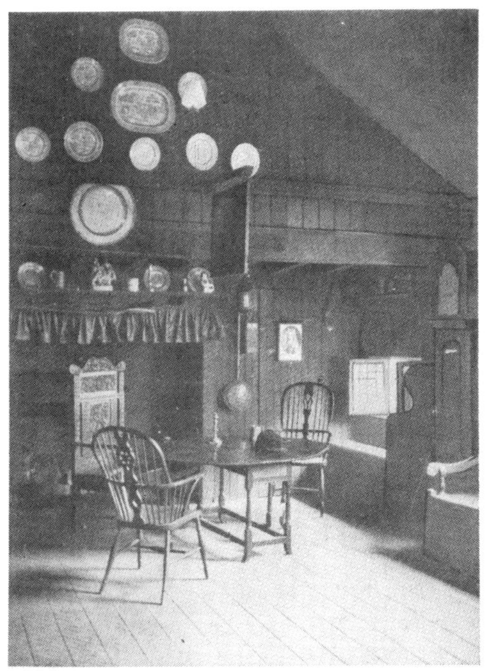

In his remembrances Clay Thomas recalled the first time he came along to the London Sketch Club.

"In 1908 John Hassall invited me to sing at the LSC then at the top of a four-storey house in Wells Street, Oxford Street, on the site now occupied by Bourne and Hollingsworth. Before leaving to go home about midnight I was elected an honorary member. To reach the Club quarters one climbed about eighty rickety stairs with a similar banister, and beer being in those days pure and potent, it has always been a surprise to me that at no time members descending did not meet with serious mishap. Therefore, I was lucky to meet many of the founders and original members. They then worked on a syllabus for two hours before the meal, and when work had ceased, each member took their lecture round to the others for comment and criticism, and it was, to me, a great joy in hearing their witty and acid comments, all taken in fun and good heart."

67

Thorpe went on rambles and hikes around Britain before it became fashionable in the 'twenties.

In 1906 Frank Reynolds gave up his Onslow Studio in Chelsea and James Thorpe took it on. It was here that George Riches, a favourite model of Phil May's, often modelled for him. Thorpe wrote:

> Riches was an interesting character, a real Cockney of the old school, with the Cockney's pride in London and utter contempt for the country. One warm summer afternoon he was posing for me in an eighteenth-century costume which he always referred to as "My Tom and Jerry". The manufacturers of a well-known whisky, for which I was doing some advertisement drawings, had that very morning sent me a sample bottle, which still remained on the table. Riches' eye spotted this at once, and he tactfully led up to the subject by announcing a slight cold accompanied by distressing dryness of the throat.
>
> I suggested that the contents of the bottle might serve to allay the irritation, and handed him a corkscrew. Mixing himself a stiff glassful he bowed with true Georgian dignity first to my friend and then to me. "Here's to you, Sir, and to you, Sir, wishing you every success and prosperity!" We returned the bow less successfully. Then he tossed off most of the drink, and there was a violent outburst of spluttering and oaths. The bottle was a dummy for use in window dressing, and the contents smelt all too strongly of eggs long unfit for human consumption.

Thorpe went on to become the first artist to design advertisements for the London Press Exchange, and he was responsible for the "Three Nuns" tobacco posters. He was also a prolific *Punch* cartoonist who turned to writing later in life, completing his autobiography, *Happy Days*, in 1933.

The last artist in this section is Will True. Born in 1866, he began life as a post office clerk in Glasgow but switched to illustration on the *Glasgow Evening News*. When he arrived in London he contributed to *Fun* and set up his own studio which had all the trappings of an oriental emporium. As a posterist he was influenced by Chéret and the Japanese school.

As Will True, Sheringham and Dulac were influenced by Japanese woodcuts, so Dudley Hardy, Tom Browne and to a lesser extent Will Owen were influenced by the Dutch realist school, with a touch of Chéret thrown in for good measure. All the poster school agreed that Phil May was master and, although he was primarily a "black and white man", many adapted his principles to their posters. James Pryde, John Hassall, Lance Thackeray and Bert Thomas all benefited from Phil May's economy of line.

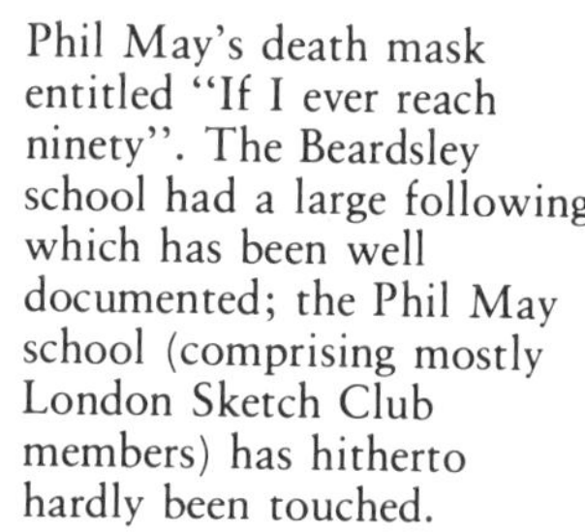

Phil May's death mask entitled "If I ever reach ninety". The Beardsley school had a large following which has been well documented; the Phil May school (comprising mostly London Sketch Club members) has hitherto hardly been touched.

CHAPTER 5

The Poster King

If Dudley Hardy was the chief influence behind the formation of the London Sketch Club, it was his boozing partner of many years' standing, John Hassall, who was the chief implementer of its aims and achievements. Hardy had revived the poster in England yet Hassall received most of the acclaim: it was Hassall who was described as the "King of Poster Artists", and he thrived in that prodigious 1890-1914 period when new colour printing processes were being exploited, printers' wages were low and paper was cheap.

John Hassall was born in Walmer, in Kent on 21 May 1868, the son of Lieutenant Christopher Clark Hassall, RN and his wife Louisa. Lieutenant Hassall was paralysed as the result of an accident and died in 1876, at the age of only 38 years. After a suitable period of mourning, his widow married General Sir William Purvis Wright, KCB.

After attending a school at Worthing, John Hassall went on to Newton Abbot College in Devon, where he had his first regular lessons in drawing. From there he went on to Neuenheim College in Heidelberg, where, according to his own account, he spent three of the happiest years of his life. He returned to England with the intention of taking a commission in the Army but failed the Sandhurst entrance examinations twice. General Wright tried to intervene, but without success.

Anxious to make himself useful after this bitter failure, Hassall joined his brother Owen in Canada and helped him on the farm. When asked whether he liked Manitoba or not he replied:

> Not much. I didn't. Manitoba spells flies. Billions of 'em. You eat flies, drink flies, breathe flies in Manitoba, and it gets a little monotonous. I don't begrudge the time I spent there. It was an experience, and I have no doubt that it did me good. One thing I have to thank Manitoba for and that is that the loneliness of the long winter evenings and the lack of society made me hunt for something to occupy my time. A dozen sketches were the result.

His first pictorial triumph occurred at an agricultural exhibition at Minnedosa, "a wee prairie town about 140 miles west of Winnipeg". John Hassall carried off the first three prizes — the highest being the magnificent sum of $16, which he took back to the homestead with as much haste as a horse and cart allowed. Encouraged by this success he sketched some Yuletide festivities and mailed them to the editor of the *Daily Graphic*. Imagine his astonishment when a copy of the paper, dated 26 February 1890, containing reproductions of his sketches, arrived. He was even more amazed when a cheque followed.

Spurred on by this early recognition, Hassall decided to return to England and become an artist. In his own words: "I was going to be a great artist, of course. The

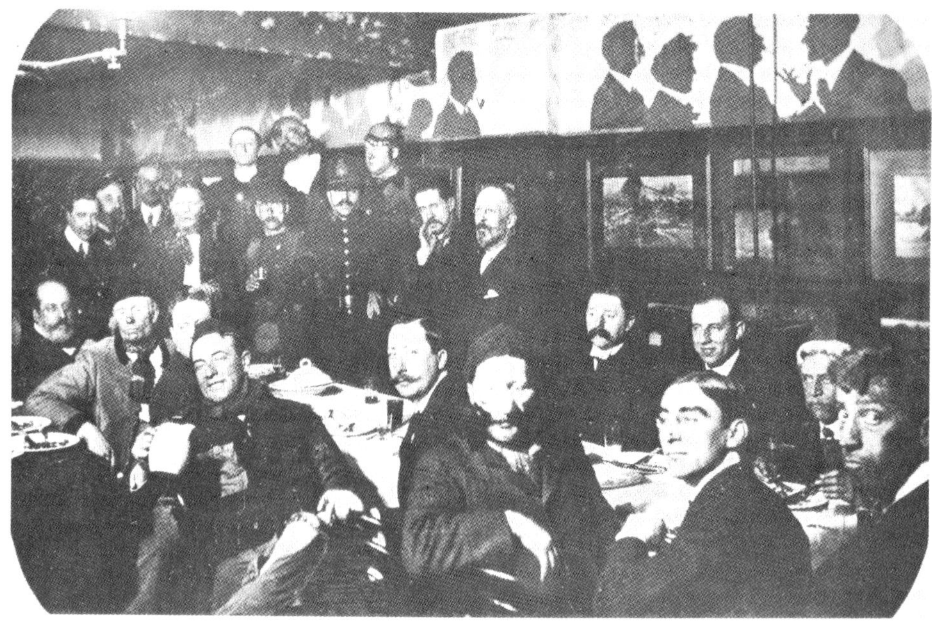

Early London Sketch Club Smoker with John Hassall (centre) in his famous policeman's uniform. Lance Thackeray is seated in the foreground holding a jug as a beer mug; behind him in cap and scarf, is Starr Wood, then Sir James Linton, bearded and looking like Edward VII. Behind Linton is Tom Browne, and Lee Hankey, also with cap and scarf, stands fourth from the left.

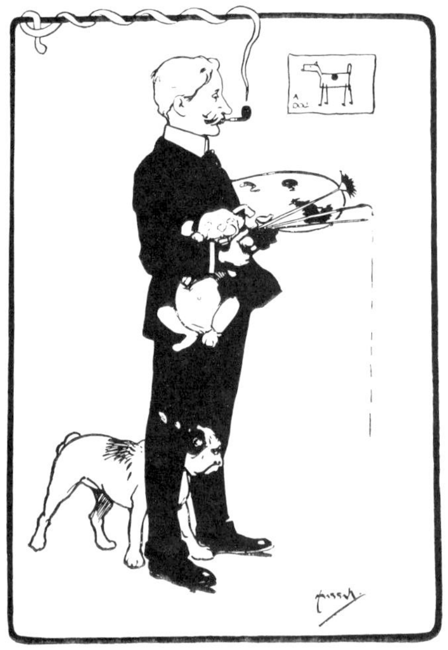

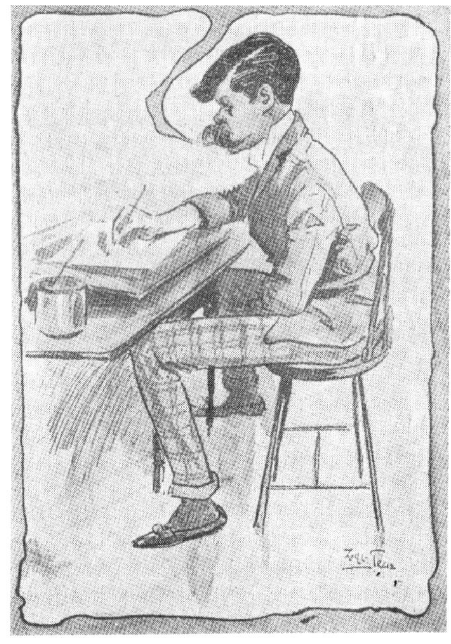

Caricatures of Cecil Aldin by John Hassall (*left*) and John Hassall by Will True.

kind of artist who paints enormous pictures and gets infinitesimal prices for them, or fails to sell them at all." It never occurred to him that there were art schools in London, but he intended to study. He obtained an introduction to Sidney Cooper, RA and went over to Canterbury with examples of his work. The elderly Academician was unimpressed and strongly advised him to give up the idea of becoming an artist.

By a stroke of luck, however, he met Dudley Hardy. Hardy had exhibited at the Royal Academy, and knew the ropes. This proved a fortunate meeting: Hassall and Hardy were to become lifelong friends. They had similar temperaments, and both being heavily moustached they looked like a couple of officers recently risen from the ranks. They drank themselves silly and sang in lusty baritones; their friendship was full of jests, jokes and jaded mornings.

Hardy, who understood his friend's financial position well, remembered a "free" Art School in Antwerp which he mentioned to Hassall. Tuition was usually expensive in those days, so to quote Hassall:

> That was just my sort, so, in my usual haphazard way, I crossed to Antwerp and presented myself at the Academy there. They asked if I had any sketches and I said I had not. While they were trying to make me understand that they must have something in proof of my aptitude, and while I was trying to make them understand that any sketches I had were in England, an old man came along. He was evidently well known there, and indeed, as I learned afterwards, was on a visit of inspection. He said, when he understood my grievance, "You vill kom to my studio, and in many months I vill make you to be an artist".

The old man was Professor van Havermaet, "Old Van". He was as good as his word: his son, Charles van Havermaet, taught Hassall everything he knew.

After six months' work Hassall was good enough to be accepted by the famous Académie Julian in Paris where he spent a further six months under Bouguereau and Ferrier before returning to Antwerp. William Adolphe Bouguereau taught some very distinguished students in his atelier, including Jules Cheret, Pierre Bonnard, James Pryde and Dudley Hardy. His influence over the students at the Académie was striking. He was a strong supporter of Alphonse Mucha and Art Nouveau.

When Hassall returned to Antwerp he met and fell in love with the very beautiful Isabel Dingwall. They were married in 1893. At times they had little money, but the faith that Isabel had in her husband kept him going and gave him confidence. They enjoyed the bohemian student life of cafés and garrets, and frequently entertained friends "mit kookskies" and "bier" at the studio of "Mynheer Hassall".

On their return to London in 1895 the Hassalls rented 88 Kensington Park Gardens and settled down to what they could eke out of a precarious artistic career. The studio at the house was an amazing room. The previous owner, who had been vicar of the church next door and an amateur artist, had had it built in what was originally the back garden and its side door was a short cut to the church. Hassall altered this to make a concealed door leading to a small workroom. The door consisted of a mock bookcase which included an encyclopaedia volume labelled "BAC to BIZ".

He worked hard. As Frank Reynolds recalled, "It was Hassall who made me realise what sheer industry meant. He was tireless turning out work like a war factory, and it was he who started me on a period of close application and hard work." Reynolds collaborated with Hassall on posters and book illustrations; he later became Art Editor of *Punch*.

The Hassall style — in essence large masses of colour and few lines — soon gained admirers and followers. One of its chief merits was that it enabled his humour to reach the working man without malice or condescension; it was used with discretion and required no explanation. In artistic terms his humour was full of "mannerism" but it was the mannerism of a forceful and determined nature. Reacting fiercely against the monochromatic delicacy of Aubrey Beardsley, Hassall did away with the fussiness and highly stylised approach of the Beardsley set.

Hassall's secret was twofold. One aspect was his technique: his treatment of flat colour masses involved heavy outlining with a black indelible pencil. The outline helped to reinforce the values of the colours and tones, and this in turn accentuated the lettering. His other strength was his humour, presented as lighthearted situation comedy. A line of copy completed the joke. In many cases Hassall's posters were no more than blow-ups of his illustrative work, the colour being added by many willing and helpful hands.

Hassall admired Mucha's *fin de siècle* sophistication: it was not unlike Beardsley's though vastly more artistic and romantic. He was himself just as good a colourist as Mucha; his large areas of colour had enormous impact. Simplification was achieved thanks to the influence of one man — dear old Phil May. The combination produced an explosive and devastating effect, as in "Bovril prevents that sinking feeling", "I think I must have left it behind" (for Andrews' Liver Salts), and the Colman's Mustard series of posters. Hassall was firm and outspoken about his selling techniques. He took a dim view of manufacturers who wanted to complicate his design by filling every space with unnecessary wording. He also grumbled that British artists were rarely allowed to sign their work, unlike their Parisian counterparts.

"The artist should be dictator of the hoardings" proclaimed Hassall and backed up his belief by using reds and yellows which withstood deterioration. "Purple, it may interest you to know, is the worst of all colours for a poster; in fact, owing to the rapidity with which it fades, it can only be used rarely."

Borwick's Baking Powder sent their poster back because its slogan "Let me help you to rise" was considered too risqué. It was not subtle enough. Nevertheless Hassall's "Dismayed but not dismantled" poster for Veritas Gas Mantles proved acceptable, as did "The only way", which showed the actor Martin Harvey (later Sir Martin Harvey) going up the steps to the guillotine while an angry Parisian mob howled at his feet. This quip, from Dickens' *A Tale of Two Cities*, was later recalled by Hassall in an interview for *The Captain*: "A bootmaker was visiting my studio whilst the poster was being completed. It seemed to have a weird fascination for him as he studied the poster in a thoughtful manner. Then, after a long time, he uttered a profound statement: 'Ah, I see now, the only way up is up them there little steps'." As Hassall remarked, "He wasn't far wrong."

In 1900 Isabel died in childbirth. Hassall arranged for her to be buried in Helensburgh in Scotland, the Dingwall family home. For the next three years Bella's haunting face was to obsess Hassall: it is repeated over and over again in his watercolours and paintings. To pass the lonely evenings Hassall played bagatelle and immersed himself in the all male company of the London Sketch Club.

Then, in 1903, Constance Maud Brook Webb visited London to see the Trooping of the Colour. She lost her way and was helped by General Sir William Purvis

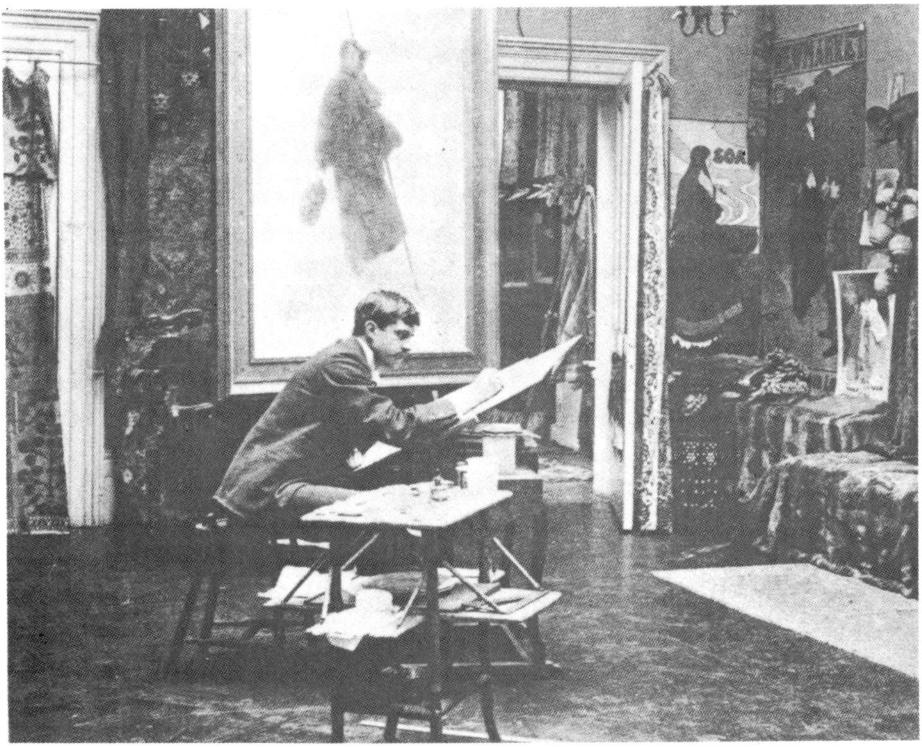

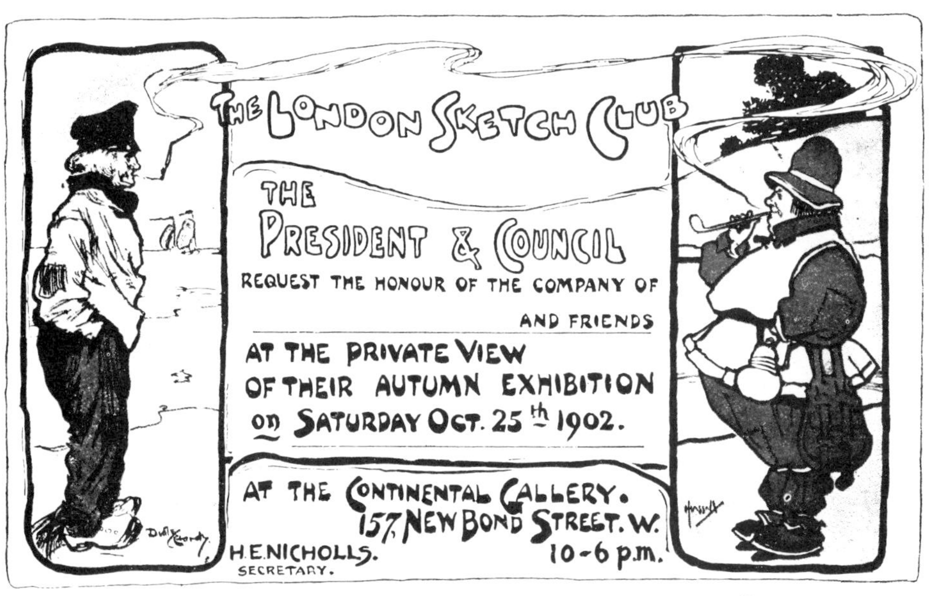

John Hassall at work in his Notting Hill studio.

Joint invitation card by Dudley Hardy and John Hassall.

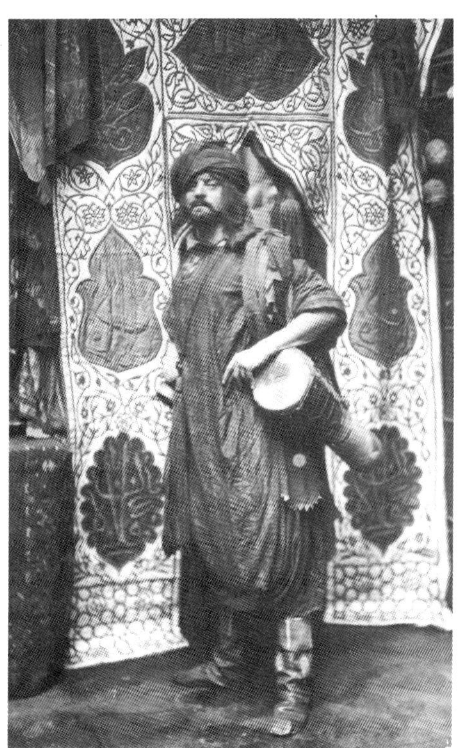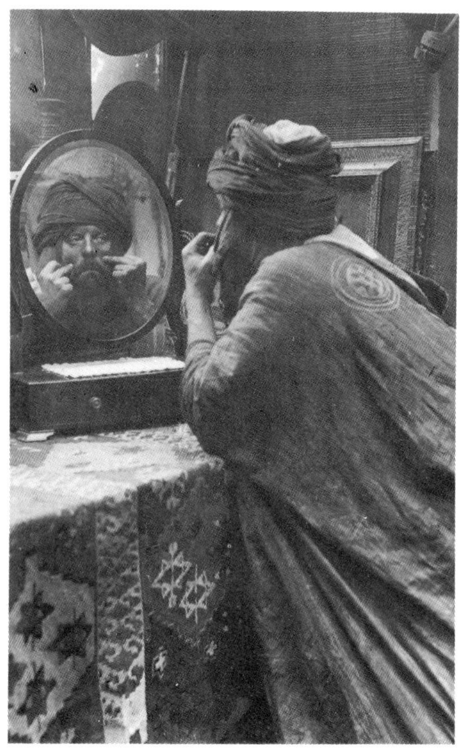

Ben Adul Hassa

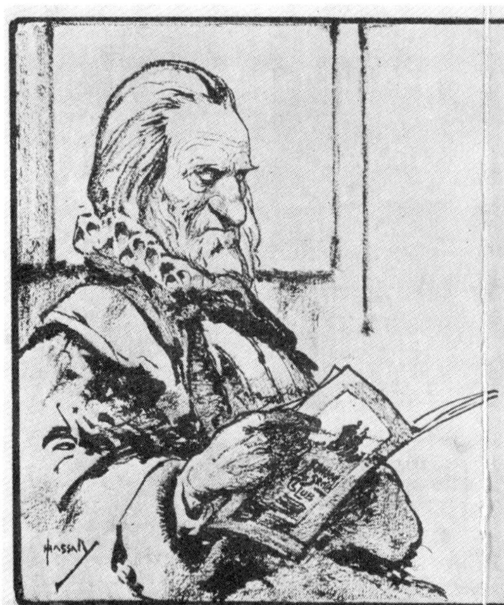

Invitation Card to The Graves Gallery, 1904.

Wright. She was invited for tea at the Wrights' home, where she met John Hassall, who had just cycled over, eating raw onions on the way. It was a propitious meeting; later that year they were married.

Constance was the daughter of the Rev. A. Brooke Webb of Dalinghoo Rectory in Suffolk. The reverend gentleman at first did his best to stop the marriage, objecting to bohemian artists, but he was eventually persuaded to give his blessing. John and Maud produced two brilliant children, Joan Hassall the wood engraver and Christopher Hassall the poet. Christopher, ingenious like his father, juggled with his talents: he was playwright, author, composer, tutor, broadcaster and administrator. He acted for the Old Vic, was lyricist for Ivor Novello, became Director of Voice at the Old Vic Theatre and poetry editor of the BBC third programme. Much of his time was spent writing libretti for composers like Walton, Bliss and Anthony Hopkins.

During this period of his life John Hassall produced some six or seven hundred posters, including one for The British Vacuum Cleaner Company which depicted a lecherous bit of machinery chasing a nubile parlour maid, and his famous "Skegness is SO bracing". The latter was produced for the Great Northern Railway in 1908 and the "Jolly Fisherman" is still used today as the emblem of Skegness Hoteliers Association; it has been incorporated into the Mayoral Chain of Office and it is a ubiquitous mascot about the town.

Hassall's poster work was so popular that, together with Charles van Havermaet, he started his own art school in 1900. Its aim was to foster originality based on a sound knowledge of drawing. The school operated from 3 Logan Place, Earls Court Road, Kensington, with Franklyn Helmore as Secretary. John Hassall himself was to attend at least three times a week. Early students included Captain Bruce Bairnsfather, H. M. Bateman, Miss Fish (who illustrated the letters of Eve in the *Tatler*), Miss Gladys Peto (who illustrated "Phrynette" in the *Sketch*), A. E. Horne, Vernon Hill (who became a sculptor in wood, ivory and bronze), Charles Bryant, Hawley Morgan, Harry Low and Sidney Strube.

A good description of the school comes from H. M. Bateman in his autobiography *By Himself*, reminiscing about 1904:

John Hassall was then at the very height of his success. Hassall was one of the most good natured of men, especially to youngsters like myself, warming themselves in the radiance he threw out and ready to help with any little odd job he might want doing to make his work go quicker and easier. His energy and output at that time was really amazing. He worked in pretty well every known and unknown medium and as like as not he would be discovered engaged on several pictures at once. It was all done as if it were a great joke, and he certainly never appeared to take his work very seriously, but there was no doubt about the results being effective.

I had known Hassall for two or three months when he told me that the man under whom he had himself studied in Antwerp, Charles van Havermaet, had come to live in London, and it might be a good thing for me to work under him for a time if he would take me as a pupil. This seemed an opportunity not to be missed if it could be managed and the long and the short of it was that in a short time I commenced work in Van's (as I soon called him) studio where I stayed for the best part of three years.

I found there were three or four other students in the place, which consisted of a large house to which the studio was attached. I think this house (3 Logan Place), with others in the same row, has since been pulled down to make room for the growth of Olympia.

Most of the rooms in the house were shut up and Van practically confined himself to the studio, a bedroom and a large kitchen on the ground floor, where we did our own cooking. It was great fun to fry sausages or an omelette for the mid-day meal, it had a true bohemian flavour which appealed strongly to me. Our housekeeping was of the sketchiest and our culinary efforts were practically confined to the limits of the frying pan in which the fat was always allowed to remain, because we said, as time went on it became richer.

There was a big stock of crockery there which we drew upon but did not always wash up after use, continuing to work upon the clean supply and allowing the dirty pieces to accumulate until someone came in or we were forced to have a big cleaning and start all over again.

The school ticked over but never made a vast profit. Neither did Hassall visit the school as often as he should; he relied heavily on van Havermaet taking the brunt. Van Havermaet's teaching did not stick to a rigid method: each student worked in a different genre and was encouraged in his own particular style. The Hassall school failed in one sense: it did not perpetuate Hassall's own theory but rather enhanced and polished these talents which students already head.

The intention of the school was to have live models from 10 am to 1 pm with the afternoon devoted to poster work and black and white. But, as Bateman explained, "We did not often have live models to work from, and never, if I remember rightly, professional models. Sometimes Van would rope in a 'striking type' off the street.'' What the students did receive was first class tuition from the very man who had encouraged John Hassall to develop his own individuality.

Frank Brangwyn had also started his own school of art, The London School of Art in Stratford Row, but Brangwyn hated teaching and, when confronted by a class, often broke out in a sweat. By 1908 he was ready to give up. Both Hassall and Brangwyn were preoccupied with commissions but Brangwyn was ready to throw in the towel whereas Hassall wanted to continue with his school.

The result was an amalgamation of the two schools, to be known as The London and New Art School, operating from Stratford Studios, Stratford Road, Kensington. Franklyn Helmore stopped on as a director of the new venture but, although Brangwyn's name appeared as a professor of the new school, it is unlikely that he ever taught there. Other tutors brought in were Philip de Laszlo, Richard Jack, C. M. Q. Orchardson and Edmund Sullivan. The last went on to teach at Goldsmiths College, where one of his pupils was the young Rowland Hilder.

The First World War decimated the school and Hassall was forced to re-think. As he said, "For 17 years I have taught drawing at the New School of Art and the London School of Art. Up to two years ago I did not believe drawing could be taught by correspondence. As a result of two years' enquiry and work I now know that it can be done." It was young Percy Bradshaw who had convinced Hassall that it was a good idea. Art could now be taught in the comfort and peace of the students' own sitting-rooms. The John Hassall Correspondence Art School was to prove lucrative and it flourished up to the 1940s in St Albans.

In retrospect, it is difficult to quantify the importance of Hassall's School of Art. Certainly none of the pupils became clones of the master. Hassall's influence was

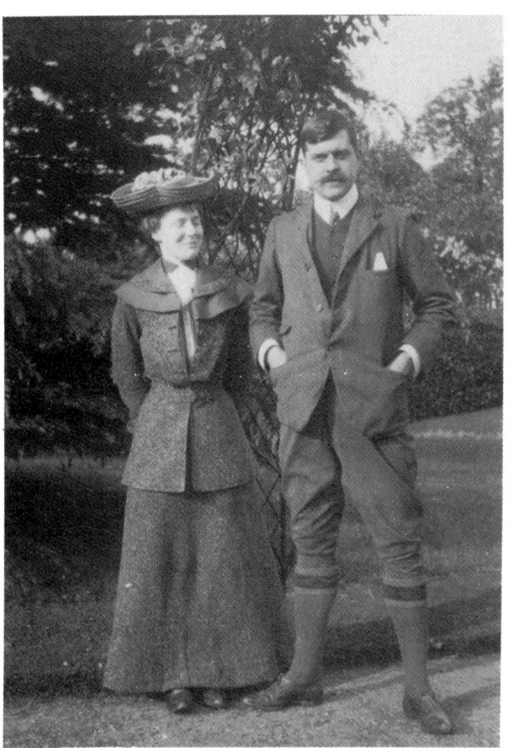

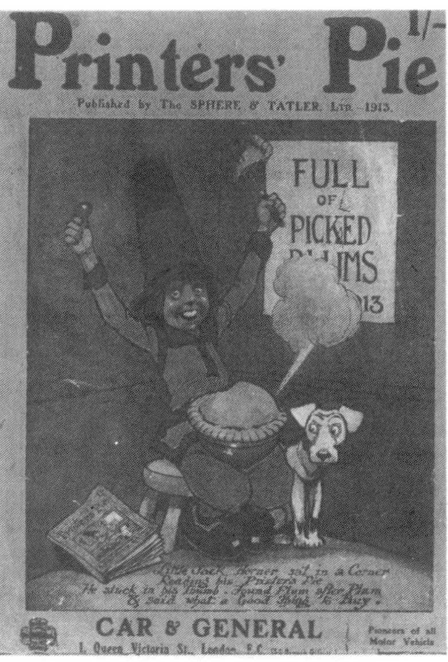

Hassall invariably designed the cover of *Printers' Pie*, to which so many London Sketch Club members contributed.

John Hassall and Constance photographed at Dalinghoo Rectory in Suffolk.

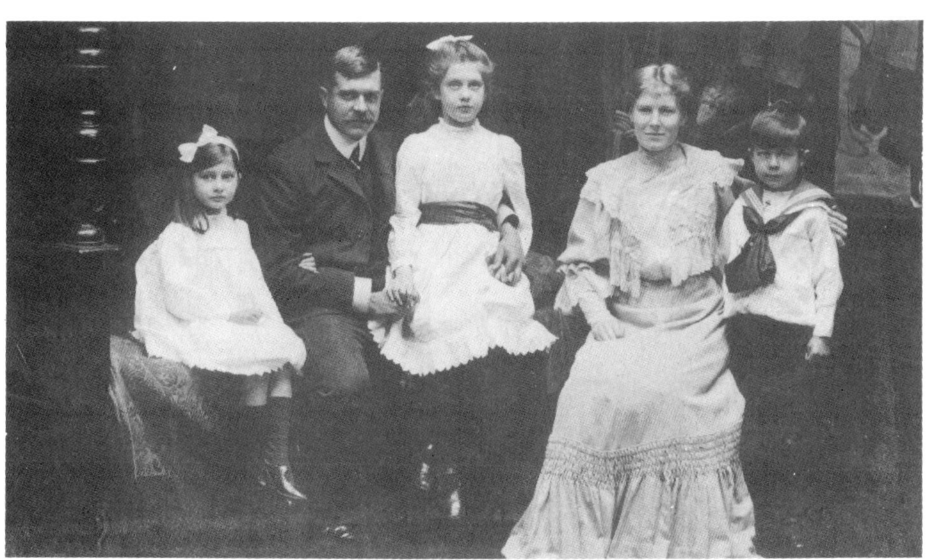

Constance inherited three children from Hassall's first marriage, Isobel, Dorothy and Ian.

John Hassall (1868-1948) was the epitome of a good all round English clubman. He was a member of the Arts Club (in Dover Street), the Eccentric Club, Odd Volumes, The Knights Club, the RI, the RMS, the Chelsea Arts Club (for a short time), the Savage and the London Sketch Club. He frequently designed menu covers and invitations, and drew lightning sketches when asked. He designed the Savage Club logo which is still used to-day. Probably the most unusual of his clubs was Odd Volumes. "The Sette of Odd Volumes" was founded in 1878 by the respected antiquarian bookseller Bernard Quaritch. They met once a month "to form a perfect sette", when a paper (usually "opuscula") was read after dinner. Other members included John Lane (the publisher), Sir Edward Sullivan (of Gilbert and Sullivan) and Vyvyan Holland (son of Oscar Wilde). Other artist members from the Sketch Club included Phil May and George Haité.

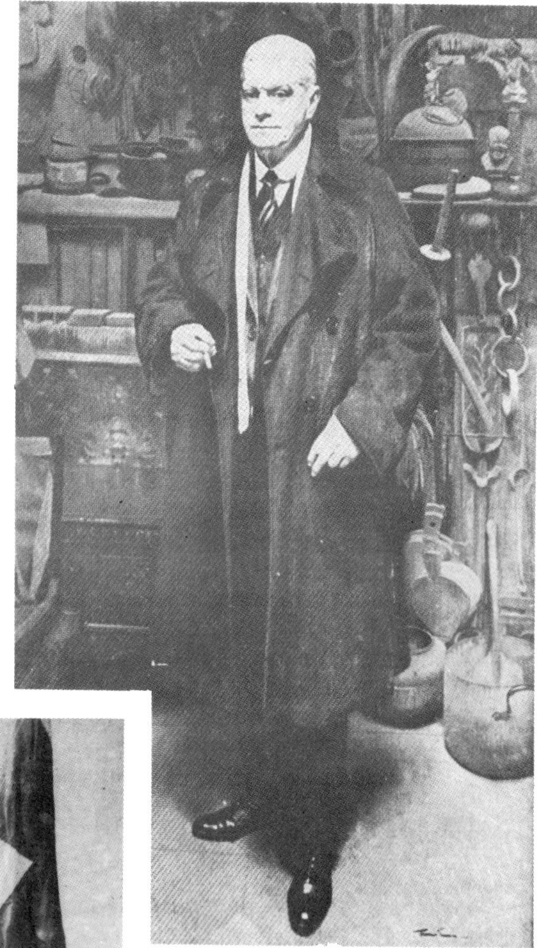

Portrait of Hassall by James Gunn.

Hassall as St George. His costume was made from bits of old biscuit tins and other discarded materials, cleverly assembled by George Parlby.

seen more clearly in contemporaries such as Charles Crombie and Frank Danton Adams. The student most influenced by Hassall was probably Hawley-Morgan (the illustrator from *The Jolly Book*) but few people today have heard of him. Nevertheless Hassall did lead the way for a time, as he advertised in his brochure.

One student who remembered Hassall well was A.R. Thomson, RA. After attending Hassall's school his career blossomed; he was to become one of the most respected Academicians of the Twentieth Century. Despite the handicap of being deaf and dumb he made friends easily and never forgot how Hassall obtained his first job.

H.M. Bateman became well known for his series "The man who . . ." and was one of the most important English caricaturists to emerge from the pages of *Punch*. Bert Thomas is well known for his "'Arf a mo' Kaiser" cartoon, designed for the *Weekly Dispatch* in the early days of the 1914-18 War. It was described as the funniest picture of the First World War by the *Daily Mail*. "Fish's" art on the other hand adorned the pages of the *Tatler* in brilliant colour and her humour sparkles with feminine wit.

One of the endearing elements which attracted people to Hassall's work was his mascot, a mongrel dog. There was a report in *Pearson's Magazine* which read:

> Every humorous artist has his favourite mascot with which he embellishes the greater part of his studies, and anyone who is at all familiar with John Hassall's work must of necessity have made the acquaintance of the mongrel dog who gives such a highly felicitous tone to many of his pictures . . . The proportions of the Hassall dog are singularly lank and ungraceful, delicately suggestive of a pedigree too complicated for words. His head is the most pronounced part of his composition, and is always touched into prominence by a highly intelligent countenance and eyes that speak of conflicting emotions. The like of this dog has never been seen in flesh and blood by any man, unless it be John Hassall, and he refrains from telling its whereabouts, but desires that it should go down to posterity known only as the "Hassall dog".

Probably the most important student of the Hassall style was Donald McGill (1875-1962) whose saucy postcards must have adorned every seaside resort in the country. His buxom ladies stem from characters in the Hassall repertoire such as the "Jolly Fisherman" and it was Hassall who suggested that McGill approach Eyre and Spottiswoode to publish his first postcards. McGill enlarged Hassall's sense of ambiguity with risqué quips: it was a winning formula that encouraged millions of holidaymakers to send a McGill card as frequently as they bought a stick of rock.

Hassall also designed some eight hundred book covers and illustrated over two hundred books. His prolific output shows the enormous demand there was for illustration in the 1900-14 period, when magazines, periodicals, children's books and illustrated newspapers were plentiful. Warren Bell commissioned Hassall to design the cover of *The Captain*, a magazine for boys, and Baden-Powell asked him to produce a cover for *Scouting for Boys*, but perhaps his most popular cover designs were those he did for the adventure stories of G.A. Henty.

The imaginative resourcefulness needed for illustrating fairy tales and other children's stories taxed Hassall's creativity. Together with Dudley Hardy he had an enormous influence on artists such as Alfred Leete, who produced the "Your Country Needs You" poster and Will Owen, father to the famous "Ah . . . Bisto" kids. Other students who benefited from Hassall's teaching were Mabel Lucie Attwell with her little cherubs, George Studdy and Bonzo, Lawson Wood with his Grandpop Gorillas and Harry Rountree with his legendary "Mansion Polish" tintop mice.

This was all to change during the First World War. Just as the pride of Britain disappeared overnight so did an army of graphic illustrators. When Hassall visited the front line and saw the real effect of his propaganda (such as his famous poster for the Public School Brigades, with the message "Fill up the ranks") he was shocked. It instilled in him the urge to do everything possible to aid the troops. Back in England he worked day and night, sometimes in all weathers, to collect money for the War Effort. A photograph taken in 1915 shows him painting in Trafalgar Square in an attempt to raise money for the troops. Another depicts Hassall and his cronies in theatrical costume entertaining at a jovial soirée in his capacity as chief fundraiser. The book in which Hassall recorded his activities constantly refers to "Free" or "Charitas" during this period. In later life Hassall was well known as an easy touch for anyone who wanted something done for nothing.

Although Hassall was too old to enlist, he became a Special Constable in 1916 and one of his many duties was to guard the gates of Buckingham Palace whilst the Grenadiers were away. He illustrated a book, which lies unpublished in Essex University, containing the comments and humorous reflections of a guardsman on sentry duty.

As his close friend Percy Bradshaw recalled, "Hassall's output was phenomenal. He was the most popular poster artist of the day, his humorous drawings were in constant demand, he designed nursery friezes, illustrated scores of books, painted serious pictures for the RA, belonged to several clubs and yet seemed to find the time for fun and games."

All this, including his evenings at the London Sketch Club where he was the star, would have drained a lesser man. Percy Bradshaw went on to describe how "One of his turns which I never ceased to enjoy was his impersonation of a Turkish refugee, who would enter in the most fearsome disguises to sell carpets or collect funds for his poor old father who kept goats in Smyrna — or merely talk the most inconsequential gibberish which the brain of a comic genius ever evolved." This emphasizes the amount of electrical energy which flowed out of Hassall, and inspired others. Other contemporaries copied his sense of humour and joined in the spoof.

His great friend George Robey often helped charities by donating his services free of charge. Hassall, too, did much work for *Printers Pie*, the charitable body of authors and artists who gave money to their "humbler brethren" in the printing trade. (It was run by Hugh Spottiswoode of Eyre & Spottiswoode.) There would be no call for it nowadays, but during the early part of the century printers were underpaid.

Unfortunately, like printers' wages, fashions in art swung wildly out of control. During the 'twenties and 'thirties the Art Deco craze took over. John Hassall, who had been famous by the time he was forty was now rejected. As old age crept up on him he became increasingly eccentric; his eyesight failed and the standard of his work declined. He splashed violent colour over his posters and his line, at one time so sure, became fussy and erratic. Repelled by anything bright, he put blankets over the windows of his studio. He covered up letters to hide their whiteness. Any light colours had to be hidden from view: he called them "out of tune". Constance returned from a holiday to find the entire drawing-room painted chocolate brown.

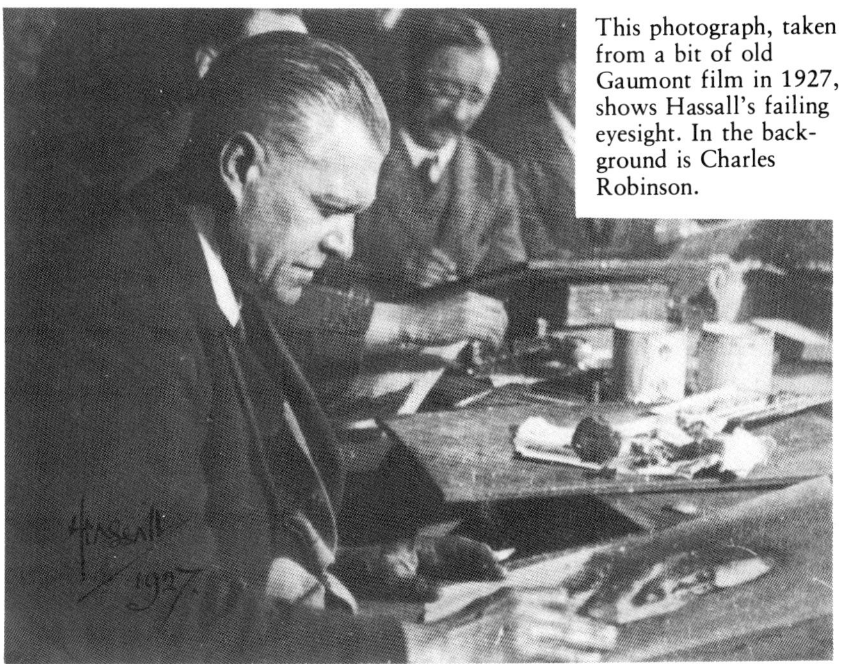

This photograph, taken from a bit of old Gaumont film in 1927, shows Hassall's failing eyesight. In the background is Charles Robinson.

Even the precious first editions she had so carefully saved had brown painted spines.

He constantly retreated to either the Savage or the London Sketch Club. He had never been one of those "greenery-yallery-foot-in-the-grave young men", products of the First World War; he was more the "hail-fellow-well-met" type propagated by Kipling and Henley. One of his great friends was the comedian Harry Tate, well known for his motoring and golfing sketches. Tate bequeathed to the formidable W. C. Fields many legendary mannerisms. Hassall was influenced by Tate in the matter of nonsense dialogue. He designed a menu card for Tate's dinner at the Savage Club using the pun "Po-Tate-O Pie": beneath it lay an assortment of down to earth dishes such as Stewed Eels, Pease Pudding and Fish Balls.

Hassall felt at home in the London Sketch Club where his own special brand of humour prevailed. Is it any wonder that he felt at home illustrating "Albert and the Lion" or "The Boatman" (with his "Per tuppence per person per trip")? This immortal selection of rhymes by Edgar Marriot (recorded by Stanley Holloway) touched the very essence of Hassall's humour. The style was simple, to the point and very effective: it reflected everything that Hassall stood for, including a hatred of pretence and pretentious people.

When asked why he didn't wear spectacles, Hassall would say, "I tried on old so-and-so's at the Sketch Club and they were no good at all", but he compromised by using a magnifying glass to work over the more difficult details of his drawings. This glass was also useful in inspecting his collection of flints. He randomly picked up stones from the sea shore and, if he recognised them as something interesting, would take them back to his studio to hoard. Eventually Hassall's collection of ancient flints became so vast and valuable that he presented them to the University of Cambridge. In addition to flint collecting, he also had a curiosity about how things worked. He was one of the first people ever to go down Wookey Hole and there is a beautiful story about him attacking Stonehenge with a hammer and chisel to test its strength.

In 1936 the urban district council of Skegness decided to make Hassall a Freeman of the Town and inscribed a roll of vellum for his first visit to Skegness. The dinner was a success and Hassall gracefully accepted the accolade. What really amused him was that he was allowed to use the deck chairs and go to the cinema for nothing.

As a businessman Hassall was not a success. Despite his enormous output and excellent book-keeping he was awarded a Civil List pension of £110 per annum in May 1939 for his services to posters. But he was disillusioned. "People do not want my work nowadays. They say I am old fashioned. I am 71 next month, and it's too late to change my ways now ... The Skegness poster took my name around the world. The last poster I designed brought me in nothing ... They asked me for help so I gave it free. But who knows that I did it? Or who cares?"

The missing factor in Hassall's Life was his old mate and mentor Dudley Hardy (nicknamed Ugly-Dugly in the Hassall household), who had died in 1922. Hassall became increasingly depressed. There were some lighter moments when he rekindled precious memories, such as nights at the London Sketch Club or the Savage, but often these nights meant hitting the whisky bottle. In the 'thirties he asked for a bank statement only to be told he had four shillings and ninepence in his account. And *he* was supposed to be a *commercial* artist! It was Frank Brangwyn, now Sir Frank, who came to his aid and suggested to the Prime Minister that Hassall should receive a pension.

Hassall's second son Christopher often accompanied him to smoker nights at the London Sketch Club but was eventually so embarrassed by his father's heavy drinking that he refused to go. Once inside the bar it was all too easy to slip down a whisky or two in convivial surroundings and possibly reminisce about Phil May. There was a difference between pre-War Britain and the Britain of the 'twenties and 'thirties: attitudes had changed. There was a cynicism about governmental control; before the war "your word was your bond". Some of the people Hassall had known before the War had amassed small fortunes. Hassall, not in the least avaricious, had none.

He had slipped into the same mould as Jimmy Pryde by accident and was paying the price. In the last years of his life it was almost as if the spirit had been thrashed out of him; he was left to ponder his fate within the confines of his studio. When he died his daughter Joan had the job of cleaning out her father's old studio. It became clear that he had been a hoarder of personal items that meant something to him. She wrote:

> When he died in 1948 the room had not been cleared for upwards of forty years. It contained a fantastic accumulation, because my father would throw nothing away which interested or amused him. There were posters, statuettes, curios, masks, weapons, costumes, the ceremonial headdress of a Red Indian Chief, suits of armour, and his Elizabethan four poster bed. Also there was a collection of flags on pins from 1914-18 Flag days, which looked like an ivy covered wall. Amongst the other objects were a sprig of heather from Nellie Melba, a lump of raw copper from Captain Scott, and Napoleon's death mask from John Tussaud. The dust that lay on the Indian gods and the ammonites was like grey sugar more than an inch thick.

CHAPTER 6

Laughter from the Trenches

The Sketch Club moved to its new premises in Marylebone Road in 1913. Bourne & Hollingsworth had acquired the block of houses in Wells Street which included No 79; they were then demolished to make way for a new store. Many London Sketch Club members were reluctant to leave their old haunt. Lionel Edwards and H. M. Bateman were not keen on the Marylebone premises. The former visited it once and then never again. Behind them they left the Aldin chimney corner, the Dulac panels in the bar and many happy memories. However, the new site in Marylebone offered entry at ground level, which made it much more attractive to older members. The first thing Hassall complained about was that the walls were too clean: he described them as being like "disinfectant!" This was not surprising since the premises had previously been used as a chapel. Hassall lit a bonfire in the middle of the room to give the walls the mellowed look usually achieved by many forgotten cigar butts and vicious pipesmoke. Thus the Marylebone studio acquired a hint of the old Wells Street bohemianism.

Exhibitions which the London Sketch Club formerly held in public galleries could now be held in the Club itself. It was said, at Wells Street, that dealers often queued outside to pick up the odd bargain. This practice continued in Marylebone. Some of the London Sketch Club exhibitions received a good press, as this report entitled "Bright Art" from the *Daily Telegraph* of November 1923 shows:

Even the most blasé arch-frequenter of art exhibitions has never found one unredeemed by some work of saving grace, yet in the welter of shows which herald the winter the enforced visitor sometimes had a feeling of surfeit. Then refreshment of the eye is required and it is often provided. One finds it, for example, in the Marylebone Road (246a), where the bright and eternally young London Sketch Club is holding its autumn exhibition. The gathering reflects the buoyant and unconquerable spirit of a brotherhood of artists who assume neither frills nor features and are determined to seek and express the beauty of Nature. Alive to the exigencies of the times, they do not appraise their art in terms of the super-tax, but obviously paint for those who desire to decorate their homes with works of colour and charm without paying old-masters prices. Montague Smyth graces the show with several works of poetic accomplishment, and he is ably supported by L. Burleigh Bruhl, Charles Robinson and Fred Taylor, among the senior executants. Another pronounced individualist is S. B. de la Bere, and one came away impressed with the merit of the luminous pictures by S. S. Bagdatopulos. One of the few portraits is a strongly-painted *chapeau de paille* subject by Charles D. Ward, and drawings of much charm have been sent by George Ayling, Alexander Lawson ("Kyle of Loch Alsh"), and J. MacWilson. A feature of the show is decidedly the series of colour-etchings, executed on a single plate without the use of aquatint by Edgar L. Pattison. Apart from their technical skill, these works are highly decorative, and it is encouraging to learn that they are finding much favour.

However, in 1913 the First World War was looming up: it was to bring losses on a scale hitherto unimaginable. Many London Sketch Club members either volunteered for active service or took on propaganda work. One of the latter was Alfred Leete with his "Your Country Needs You" poster of Kitchener with the famous pointing finger. Alfred Chew Leete (1882-1933) was the son of J. A. Leete, a Northamptonshire farmer. He was born at Thorpe Achurch and educated at Weston-super-Mare Grammar School. During the War Leete designed several posters and a number of war cartoons for magazines such as *The Passing Show* and books such as *All the Rumours* and *The Worries of Wilhelm* (both published in 1916). He married Edith Webb and they had one son.

If Leete's "Your Country Needs You" was the most famous poster of the First World War, then Bert Thomas's " 'Arf a Mo, Kaiser" was the most famous cartoon. Created for the *Weekly Dispatch* tobacco fund campaign, it raised some quarter of a million pounds to provide "Smokes for the Tommies". Private Bert Thomas of the Artist Rifles was also commissioned to design a series of War Loan posters. One, which was 75 feet long, was completed on scaffolding outside the National Gallery. Herbert Thomas (1883-1966), known as Bert, was the son of Job Thomas, a Welsh sculptor and stonemason who, as a young man, had worked on the new Houses of Parliament. Bert later remarked that he could "claim to have inherited the family passion for making graven images". He left school at the age of fourteen to work for a Swansea engraver. His entrée into the world of illustration and caricature came through the *Swansea Daily Leader*, *The Daily Post* and *The Echo*, where his sketches and cartoons appeared regularly. His theatrical cartoons caught the eye of Albert Chevalier and the comedian commissioned Thomas to design a huge poster. This netted Thomas five pounds (a considerable sum in those days) and an invitation to London, where he mounted an assault on Fleet Street. In 1905 he started drawing for *Punch* and a year later was a regular contributor to *London Opinion* (this association lasted until the journal's demise in 1954). Thomas also had a variety of other outlets for his cartoons including *The Humorist, The Sketch, The Bystander* and *The World*.

The most memorable book illustrated with his caricatures was *Meet These People* by Reginald Arkell, published in 1928 by Herbert Jenkins. Thomas is probably best remembered today for his cartoons in the now defunct *Evening News* in the 'twenties and 'thirties. He would often produce four or five drawings a day.

In 1928 Methuen published *In Red and Black*, a collection of his two-colour cartoons from *The Sketch*.

In 1923 Thomas moved to a spacious farm at Pinner in Middlesex where he remained until 1947. A visiting writer recalled "the presence of two easels, a beige-draped billiard table which served as a filing centre, a large wireless set on the window ledge, one white parrot and Bert Thomas the artist — a short restless, outspoken chain-smoker in sweater and flannels." Thomas had married in 1909 at

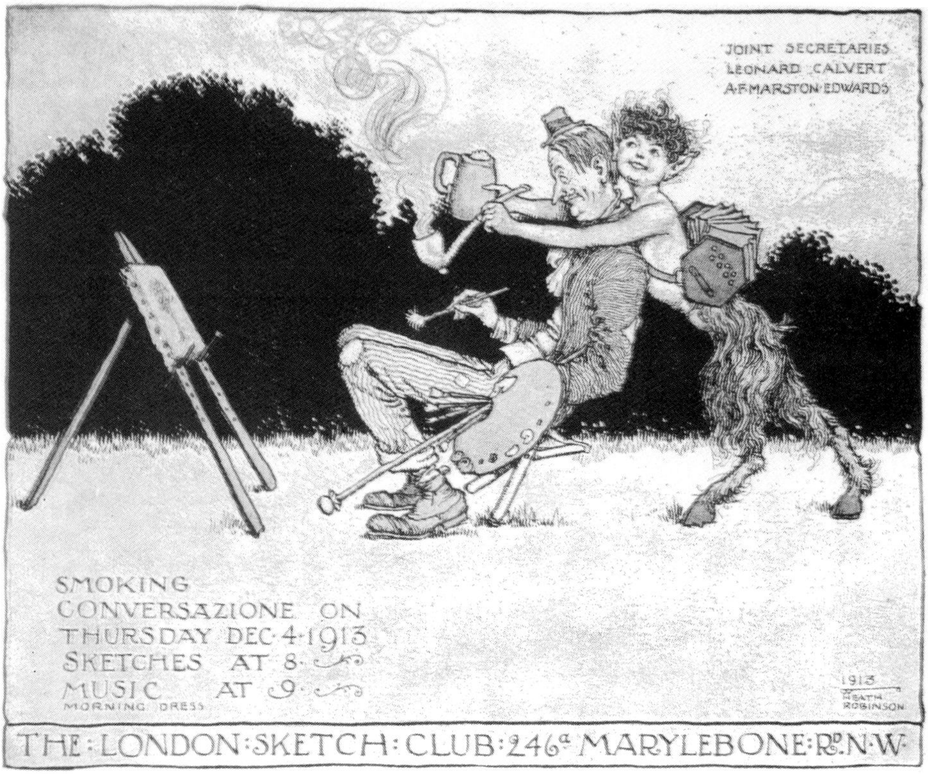

This invitation card by W. Heath Robinson is mild in comparison with many of his strangely prophetic cartoons. Although he made the most of his reputation for being a bit odd, he clearly foresaw a bureaucratic nightmare, with the country's institutions being held together with bits of string in an amateurish, homespun kind of way. He was one of the great satirists of our time.

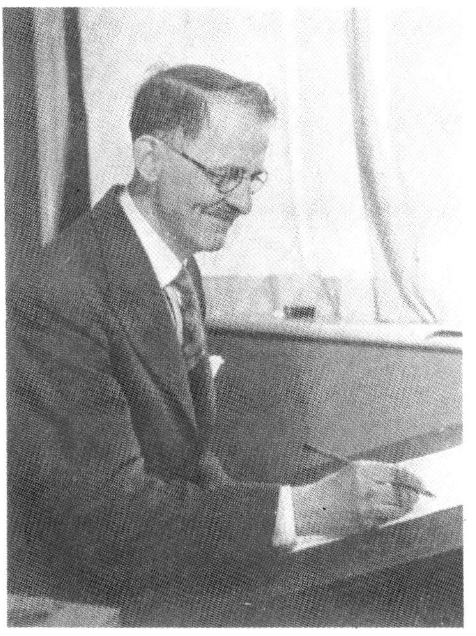

W. Heath Robinson at work. His son Oliver Robinson followed in his father's footsteps by joining the Club in 1936, eventually becoming a Trustee of the London Sketch Club.

the age of twenty-six and had four sons and two daughters. He kept his own horses and rode regularly to hounds before breaking his collar bone at the age of fifty. In 1918 he was awarded the MBE for his contribution to the war effort and he was described in his *Times* obituary as "stocky and short and as friendly as a Toby jug."

A near neighbour of Thomas in Pinner was W. Heath Robinson. Even before the war Heath Robinson's contraptions had caught the public's imagination. His drawings in *Am Tag* showed what might happen if the Germans invaded Britain. He was the first artist to caricature inanimate objects but he also succeeded in making the German army look like a bunch of pompous poltroons.

The absurdities Heath Robinson (the 'Gadget King') dreamt up were to remain his trademark for the rest of his life. He was the only London Sketch Club artist whose name actually entered the English Language. There was a definite Hassall influence in his early illustrations for *The Adventures of Uncle Lubin* (1902) and *Bill the Minder* (1912), but in his later work even Hassall could not have matched Heath Robinson's imagination. During the War his cartoons appeared in the *Sketch* and *Bystander* and prompted a flood of correspondence. One of his inventions was the "Subzeppmarinelin", a cross between a submarine and a zeppelin, which was seen attacking an innocent elderly lady in a rowing boat. Other ingenious devices included "The American Suction Tank", which extracted the enemy from his dugout with a vast suction pump, and "American Barb Trousers" which enabled troops to extricate themselves if caught up in barbed wire. Most of Heath Robinson's war pictures appeared in book form in *Some Frightful War Pictures, Hunlikely* and *The Saintly Hun*, published by Duckworth.

W. Heath Robinson (1872-1944), known as "Will" in the London Sketch Club, had come from an artistic background. His father Thomas Robinson was an illustrator and two of his brothers, Charles and Tom, were also artists. He trained at Islington and the Royal Academy Schools before becoming an illustrator himself. He joined the London Sketch Club in 1910 through Frank Reynolds and used the same agent, A. E. Johnson, as did Hassall, Dudley Hardy, Tom Browne and Lawson Wood.

Another memorable artist of the First World War, and one of Hassall's earliest students, was Captain Bruce Bairnsfather, famous for his character Old Bill. Bairnsfather (1888-1959) was born in Murree, India, the son of an Army officer, and was commissioned in the Royal Warwickshire Regiment in 1911. He left to study art but at the outbreak of the First World War hastily rejoined his regiment. Old Bill first appeared in *The Bystander* but was eventually published in *Fragments from France*. His catchphrase was, "If you know of a better 'ole go to it!" Bairnsfather always declared his character was based on a variety of people and *not* on his old tutor John Hassall, but the likeness cannot be ignored.

The London Sketch Club's wartime efforts were a boost to morale at a time when there was little to laugh about. Of the many magazines of the period (there were dozens of propaganda publications such as *Keep Smiling* and *Ye Berlyn Tapestrie*, (both illustrated by John Hassall), probably the most ambitious was *The Fledgling* (later called *Roosters and Fledglings*). This was the RAF journal, originally devoted to No 2 Wing of the RFC in 1917. It was edited by Basil Macdonald Hastings and included illustrations by Bairnsfather, Hassall and Arthur Ferrier and literary contributions by Joseph Conrad.

The most controversial artist at this time was Christopher Richard Wynne Nevinson (1889-1946). Born in Hampstead the only child of Henry Wood

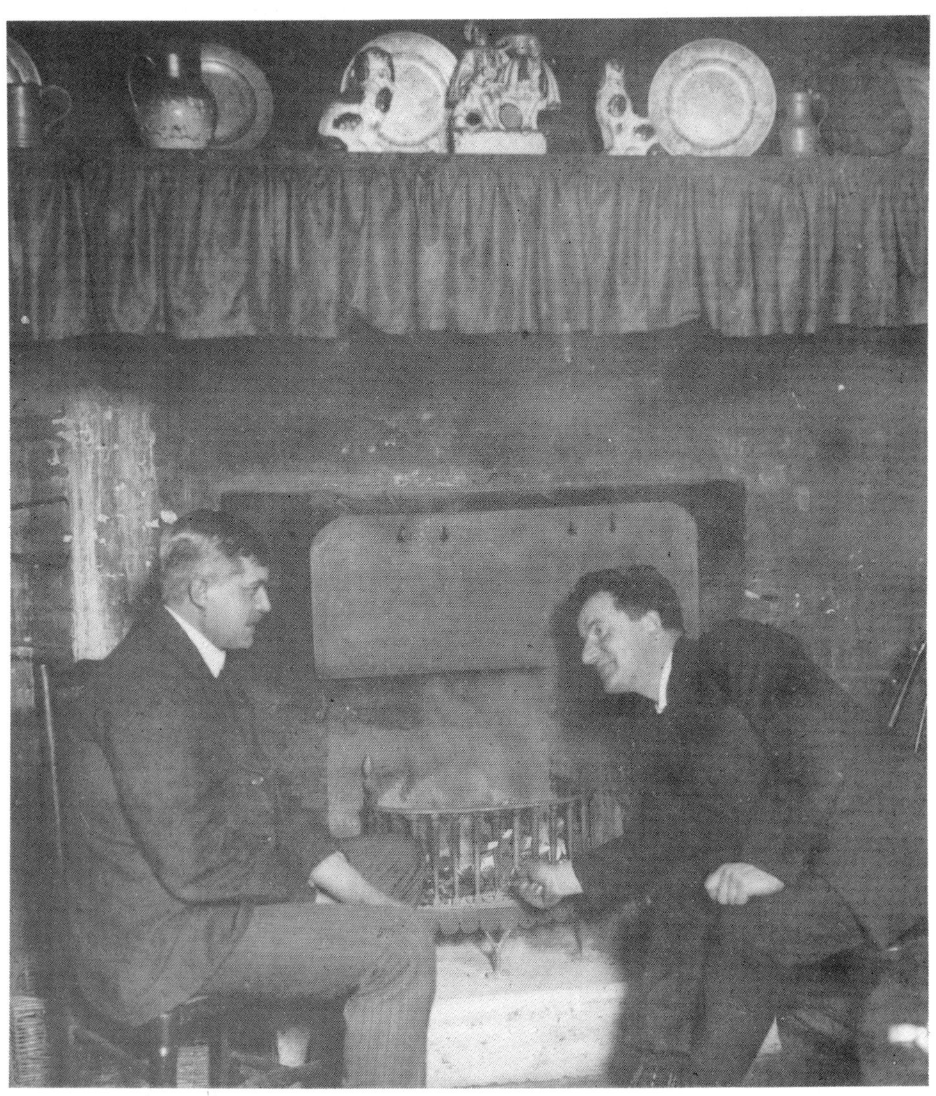

The caption to this photograph might have been "Two publicity seekers seeking publicity" according to Nevinson's critics of the 1920s and '30s. John Hassall on the left is talking to the young C.R.W. Nevinson in the old tavern chimney corner designed by Cecil Aldin in the Wells Street studio. Nevinson was pilloried for his publicity seeking in later life.

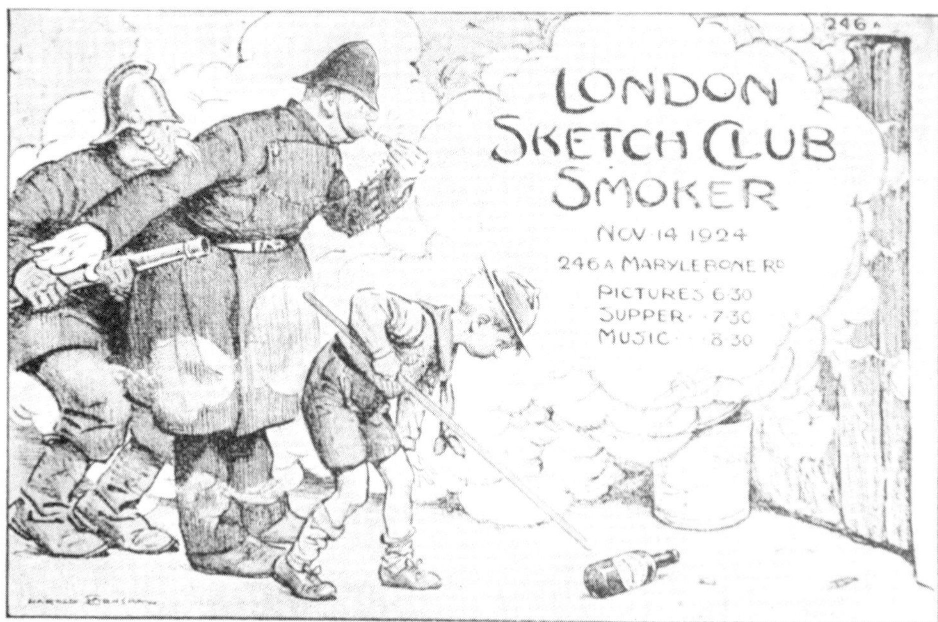

(*Above*) Invitation card by Harold Earnshaw.

(*Right*) Portrait of Harold Earnshaw by Charles Ward, another good London Sketch Club member.

(*Below*) Charles D. Ward, ROI, who painted Earnshaw's portrait, probably during a two-hour sketching session at the London Sketch Club, was known simply as Chas. Born in Taunton in 1872, he studied at the Royal College of Art. He married Charlotte Blakeney, and was elected to the ROI in 1915.

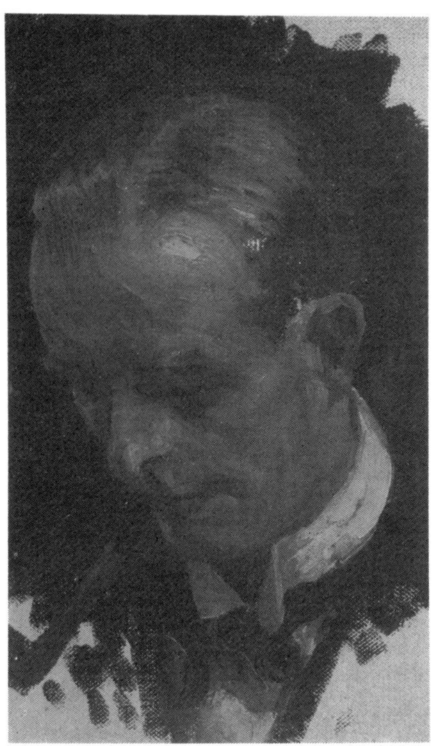

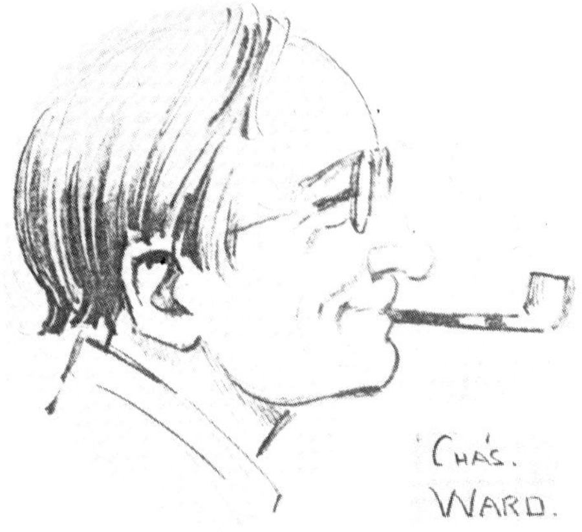

Nevinson, the celebrated war correspondent, and his first wife Margaret Wynne, he was educated at Uppingham, which he hated. He enrolled at St John's Wood School of Art in 1907 and from there went on to the Slade (1909-1911), where his fellow students inlcuded Stanley Spencer, Mark Gertler and Edward Wadsworth. At the Slade Henry Tonks (arguably one of the greatest art teachers of all time) told Nevinson that he was without talent and unqualified to become a painter (this was despite some favourable reviews of his work in the 1910 Friday Club Exhibition reported in *The Sunday Times*). As a result Nevinson decided to follow his father's career in journalism, and in his time in Fleet Street interviewed Little Tich and Marie Lloyd.

Meanwhile he joined the London Sketch Club, which offered a very different hospitality to that of Tonks. He visited Paris in the years 1911 to 1913 and for a time shared a studio with Modigliani, enjoying the company of fellow artists with whom he could swop ideas and opinions. One of the artists he met, over lunch with Roger Fry and Clive Bell, was Severini. It was the start of a lifelong friendship with the Italian Futurist; Nevinson will always be associated with the Futurist movement, despite his involvement with the Vortists.

At the outbreak of the First World War, Nevinson, whose health was never good, joined the Red Cross because he heard they were short of ambulance drivers. Subsequently stationed in Belgium he took on the roles of nurse, stretcher-bearer and interpreter, as well as driver, and eventually joined the Royal Army Medical Corps, serving as an orderly until he was invalided out of the Army with rheumatic fever in 1916.

Before 1914 the name of Christopher Nevinson was known only to a handful of artists, mostly his own circle. However, after the Spring of 1915, when he exhibited his first three war pictures at the Goupil Gallery, his reputation travelled far and wide. He was the first artist to make his reputation from the battlefields. Later he turned to more lyrical subjects but these did not have the impact of his war pictures. Nevinson was a rebel all his life, yet was humane. His memories from the First World War remained with him. Except during a brief period in 1917 when he was sent to the Western Front as an Official War Artist and produced paintings which did not have the same bite, Nevinson was a controversial figure. He was often ridiculed in the press and caricatured by fellow artists. As he became older and more tetchy he made an easy target, encouraging cynicism with articles in the popular press such as "Do beautiful women get away with it?" or "Pretty women: are there any left?" He gave parties in his studio off Haverstock Hill which were crowded with celebrities of stage and screen, usually with Nevinson talking loudly at the centre of the room. "Poor girls, poor girls" he was reputed to have said, "sooner or later they all tell me I'm the love of their lives! I give up. I can't explain it. I'm fat, ugly, promiscuous and indifferent. What do you make of it?" Nevinson became an associate of the RA in 1939 and wrote his autobiography *Paint and Prejudice* which was published in 1937.

Everyone from the London Sketch Club did his bit in those war years. Conan Doyle wrote profusely abut tactics, comparing them to those of the Boer War. The young Stanley Holloway was commissioned as a 2nd Lieutenant in the Connaught Rangers and served with the Green Howards. John Keble Bell, also a 2nd Lieutenant, wrote his wartime memoirs, *An Author in Wonderland*. It would seem that everyone heeded the old adage "In life, the Great Call comes only once!" Members who were too old for active service, such as John Hassall, James Pryde and

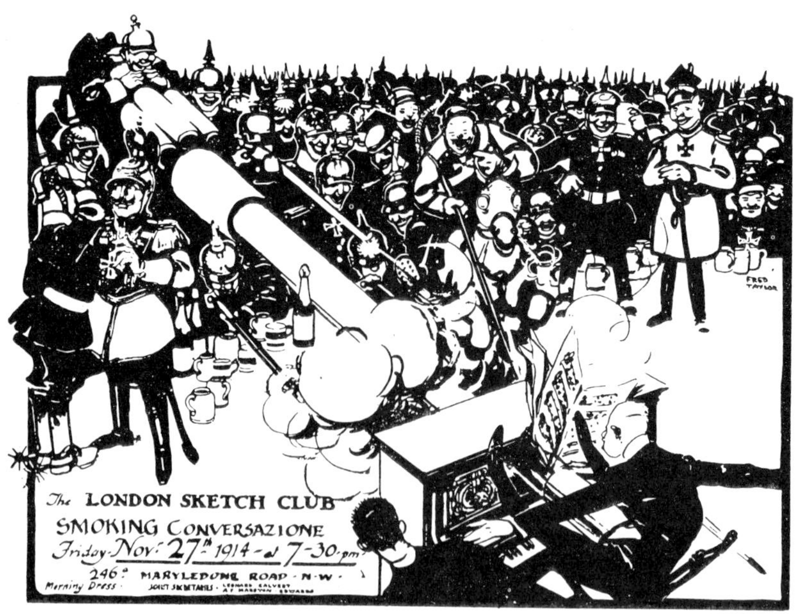

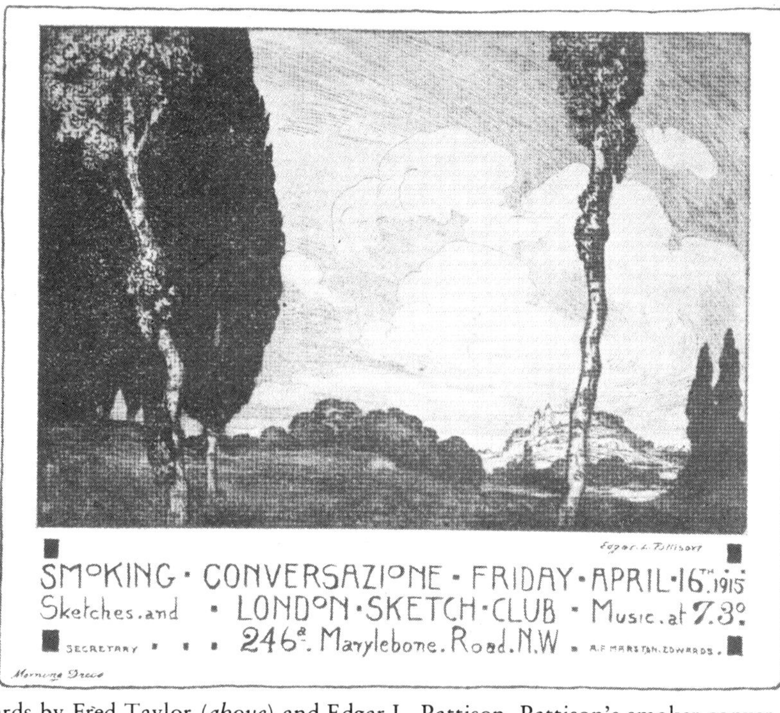

Invitation cards by Fred Taylor (*above*) and Edgar L. Pattison. Pattison's smoker conversazione of 1915 contrasts heavily with the horrors of war. In place of barbed wire, stinking trenches and shell holes is a serene landscape full of escapism. Pattison, who was born in 1872 and trained at Lambeth Art School, was an etcher designer. Fred Taylor's message is simpler: "Who shot the piano player?"

90

Percy Bradshaw, volunteered as special constables. Those rejected on medical grounds, as H. M. Bateman was in 1915, were left feeling miserable and depressed. Bateman recalled:

> The years that followed were little better than a nightmare for I suffered much from debility and the depression which goes with it. But mercifully I could work — it is less exhausting physically to wield a pen than to carry a rifle and equipment — and I threw myself heart and soul into drawing, because it was about the only thing for me to do. All my friends were away at the front, and feeling thoroughly out of it I went down to Dartmoor which was about the best and the worst place for me to be in at the time. It was healthy but very lonely, and there was nothing else for me to do but fish for small trout and work and think. I thought a great deal, and on leaving Dartmoor found I was too restless to settle anywhere for long. Frank Hart, who was away serving, lent me his studio in Chelsea, where I did a lot of work in a rather hysterical condition, being up one day and down the next.

Luckier artists such as Lionel Edwards, who served in the Army Remount Service, René Bull, who served with the RNVR and latterly with the RAF, or George Studdy, who did VAD work, all survived the War. Some were highly decorated: Lawson Wood from his time as a balloonist observer with the RFC; Ellis Silas from his time with the Anzacs. Most of the younger members served with The Artists (The Artists Rifles). They included James Thorpe, Harold "Pat" Earnshaw, Bert Thomas and Fred Buchanan. Those commissioned included Lieutenant Hughes-Stanton and W. Lee-Hankey. Even the fifteen-year-old Ian Hassall rushed off to join The Artists until his father found out. Eventually he joined the London Scottish.

There were of course casualties. Lance Thackeray, who enlisted at the outbreak of hostilities, was seconded to Egypt with The Artists and died on active service in 1916. Thackeray left a plethora of photographs in which he was always smiling — what a wonderful epitaph! Another casualty in the Middle East was Charles Orchardson (1873-1917) who served with the Camel Corps. He was awarded the Military Cross. The son of Sir William Quiller Orchardson, RA, he had been a tutor at Hassall's School of Art and was a member of the Chelsea Arts Club. A third casualty in the desert was a promising young illustrator, Will Houghton.

Probably the worst injury was the amputation of Harold Earnshaw's right arm in 1916. For a right-handed artist this was unbearably cruel, but Earnshaw determined to learn to draw with his left. He possessed a pleasant, easygoing, boyish sort of character. Whilst recuperating in hospital during the War he drew a series of humorous sketches of fellow patients and nurses which appeared in *The Tatler*. This was the first time he had drawn with his left hand.

Earnshaw (1886-1937) had studied art at St Martins School of Art, where he met Mabel Lucie Attwell whom he married in 1908. He introduced her to many Sketch Club contemporaries such as Charles Ward and Harry Rountree. He had a good light tenor voice, singing ballads such as "Absent", "Because", "Where My Caravan has Rested" and "Until" at London Sketch Club Smokers. He was keen on billiards, playing with his left hand and a special hook to screw into his false right hand as a cue rest. He also enjoyed golf and was part of the Sketch Club team. He was one of *The Jolly Book* illustrators, with George Studdy and Hawley-Morgan.

Another casualty that affected the Club was Cyrus Cuneo, a member of the Langham not the Sketch Club. A handsome man who had seen off the trenches and

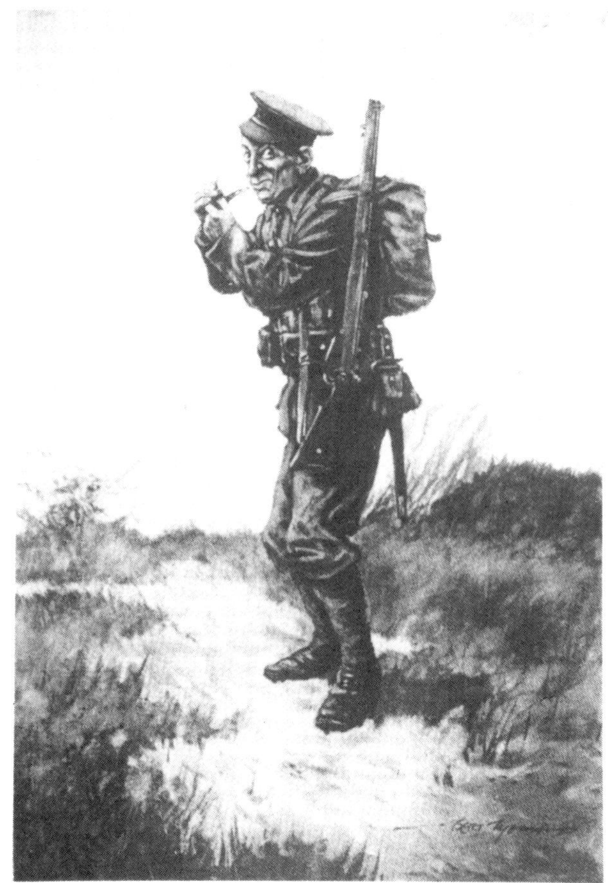

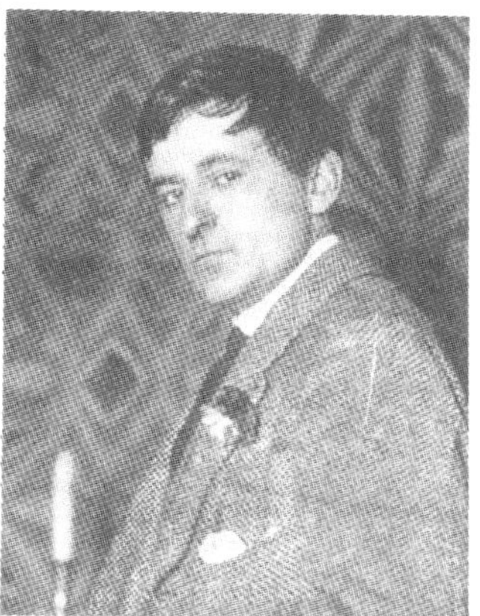

Bert Thomas (1883-1966)

Bert Thomas's "''Arf a mo, Kaiser!'' cartoon. The original "vanished" shortly after it was engraved and has not been seen since. Both Bert Thomas and W. Heath Robinson were also members of the Savage Club.

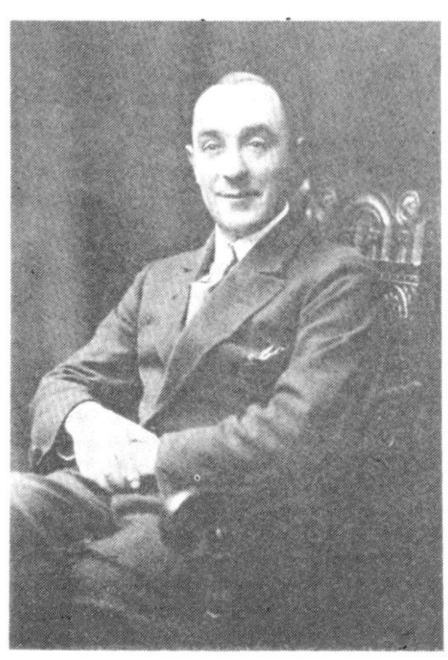

Clay Thomas during the First World War, when he served as a Special Constable. With Stendale Bennett and Herbert Collings he organised concerts for the troops serving in The Artists Rifles. They helped lighten those dismal war years. In later life Thomas recalled a wonderful anecdote concerning E.J. Odell and John Hassall: "Odell was leaving the Savage Club in the early hours of the morning when he saw a body lying in the gutter. Looking down, he saw it was a fellow Savage who muttered, 'Get me up. I'm drunk,' to which Odell replied, 'My dear chap, I am not capable to lift you, but I can keep you company,' and proceeded to lie down beside him. A little later John Hassall left the Club and, seeing the two bodies, said, 'Well, you two drunks, I can't help you up but I can join you.' And thus they lay till dawn.'' As a footnote Thomas added that in those days Adelphi Terrace, where the Savage Club was situated, had no passing traffic.

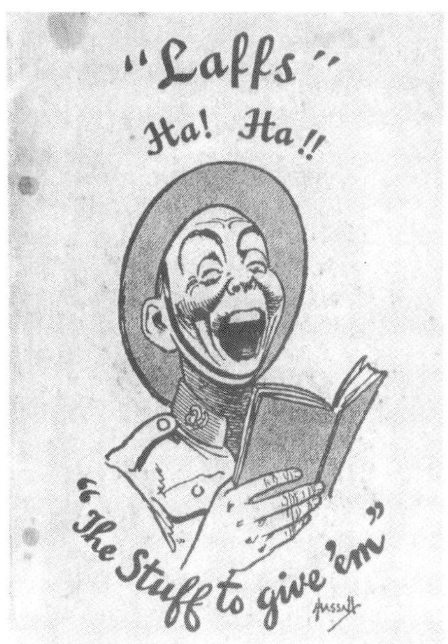

Hassall's cover design for *Laffs* by John Ross, dedicated to The Glasgow City Business Club which collected £50,000 for the Earl Haigh Fund between the years 1922 and 1939.

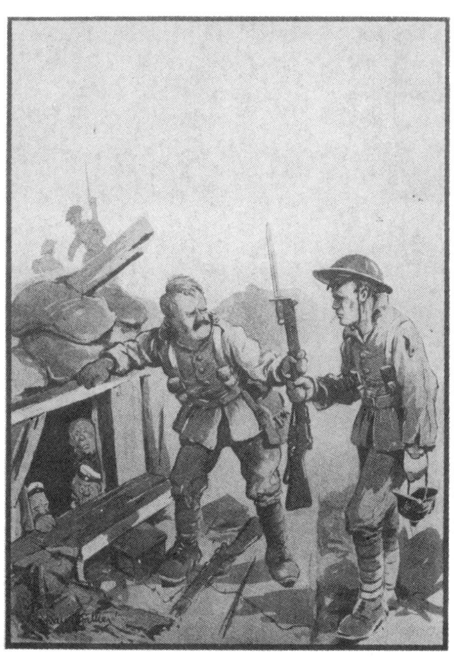

A Bruce Bairnsfather cartoon from *Fragments from France*: "Coming to the Point: 'Let's 'ave this pin of yours a minute. I'll soon 'ave these winkles out of 'ere.'"

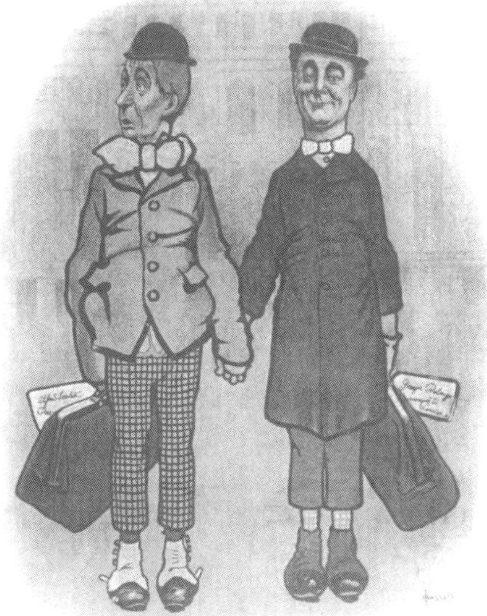

Hassall's illustration of the Bing Boys. London Sketch Club member Alfred Lester is on the left whilst George Robey is on the right.

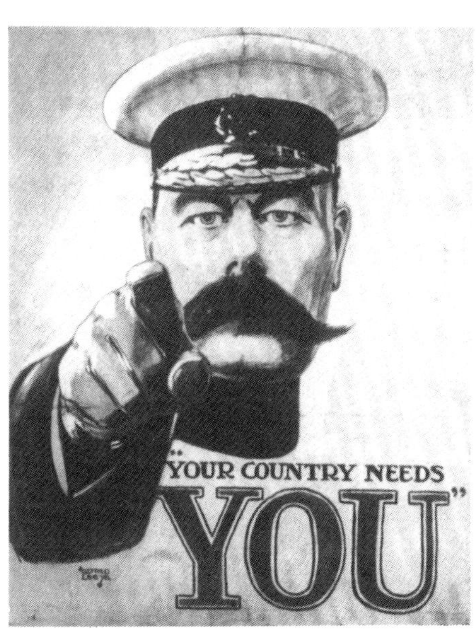

Alfred Leete's famous poster, "Your Country Needs You".

come home safely, he attended a dance where an accidental graze from a lady's
fingernail turned gangrenous. He died a few weeks later.

During the Boer War there was a demand for reporter artists but by the time of the
First World War photography had taken over the function of recording scenes
accurately. However, what the camera did not possess was a sense of humour. In this
area Sketch Club artists excelled themselves and their humour was a great boost to
the troops' morale.

Many a soldier's sanity also depended on music hall humour and the stage when
he returned home on leave. Musical comedies, revues and light operas enjoyed record
runs. Shows such as *Chu Chin Chow, The Maid of the Mountains* and *The Bing
Boys* ran throughout the War. It was the heyday of the music hall: the vast selection
of sing-along songs included "Pack Up Your Troubles" and "Drunk Last Night
and Drunk the Night Before ...".

In 1915 two members of the Sketch Club decided to cross the Channel and
entertain the troops in France: they were Alfred Lester and John Hassall. Lester was
one part of the Bing Boys, playing opposite George Robey. (The big hit from *The
Bing Boys* was "If You Were the Only Girl in the World", still popular in the
'fifties!) When the pair arrived after a rough crossing John Hassall was quoted as
saying "He will sketch and, if encouraged, talk a bit. Prices for these works of art nix
... nought." The troops appreciated their turns and Hassall commented, "You
never saw such a cheerful bunch even though they had their arms in slings and were
bandaged up." The troops were English, Canadian and Australian forces.

Not that it was hunky-dory back in Britain. There were air raids from zeppelins
and occasional catastrophes, as John Hassall found out on 19 January 1917. He
received a phone call that led to his helping to clear up the devastation left by a
munitions explosion in Silvertown. A fire had broken out in the upper part of
Messrs Brunner, Mond & Company Chemical Works of Crescent Wharf, Silvertown. The fire brigade had been called but could do nothing to prevent the
consequences. Ten minutes later a red glow lit up the sky over East London and the
explosion was heard as far away as Slough. Doors, hand barrows and shutters were
used as stretchers as rescue workers fought to save lives. The final death toll was 72,
with over four hundred people injured, some seriously, and over a thousand made
homeless. The crater left by the explosion was some fifty yards in diameter. It took
days to clear up the mess and count the dead whilst an acrid smell hung over the
scene. Hassall made several trips to the disaster area and later suffered badly from
recurring nightmares, waking up in a sweat.

When the war finally ended there was much disillusionment. Hardly a home in
the country had not been affected. Men had joined up because it was their duty but
many even thought it was going to be a glorious adventure! Nothing could have been
further from the truth. It was no J. A. Henty story! As James Thorpe recorded:

What it was all about or why we were fighting, none of us knew. It was, like
most others, a politicians' war, and hatred between the combatants had to be
stimulated and encouraged by them. All their wild promises, foolish as we
then knew them to be, we have since seen broken and conveniently forgotten.
It left us all tired, poor, disillusioned and wondering, wondering still more
when we came home to find how well the cunning ones who stayed in England
had looked after their own interests, and how they pitied and despised our
foolishness.

CHAPTER 7

The 'Twenties

During the 'twenties the London Sketch Club came into its element. All Hassall's
protégés were now becoming well known and respected artists in their own right.
The Club was financially secure and 246A, Marylebone Road became known as one
of the best bohemian haunts of London. As Leonard Crocombe recorded in 1928:

> At the far end of a long, dark, narrow alley off the Marylebone Road there are
> some old studios with walls that ramble in quaint angles . . . The main front
> door of these genial studios was once the door of the condemned cell at old
> Newgate. You can take your first peep at the London Sketch Club through the
> inspection hole used by the warders to watch those condemned to die. Over an
> inner door is the lamp that once shed its brilliance over the Empire stage door
> . . .
>
> Alfred Leete hurried across the room to greet me. I gripped his hand, and
> pulled mine away with a hot baked potato squashed in it . . . George Studdy,
> crouched up in a corner, drawing board on knees, was engrossed in a sketch. I
> hailed him, cheerily, "Hallo Studdy, learning to draw?" Studdy, famous
> throughout two continents, growled solemnly, "That's what we're here for,
> isn't it?"
>
> Fred Buchanan is the Club's low comedian, John Hassall and Harry
> Rountree are its leading characters, Stan Terry its flipper of bread pellets and
> Wilton Williams its heavy-weight. Thomas Downey holds the record for
> pickle-eating — or he did at the last tramp supper when I tried to get hold of
> the jar.

Crocombe then related his remembrances of that supper:

> The last supper at which I was a guest was the Tramp Supper. Many of the
> men had spent considerable time and trouble on making themselves look
> disreputable.
>
> We ate cold ham, hot potatoes in their jackets, salad, bread and cheese, and
> apples washed down with beer served in hefty earthenware jars. Candles stuck
> in beer bottles adorned the long tables, on which there were plenty of clay
> pipes and many jars of good strong shag.
>
> It was great to watch John Hassall, fearful and wonderful in an indescrib-
> able medley of ancient clothes, impersonating a Russian peasant who had just
> arrived in London and wandered in by mistake. One entertainer, looking more
> like a much-scrubbed and genial navvy than a tramp, gave us a funny one-man
> pantomime. Others sang or played or told stories during the evening, for the
> talents of the "Sketches" are not confined to their brushes and are of a higher
> order.

George Parlby (1856-1944) frequently exhibited at the Royal Academy.

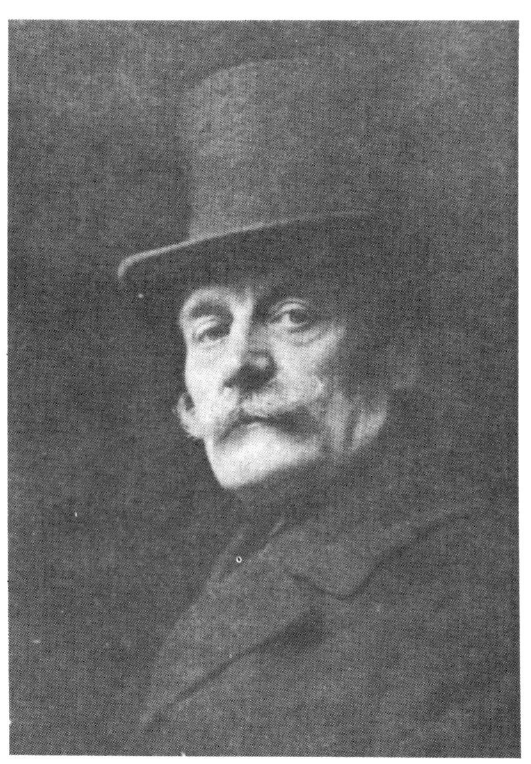

George Parlby is seated on the extreme left; Hassall in his policeman's uniform is on the right.

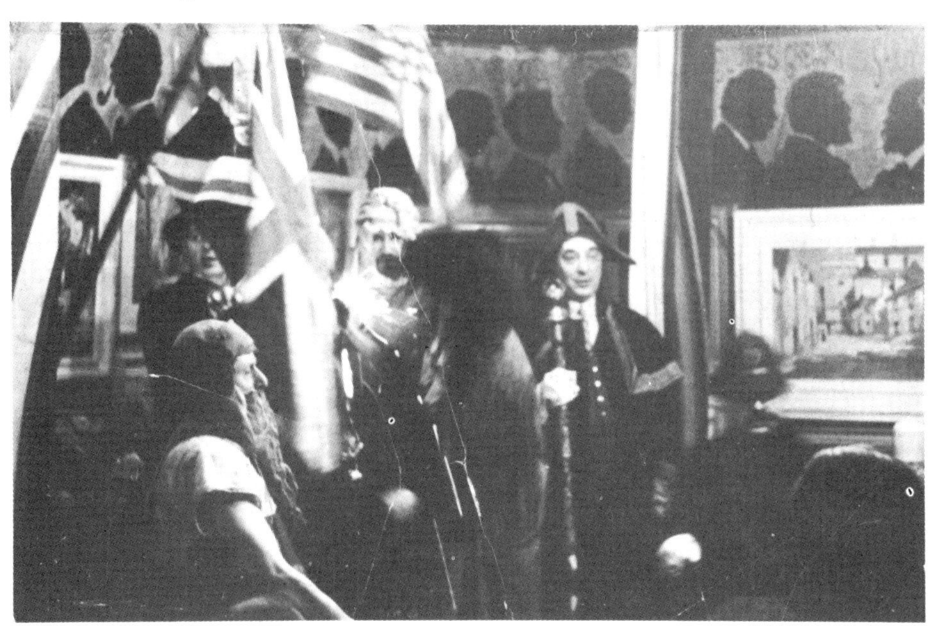

All this, in cold type, may seem rather trivial, but the humour provided is often better than that of the average variety theatre. On one of these festive nights the Club indulged in an elaborate bull-fight. The Club has, you must know, its Master of the Revels, this important office being most efficiently filled by George Parlby.

The reference to George Parlby, sometimes nicknamed the "Grand Old Man of the London Sketch Club", was most significant. Parlby was a tall, distinguished looking stained glass artist. He dressed as if he had just stepped out of a Dickens novel and he was a man full of invention. For years he was Master of Ceremonies, whether it was for the opening of the London Sketch Club Ball or simply taking charge of the entertainment at Friday evening suppers.

Parlby's studio in Chiswick was typical of the man, as Arnold Beauvais recalled:

It was a large studio on the top floor, filled with an accumulation of furniture, costumes, junk, etc, etc, a collection of armour around the walls. When he detached a suit of armour from its hook, he was almost obliterated by the falling dust, and I was surprised to find that it was made of cardboard, painted with silver paint! He made all his historical costumes out of bits and pieces; many period hats were made out of old bowlers: one method was to soak the hat and, using an ordinary flower pot, drag the felt over the top. When set, add a broad brim or other addition, and you had a period hat rather like the Charterhouse uniform. The Presidential chain of office of the LSC was made by Parlby out of odd bits and pieces, and on his desk I notice a wad of 10/- notes nailed to the top. As a member of The Bourjeois Club (pronounced Bojoys), he was presented with a casket containing 10/- notes, to celebrate his 80th birthday. When I asked how many notes there were he replied, "Dear me! I would never think of counting them." (I presume there must have been 80.) He said it was very convenient to detach one when required.

Most of the costumes he made were stored in the attic that could only be reached by swinging on a rope that was attached to the ceiling on the top landing (that was also a bathroom) into the door of the attic, just above the bath, which prevented a ladder being placed under the attic door. Therefore the ladder was placed against the opposite wall, and by climbing it and using the rope you could swing over the bath and into the attic.

George showed me how he did it and bade me follow, and I can never think of this incident without being reminded of Shakespeare's *Julius Caesar*, when Caesar said to Cassius: "Dar'st thou Cassius, now leg with me into this angry flood, and swim to yonder point?"

What a kind fellow he was, such a clever artist, and a most enthusiastic entertainer, too enthusiastic for many members of the LSC who thought that the terrific energy he always put into his "turns" might bring on a sudden collapse, or set fire to the premises with his box of fireworks. I remember one "turn" in which he put a lighted candle in his pocket, thinking it was extinguished, and set fire to his clothing.

Parlby went to the town of Beauvais in France every year for a short holiday and he always sent me a postcard inscribed "from Beauvais to Beauvais". When I asked him why he made this annual pilgrimage, he told me, in strict confidence, that each time he re-visited a certain forest that in the past (on

honeymoon) he had walked with his late wife; he felt her presence so strongly
that it was as if she were still with him.

Parlby's props included buttons, threads, cottons and curios and his armour was
constructed from old biscuit tins. On certain occasions he would don one set of
clothes over another so that when he had finished his act he would strip off his
"garb" to reveal a smart set of evening clothes underneath.

During one of the Friday evening entertainments Parlby arranged a firework
display and when a particularly vicious banger went off, Thomas Downey complained that he had gone deaf in one ear; unperturbed Parlby simply continued with
his act.

At the Christmas Dinner it was Parlby's generosity that ensured each LSC
member receive a present. He would produce a sack of novelties to hand to each
member as they filed past for dinner: each had to bow and thank him personally
before opening his package.

On one occasion the intrepid Parlby was arrested on his way to a tramp dinner: no
doubt the sack of novelties slung over his shoulder did not endear him to the
arresting officer. Once at the station, Parlby's explanation was verified by the acting
sergeant; he then proceeded to amuse the constabulary with his act before leaving.

Parlby's eccentric way of life stemmed largely from his honesty. He could
completely disregard his surroundings, as happened once on Victoria Railway
Station. Parlby noticed a friend at the other end and proceeded to greet him in a loud
voice. The repressed recipient of the greeting was so embarrassed at having his name
shouted the full length of the platform that he pretended not to notice. A passer-by
was heard to comment, "He must be a theatrical man."

Parlby exhibited some 44 paintings at the Royal Academy during his lifetime and
frequently stood in as a portrait model to the Sketch Club crew when no other model
turned up. He was in every respect a gentleman who disliked smutty stories, but he
would patiently listen and smile obligingly afterwards.

Crocombe's account of the Sketch Club in 1928 concluded:

> A Friday evening. About twenty earnest men seated in various attitudes
> around a large table, busy picture-making with brushes and pencils. Watching
> them at work, as I did — why do so many modern artists look like smart
> London businessmen? — one marvels at their dexterity, the speed and sureness
> of their hands. The time sketches made at the Club are by no means mere rough
> sketches. In many cases paintings in oils or water-colours have been produced
> in the space of two hours worthy of a place on the walls of any connoisseur —
> Pictures freshly vivid with imagination and vibrant in expression. The united
> output of these enthusiasts in the course of a year is something like one
> thousand pictures.
>
> As with their work, so with their play — these merry men rely upon
> spontaneous inspiration rather than upon a laboured effort. And well do they
> succeed.

It was unthinkable that this talented band of artists could remain secluded in their
safe haven of the Sketch Club without someone trying to manipulate their skills:
this job fell to the entrepreneural Percy Venner Bradshaw. Born in London, the son
of a commercial traveller and grandson of an ardent Baptist minister, Bradshaw had
joined the Club back in 1912 as a lay member. His entrée into illustration had come

(*Right*) Curiously Sidney Strube (1891-1956)
was *not* one of Percy Bradshaw's Press Art
School students. Instead he studied
at John Hassall's School of Art in
Kensington. Within the
London Sketch Club
Strube was known
as George.

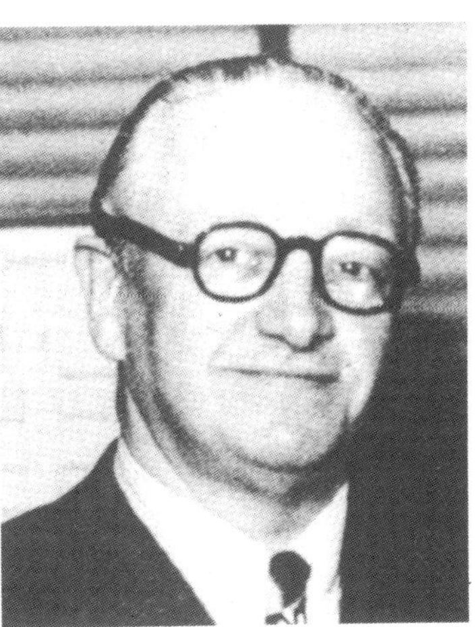

Percy Venner Bradshaw, who
died in 1965, was responsible
for many publications, the most
memorable being *Art in Advertising* (a massive tome) which
he published through the Press
Art School.

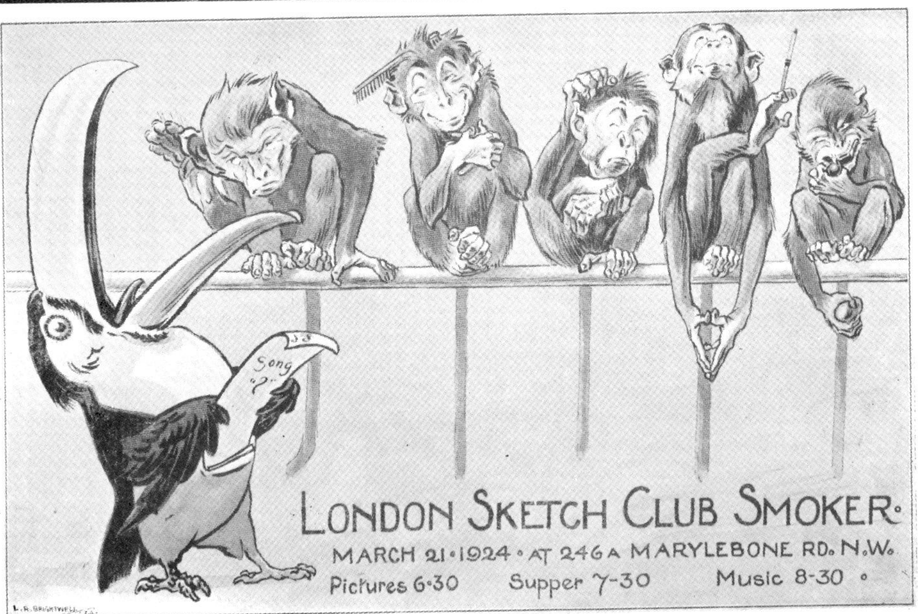

L. R. Brightwell invitation card. Leonard Robert Brightwell, FZS was born in 1889 in
London and spent his early childhood drawing animals in and around Chiswick. He studied
at the Lambeth School of Art and illustrated numerous books. The bespectacled Brightwell
was President of the London Sketch Club in 1928. During the First World War he had
served in France and was an air raid warden in World War II.

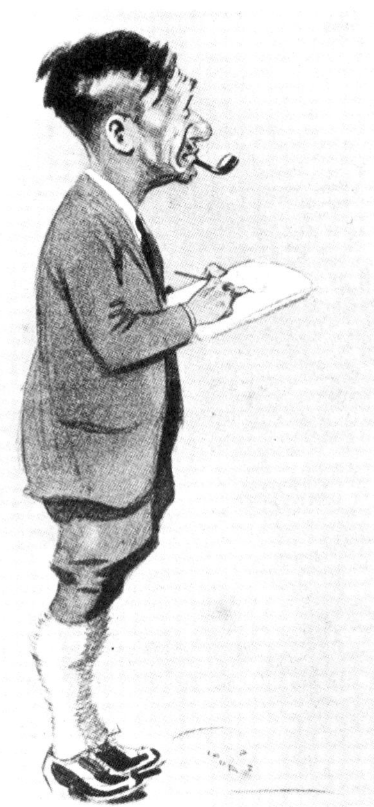

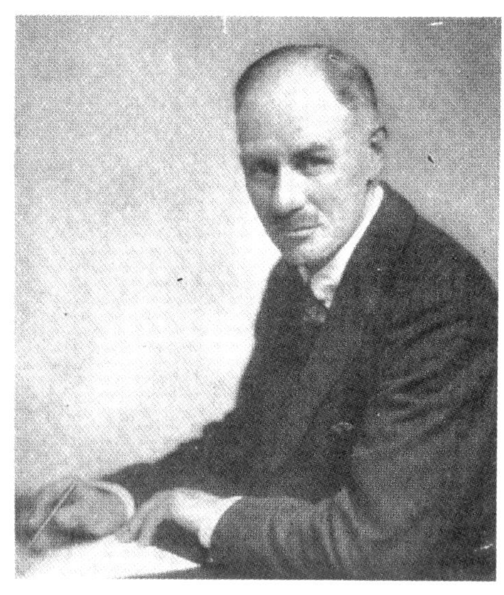

Caricature of H. M. Bateman by James Thorpe (*left*), and photograph of Bateman (*above*).

(*Below*) Invitation card by H. M. Bateman.

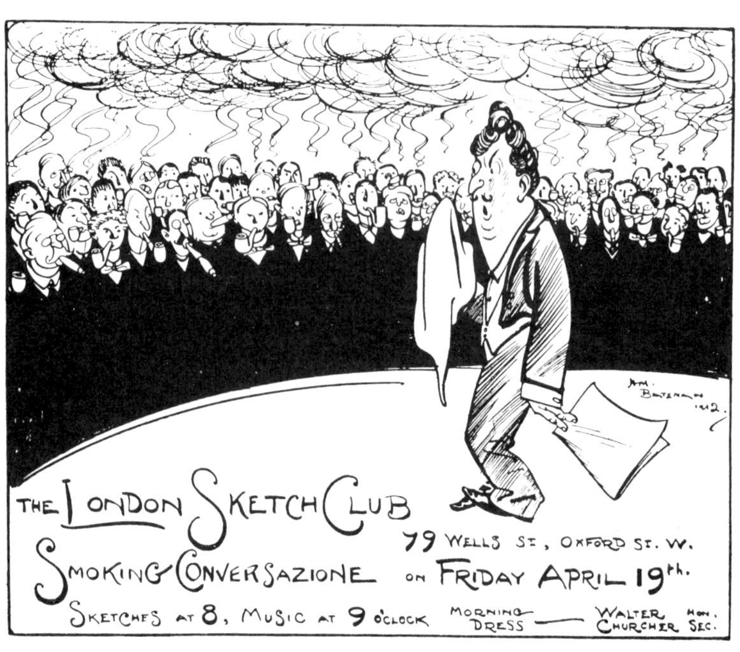

by way of the *BOP (Boy's Own Paper)* and for a time he worked for Harmsworth on *The Daily Mail* before being sacked. Bradshaw was also a good member of the Savage and wrote *Brother Savages and Guests (A History of the Savage Club 1857-1957)* which was published in 1958. However his most significant contribution to art was to set up the Press Art School in 1905, using many LSC members as tutors.

Hassall had started his own art school, like Sauber before him, and Lenfestey and Harry Clifford had started their Technical Art Correspondence College in 1897, but it was Bradshaw's Press Art School that was to flourish and prosper. Operating originally from his home, Bradshaw was forced to look for outside accommodation after getting married in 1910. By 1913 he had found suitable premises in Tudor Hall, in Forest Hill, London.

Tudor Hall was originally built for the use of Queen Victoria's children; it boasted a grand façade of mock Gothic respectability. For a time it had been the home of Queen Victoria's lady-in-waiting Baroness Burdett-Coutts, then the residence of a famous judge, and later a hostel for the Select Academy for the Daughters of Gentlewomen before Bradshaw requisitioned its 22 rooms for the Press Art School.

Over the years Bradshaw's School claimed to have helped many artists, mostly illustrators or cartoonists, to achieve recognition. Barry Appleby of Gambols fame, Leo Cheney of Johnnie Walker fame, "Fougasse" (the nom-de-plume of Kenneth Bird). David Ghilchik (more of him later), Illingworth of *The Daily Mail* and Norman Pett, who created Jane in the *Daily Mirror*, were but a few. There were also one or two surprises such as the eminent portrait painters Edward Halliday (an excellent after dinner speaker) and Leonard Boden (later a member of the London Sketch Club); later still came the young Ralph Steadman, who said of Bradshaw: "He was a real Victorian gent — like something out of another age!"

Although the Press Art School enjoyed a prestigious reputation at Tudor Hall, it finally came to rest in Aldermaston Court, in Aldermaston, which achieved a totally different reputation a few years later for its Ban-the-Bomb marches.

The tutors Bradshaw requisitioned from the Sketch Club included Frank Reynolds, Harry Rountree, Lawson Wood, Bert Thomas, H. M. Bateman, Claude Shepperson and W. Heath Robinson. Then came Tom Webster and Alfred Leete. Two of the tutors used anthropomorphic themes in their work: the first was Harry Rountree, who specialised in birds, beasts and fishes; the second was Lawson Wood who specialised in monkeys. There was also a third, who did not work for Bradshaw, and this was George Studdy.

Studdy's chief creation, Bonzo the dog, became legendary, a beloved mascot like Grandma in Giles' cartoons or Snoopy in Schulz's *Peanuts*. No one was surprised by Bonzo's bizarre, outrageous behaviour: the bottle of whisky may have been hidden under the bed, the cigars suitably removed from sight, but Bonzo's problems captured the public imagination and he remained popular for twenty years. All sorts of publishers jumped on the Bonzo bandwagon and hundreds of trinkets, from mustard pots to toasting forks, bore his profile. Yet George Studdy never shared the limelight as his artist: one of the reasons could have been that Studdy loathed personal publicity and kept himself to himself.

His small London flat was a far cry from the picturesque village of Stoke Damerel in Devon where George Studdy had been born on 23 June 1878. His father Ernest Holdsworthy Studdy was then a Lieutenant in the 32nd Regiment; as he rose in rank he hoped that his young son would follow in his footsteps. George was sent to

Clifton College Preparatory School in Bristol, which has connections with Sandhurst: many boys from Clifton went on to Sandhurst. One was Douglas Haig, later the famous First World War Field Marshal. Unfortunately young George was expelled from Clifton. After completing his preparatory education at a local Devon school he gained a place at Dulwich College, another public school with military emphasis.

One of many mishaps which befell young Studdy was an accident with a pitchfork which went straight through his foot and left him with a limp for the rest of his life. Like Donald McGill, who had to have his left foot amputated as the result of a rugby accident, he turned his attention to art. The injury exempted Studdy from army service and limited his physical activities. During the latter part of the 19th Century most public schools placed much importance on "playing games"; since Studdy was incapacitated for the usual "blood sports" such as cricket or rugby he turned to gymnastics. He excelled on the parallel bars, rope and rings which did not require leg work.

When he left Dulwich in 1896 his father, by now a Major, ensured that George found work in the City. He entered a stockbroker's office, which was, however, within easy reach of Fleet Street: he soon turned to the more flamboyant aspirations of illustration, neglecting the stock market.

Studdy had long been influenced by children's illustrated gift books and periodicals; he had grown up with such characters as Ally Sloper, Weary Willie and Tired Tim. He was often found doodling in the office when he should have been working and tried to persuade his father to let him turn to a career in art. His father was reluctant to let his son abandon an assured income (artists were considered by some to be "slackers, drunkards and probably immoral"), but he eventually agreed that his son should follow that precarious profession.

Studdy enrolled at Heatherley's School of Art, where he met Mabel Lucie Attwell and her future husband Harold Earnshaw. All three were influenced by the work of John Hassall, who by 1900 was already famous: his bold dark outline and flat masses of colour were both revolutionary and appealing. It was Hassall who introduced Studdy to Harry Rountree and Lawson Wood: it is curious that all three became well known for their adopted animals (Rountree for his mice, Lawson Wood for his gorilla and Studdy for his dogs). Attwell did not follow this trend and probably developed a style which was closest to Hassall's own with her toddlers and their teeth-aching baby talk and dolls called "diddums".

Hassall encouraged their poster work and soon obtained commissions for them: Attwell was asked to produce designs for Swan Fountain Pens and Eucryl Toothpowder, whilst Studdy was commissioned by Pan Yan Pickle. Moreover Hassall gave Studdy the best piece of advice he was ever to receive, when he said: "You need a peg on which the public can hang its hat." It could have been this advice that prompted Studdy to produce Bonzo.

The history of Bonzo is interesting, if only because of the wild speculation surrounding his debut. Indeterminate dates have been bandied about between 1920 and 1930, but in fact he was created as early as 1918. In an article in *The Sunday Sun* dated 1929, Studdy confessed:

> Shortly after the peace celebrations [1914-1918 War] Bonzo was born. A certain professor had declared that in time we should all make use of mechanical men, not only to do everything in the home, or office, but even to

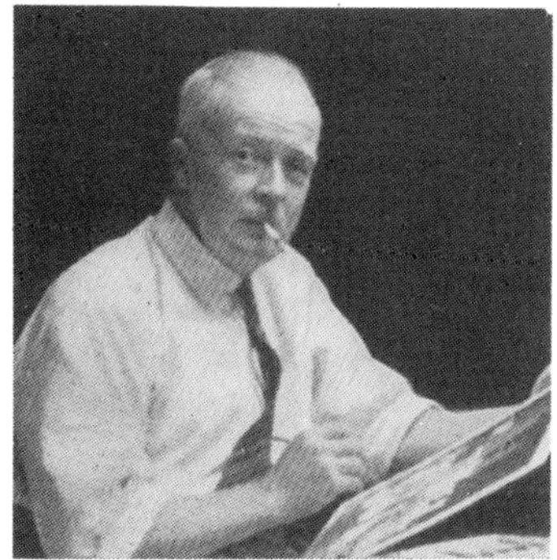

The mercurial Harry Rountree who retired to St Ives in Cornwall. On his arrival he took a shine to the daughter of Lamorna Birch, RA, but his advances were not reciprocated. Although he was principally a book illustrator, he was also responsible for many well-known advertisements, including Ronuk polish, Quaker Oats and Derry & Toms store in Kensington. He also designed the cover of *Animal Ways*, the RSPCA journal.

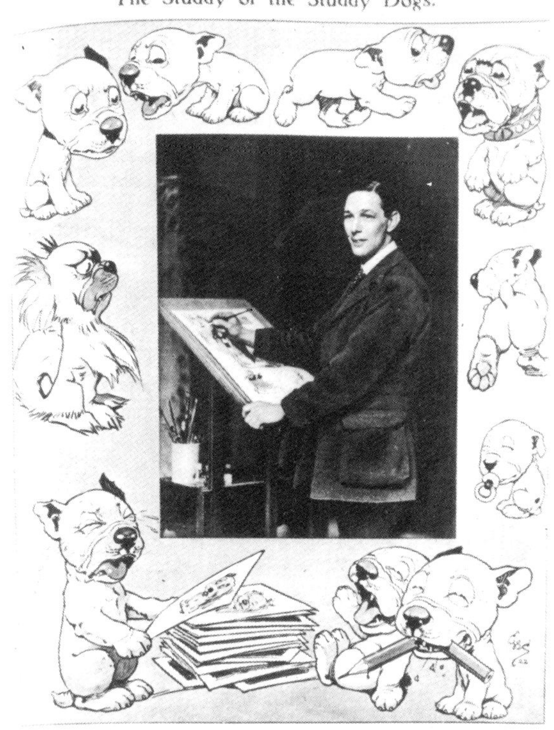

George Studdy

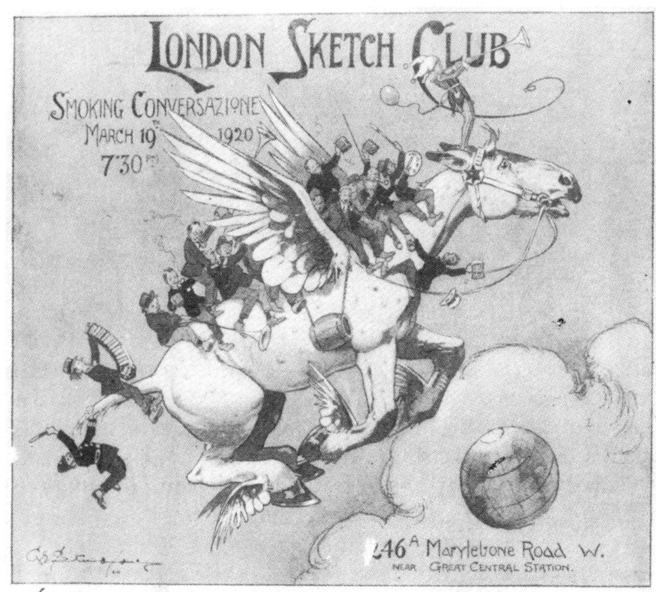

George Studdy
invitation
card

carry us from place to place. The idea struck me as funny. I drew an old lady riding such a robot, and it appeared as a large dog-like animal. But since the lady was somewhat stout, only the legs of this creature were shown.

Nevertheless, those legs were enough to impress the editor. He asked for more. They were the first Bonzo pictures. In those days he was never the same for two weeks running. I was continually trying to make him funnier. One week I altered a leg, then an ear, and the next week, perhaps the entire shape of his body. Now he is as absurd as I can make him. When the editor first christened him "Bonzo" I hated the name. To-day I am used to it, and would not change it for anything.

Studdy's upbringing called for modest restraint whereas Bonzo could let rip. True, Bonzo did not come into commercial use until the 1920s, when his one black ear, few spots around his face and perpetual grin caught the public by surprise. They were soon to fall in love with this mischievous pup, and even made him a film star. It was to be a short-lived cinematic career: in 1924 animator William A. Ward made 26 films of Bonzo, enough, perhaps, to influence Walt Disney. One might be forgiven for thinking that the inspiration for Mickey Mouse rested on Bonzo's shoulders. However, whereas Mickey Mouse was to become the superstar of animated cartoons, Bonzo subsequently became a legend in picture book annuals.

There was a comic strip which appeared for a short time in one of the dailies and in 1927 Bonzo appeared on the cover of *Toby* magazine, a popular children's monthly. This eventually led Dean's to produce *The Bonzo Annual* which was to run for over 25 years. These days Bonzo has practically disappeared from the scene: only the "Bonzo Dog Doo-dah Band" perpetuated the memory of his name. It is left to the postcard collector or memorabilia fanatic to unearth him from the past. A treasury of postcards were produced by Dean's, F. Warne and Valentine's and the Bonzo annuals are now collectors' items.

It is interesting to note that both Attwell and Studdy used Francis & Mills as their agents. As an art agency they were a good deal more than mere business representatives: they took complete control of their clients' affairs and provided a constant flow of work for them. This gave Studdy plenty of time for relaxation and lessened the arduous task of seeking work which most artists find objectionable. Studdy was fond of fishing and frequently went on trips with H. T. Sheringham, *the* authority on fly fishing and brother of fellow Sketch Club member George Sheringham. Studdy even illustrated one of Sheringham's books as a personal favour.

Nevertheless it was Bonzo who provided Studdy with most of his work. He was a popular mascot on jugs, mugs, petrol caps and children's games. During the 'twenties he appeared on stage for the first time in the pantomime *Aladdin*, where he stole the show and outclassed the rival production of *Robinson Crusoe* at the Lyceum. Bonzo was portrayed by a costumed actor in a larger than life creation opposite Mr Lupino Lane as the energetic Pekoe. By 1924 Bonzo was even advertised as a very attractive Yuletide present — soft and cuddly in champagne and mauve velveteen — still a big favourite! You could buy a 10″ Bonzo cuddly toy for 10/6 or a smaller one for 3/6. The fact that Bonzo appeared on all sorts of ornaments, ashtrays to pin cushions, showed how universal was his appeal. One of the most successful productions was the William McBonzo game for children, a sort of hoop-la using a kilted Bonzo as the target.

In his private life George Studdy was a quiet, modest man who usually took a

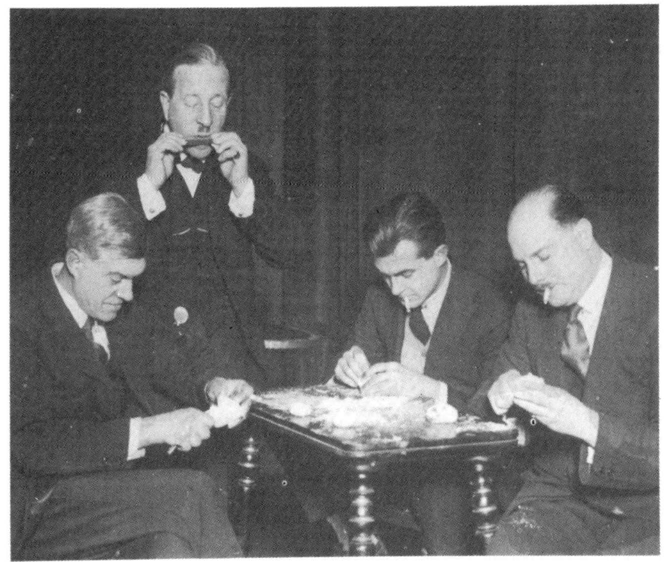

A Sculptors' Exhibition in St Georges Hall. V.V. Robinson, the Canadian entertainer seen here playing the mouth organ, held an exhibition at which several well known members of the London Sketch Club were asked to carve something out of a beach pebble with a penknife in five minutes. From left to right are John Hassall, V.V. Robinson, Ian Hassall and Wilton Williams.

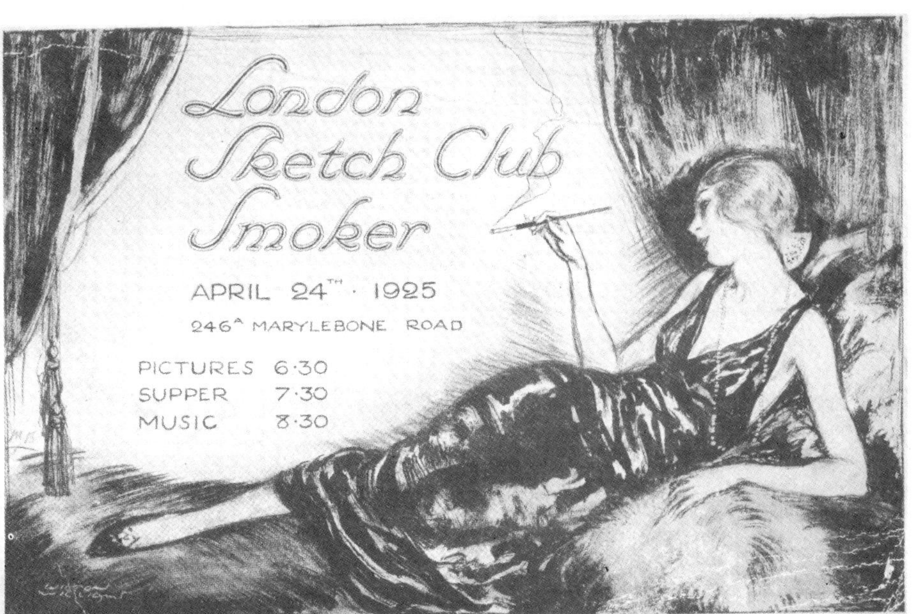

Wilton Williams invitation card.

back seat. He often said, "I could have made a fortune out of Bonzo"; instead he chose the peaceful cloistered life of a lonely bachelor with his dogs and gentlemen's clubs. He did in fact marry as a young man and had a daughter, but the marriage was a disaster and only lasted a few weeks. His estranged wife returned to France and they never saw each other again although his daughter Vivien was still alive a few years ago.

It appears that Studdy "got on" with most people, yet there seems to have been a rift between him and Lawson Wood. Did Lawson Wood steal his Grandpop Gorilla idea from Studdy? A drawing dated 1907 which appeared in *Printer's Pie* depicts the prototype of Lawson Wood's gorilla character. There were no such difficulties with Alfred Leete, Bert Thomas and J. A. Shepherd with whom Studdy relaxed in the clubbable atmosphere of both the London Sketch Club and the Savage. In fact he remained a stalwart member of both clubs until his resignation in 1934.

Oddly enough Studdy had only one major exhibition during his lifetime, at the Brook Street Art Gallery in London. For most of his life he lived in the small Kensington flat but at the outbreak of the Second World War he moved to Portsmouth where he worked as a draughtsman for the Admiralty. Studdy was a chain-smoker and it is rare to see a photograph of him without a cigarette dangling from his lips. When he died in 1948, the same year as his great friend and tutor John Hassall, his family blamed air pollution from the constant bombing of Portsmouth for his fatal lung cancer.

There is something essentially English about dogs as pets, a homeliness which relates to every child's upbringing. Perhaps this is why Bonzo was accepted so readily and has become part of English folklore. Whether or not Studdy's Spaniel Ben sat unknowingly for some of Bonzo's strange adventures we can never be sure, but what is certainly true is that Studdy was one of the most remarkable exponents of anthropomorphic art.

There was another member of the London Sketch Club who shot to prominence in the 'twenties and that was H. M. Bateman. His large double-page spread cartoons of "The man who . . ." appeared in *The Tatler* and caused a sensation. *The Tatler* at this time had a considerable following and circulation. It contained photographs of 'twenties jetsetters, their parties and race-meetings, which contrasted heavily with Bateman's gaffes, usually caused by the inoffensive middle classes.

Bateman was himself a shy, introverted man, the son of a domineering father and resolute mother. Bateman's decision to become a humorous rather than a "serious" artist caused him much distress and led to a nervous breakdown at the age of twenty-one. His mother, who had purloined Phil May, sent some of Bateman's drawings to him and asked for help. Phil May replied saying that he thought the boy had talent and should go to Westminster Art School to work under Mr Mouat London. This was followed by a period at Goldsmiths until Hassall advised him to work under *his* old tutor Charles van Havermaet.

Bateman joined the London Sketch Club in 1907 and recalled the event in his autobiography published by Collins in 1937:

> Now I joined that jolly band of men who constituted the London Sketch Club,
> a gathering of artists and others connected with the Arts who met on Friday
> nights at a picturesque garret in Oxford Street for sketching, supper and song.
> It was a sort of offshoot of the Savage Club, and truly bohemian in character.

After this, Bateman was not to be short of work for the rest of his life. At the peak of

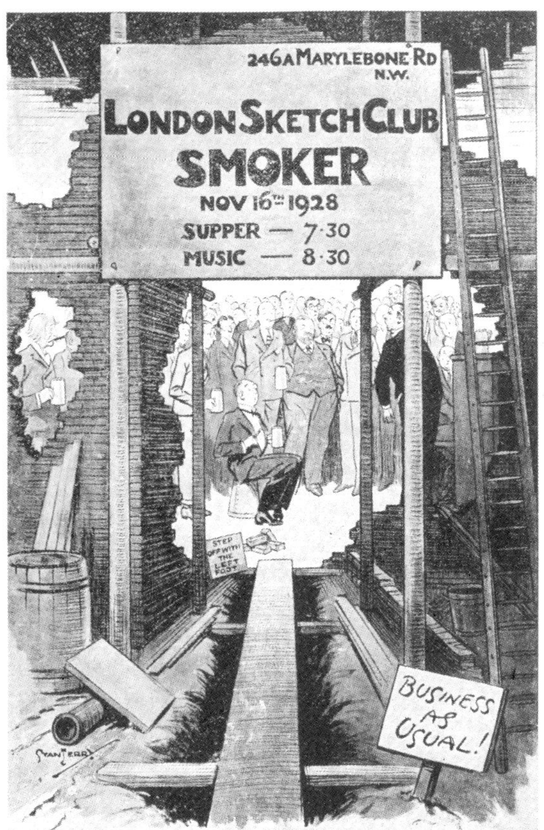

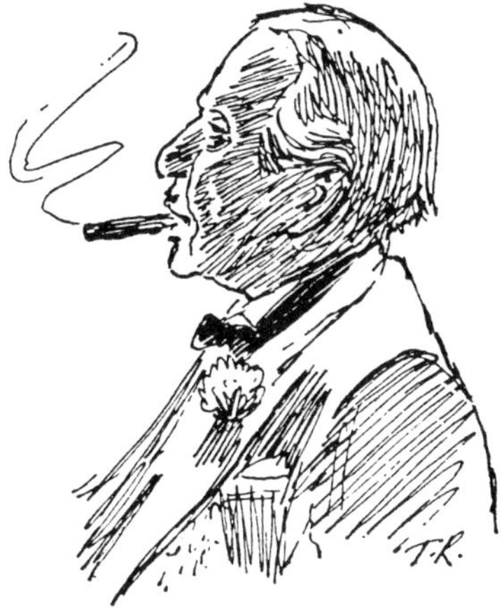

Caricature of Montague Smyth, RBA, ROI by Tom Robinson. In the 'twenties Smyth regularly attended Sketch Club smoker evenings and in 1963 he was honoured with a special dinner for his centenary. In his youth he had been friendly with George and Gerald Du Maurier, he remembered Oscar Wilde in the Café Royal and Aubrey Beardsley's long black cloak. Smyth (1863-1966) considered himself part of the Barbizon School.

Invitation cards from the 'twenties: (*above*) by Stan Terry and (*below*) by Norman Keene.

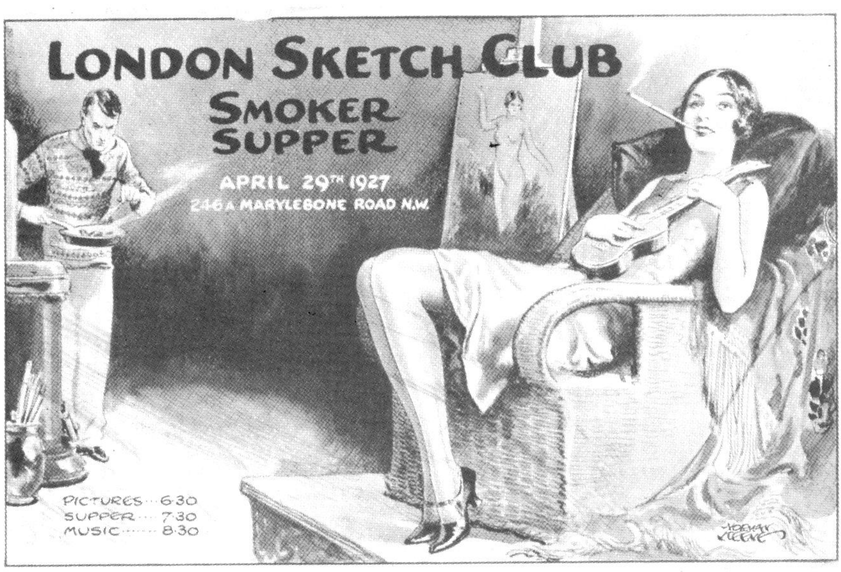

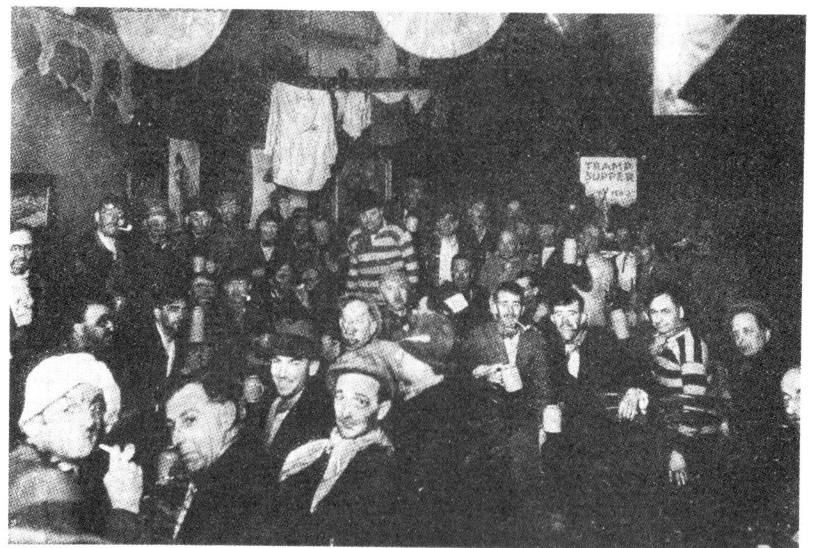

Tramp supper in the Marylebone Club. The gent in the middle of this photograph dressed in rugby shirt, bowler and scarf is Wilton Williams, whilst Arthur Ferrier is seated fourth from the left in cap and scarf.

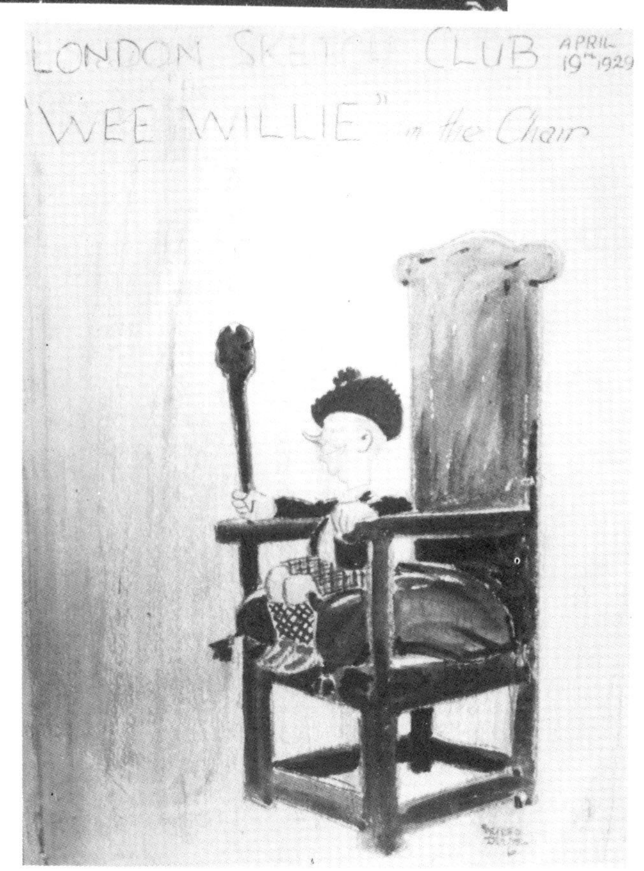

Invitation sketch by Alfred Leete when "Wee Willie" took the chair on April 19th 1929. The skit was probably based on the successful book *Wee MacGregor* by J. J. Bell, published at about this time and illustrated by John Hassall.

his career he earned between four and five thousand pounds a year (probably a bit more), no mean sum in the 'twenties and 'thirties. He drove the latest cars, built himself a house in Reigate, Surrey and enjoyed fishing as a pastime. Sadly the Inland Revenue caught up with him and in later life he became obsessed by correspondence with the Tax Department. Eventually he divided his time between his cottage on Dartmoor and Malta, where he spent his winters. He died in Gozo in 1970.

Bateman was yet another artist who admired Caran D'Ache. Like René Bull and Frank Reynolds before him, Bateman was greatly influenced by this unique Frenchman who was little known in England. Caran D'Ache was the pseudonym of Emanuel Poire who had been born in Moscow in 1858. When *Caran D'Ache The Supreme* was published in 1933 by Methuen, Bateman wrote the Introduction, showing the versatility of the man. He was pleased — no, he was honoured — to introduce Caran D'Ache to an eager, unsuspecting English public.

In a belated article left with *The Artist* magazine, Bateman recalled his early days with the Sketch Club:

> The London Sketch Club existed for work and entertainment, and I must begin with a description of its premises as, without doubt, these were the foundation on which the active spirit and success of the Club rests.
>
> For the purpose the premises were ideal. They were situated in Wells Street, off Oxford Street, and consisted simply of a huge top-floor room, or garret, complete with ancient beams and a chimney corner of the old sort, all redolent of Bohemia. It was reached from the street by a steep enclosed wooden staircase, so narrow that two persons could barely pass on it.
>
> We had a small bar, where beer in solid stone mugs and a few aperitifs were supplied, and we had a small stage about ten feet square centrally placed for short performances. A remarkable feature was a frieze of silhouette portraits, all life-size, of every member, which ran just below the ceiling, right around the room. I remember sitting for my silhouette in the small darkened office, with a lamp to throw my shadow, when the member responsible for making them operated on me soon after my election. I did not obtain election on my first attempt — when I submitted a highly-wrought oil painting it smacked rather too much of the art student, I believe — however I tried again a bit later with something more imaginative, which succeeded, and I was duly admitted into the fold. I was then the youngest member of the Club, a distinction I enjoyed for a number of years until another youngster arrived on the scene to oust me from that position.
>
> The black-and-white men, prominent illustrators and humorists of those days, were, in point of numbers, the biggest section. Among them were: Tom Browne; Lawson Wood; Starr Wood; John Hassall; René Bull; Frank Reynolds; Frank Hart; Lance Thackeray; Bert Thomas; Heath Robinson; and there were some notable serious artists with: George Sheringham; Hugh Stanton; Edmund Dulac; Charles Dixon — a marine painter; Geoffrey Stahan — a most promising young painter, alas killed in Gallipoli; Dudley Hardy, so versatile; Joseph Harker, the scene painter who was responsible for much scenery in Beerbohm Tree's stage productions. Colonel Baden-Powell, the hero of Mafeking and founder of the Boy Scouts was, I believe, a member or honorary member, at any rate he appeared there on occasions. Baden-Powell was uncommonly good at pencil drawing ...

We met on Friday evenings ... and two titles were given. We worked for two hours on whichever subject we liked, and then put our work on show for discussion and criticism. Needless to say the variety of interpretations of the same title were often extraordinary. By this time the lay members began to arrive and joined in the general review — they were not expected to show up during the working period — and the long table was being laid for supper of the boiled beef and carrots order, though roast joints were frequent, and the occasional steak and kidney pudding evening was something of an event.

After supper an impromptu smoking concert followed, and that could go on till the early hours of the next morning if there was enough talent on hand. Many of the lay members were professional entertainers of one sort and another; singers, musicians, reciters — all very skilled and generous in their readiness to do a turn. And many famous figures in the entertainment world, when performing in London, were brought along by somebody who knew them. It was almost the thing to do to visit the London Sketch Club and do a short turn there. When the winter ended we had a full-scale exhibition — the only time when ladies were admitted to this all-male stronghold. It came to an end when the lease on the place ran out and could not be renewed. The club moved into smaller quarters in the Marylebone Road and did its best to carry on there. But something was lacking, some of the old vitality had gone, and we put it down to the loss of that atmosphere which had prevailed in our unique Wells Street top floor.

The inference that some of the members were not happy to move to Marylebone was there. Just as Lionel Edwards had said a few years earlier, artists are just the same as ordinary people — they don't like change. Reminiscing all those years later Bateman liked to remember the Club as it was when he was a youngster. The other big factor to affect the Club in the 'twenties was the advent of radio: however the Club stuck to its format and instead of decreasing the standard of entertainment, somehow it enhanced it.

If Bateman was not happy with the Marylebone premises, Frank Reynolds felt quite at home there. Reynolds even sketched the interior which appeared in *Punch*, showing his affinity for the place. There was one slight hiccup in 1922 when a special meeting of the Council was held on 9 June, at 7 o'clock, to discuss urgent business. The reason was the dismissal of Dickinson, the secretary: what the row was about can only be conjecture after all this time.

Certainly the Club was left the poorer for Dickinson's dismissal. It prompted Thomas Downey to stress the importance of financial matters in his presidential letter of 1923, where he wrote: "I am fully aware that the artistic soul is a little above financial matters, yet I must (officially) mention that the Hon. Treasurer has no objections to members paying their subscriptions promptly."

The tradition of the annual challenge between the Langham Sketching Club and the London Sketch Club continued. Adrian Hill, who gained fame in later life through his series of "How to Paint and Draw" classes on television, was President of the Langham in 1929 when members presented him with a circular pewter cigarette box on the occasion of his marriage. As he recalled, the challenge was usually of an artistic nature and was "always made by the London Sketch Club".

CHAPTER 8

Come to the Ball

After the First World War, Britain benefited from a brief period of stability. Children who remembered how their parents enjoyed the freedom of the Edwardian era now wanted to enjoy a freedom of their own. The result was the Roaring Twenties which put much emphasis on youth. After all, so many young men had had their youth taken away in the filth of the trenches on the battlefields of France.

It was in this carefree atmosphere of fun and frivolity that the London Sketch Club Annual Ball flourished. Many values were turned upside down and fashions strayed erratically. One of the casualties was the magazine *Ally Sloper's Half Holiday*, started in 1884, which closed its doors in 1923. The character Ally Sloper had first appeared in the pages of *Judy* back in 1867 as the original comic anti-hero, a sort of Victorian Arthur Daley. The bulbous nosed chancer was regularly seen sloping down East End alleys to complete some shady deal, the police in hot pursuit.

Other magazines emerged: *Passing Show* (in 1915) and *London Calling*. The former was a cheaper version of *Punch*; *London Calling* was edited by London Sketch Club member Reginald Arkell. It has always struck me as odd that no one appears to have written a history of English magazines and periodicals; there has been such a variety of them. Others were *London Opinion*, which Arkell went on to edit, and *Blighty*, which appeared in 1916, and *The Flag*, the official magazine for the Union Jack Club, published by the *Daily Mail*.

Most London Sketch Club members, however, were happy to contribute to *Punch* which in the 'twenties was still the leading humorous magazine in Britain. Fred Buchanan, Bertram Prance, Frank Reynolds, James Thorpe, Bert Thomas, the young Lunt Roberts, David Wilson, Gilbert Wilkinson and Charles Harrison were but a few of these. *Punch* had been Phil May's vehicle to fame and posterity and there were plenty of artists prepared to follow suit.

On the arts scene there emerged the name of Picasso. This artist more than any other was to annoy London Sketch Club members. Although he had a keen following in Britain, just as many artists hated his work. One author who mocked Picasso was Jan Gordon in his book *Art Ain't All Paint*, to which H. M. Bateman added a brilliant set of illustrations. Other London Sketch Club cartoonists ridiculed Picasso's search for modernism in the pages of *Punch*. The trouble with Picasso was that he shattered an already disjointed art scene into splinters, satellites of which still argue among themselves to this day. Picasso was an able draughtsman who seemed to treat draughtsmanship with contempt; London Sketch Club members knew the importance of drawing. In 1931, less than thirty years after Phil May's death, James Thorpe wrote: "Considering the wide popularity he [Phil May] enjoyed in life it was disturbing to find how very completely May's great genius had been forgotten!" The problem was England enjoyed a wealth of superb draughtsmen all at the same time.

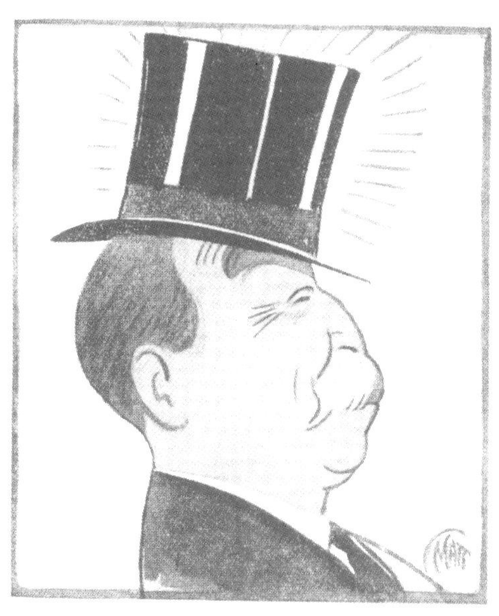

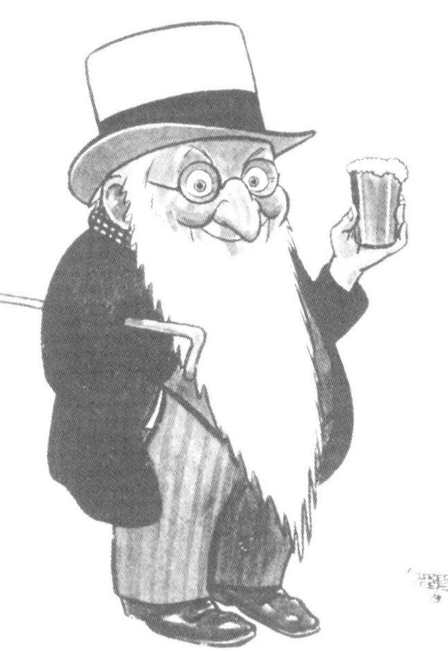

Caricature of Sir George Younger by "Matt".

Alfred Leete's "Father William".

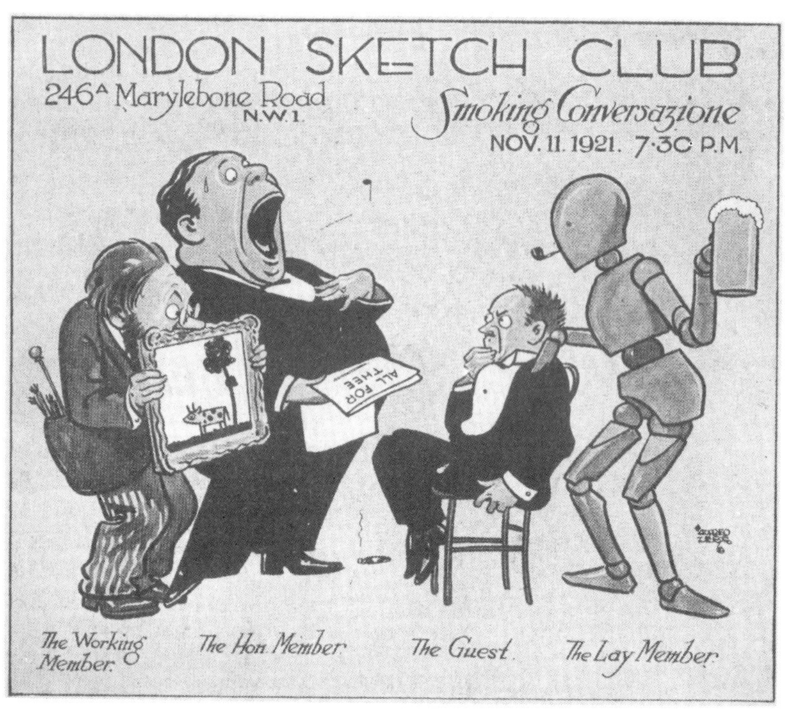

Alfred Leete's invitation card.

By the 'twenties a visit to the Sketch Club had become something of an "experience". Members such as Lee-Hankey, Hughes Stanton, Lawson Wood and H. M. Bateman, by now were middle-aged, made way for younger men. Some older members, John Hassall, Harry May Hemsley, Montague Smyth, George Parlby and others still, however, played active roles and strove to retain their youth. The younger generation taking over included Thomas Downey, Edgar Norfield, Stan Terry, Alex Lawson and Norman Keene.

When I mention the word younger I have to be careful because Sir George Younger MP was a lay member of the Sketch Club. His was one of those peculiar memberships like that of Baden-Powell. In 1922 when he was Tory Party Chairman he was reported to be "seventy years old — but looks Younger!" In the Sketch Club he was simply known as George and it was through his association with the Club that Alfred Leete was commissioned to produce a logo for Younger's Ales. The result was a drawing called "Father William" which is still used today. Sir George had inherited the brewery at the age of seventeen, on the death of his father; this may explain why so much Younger's beer was drunk by London Sketch Club members in the 'twenties. The idea for Father William came from Thomas Downey's initial drawings of monks imbibing. The idea made sense as the brewery in Edinburgh was built on the site of an old abbey. However Downey's drawings were rejected by an outraged clergy. Alfred Leete was then consulted and after acceptance of his "Oi be 101 and getting Younger every day" (reproduced here) he came up with "The Younger Generation" in 1924.

Another noticeable change in the 'twenties was the virtual disappearance of studio parties or conversaziones which before the War had been commonplace especially in the Bedford and Holland Park areas of London. Cecil Aldin had held soirées, entertaining Dudley Hardy, Tom Browne, Walter Churcher, Lance Thackeray and that old Savoyard Harry Lytton. At these suppers the plot of an impromptu play was enacted after the meal by Dudley Hardy, Sydney Brough and Lal Brough. All the artists eventually joined in, improvising to cover any gaps in the plot with a string of gags. This was before the Sketch Club came into existence. By the 'twenties Hardy, Browne and Thackeray were all dead; only Walter Churcher was left to continue these traditions. A rare photograph of one of Churcher's informal gatherings, when the arts world would be put to rights, shows a number of early London Sketch Club members at table including Sir George Frampton, Walter Churcher, Albert Toft, Rene Bull and John Hassall. Back in the Sketch Club itself the traditions which these men had laid down were rigorously adhered to. Ale was served in earthenware tankards, members called each other "Brother Sketcher" and a deafening "For ...!" filled the room as the chairman of the evening was announced.

Although the London Sketch Club was an all male preserve, members could go to town at the London Sketch Club Annual Ball. In the 'twenties this was a highlight of every young débutante's diary. Held at the Wharncliffe Rooms of the old Marylebone Hotel, just next door to the Club itself, revelries often went on until the early hours of the morning. Always star-studded by popular celebrities, it was an occasion not to be missed.

Everyone appeared in fancy dress and there was a prize for the most original costume. In 1924 the winner was Lawrence Holman, in 1925 Ellis Silas, in 1926 Fred Buchanan. Much effort went into preparing for the Ball. There was a special Dance Committee (see Appendix II); in 1927 this comprised L. R. Brightwell,

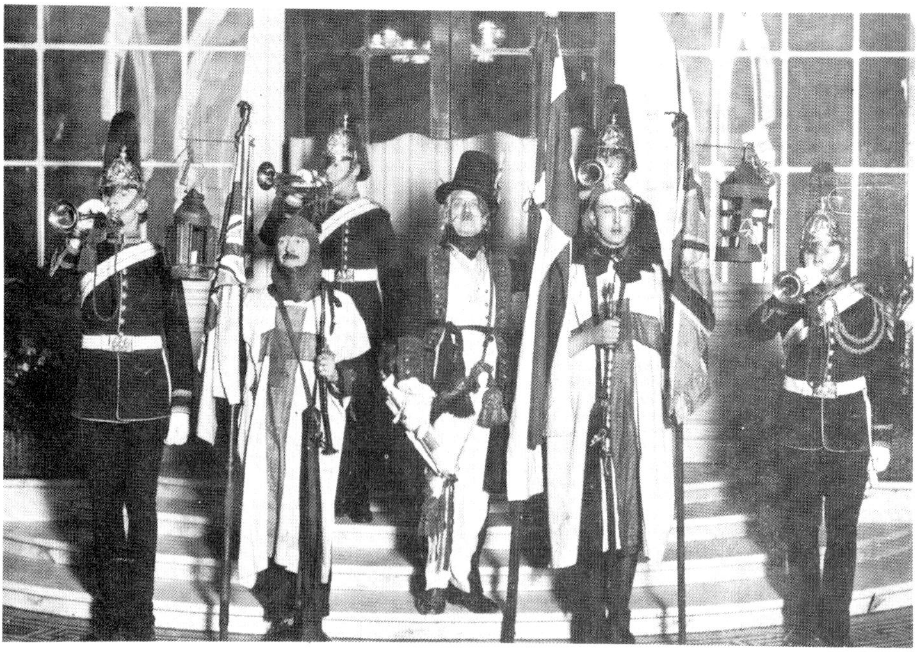

George Parlby opening the London Sketch Club Ball.

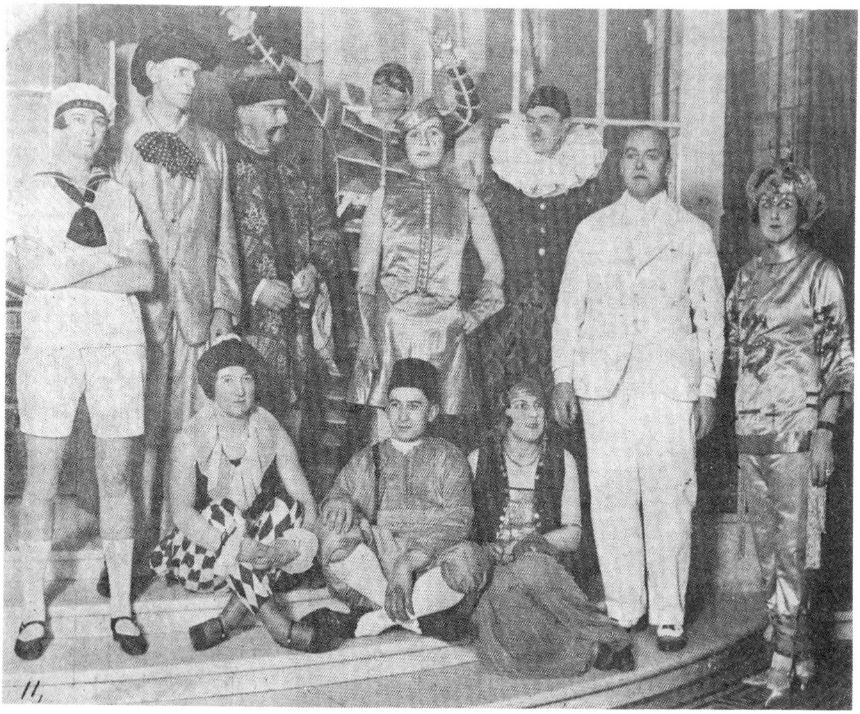

A group of revellers.

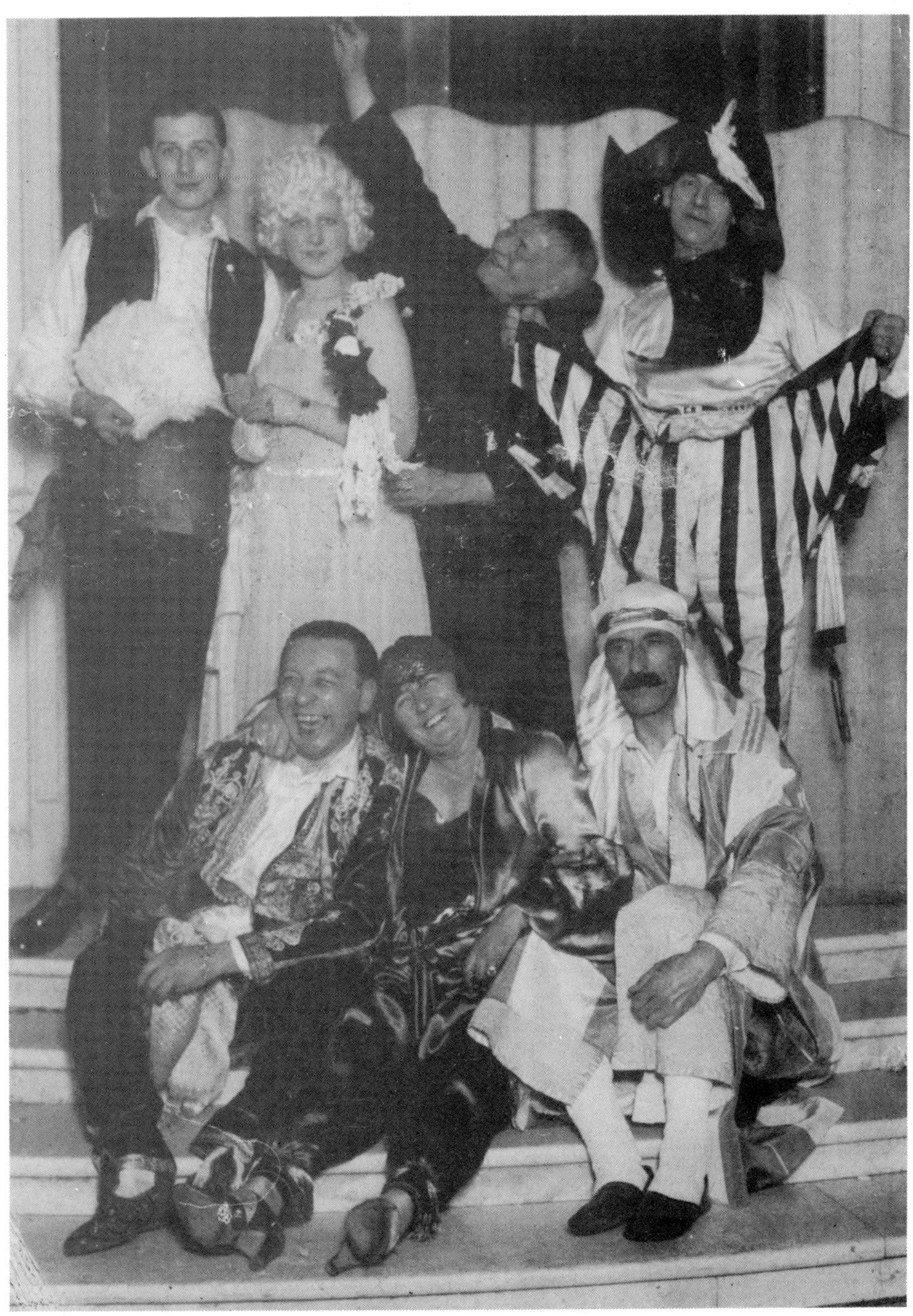

More revellers. The group seated on the steps look like Wilson, Kepple and Betty,
well known for their famous sand dance.

Norman Keene, Edgar Pattison, Charles Robinson, Ellis Silas, T. Somerfield, MacMath Wilson and Frank Wright.

The Ball always commenced with a fanfare from the trumpeters of HM Life Guards, after which George Parlby, the Master of Revels, would officially open the proceedings. Thereafter it was a bun fight: anything could happen and often did. The orchestra was invariably provided by Marius B. Winter. Surprises such as community singing, puff-ball or cabaret turns were interspersed throughout the evening: one favourite was the tug-of-war. Dances included the foxtrot, charleston, waltz and conga.

The origins of the London Sketch Club Annual Ball were in the old Royal Institute of Painters in Watercolours Balls held in Covent Garden before the Great War. In 1906 Hassall attended dressed as Richard Coeur de Lion, and George Parlby as Blondel. On another occasion George Parlby went as Guy Fawkes, firing a barrel of gunpowder. Photographs were taken of these artists but sadly are so faded that reproduction is impossible. At yet another RI Ball John Hassall was dressed as a Viking, his wife Constance as a Viqueen, partnering Walter Fowler and his wife. Once again the photographs have lightened beyond recognition.

The London Sketch Club Ball was not meant to rival the Chelsea Arts Club Ball — quite the reverse. In 1911 all three societies, the London Sketch Club, Chelsea Arts Club and Royal Institute had teamed up to stage The Three Arts Ball. It was held in the Albert Hall; Marie Lohr, then at the height of her fame, was present. Arthur Bourchier, the actor, dressed as Santa Claus, made a triumphal entrance under a blanket of artificial snow and a blaze of coloured lights and distributed small presents made by Walter Crane, John Hassall and E. J. Sullivan. Then the dancing began. It was the Chelsea Arts Club who in 1912 took over the management of the Ball when they formed the Chelsea Arts Ball Limited, which cut out the other two societies.

The Sketch Club was left out on a limb and so devised their own Ball which, apart from the years 1914 to 1918, produced a wonderful alternative. The great advantage of the London Sketch Club Ball was that it was held next door to the Club. When the Ball was over members could retire to the convivial surroundings of the Marylebone Club bar. As Bert Wilson remembered:

> The highlight of the year was the annual fancy dress dance held in the Wharncliffe Rooms in the old Marylebone Hotel, which was next door to the Sketch Club. There must have been anything up to 400 people present, with quite a number of famous film and stage stars.
>
> After the dance, which I think finished about 2 am, those who didn't go home returned to the Club where the bar used to be open until about 7 o'clock in the morning. It always amused me to see people waiting for taxis or buses around the coffee stall, which used to be about 50 yards from the Club, still in fancy dress, much to the consternation of people going to work.
>
> One amusing character was Eddie Morrow. He was the brother of *Punch* cartoonist George Morrow and known as the secret eater, because no-one had ever seen him eating. He had a big underlip which he used to say was caused by the weight of pint tankards. Eddie used to go to the dance with a doctor's wife, a Mrs Bell, but never got there as they were always too boozed. I remember seeing him and Mrs Bell arriving in a taxi once. They managed to get halfway up the stairs to the ballroom before they both rolled down again and were promptly put back into the taxi.

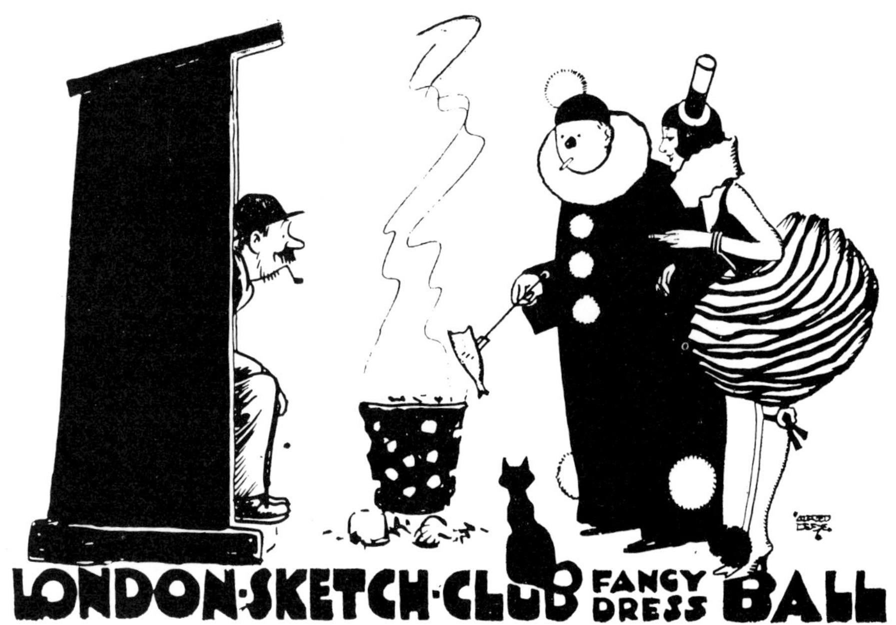

WILL BE HELD AT THE

WHARNCLIFFE ROOMS, GT. CENTRAL HOTEL, FRIDAY, FEBRUARY 28th, 1930.

TICKETS, ONE GUINEA EACH, INCLUDING SUPPER.

MASTER OF REVELS :—Mr. GEORGE PARLBY.

A "GRAND NATIONAL STEEPLECHASE" WILL TAKE PLACE DURING THE EVENING. ORIGINAL PICTURES BY MEMBERS OF THE CLUB BEING GIVEN AS PRIZES.

AS THE NUMBER OF TICKETS ISSUED IS STRICTLY LIMITED, EARLY APPLICATION, ACCOMPANIED BY REMITTANCE, SHOULD BE MADE TO THE HON. SECRETARY, LONDON SKETCH CLUB, 246a. MARYLEBONE ROAD, W. 1. FANCY DRESS FOR MEN ESSENTIAL.

MARIUS B. WINTER'S ORCHESTRA.

DANCING, 9 p.m.—3 a.m. . . SUPPER, 10.45 p.m.

Organising Secretary : EDGAR L. PATTISON. Tel. Chiswick 2401

All Tickets are issued subject to the discretionary powers of the Council.

Alfred Leete's design of 1930.

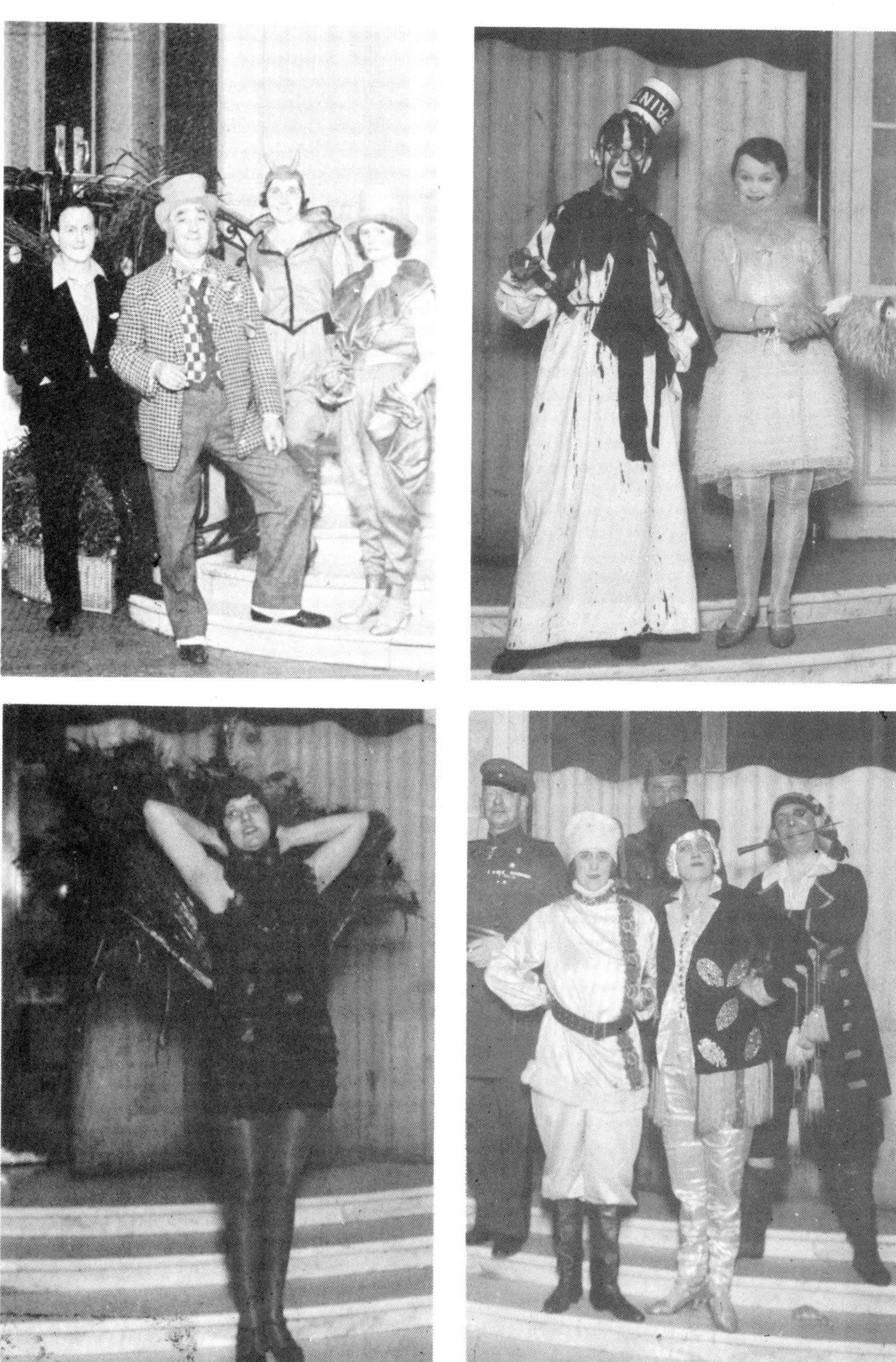

G. Ceci, Clay Thomas, Ruby Shepherd and Mrs Ethel Thomas (all top left), together with other revellers who attended the ball.

Eddie Morrow was one of eight sons of a Belfast house decorator. Curiously five of the Morrow boys became artists. George Morrow was probably the most famous, although Eddie (short for Edwin) achieved a reasonable reputation for his black and white work. The other brothers were Norman, who died in the Great War, Harry and Albert.

As for the other guests, they were usually photographed before they went into the Ball. This was a sensible decision — they may have been less photogenic on their way out. One member who always had a pretty girl on his arm was Montague Smyth, a handsome man who reached the grand old age of 103! Montague Smyth ROI, president of the Sketch Club in 1912, had a painting accepted for the RA Summer Exhibition on his hundredth birthday. He always had a flower in his buttonhole and a twinkle in his eye. Almost a founder member, he achieved in the London Sketch Club what Captain Adrian Jones achieved in the Chelsea Arts Club, an unbounding respect due to longevity. They celebrated his century with a special dinner.

In his early days Smyth kept fit by playing cricket for his College at Cambridge, and he made a useful member of the LSC Cricket Team. As the years drifted by he became the Grand Old Man of the Sketch Club. Even at the age of ninety he was able to get up and tell a good story at Friday night suppers!

One member who dreaded the London Sketch Club Ball was Webster Murray, whose cottage was only a stone's throw away from the Club. If anyone had had over the odds to drink it was just the place to sleep it off: his hospitality was often called upon.

The son of a clergyman, Webster Murray had immigrated from Canada before the 1914-18 War and studied at the Slade. He was surprised by the exuberant hospitality of the Sketch Club, having expected to meet the great British reserve. His life was changed by the War when he saw action as a Company Commander on the Western Front. He was one of the lucky ones who returned. For a while he tried to live on his severance pay, then resumed his career as an artist.

Today the name of Webster Murray is probably known only to a handful of cartoonists and illustrators. He was one of the band who illustrated *Pan*, a short-lived periodical — others included Victor MacClure, Tom Purvis, Walter Barribal and Gilbert Wilkinson (all from the London Sketch Club). Later Webster Murray completed some double-page spreads for the *Tatler* and contributed to *The Sketch* and *The Bystander*.

The 'twenties was the age of cloche hats, bobs and camibockers: Barribal, mentioned above, was quick to capture these fashions. He was a lightning quick draughtsman who could portray the delicacy of femininity in the same way that had made Shepperson's reputation.

Walter Barribal soon found work from Schweppes, Condor hats, Masterfront corsets and Price's buttermilk soap. Affectionately known as Barry within the confines of the Sketch Club, his success often prompted the question; "Have you seen the latest Barry?" wherever a new advertisement or show card appeared on the hoardings or in a magazine. His most memorable design was "The Rose Girl" which Percy Bradshaw described as a "face appearing through the petals of an open rose, the treatment being so fresh and charming that the design was bound to force its attention upon the public".

It became known, during the 'twenties, that membership of the London Sketch Club was a stepping-stone to the more celebrated Savage Club. Artists such as Webster Murray, with his moustache and "lady-killing saturnine grin", or Walter

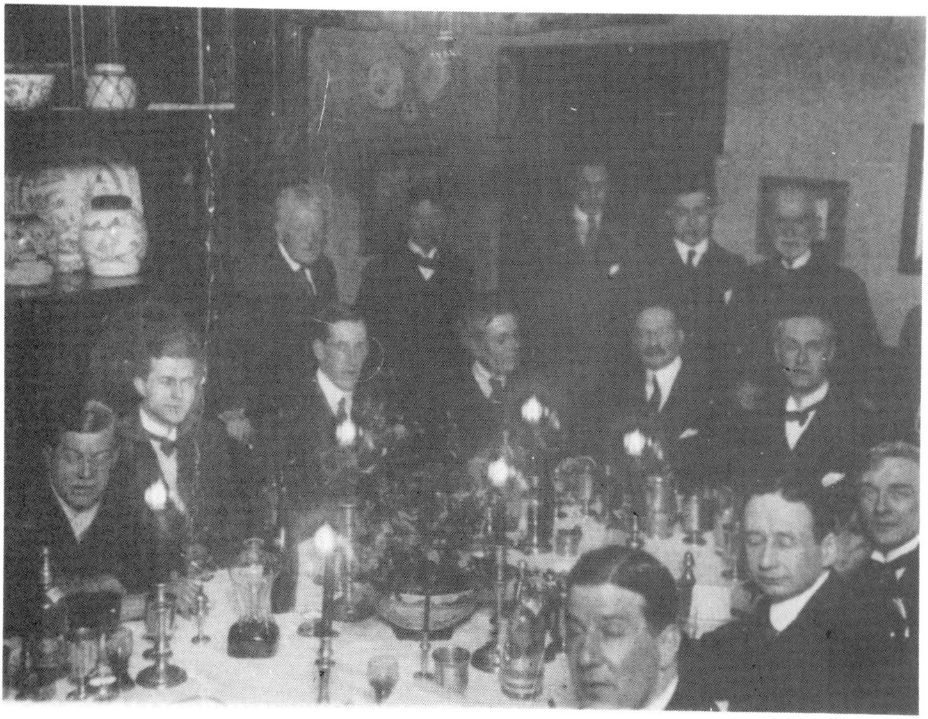

Walter Churcher's conversazione showing (left to right, back row): Harry Nicholls, Pett Ridge, Brian Churcher, Sidney Nicholson, A.D. Thomson; (at table): John Hassall, Christopher Hassall, Alec Miller, Sir George Frampton, Jeremy Mathews, Walter Churcher, Albert Toft, René Bull and Harry Riley.

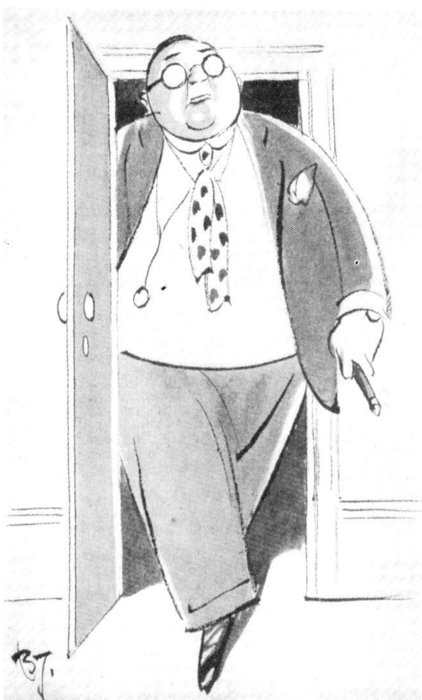

Caricature by Bert Thomas of Aubrey Hammond (1894-1940). Hammond was born in Folkestone, Kent. He studied at the Byam Shaw School of Art and at Julian's in Paris. For a time he taught commercial and theatrical design at the Westminster School of Art but will be remembered for his art deco style, so popular in the 'twenties. A member of the Savage, he often designed invitation cards for house dinners. As a caricaturist he was noted for leaving out people's noses, relying on eyes, mouth and hairline to convey character. Bert Thomas's caption was "So much of you to come!" Hammond was used to such jokes, often turning them on himself.

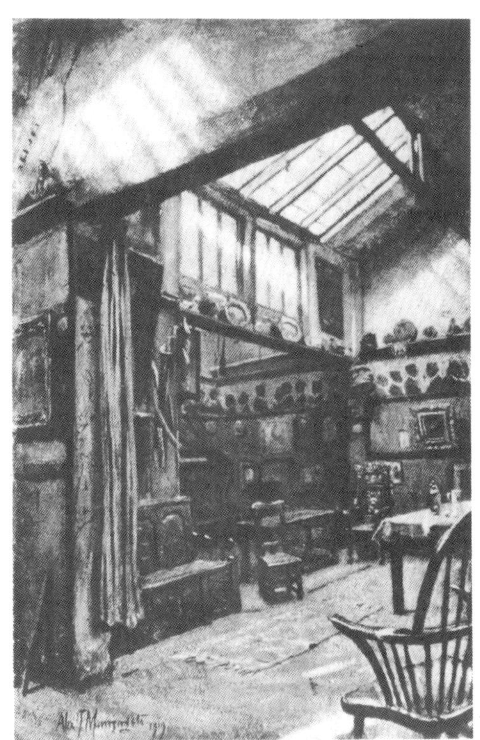

(*Left*) Interior of the London Sketch Club in Marylebone Road from a painting by A. J. Mavrogordato.

(*Below*) In the early 'twenties an extra floor was added, with a gallery which increased the quaintness of the studio. From a *Punch* drawing by Frank Reynolds.

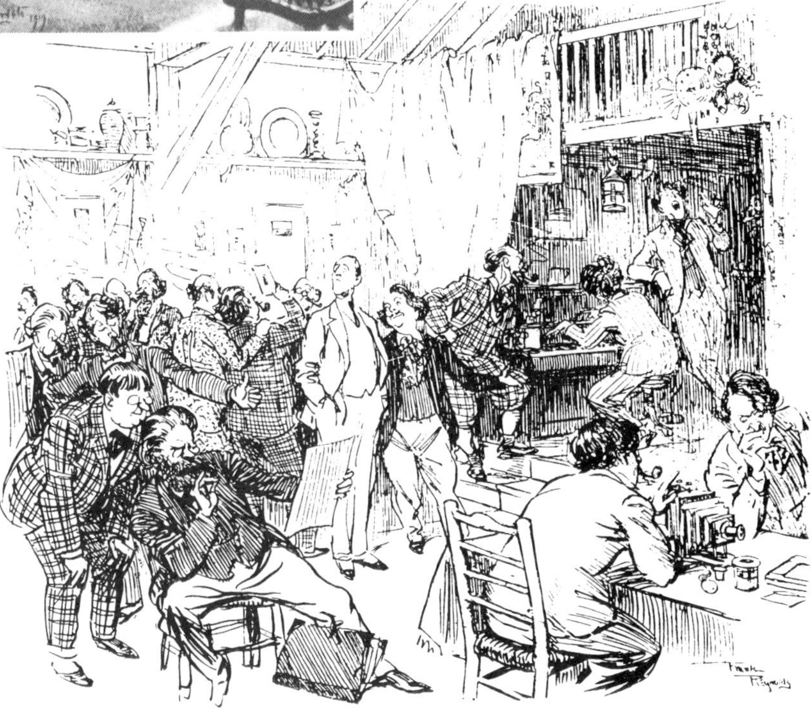

Here one gets the real atmosphere.

Harry Riley and the Empire Stage Door.

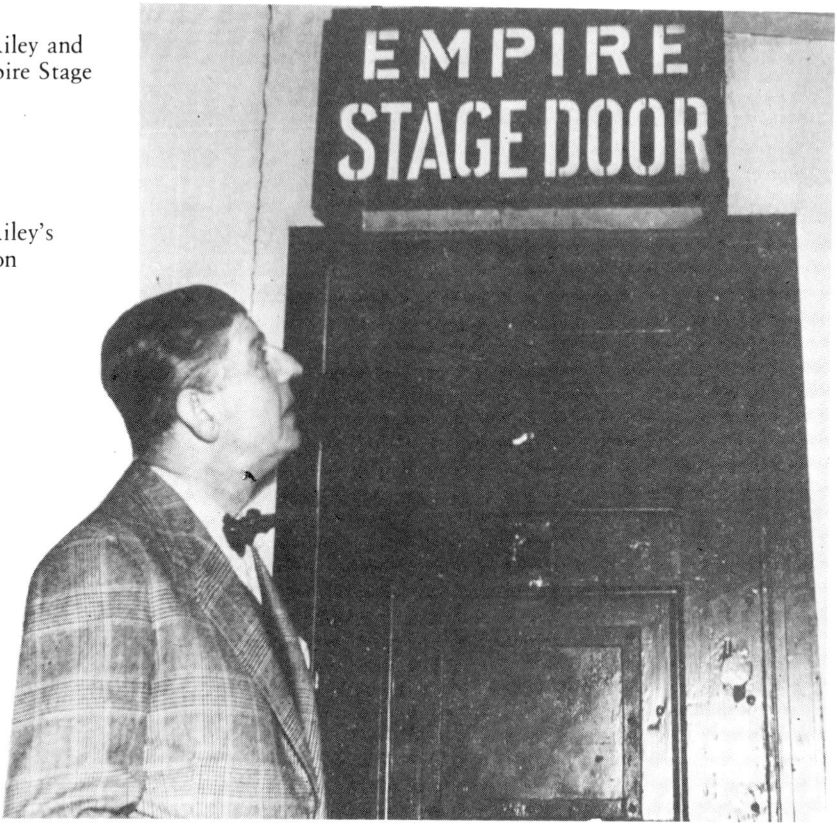

(*Below*) Harry Riley's invitation card.

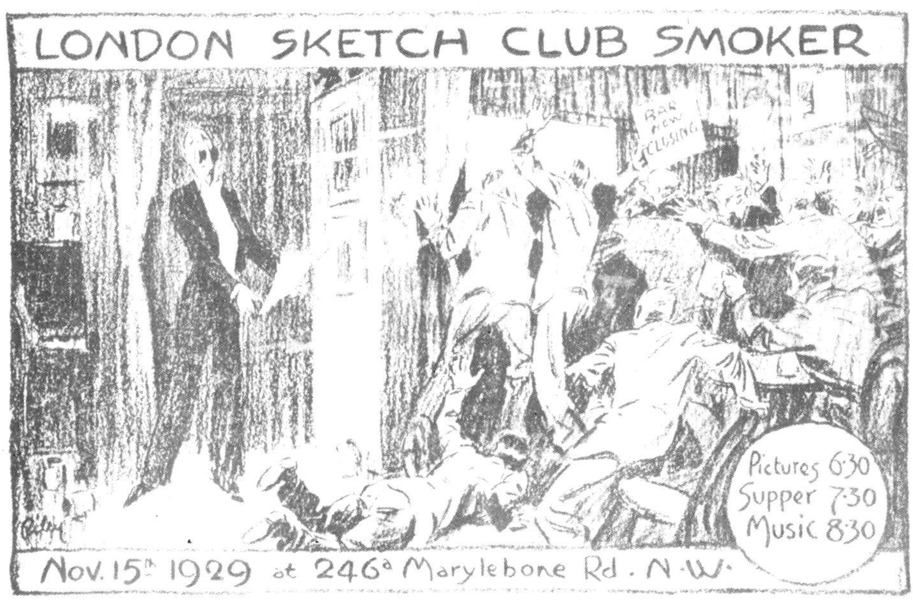

Barribal, Strube and Gordon Nicholl RI, were all members of both clubs. It had been the same with the previous generation: Phil May, Tom Browne, John Hassall, Heath Robinson, H. M. Bateman and Bert Thomas were some of those who had enjoyed joint membership. Another member of both clubs was Aubrey Hammond, who must have hated jokes about his massive physique. Hammond was indeed a large man who took the brunt of many jokes about obesity, but he will chiefly be remembered as a stage designer, often working in collaboration with Joe Harker. Also a member of both clubs was A. P. Herbert MP, Petty Officer, playwright and novelist, whom some people will be surprised to discover was extremely shy. After his death the BBC presented an entertaining series of court room battles based on the life of A. P. Herbert, with Roy Dotrice in the starring role. Both Hammond and A. P. Herbert enjoyed the London Sketch Club Balls. Between the wars A. P. Herbert's barge was moored on the Thames next to that of Ian Hassall. Daphne Silas remembered being invited back to A. P. Herbert's place after a London Sketch Club Ball. She was nervous about walking such a slim gangplank but A. P. Herbert is reputed to have encouraged her with "Just lift your skirts and join us!"

The other literary connection at this time was Reginald Arkell, who, after editing numerous magazines, went on to found *Men Only*, published by George Newnes. Arkell enjoyed a substantial following in horticultural circles with his books (published in the 'thirties and 'forties) *Green Fingers*, *More Green Fingers* and *Green Fingers Again* (illustrated, incidentally, by Edgar Norfield). It is unlikely that Arkell would have approved of *Men Only* as it is published today. His idea was to encourage literacy through humour, adding a chic sprinkling of female naughtiness. The titillation then was mild and suggestive, in contrast to the blatant, almost pornographic material in today's magazine. Arkell's sketches of scantily clad females bordered on stereotypes. Illustrators who worked for him included Webster Murray and Arthur Ferrier. *Men Only* continued in much the same way in the 'fifties under the editorship of R. J. Minney but when Paul Raymond bought the magazine he threw out Arkell's original idea, concentrating on gynaecology which leaves little to the imagination.

Inside the club, members often left artefacts or souvenirs lying about. The Wells Street studio had a large collection of pewter, thanks to Walter Churcher, and a selection of old posters; the Marylebone Club had an equal selection of theatrical props such as spears, imitation guns, pikes, shields and swordfish teeth hanging around the walls. One of the most unusual additions was the Stage Door sign from the old Empire Theatre in Leicester Square. It was placed above the Newgate prison cell door and lit up as members went through. Ian Hassall had rescued the sign in 1927 when the Empire closed its doors as a theatre. This was probably possible because Arthur Aldin, brother of Cecil, was manager of the Empire. When it reopened as a cinema on 8 November 1928, the first film was *Trelawney of the Wells*. By this time the old stage door sign was safely implanted in the Marylebone studio of the London Sketch Club.

Another member of both the London Sketch Club and the Savage was Harry Riley. Born in 1895 in Chelsea, Riley spent the early part of his childhood in the Leicestershire countryside where his father had a smallholding. He left school at the age of fifteen to study art at the Hammersmith School of Art. After only a few months he secured a job as a junior artist in Fleet Street whilst continuing to study at the Bolt School of Art (1910-1915) in the evenings. During the war he served in Salonica, Palestine and France with the 3rd County of London Yeomanry and after the War achieved a reputation as a humourous artist working for journals such as *London Opinion*, *Blighty* and *The Humorist*.

Riley was a versatile artist but not as talented as contemporaries such as Barribal, Gilbert Wilkinson or Fred Taylor. Nevertheless what Riley lacked in talent he made up for in his work for the London Sketch Club. He took over the job of organising the entertainment from Wilton Williams and worked tirelessly on numerous projects for the wellbeing of the Club. He was an excellent raconteur and often filled many a slot at a minute's notice. George Baker, Secretary of the Savage Club, wrote of him: "When I want a drawing, and want it in a hurry, I ring up Harry Riley, and although he may grumble that he doesn't know how he can possibly do it with all the work he has on hand, lo and behold, the next morning the job is done and delivered, and mark you all done for the deep and abiding affection he has for the Club and its members."

Riley was the epitome of the self-employed artist, ready to tackle anything and often put upon for little reward. He designed his own house in Dunstall Road, Wimbledon and was a member of a number of London clubs. Latterly he worked as a cartoonist for the now defunct *Sunday Chronicle* and after the Second World War was one of the tutors with Galleon Painting Holidays, which I will explain a bit later.

One incident which went down in Sketch Club records involved Harry Riley and Wilton Williams. The pair tried to pull a prank on Captain Adrian Jones which backfired badly.

> Wilton Williams, one night, suddenly picked a quarrel at the table with Harry Riley, who, goaded to fury by Wilton's insults, drew a revolver and shot him. Wilton's body was then solemnly covered with a tablecloth and carted out of the Club. This episode had been staged to impress Captain Adrian Jones, the sculptor of the *Quadriga*; but as Adrian suffered from almost total deafness, the venomous dialogue was wasted.

The same lighthearted humour was manifested in the London Sketch Club Balls. One year "Living Pictures" were a feature: professional models and Club members were shown as silhouettes, the subjects ranging from the sublime to the ridiculous. After a most alluring model had disrobed as Venus, one of the Sketch Club members followed as Apollo, reducing his classic pose to banality by relaxing and lighting a pipe in view of the audience. Elaborate bull fights were staged in full costume, bicycle races, polo matches and other sporting events for ladies and men were arranged, with the fun often continuing throughout the night for the hardiest of revellers, who would sometimes be found dancing at the Club at breakfast time.

One year a member went to great pains to disguise himself as a statue. Wearing a leotard and covered with lashings of grey paint, he kept so perfectly still he convinced partygoers until one young débutante, curious about statues, went up to inspect him. She nearly fainted when he opened one eye. Such was the preparation that went into these Balls ...

Although there was a certain amount of financial risk in the early days of the Ball, it was soon discovered that they were making the Club a healthy profit. In 1925 the Puff-Ball Final saw Miss Evelyn Laye as Captain of the Fair Team and Miss Mai Bacon as Captain of the Dark Team. Other events that evening included "Spot Pictures" which involved piercing a picture with pins: those nearest the spot on the reverse won prizes, and Ping-Pong Dances. In 1927 there was Puff-Ball again with

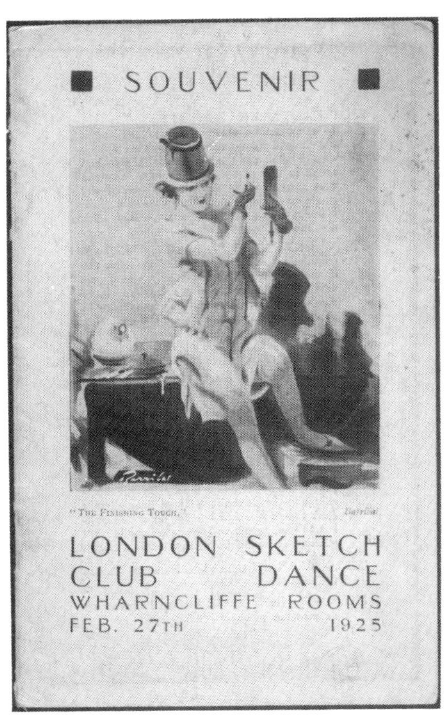

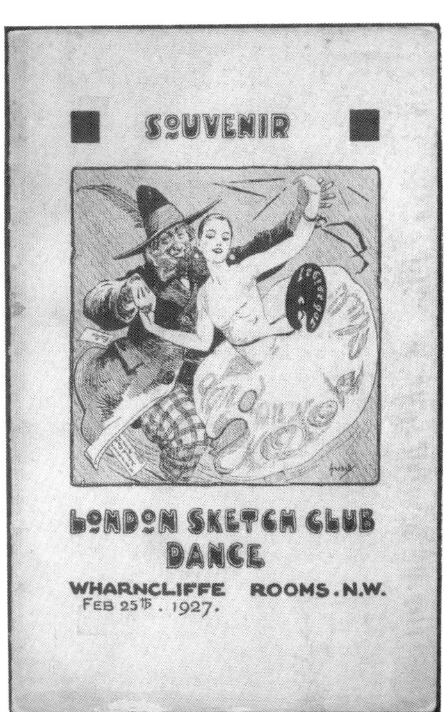

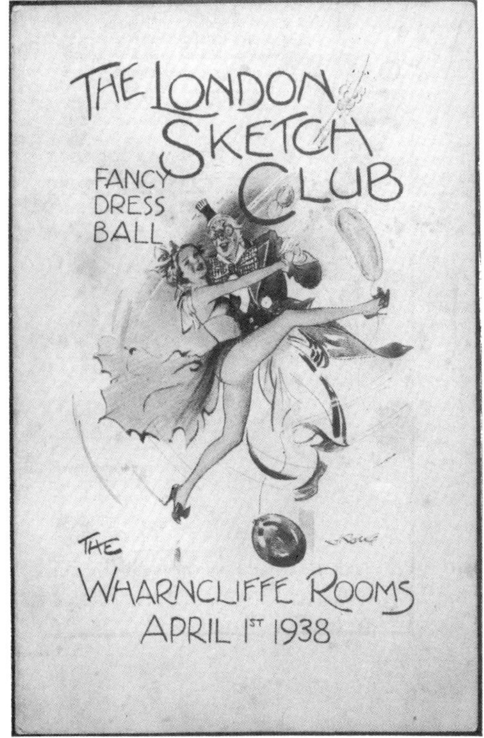

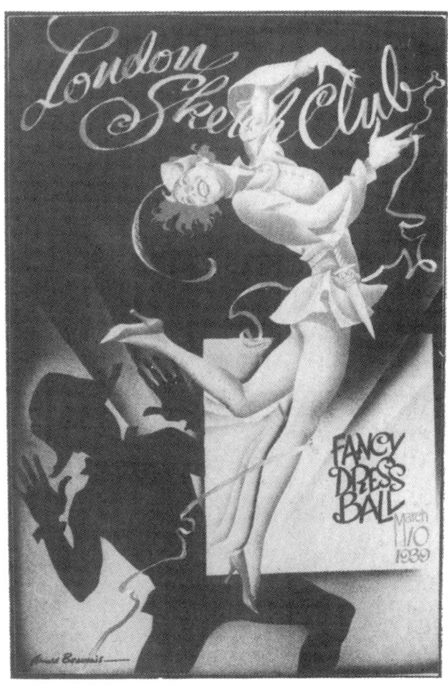

London Sketch Club Souvenirs of 1925, 1927, 1938 and 1939 by Walter Barribal, John Hassall, Norman Keene and Arnold Beauvais.

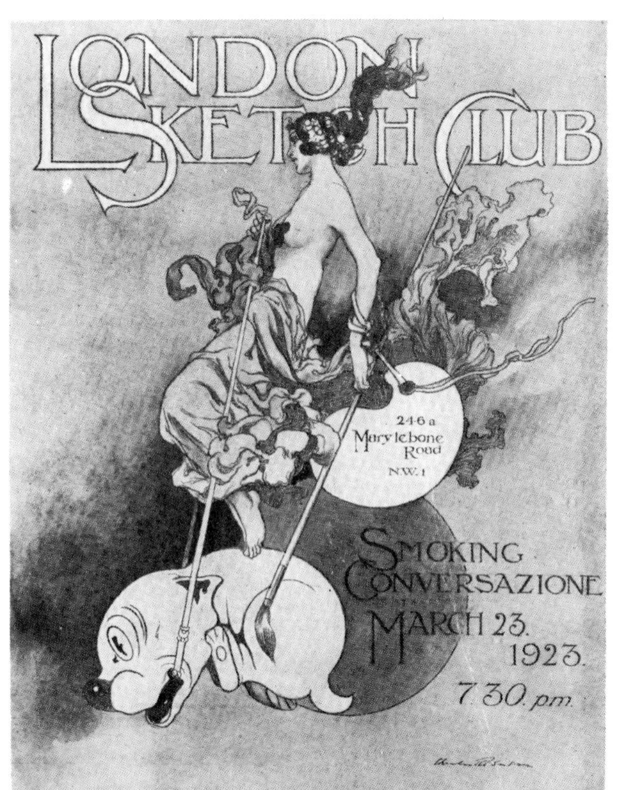

Invitation by Charles Robinson, 1923.

(*Below*)
Invitation by Mac Wilson, 1922.

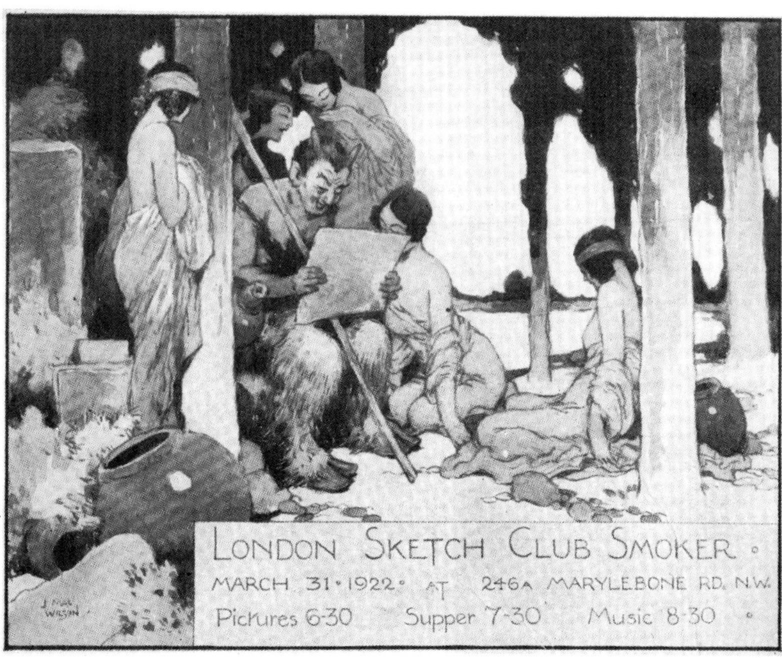

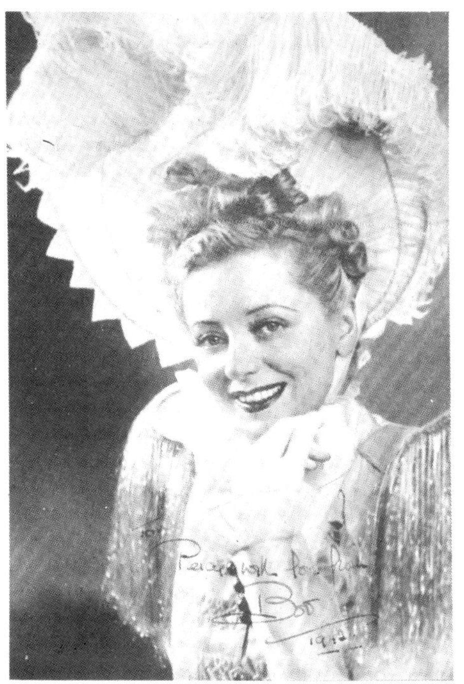

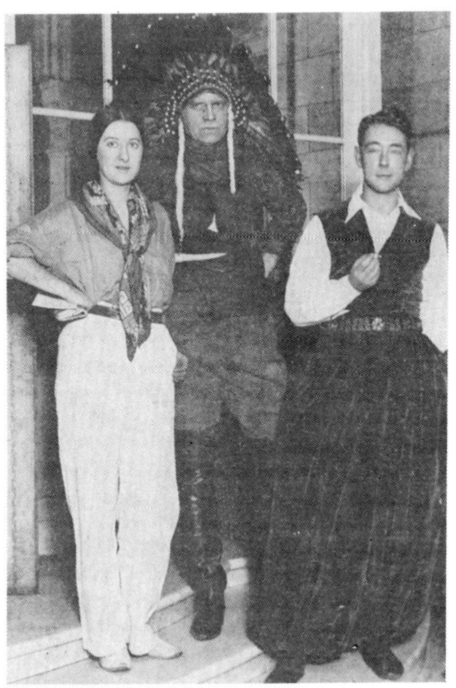

(*Above, left*) Evelyn Laye, Captain of the Fair Team in the 1925 Puff-Ball Final.

(*Above, right*) John Hassall in Indian head-dress, accompanied by Christopher Hassall (lyricist for Ivor Novello and, later, William Walton).

(*Left*) A selection of sketches inside the London Sketch Club Souvenir of 1925. They are by Albert Hindle, Kenneth Denton Shoesmith, Charles Ward, Eddie Benfield, Harold Earnshaw, George Studdy, J. MacMath Wilson, Leonard Brightwell, Thomas Downey (a caricature of Evelyn Laye) and one other with an indecipherable signature.

Miss Joan Barry as Captain of the Fair Team and Cicely Courtnedge as Captain of the Dark Team. This year there were Hidden Masks in both ballrooms and prizes were given to the first four complete set of six masks.

In the early 'twenties the Club decided to organise a Life Class on a different night from their working meetings. Friday night working meetings always seemed to end in frivolity and lightheartedness; the Tuesday night Life Class was a more delicate affair: it gave members a chance to draw from the model, and it was taken seriously. Charles Robinson ran the class for years. Indeed it was also his great efforts which make the London Sketch Club Balls so enjoyable: he worked tirelessly for the Club.

A number of the models who posed for the Sketch Club Life Class were of Italian extraction. In addition to their modest fee, Club members showed their appreciation by entertaining them twice a year. The first of these two functions was a Spaghetti and Chianti Night: the girls cooked the spaghetti and members provided the Chianti. The second was a Christmas Lunch at which the models were waited upon by members; the chief attraction was a large bowl of punch!

The Friday Smoker Nights were a different matter. One night a famous explorer was a guest of the Club; he brought with him some big wooden crates. During the entertainment after supper he opened his crates, from which emerged three live alligators and some venomous snakes. Members were so shocked they decided unanimously to sign the pledge! However, the following Friday Harry Riley and Fred Buchanan staged such an outrageous burlesque of the explorer's entertainment that the pledges were broken.

Other visitors included the British and Welsh All-in Wrestling Champion who gave a demonstration that was a huge success with the sporting element of the Club. Harry Riley scored an even greater triumph when he appeared on stage a week later in an approved wrestling costume and parodied the event with a particularly gory bout with, of all things, a kitchen chair! This interest in sport led to the Belsize and Polytechnic Boxing Champions giving exhibition bouts in the Club, no doubt encouraged by Wilton Williams, something of a boxing buff and himself quite a useful boxer. On another occasion Williams brought Georges Carpentier to the Club to give a boxing demonstration and proceeded to knock him out (by accident, of course).

This interest in boxing was to remain within the Club during the 'forties and 'fifties. David Langdon remembered a boxing exhibition held in the Marylebone Club during one of his visits in the Post-War years when he met Sir Arthur Tedder. It was continued when Bill Bavin an ex-estate agent of South London turned author, joined the Club in 1955. He was also a big chum of Freddie Mills the boxer, whom he brought along as a guest of the Club.

Meanwhile Wilton Williams was always up to pranks. One night he arrived at the Club heavily disguised as his own brother. Members were so convinced by his make-up that they bought him drinks all evening and entertained him royally. Not that Wilton Williams should be confused with Terrick Williams. Terrick Williams had joined the Sketch Club back in 1903 and had achieved an enormous reputation. He had become a member of the RI in 1904 and was elected to the RA in 1933. Together with Albert Toft, Gilbert Wilkinson, Percy Bradshaw, Leonard Richmond and Gordon Nicholl he contributed articles regularly to the *Artist* magazine in the 'twenties and 'thirties.

No doubt Terrick Williams had a large influence on the work of Ellis Silas, S.T.C. Weeks and Leonard Richmond. He was one of those artists, like Lee

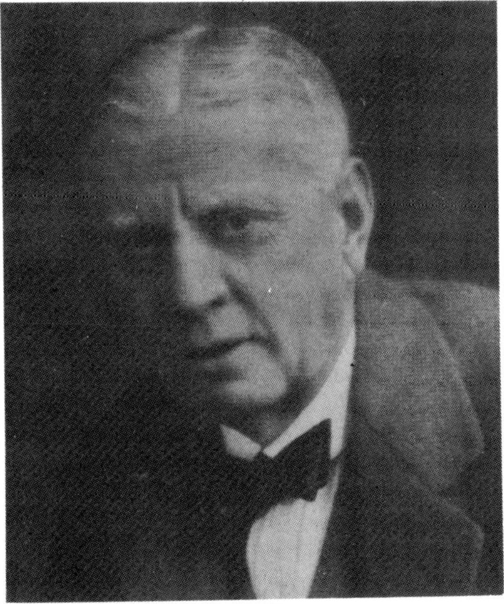

Terrick Williams (1860-1936) was born in Liverpool and studied art in Antwerp under Verlat (1885-6) and in Paris at the Academie Julien under Bougereau and Robert Fleury (1887-9). He was President of the RI in 1934.

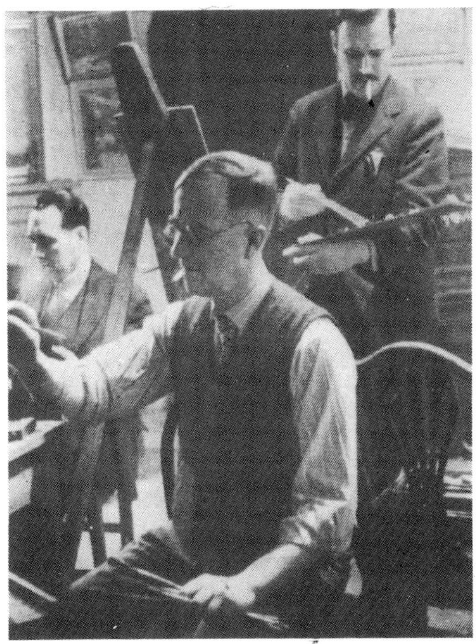

Leonard Richmond, ROI, RBA, at work in the London Sketch Club. Richmond, who died in 1965, studied at Taunton School of Art. He was also a writer, being responsible for many a treatise on art. He wrote for the *Artist* magazine and had books published by Pitmans. He illustrated *Devon and Cornish Days* and *Come Abroad With Us* by E.P. Leigh-Bennett, both published by the Southern Railway Company.

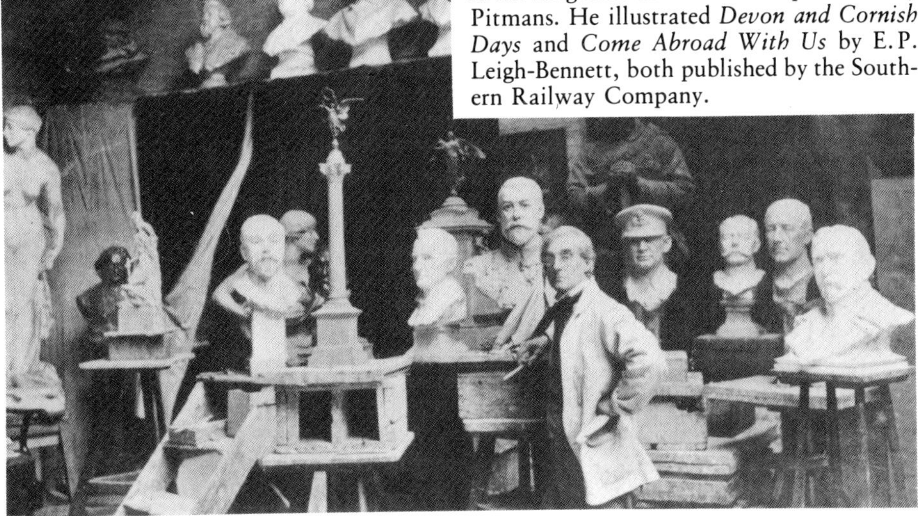

Sir Albert Toft (1862-1949) was born in Birmingham and studied at Stoke-on-Trent and the Royal College of Art. He was a regular exhibitor at the Royal Academy and permanent works can be seen in the Tate Gallery, Walker Gallery, Birmingham, Newcastle, Preston, Glasgow, New York, Melbourne and at the London Sketch Club. He was also a teacher, often finding more satisfaction in his students' success than his own. His brother J. Alfonso Toft was also an artist, specialising mainly in landscapes.

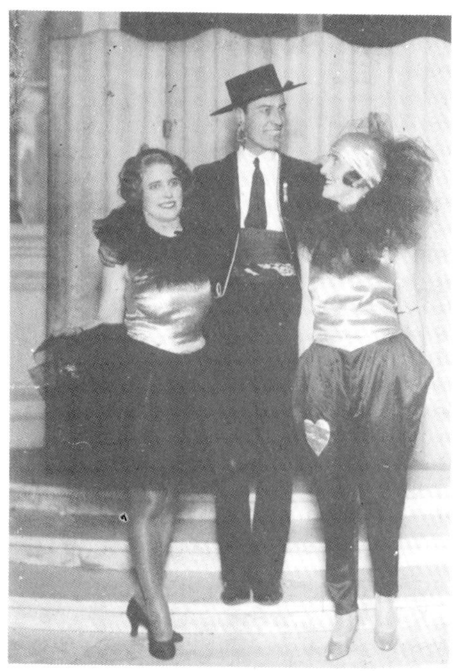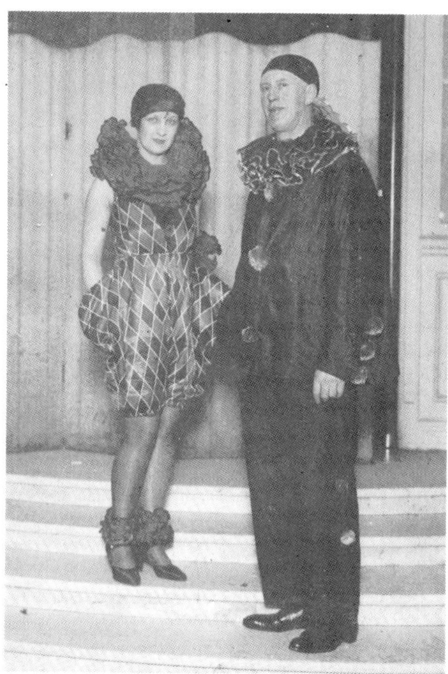

Two photos of revellers at the London Sketch Club ball, which evoked so many happy memories for members and guests.

Hankey, who found fame and, to a lesser extent, fortune towards the end of his life, having exhibited at the Royal Academy without a break since 1889. His art schooling had been similar to that of John Hassall but whereas Terrick Williams regularly exhibited his paintings and thus increased their value, Hassall stuck with illustration.

Terrick Williams enjoyed a notable following like that other early London Sketch Club member Herbert Hughes-Stanton. The pair had an enormous impact on the arts world of the 'twenties. Hughes-Stanton, who had been President of the Sketch Club back in 1906, was elected to the RA in 1920 and was knighted three years later.

It is interesting to note that the Sketch Club made no differentiation between fine artists, graphic artists, cartoonists and illustrators. In this regard it was most unusual. Every member was treated with the same respect.

CHAPTER 9

The 'Thirties

If Bateman shot to prominence in the 'twenties, the other Hassall protégé who became well-known in the 'twenties and 'thirties was Sidney Strube of the *Daily Express*. "How does Strube do it day after day, year after year?" puzzled the writer H. V. Morton. "I cannot tell you, neither I think could he. It is a gift brought to perfection by hard work and experience. He always has three ideas for a cartoon and his greatest difficulty is which one to choose. He is always working against the clock, sometimes with his eye on every ticking second. And he never fails!"

Strube's "Little Man" was the suburban commuter or man next door; with his umbrella, bushy moustache and bowler hat he was the epitome of British life, a lovable, inoffensive little man, often henpecked, always good mannered, suffering under bureaucratic pressure or the tax department. He took a heap of trouble on board because essentially he cared about his country and the way it was going. Strube's creation was Everyman, the hero of a hundred epics who typified lower middle class England and who, despite national catastrophes, kept smiling. He was the goose being cooked in the proverbial oven, regulated by irksome laws but uncomplaining.

Strube (1891-1956) was born within the sound of Bow Bells — Strube was his real name, despite many assumptions that it was a pseudonym — and he remained a true Cockney throughout his life. He started work as a junior draughtsman with a furniture firm designing Shades of Sheraton, but he was determined to become a professional artist. He enrolled at John Hassall's school of art in Kensington, then became a freelance cartoonist in 1910; two years later he joined the staff of the *Daily Express*. He remained with the *Express* for 36 years, during which time he established himself as one of the foremost cartoonists of this century. Apart from a brief spell during the First World War when he served with the Artists' Rifles on the western front he regularly contributed to the *Express* and *Punch*. Sometimes his Little Man would appear as Henry or George; he was always the henpecked loyal husband who crystallised the British way of life.

As H. V. Morton said, "I know only one secret about his cartoon-making and this from my own observation. When he is sorting out his ideas he takes a piece of drawing board and his pencil begins to dance over it, making little rough scrawls which resolve themselves into Mr Baldwin's pipe, Mr Ramsay MacDonald's moustache, a tall stove-pipe hat to which becomes added the face of Sir William Hicks. All the time drawings are appearing Strube's face is set and solemn. Then his pencil stops. Strube smiles!" The most memorable of Strube's cartoons was "Business as Usual", which appeared in the *Daily Express* of 19 May 1926. The General Strike is over and a victorious British Lion, complete with cigar, sits in the chair dictating to his secretary: "Now where were we Miss, when that fellow interrupted us?" he is saying as a character with "General Strike" written across his chest blocks the doorway.

This same use of understatement appears in a cartoon of November 1940 in which Strube's Little Man inspects a cucumber in the garden after an air raid. Everywhere is destruction around the air-raid shelter, where his wife is busily knitting. "Is it all right now Henry?" she calls from inside the shelter. Henry, looking at his cucumber, replies, "Yes, not even scratched!"

Strube was a quiet, sober man who always dressed in a suit, was clean shaven and married; he rarely looked out of place in a crowd. Constantly aware of current events, Stanley Baldwin remarked: "David Low is a genius, but he is malicious, whilst Strube is a little genius". In 1933, Sidney Strube was offered ten thousand pounds by the *Daily Herald* to leave the *Express*. Beaverbrook instantly matched the *Herald*'s offer and Strube continued with the *Express* until 1948 when he was forced to retire due to ill health. He continued to make odd visits to the London Sketch Club and the Savage Club until his death in 1956. The last word came from his old friend Morton:

> Is there any need to analyse Strube's uncanny genius for interpreting a situation in terms of simple and frequently biting, but never unkind, humour? Surely Strube's kindness was one of his most attractive attributes.

One member of the Sketch Club whom I have failed to mention yet was Charles Harrison. Harrison had sat out the ups and downs of the Club's fortunes. His own style of humour and draughtsmanship could best be described as quirky, and his work had frequently adorned the pages of *Punch*. Harrison, a Londoner by birth, had family connections with the stage and made his acting debut in *Oliver Twist*, with Henry Irving playing Bill Sykes, J. L. Toole as the Artful Dodger and Lionel Brough as a police officer, back in the last century. He was torn between the acting profession and art but his decision to follow an artistic career in favour of a theatrical one was well justified. He was one of those Strand artists whose number included Hassall, Browne, Owen and Lewis Baumer. Harrison's work was influenced by Japanese and Egyptian art and he was considered by his contemporaries to be much in the same mould as E. T. Reed.

Harrison was already an old man in the 'thirties but he was rarely without work. As Hammerton said: "He has often reached home late at night to find a messenger waiting with instructions for a picture to be delivered the next morning. But working under journalistic pressure and for rapidly printed papers, he had developed a remarkable facility for simple and effective outlines, and although his drawings are essentially mannered in their style — that style is entirely his own". He had worked as a cartoonist on the *Daily Express* before Strube, and when he died in 1943 *The Times* featured an obituary.

Certain members of the Press were welcomed to report on proceedings at the London Sketch Club in the 'thirties, although it was still strictly a private Club. This report appeared in *Quex* in 1931 entitled "A Man about Town":

> It was hard in the fog to find the number, 246a Marylebone Road, and then there were some yards of openair passageway, and after that an indoor corridor that led to a dark door. But a man in a cap, who came silently out of the fog, said there were studios up the passage. Besides which, when the dark door suddenly opened, a stream of light and the sound of many men talking and

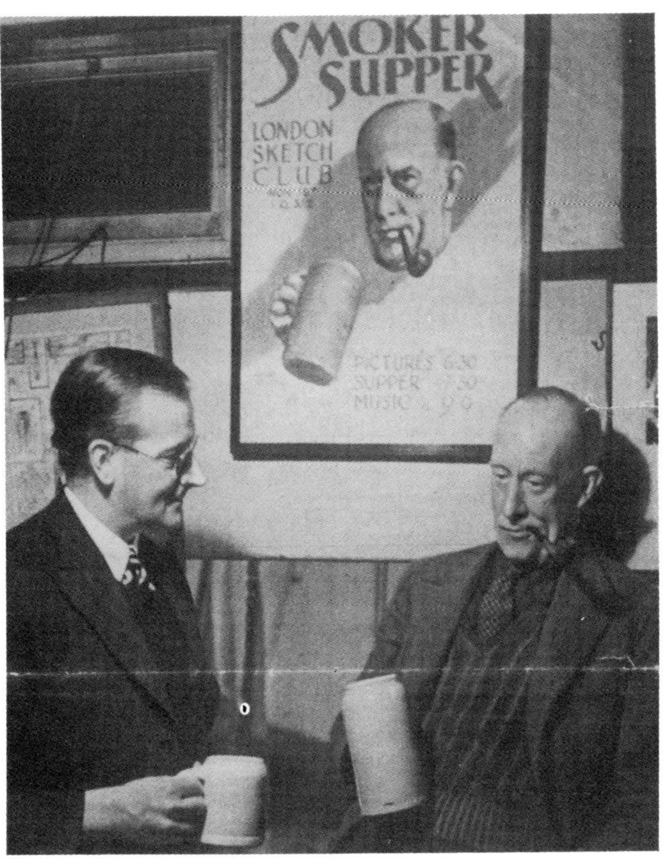

George Dixon (*left*, with glasses) talking to S. T. C. Weeks. Dixon was President of the London Sketch Club in 1938 whilst Sidney Weeks was President in 1932.

Invitation card by George S. Dixon.

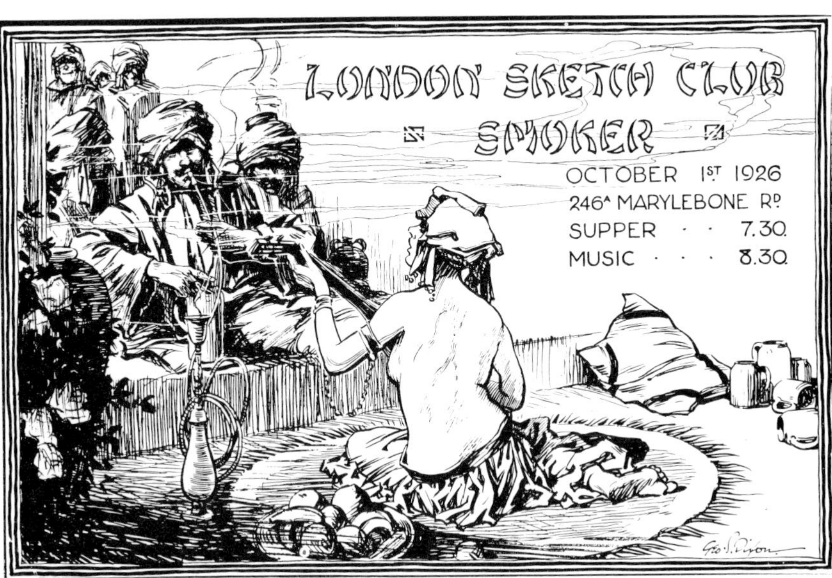

Invitation card by Cecil Wade (signed Royle, his pseudonym) depicting George Parlby on the floor and Arnold Beauvais as Britannia, with a brush and palette instead of a trident and shield.

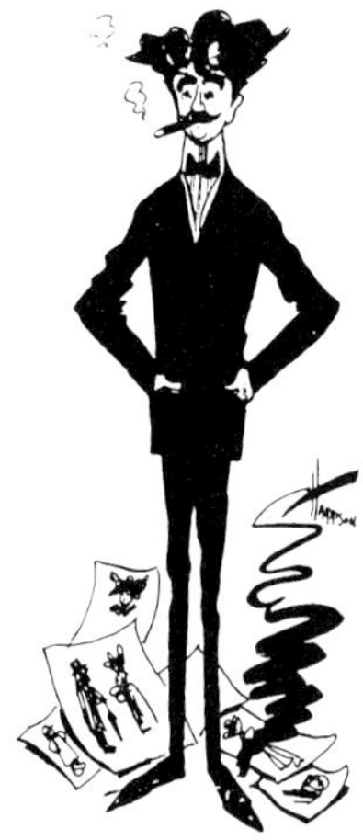

Caricature of Charles Harrison by himself. Harrison sometimes signed his work "Harry's Son"!

Invitation card by Charles Harrison. His style was distinctive and unique.

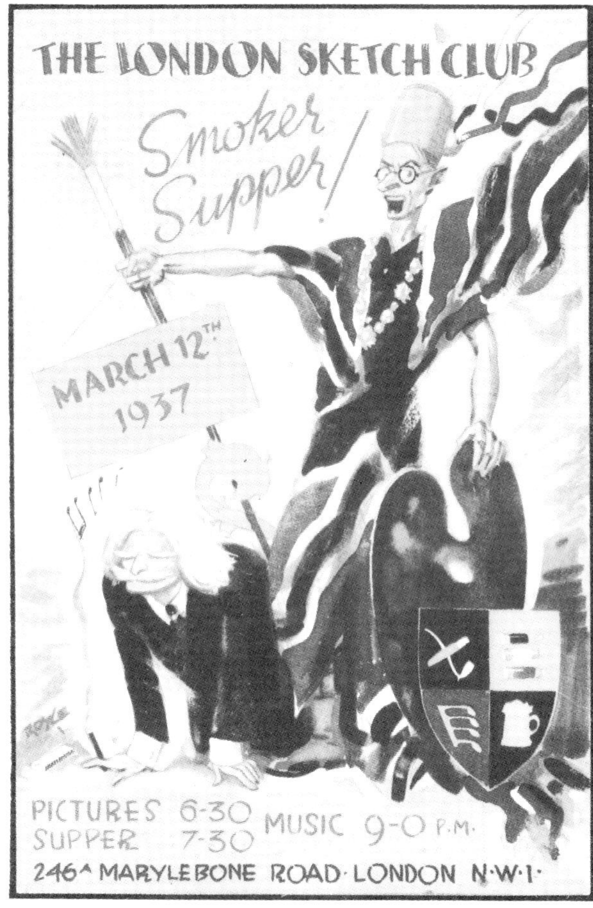

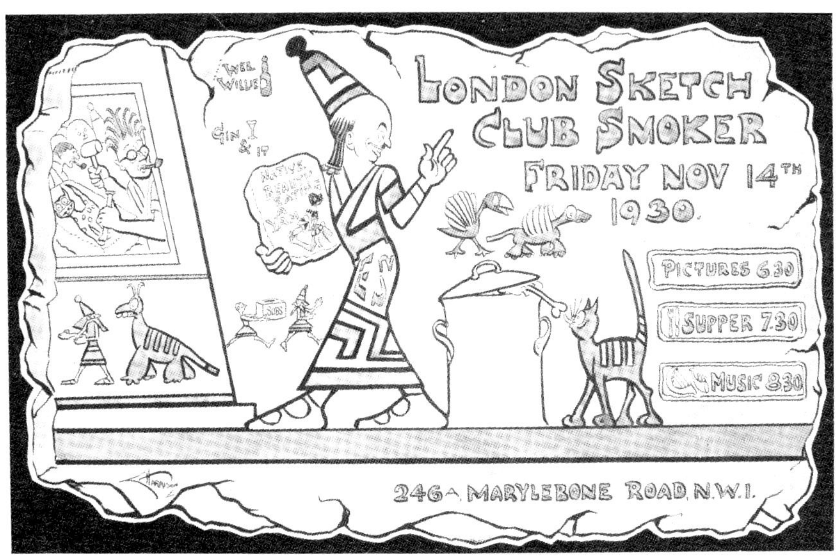

laughing came through, and I had a swift vision of gay-coloured streamers and Chinese lanterns; and soon after I saw Mr John Hassall, got up as a highwayman, with his hair all a rat-tailed tangle and a slack cartridge belt that dropped queerly in front. That was for his stage performances later as the world's greatest trick sharp-shooter. And anyway it was proof that I had found the London Sketch Club on the night of its annual Christmas dinner and entertainment.

Later in the evening Mr Tom Downey and Mr A. J. Wilson, the lay member from the City, who is Hon. Treasurer of the Club, showed me another door — a brown painted one — now propped against the wall of the passage. "That", said Mr Downey, "was the door of the condemned cell at the Old Bailey." "I didn't expect it to have a letter-box," I said. "Ah", went on Mr Downey, "we had that put in when the Club used it as their front door, which it is not now. That small hole above the letter-box is where the warders used to look through at the prisoner".

It was a squeeze to get to the dining tables, for the studio was hardly big enough for the 80 members and their 120 or so guests. The dinner was done in two relays, 7 pm and 8 pm, and members who had sat down at seven helped as waiters at the second relay. I was put next to Mr Ernest Moore, the portrait painter, and Mr Walter Barribal, the President, came to say "How do?" The roast beef was borne in, great steaming hot dishes of brussels sprouts and cabbage were set before us and vast loads of potatoes in their jackets; and it was during this time that I noted that among the diners were Mr Heath Robinson, Mr Alfred Leete and that friendly giant, Mr Aubrey Hammond, who long ago told me the tale of the Scotsman, his purse, and a moth that flew out, which story I was first to publish, and which since has gone right round the world. And it was also about this time that I caught sight, on the wall above the bar opening, of the weird, devilishly clever plaster head that Phil May did of himself — "if ever I get to ninety".

And then came the entertainment. We were ordered to scramble for seats on the wooden forms arranged in front of a tiny stage, and take our beer with us. There were tall stone jugs that as time went on tested the strength of the wrist. The veteran and courtly Mr George Parlby, the celebrated worker in stained glass, came down the stairway at the side, playing an instrument that made sounds like tissue paper on a comb. But he led a serious party, garbed in picturesque costumes — Mr Parlby is a master of make-up, can make astonishing dresses out of a rag bag — and very delightfully they sang "Good King Wencelas" and "Noel". And it was while they and we sang "Hark the Herald Angels Sing" and marched round in single file that Mr Parlby became Father Christmas and, as we passed the stage, handed out gifts of toys and drums and whistles from a painted gallery that descended from above.

Then followed the unprecedentedly great circus show on the tiny stage, particularly the putting up of the tight-rope and the actual tight-rope walking which was done in the dark, and the elephant turn, and the comic singing of Mr Arnold Beauvais and the masterly showman of Mr Harry Riley. And on the walls were posters that would entice visitors into any show. And everyone voted it a great evening and I learned that the Club was one of the arts clubs that really is doing well. The Friday evenings, when the members come to sketch, remain a feature of the art life of London.

One of the most promising talents to join the London Sketch Club in 1931 was Terence Cuneo. His credentials were impeccable. He was the son of that talented yet unlucky illustrator Cyrus Cuneo, and was eager to make his mark on the world of art. As he put it in his autobiography:

> Their premises were then in the Marylebone Road and the dear old ramshackle place was a friendly haven full of character and an atmosphere of easygoing camaraderie. One of its attractions for me was the Friday night sketching sessions. We would be given the choice of two subjects, figure or landscape and the object was to complete one or other within two hours from memory. The figure subject, for instance, might be "The Watcher" and the landscape "Frost on the Heath". Or, again, "The Worker" and "Mist on the River", and so on. I enjoyed these working sessions and seldom had trouble in turning out a reasonably finished sketch within the allotted time. Afterwards the sketches were stood up in rows and then, after fortifying ourselves at the bar, we gathered round, criticising and admiring each other's efforts. It was interesting and it was fun, but it also did much to foster my inclination towards versatility.

At this point Cuneo was undecided which path to follow in his career, that of illustrator, like his father, or that of painter. His mind was made up by talking to John Hassall, whom he does not mention by name but who is clearly implicated in this quote:

> One night I returned from The Sketch Club in a depressed state. I had been talking to another illustrator, a man supreme in his field, well-established, a fine draughtsman with a mass of work at his fingertips. But as we had chatted I saw only a tired, over-worked man in late middle-age; a man whose house and family spelt heavy responsibilities and a man so set in his ways that he was unable to break into new fields of expression. Suddenly, I saw myself, in my fifties or sixties still slogging away as a hack illustrator. The prospect appalled me.

It was this conversation that helped Terence Cuneo make up his mind to ditch illustration in favour of painting. Although he was to resign from the Club a few years later because a certain member exhibited one of his paintings on the back of the kitchen door, Cuneo was to become one of the most respected painters of the twentieth century. Indeed he has been the inspiration for many other painters who have made their reputations in recent times. He painted a clutch of notable portraits including those of Queen Elizabeth II, Montgomery and Edward Heath, and often included a mouse in these paintings. One could be forgiven for thinking Cuneo had pinched this anthropomorphic idea from Harry Rountree, who left the Marylebone Club with pictures of *his* mice in every nook and cranny. During the 'thirties at Marylebone cobwebs generously intermingled with relics profusely dotted around the room; the skylight leaked and Mabel, the club cook, had to cope with impossible odds on Club smoker nights. Rowntree deposited mouse paintings in places where mice usually entered the Club! He was following the tradition Edmund Dulac had started, painting panels behind the bar in the Old Wells Street Studio.

On 8 June 1934 the London Sketch Club was invited by the Canadian Pacific Railway Company to visit the *Empress of Britain* liner docked at Southampton. The reason for the invitation was that the cocktail bar had been decorated by W. Heath

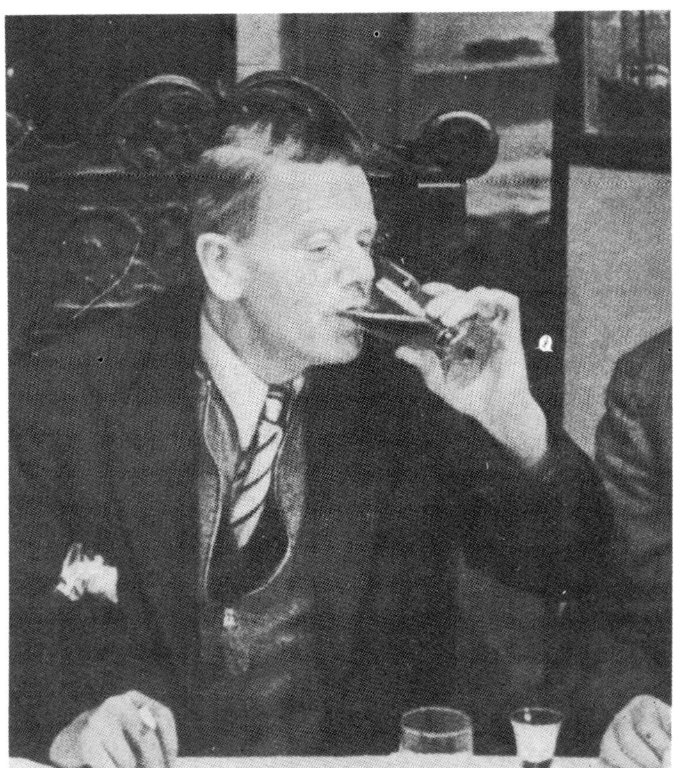

Fred Charles Buchanan (1878-1941) served with the Artists' Rifles in World War I and was a *Punch* cartoonist. He also worked for *Strand* magazine and was a long time member of the Ilford Dramatic Society. Latterly he and his wife moved into the flat beneath Harry May Hemsley in Telford Court, Streatham. They constantly played practical jokes on each other.

Invitation card by Buchanan.

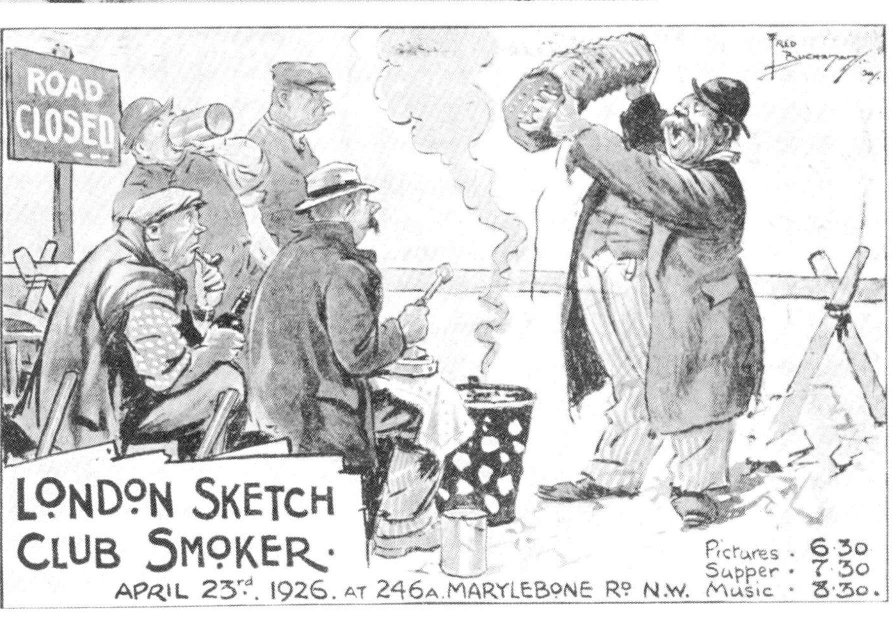

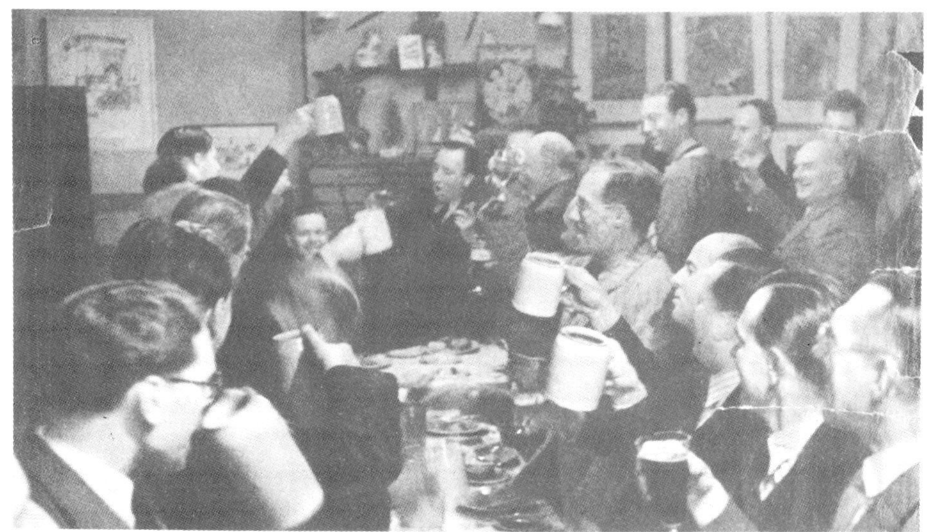

When Fred Buchanan took the chair in 1939 the members all raised their earthenware tankards and yelled "For ...!", a shortened version of "For he's a jolly good fellow".

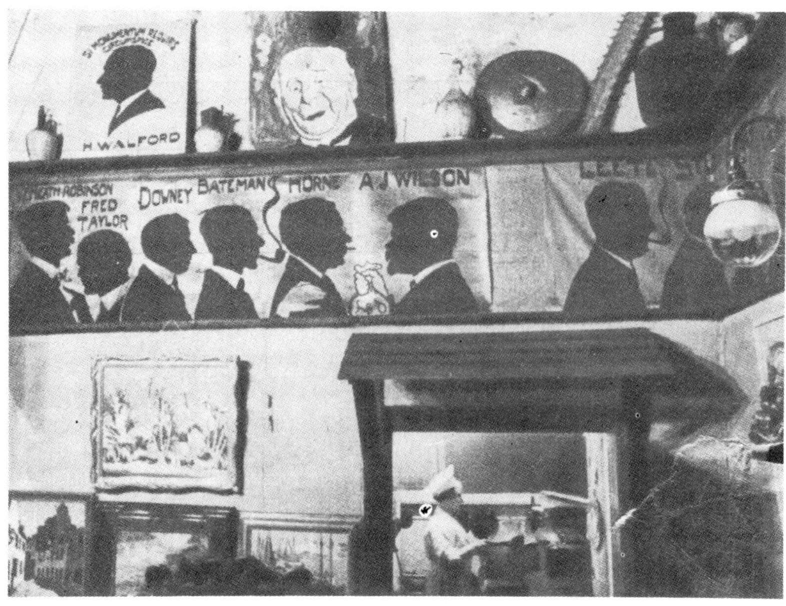

Mabel, the Club cook, coped with Friday evening dinners. She started cooking for Club members in 1933 and on men only nights was the only woman allowed in the Club.

Robinson and the Company was so delighted with the result that the entire Club was treated to a day out. The party was given First Class train tickets at Waterloo Station and entered a railcar stocked with adequate refreshments. At Southampton the railway carriage was detached and shunted to the docks where it stopped right next to the liner. The jovial Captain had obviously heard about Sketch Club humour: he greeted them with a "cod" cocktail (water and a cherry!)

Once introductions were over the party was escorted to a very large room, like a baronial hall, where unlimited bottles of champagne were uncorked; there was also a caviar buffet on hand. Then they were taken on a guided tour of the liner, which included the Captain's bridge and engine rooms. This was followed by lunch in the dining-room where the menu was written on palettes and placed on miniature easels in front of the guests. The party eventually left at 6 pm; the rail coach was waiting to take them back to London. Sadly the *Empress of Britain* was sunk by the Germans in the Second World War.

One member of this party was Arnold Beauvais. Beauvais, the son of Charles Henry Beauvais and Anne Corfield, was born in Catford in 1886. He started off in his father's studio, working on lithographic and poster design but in the evenings studied at the Bolt Court Art School in Fleet Street. In 1903 Beauvais went to Paris to further his studies, later joining his father in Marseilles, where he spent two years working in a commercial vein. His father died in 1911 and two years later Arnold returned to London "setting up his stall", as he put it, in a studio in Chancery Lane. These fruitful and financially rewarding years saw him working for Walt Disney productions, Danny Kaye films and the publishing house Collins. In the 'thirties he produced a set of caricatures of film stars for the magazine *Film Weekly* and a series of promotional advertisements entitled "Where's George?" for Lyons.

Beauvais (1886-1984) was also an operatic star, making his debut at the Old Vic, playing the part of Fernando in *Il Travatore*. This was followed by leading roles in *The Magic Flute, Rigoletto, Aida, Faust, Carmen* and *Don Giovanni*. This schizophrenic existence, working in the studio by day and singing by night, eventually took its toll and Beauvais was forced to decide between singing and art. His choice was made easier by his joining the London Sketch Club in 1929. To quote his own words: "I first visited the Club when my daughter Paula attended St Martins Art School and there met Mina the daughter of Fred Buchanan, and told her I was a singer at the Old Vic. Then Fred Buchanan invited me to the Club and, like Tommy Tucker, I sang for my supper." One of the most popular duets at this time was "There's a hole in my bucket, dear Liza, dear Liza", which Beauvais sang with Harry Riley. In later life Beauvais taught at the Bolt Court Art School, and devoted more and more of his time to painting and fine arts. He was President of the London Sketch Club in 1936 and, in contrast to someone like Buchanan noted for his heavy consumption of alcohol, Beauvais was a moderate man. He was even nicknamed "sobersides" by one or two of the more convivial members of the Club.

During the same year that Arnold Beauvais was President of the Club, a few members got together and decided to hold a public exhibition. The theme was "London and the Thames", the date 16 April 1936 and the place the Arlington Galleries. To publicise the show members produced posters and paraded through the streets with billboards like sandwichmen. The exhibition received a good review from the *Daily Telegraph*:

The London Sketch Club has had the happy idea of devoting its exhibition at the Arlington Gallery to London itself. It is a magnificent subject, yet painters are curiously shy of attempting it. By resolutely abandoning "beauty spots" on this occasion, the Club has given a useful lead in actuality.

The Thames, of course, receives most attention. L. Richmond paints St Paul's from Bankside with unforced fidelity, and achieves the harder tasks of making a delightful composition out of Hungerford Bridge. A. Beauvais' "The Pool" weaves tramp steamers, water and cloud in a glistening impression, while J. Hassall's "The Thaw, 1895" captures the river's darker mood. C. R. W. Nevinson shows a vivid glimpse of the rainswept Strand, but depends on the river for the final pattern of "Swim End Barkes". C. Bryant's "The Dome", well-conceived and triumphantly carried out, catches the majesty with which St Paul's rises over huddled roofs and chasmal streets. He too seeks the Thames for a glowing Waterloo Bridge.

After the river and the cathedral, the parks come next in popularity as a subject. G. W. Allinson's "Riding Lesson" is a quick and amusing vision, and G. Wilkinson's "The Talkies" is an impressive study of an orator and his audience. The opportunities afforded by the Changing of the Guard have been successfully grasped by G. Irwin and G. Nicholl, who also provided an indispensable "Eros".

Frank Taylor brings off a *tour-de-force* in his large, gaily-crowded watercolour of a Bank Holiday on the Heath. London taverns are represented in E. R. Parker's "Round at Tom's", and the town's natural history in L. R. Brightwell's "Cat in Clover" and "A London Sparrow". The exhibition is a synthesis of the City's pictorial appeal; it is a good painting, well seasoned with London relish.

Another report from the Daily Herald:

Sandwichmen made happy artists advertise in Bond Street — A happy sandwichman walked proudly along Bond Street yesterday with a board that flamed with colour. Members of the London Sketch Club are the sandwichmen's benefactors. They are holding a Jubilee show at the Arlington Galleries, Old Bond Street, and decided to advertise themselves by painting posters of London scenes. Most of the artists are Fleet Street men who earn their living as magazine and newspaper illustrators. Gilbert Wilkinson, whose drawings appear each week on the cover of Passing Show, has added a touch of humour to the exhibition with a picture of a butler out with a Pekingese. The exhibition remains open until 3 May.

In total the works numbered 84 and other artists not mentioned in the *Daily Telegraph* report were S. T. C. Weeks. Harry Riley, S. Van Abbe, H. Dixon, W. Barribal, Charles Robinson, George Ayling, Bertram Prance, M. C. Gaffron and Chas. W. Norton

The Times wrote rather unfairly:

With a wide interpretation of the "terms of reference" the present exhibition reflects the general objects of the Club "to encourage and facilitate spontaneous execution and to discipline the artist to look to the inspiration of the moment, rather than depend on the more laboriously thought out effort", and the majority of the pictures are distinguished by workmanlike "slickness" rather than by profound research.

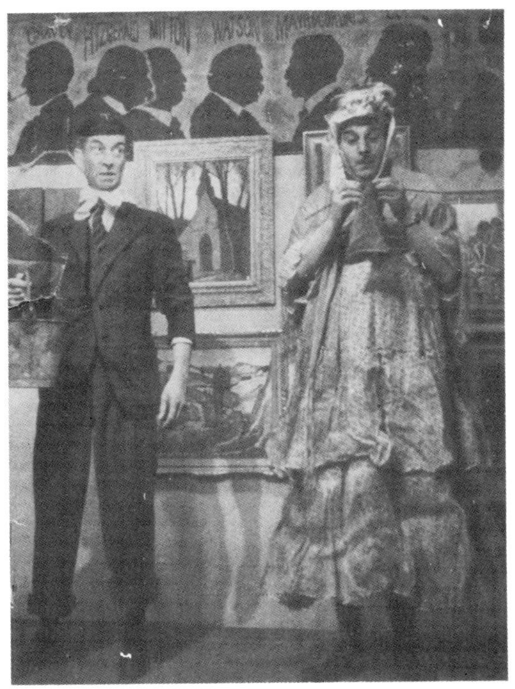

Entertainment after the meal included Arnold Beauvais (*left*) and Harry Riley (*right*) singing "Dear Liza and Dear George" . . .

. . . whilst members enjoyed the entertainment. The three in the foreground of this photo are Ellis Silas (recently returned from the South Sea Islands), Harry Hemsley (the music hall artist) and Alan Stainer (conjuror).

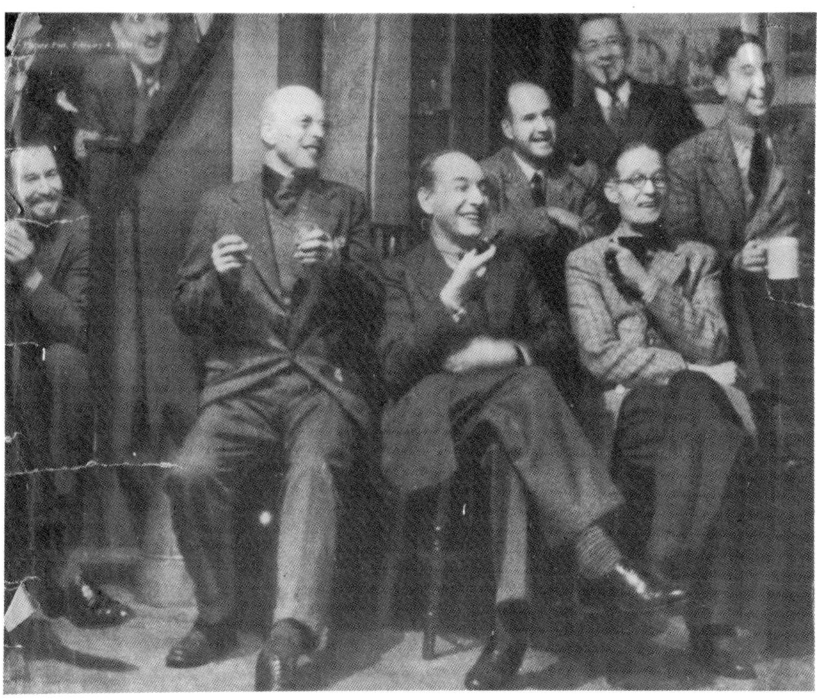

To continue, the *Daily Express* added:

> Before passing, note the very charming "Design for a London Stained Glass
> Window" by Mr George Parlby, and the vigorous "Bloke" by Mr Albert Toft.

The exhibition was a success and it showed that the Club was still as active as
ever, but it was difficult to disregard *The Times'* opinion that the one thing the
exhibition lacked were sketches. There were many polished paintings but few, if
any, spritely preparatory drawings, the one thing the Club had thrived upon in earlier
years. Had the Club continued with public exhibitions, it would be more widely
known nowadays. It did not repeat the '36 show, retreating instead to the confines
of the Club premises in Marylebone.

Other noticeable omissions from the 1936 exhibition had been the work of
Heath-Robinson, H. M. Bateman and Edmund Dulac. All three had achieved an
enormous following, yet the Club was relying on old-timers like Hassall, Nevinson
and Charles Bryant to see them through. Of the youngsters there were many talented
and enthusiastic members such as Stan Terry, Thomas Downey, William Wilton
and Norman Keene, but these artists, successful as they were, were not in the same
class as their predecessors. However, Heath-Robinson did come to the Club's aid
when his autobiography "My Line of Life" was published in 1938. He says of the
Sketch Club:

> Here you may meet the perennial George Parlby, the stained-glass window
> designer. I can remember George Parlby in the days of the Yorick Club, some
> forty years ago. He seemed no younger then, than he is today. I have known
> that true humorist and artist John Hassall, almost as long, yet he too does not
> grow old. It was at the London Sketch Club that I first met Reginald Arkell.
> He was not so well-known in those days. But those of us who had read that
> delightful fantasy called Columbine, and the verses with which it was
> published, knew that here was a real poet.

It was Reginald Arkell who, on the 40th Anniversary of the founding of the Club,
wrote a short history, but sadly I have never seen a copy of it. It was presented as an
illustrated souvenir to members at the London Sketch Club Fancy Dress Ball in
1938.

The 'thirties had begun with Ellis Silas as President of the Club in 1930-'31. Silas
(1883-1972) was the son of the Dutch flower painter Louis Silas and grandson of
Edouard Silas the composer. He studied first in his father's studio, designing
furnishing fabrics and interior decor, and then under W. R. Sickert, before deciding
to try his fortune in Australia. Unfortunately the First World War interrupted this
project but after the War he spent three years living Gauguin-style among the natives
of Papua, which he recalled in his book *A Primitive Arcadia*, published in 1926.
During this time he captured the innocence of native life in his illustrations and
remembered how the Papuan children would line up each morning to watch him
brush his teeth!

On his return to England he married Daphne, with Charles Robinson as his best
man, and settled down to married life, having promised his future spouse that his
"wanderlust" days were over. The couple bought a house designed by William
Morris at 84 Brook Green in London, where they were to spend the rest of their lives;
sadly, they had no children. After Silas's death, Daphne involved herself with the
London Sketch Club's social life, sometimes coming to Ladies' Nights and

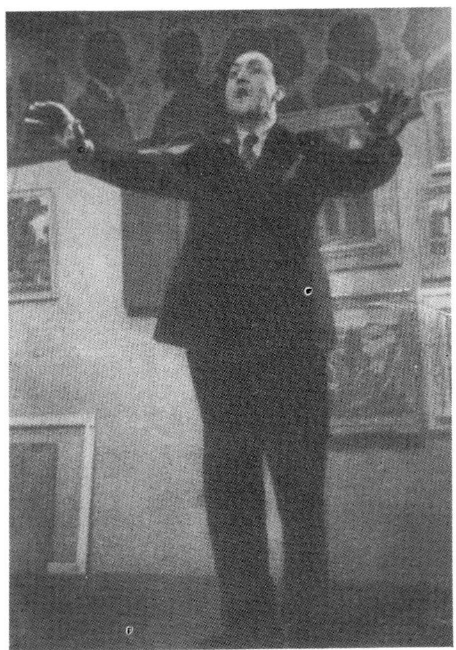

"O Solo Mio" performed by the tenor Giuseppe Ceci, who joined the Club in 1920.

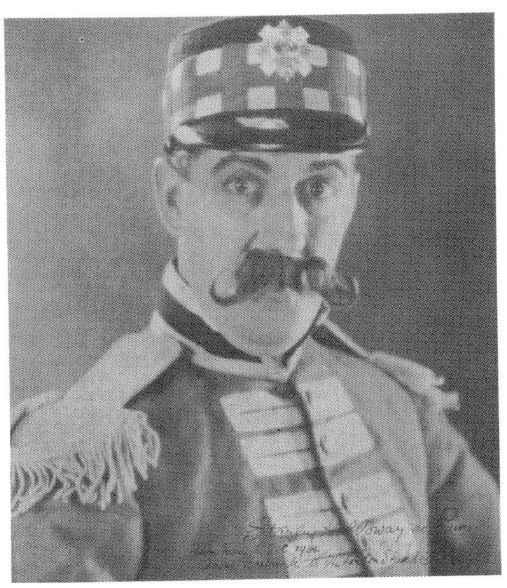

Stanley Holloway joined the London Sketch Club in 1934. This photo was taken from *The Co-optimists*.

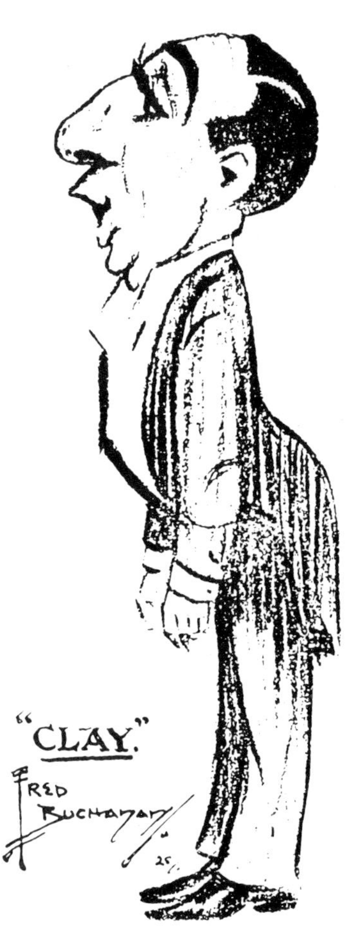

One of the most popular entertainers at this time was Clay Thomas. This caricature of him was drawn in 1925 by Fred Buchanan.

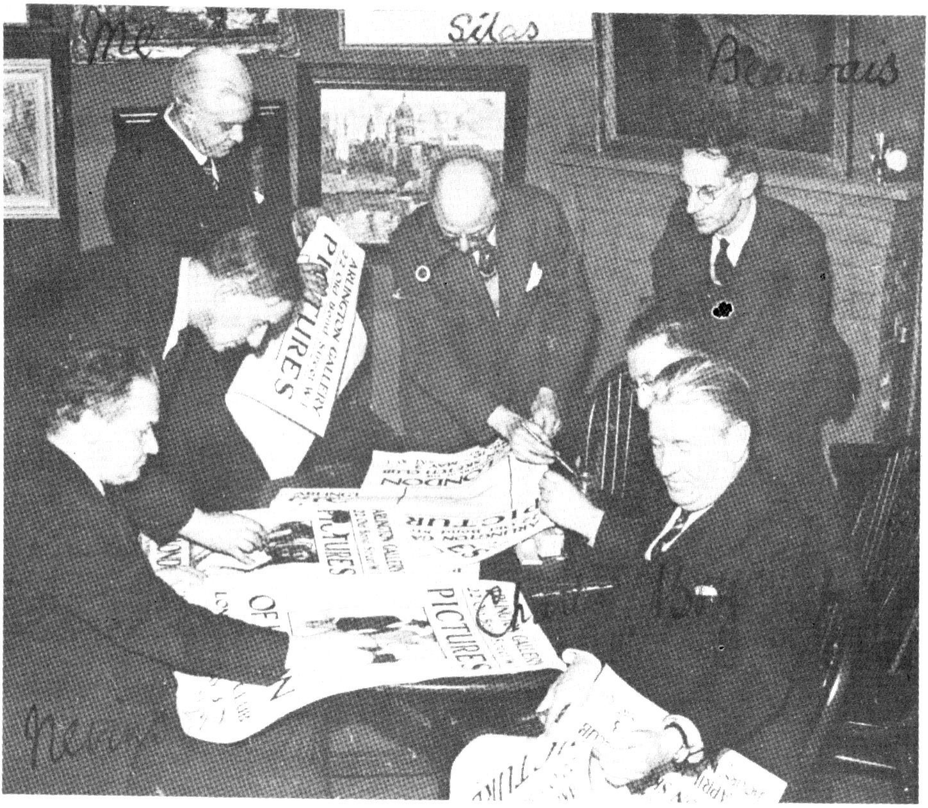

The 1936 Exhibition.
Pictured are, left to right, C. R. W. Nevinson, unknown, John Hassall, Ellis Silas, Arnold Beauvais, S. Van Abbé and Charles Bryant.

A year after the above photo was taken Charles Bryant died at the age of 54. Born in Australia, he was educated in Sydney, starting work as a bank clerk but studying art under W. Lister. He exhibited at the Royal Art Society before coming to England in 1908. He studied at John Hassall's art school and under Julius Olsson before his first picture was accepted at the RA in 1913. He was official artist to the Australian Imperial Forces on the Western Front in 1917 and in 1923 official artist to the Commonwealth Government when visiting New Guinea.

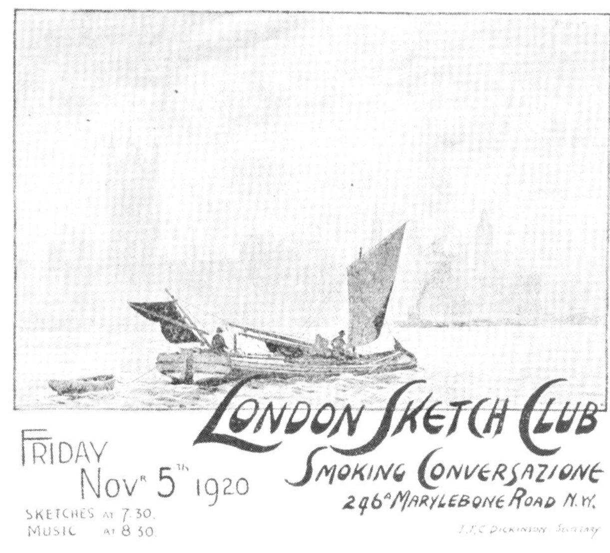

attending Club exhibitions. When I visited her for Sunday tea in 1975 she told me that her last visitor had been David Attenborough who wanted to look through Ellis Silas's notes in preparation for a possible television programme.

The highlight of Silas's career came shortly after his return from Papua when he staged an exhibition at a Bond Street gallery. It received a Royal Command: it was requested that the entire exhibition be sent to Buckingham Palace, after which Silas was given a private audience with His Majesty the King and Queen Mary. It was Ellis Silas who designed the sign which once hung in the Marylebone Club "The Sketchers Arms" (it was transferred to Dilke Street, Chelsea when the Club moved in 1957). There is also a small original water-colour hanging in the Horniman Museum in Forest Hill, South London of his time in Papua. Ellis Silas was a careful, sensitive man who often hid under a cloak of modesty. Just as he had begun the 'thirties as President of the Sketch Club it was Solomon Van Abbé who began the new decade (1940-41). In many ways both men had similar temperaments: they enjoyed the banter and camaraderie of the Sketch Club but took back seats as far as entertainment was concerned.

There was however one vital difference between the two. Silas was slim, fit and a bit short of hair whereas Van Abbé was grossly overweight and suffered from angina. For many years Van Abbé had belonged to the RE, a society that receives far too little press. The Royal Society of Painter-Etchers and Engravers was founded in 1880 under the presidency of Sir Francis Seymour-Haden. Over the years it has included a great many talented artists in its membership: Van Abbé was one of its most staunch supporters and his output was prolific. There was nothing whimsical or fanciful in Van Abbé's work. Everything he did was carefully calculated and well researched.

Van Abbé housed an immense collection of "reference" books which he kept "with considerable system". In his house in South London there were massive cupboards full of information on just about every subject available from love-making to rough-housing and costume to shipping. Van Abbé spent a good many evenings leafing through periodicals and books, excerpting promising items. Van Abbé's wife disapproved of her husband's Sketch Club circle. They were too boozy, too male or too much of a threat to her married life. It was not uncommon for members' wives to dislike the all-male preserve that their husbands wandered into so freely. Hassall suffered in the same way: Constance, his second wife, never came to terms with the fact that her husband enjoyed all-male company when he should have been at home. It was all right for the younger bachelor element of the Club such as Don Blake, Hindle and Cunningham, but for the middle aged group it could be awkward, especially if their wives were domineering.

Of course there were two Van Abbés, and both were members of the London Sketch Club. Solomon and his brother Joe, who died in 1954 by choking on a fishbone, were etcher illustrators. Solomon was the better known of the two — his nickname was "Jack" in the London Sketch Club but when it came to designing book covers he would often use the *nom de plume* J. Abbey. On the rare occasions that Edmund Blampied his agent thought he was getting too much work under that *nom de brosse*, he would sometimes use the name of C. Morse (after a distant cousin living in the USA).

It was in the late 'twenties or early 'thirties that Hassall had invited a well-known MP, who had just written a book on *The Black Shirts* to the Club. The MP who was full of himself (as most MPs are) proceeded to expound the advantages of his

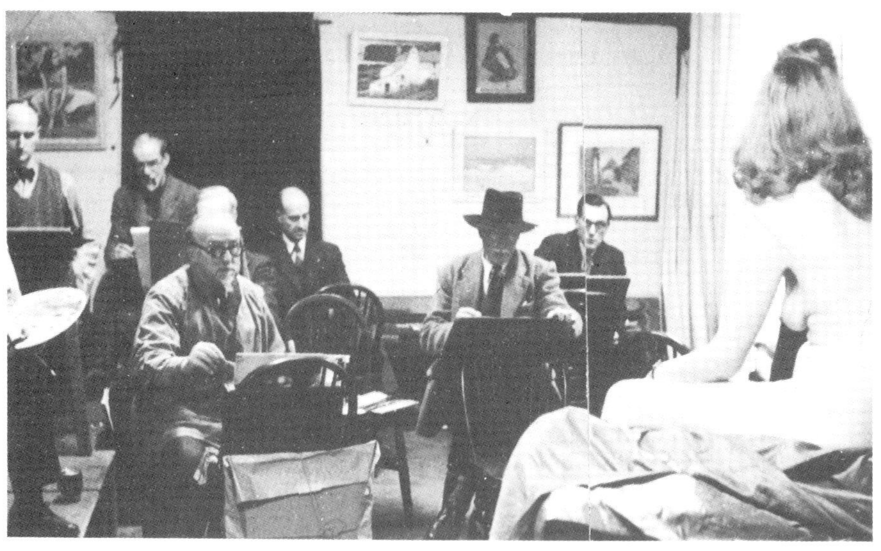

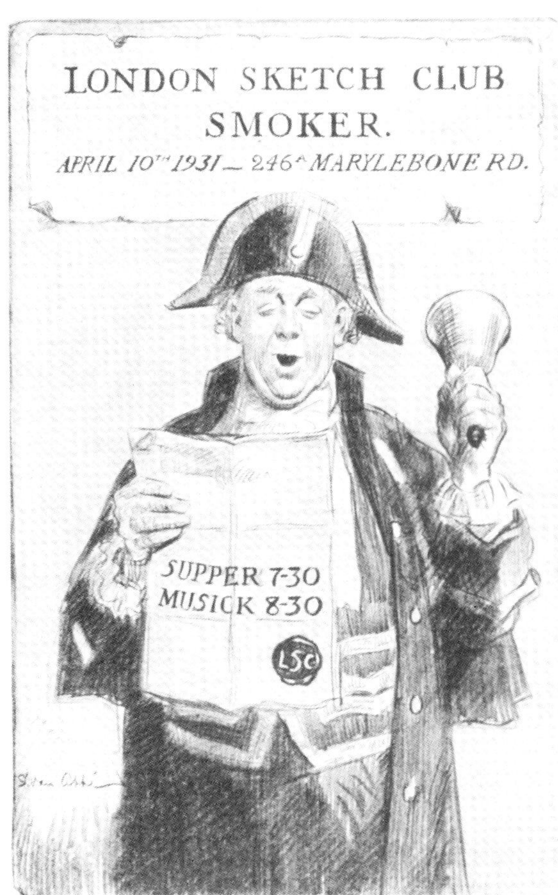

In the 'twenties and 'thirties, the London Sketch Club organised a life-class to run separately from their working evenings. In this photograph are, left to right, F. Donald Blake (President in 1944), Henry Collier (President in 1955), S. Van Abbé (President in 1940), Kenneth Brookes (President in 1952), Ellis Silas, with hat (President in 1930) and one other, sketching the model.

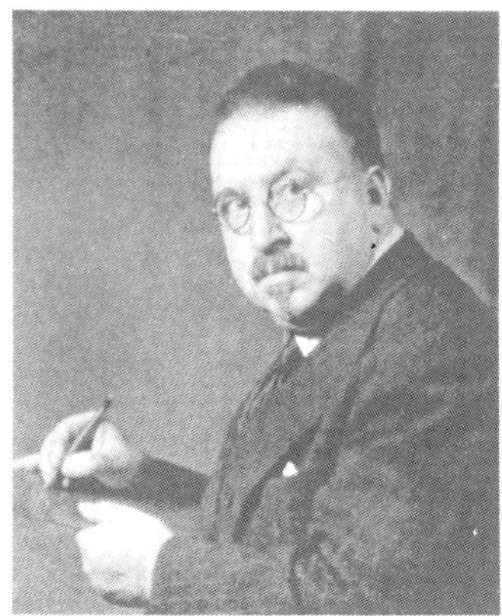

Van Abbé (1883-1949).

Invitation card by S. Van Abbé.

political views and his book. George Studdy, who was no politician, took exception to these views and, after containing himself for some considerable time, eventually burst out: "In this Club we never discuss politics or religion and as long as I can remember we don't care if a fellow chooses to wear a black, pink, green or yellow shirt — we don't talk politics." At that the MP shut up, but Studdy was "as white as a sheet" and the incident may have had some bearing on his resignation. For political views to be brought into a private Club was considered an invasion of privacy.

The Sketch Club had encouraged a great many talents from all over the world. Harry Rountree from New Zealand, Charles Bryant and H. M. Bateman from Australia, Edmund Dulac from France, David Ghilchik from Rumania, Bagdatopolous ("Bags") from Greece and Mavrogordato from Italy were but a few. That S. Van Abbé came from Holland was purely coincidental. Studdy wanted none of the National Front bully-boy tactics and he probably would have disapproved flatly of the Unions' stranglehold on Britain in the 'seventies with the thick-skinned arrogance that nearly brought the country to its knees.

Meanwhile entertainment in Marylebone in the 'thirties was excellent. There was an assortment of new up-and-coming talent — including a young Cyril Fletcher who appeared regularly between 1936 and 1940. Another rising star was the actor Stanley Holloway, who joined the Club in 1935. Holloway had already established his reputation in *The Co-optimists* (circa 1921) but was to achieve an even bigger reputation in later films such as *The Lavender Hill Mob* and *My Fair Lady*. Holloway regularly entertained Friday night (Smoker night) audiences with his monologues. Who can forget "Sam, Pick oop tha' Musket" or "Albert and the Lion", chiefly written by Marriott Edgar (brother of Edgar Wallace) and in book form illustrated by John Hassall? These monologues were to last for half a century and are still repeated to this day.

Stanley Augustus Holloway, born 1 October 1890 in Manor Park, East London was a one-off in the world of entertainment: part monologist, part singer and part actor, he could play the piano as well. He was one of that special down-to-earth type of character that "got lucky". From his early beginnings, admiring the great names of his generation such as Jack Buchanan and George Robey, Stanley Holloway was content with a quiet retirement in East Preston in Sussex. Sadly in the latter part of his life he was taken up with visits to the chiropodist, dentist and eye specialist which must have been an awful nuisance to him, as parts of his once active physique failed him bit by bit. He published his autobiography *Wiv a Little Bit o'Luck* in 1967 (Leslie Frewin publishers).

One of the Club's female entertainers was Harry Dixon's wife Mabel Mann, a most promising contralto after Clara Butt. Mabel Mann was a high spirited and handsome woman who had a keen eye "for the fellers". Her renditions at Ladies' evenings were much appreciated. G. Ceci had a throaty Italian tenor voice but was always pleasantness personified; Beauvais, on the other hand, had a thin, typically English oratorio voice but never compared to that other constant attender Parry Jones. Then there was Walter Widdop, who always looked as if he was going to burst a blood vessel when he took a top note, and another old faithful was Peter Dawson, an Australian who probably spent more time in the Savage than he did in the London Sketch Club.

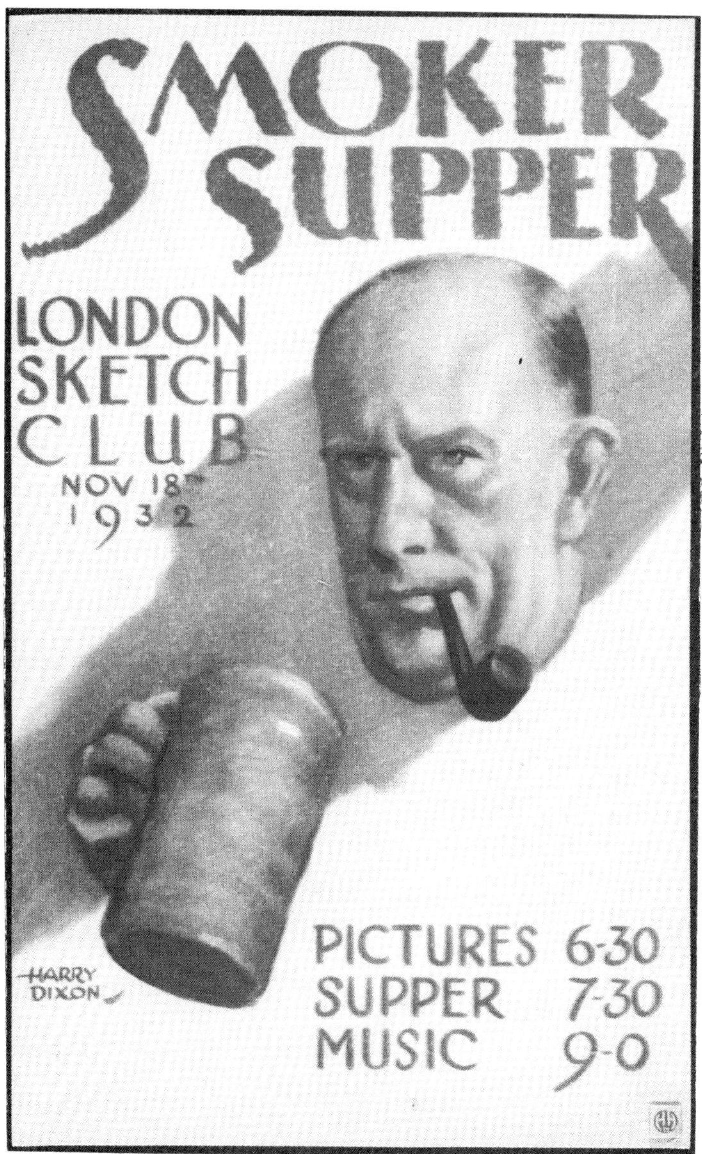

Sydney Thomas Charles Weeks (1878-1949) studied at Heatherleys and started his career as a cartoonist in *The Encore*, a music-hall paper. Then he worked for the Avenue Press, where he designed many posters, including some memorable examples for the London Underground. His first Zoo poster, which appeared in 1913, was regarded as a landmark in poster design. In 1918 he was engaged by the Ministry of Labour to produce posters for their campaign to get people back into the right jobs after serving in the Naval Air Service. In addition to the London Sketch Club, Weeks was also a member of the Savage and the Highgate Artists Society (serving as their Hon Sec). He was awarded the Freedom of Islington for his services to local history, and examples of his work can be seen in Islington Public Library. This portrait of Weeks is by Harry Dixon (1861-1942), who should not be confused with George Dixon.

CHAPTER 10

War Again and the Post-War Years

In the middle of September 1940 the German Luftwaffe started its "Blitzkrieg" against London. Casualties included Langham Chambers: the Langham Sketch Club lost not only its vast collection of costumes, books and memorabilia but also its home. The London Sketch Club quickly came to its aid, offering temporary accommodation — and continues to do so more than fifty years later, although the Langham Sketch Club is a shadow of its former self, with just 34 members in 1979.

Its heyday was in the 1850s when membership was two hundred plus. Number 1, Langham Chambers, All Souls Place (near Broadcasting House) was built for the use of members like Charles Keene and that wonderful Victorian illustrator Fred Barnard.

The RI was also bombed twice and nearly demolished. Another casualty suffering severe damage, was the Savage Club which was hit by two incendiary bombs. The first brought all the windows of the upstairs lounge splintering through the curtains; the second sent a taximan spinning through the double doors downstairs. He was found in the front hall "walking round and round in a small circle like a chicken that had been hit on the head!" Other London clubs affected by the Blitz included the Union Club, Carlton Club and The Reform, but fortunately the London Sketch Club escaped.

Cartoonists from the London Sketch Club who had been predicting this catastrophe included Strube, Gilbert Wilkinson and David Ghilchik. David Ghilchik's humour was so cutting that he was placed on Hitler's black list, joining the likes of David Low and Illingworth. Ghilchik (1892-1974), a Rumanian by birth, was brought to England at the age of five and became a nationalised British subject. He studied at Manchester School of Art, along with Bert Wilson and Henry Coller, under Valette. He continued his studies at the Slade before winning a travel scholarship to Florence and Venice. In those early days Ghilchik contributed illustrations to *Passing Show* and *London Opinion* before his cartoons were accepted by *Punch*. During the First World War Ghilchik volunteered for active service but was only accepted after the authorities had tried unsuccessfully to persuade him to join a Rumanian contingent. He was one of the cornerstones of *Punch* in the inter-war years and joined that band including Bertram Prance, Bert Thomas, Frank Reynolds and H. M. Bateman who did so much sterling work.

Although the public were well aware of David Ghilchik the cartoonist, few people realised he was also a highly competent fine artist who was elected to the ROI. There is a painting of his entitled "Out of the Ruins" in the Guildhall Art

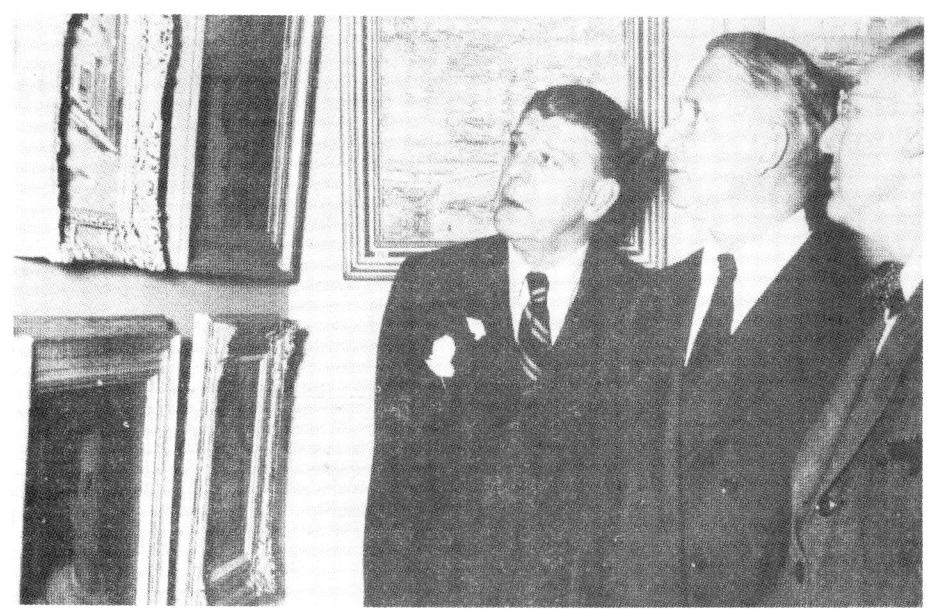

Art critics Harry Riley, RI, Lord Tedder and Edward Bishop, RBA.

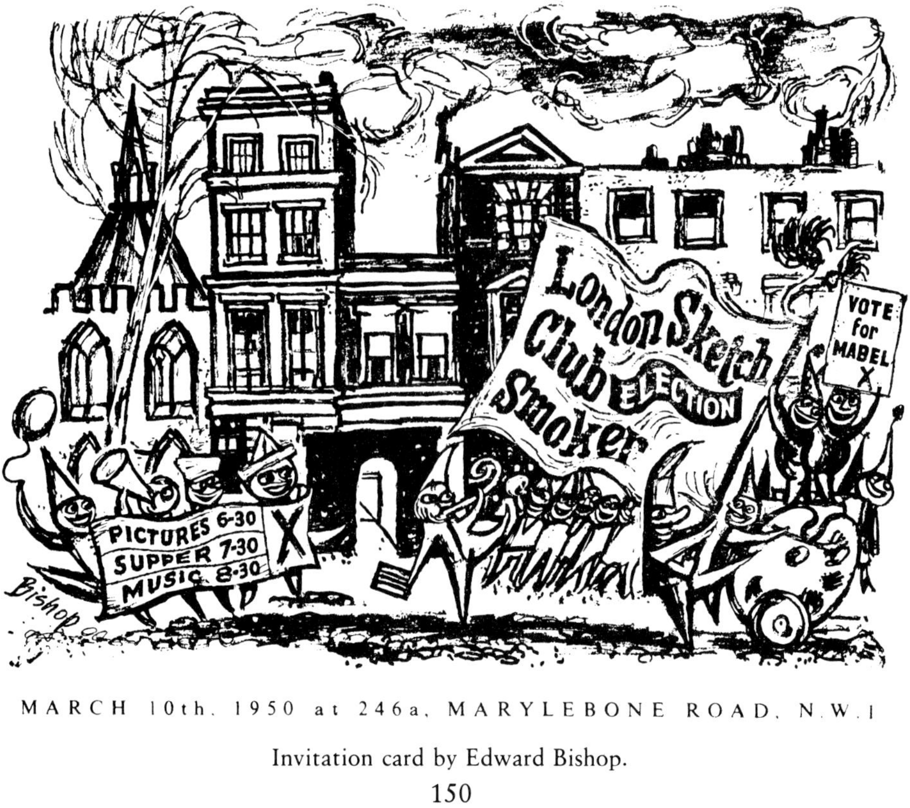

MARCH 10th. 1950 at 246a, MARYLEBONE ROAD. N.W.1

Invitation card by Edward Bishop.

150

Library, which depicts the bomb-shattered waste of the Cripplegate area during the Second World War. A fine portrait of George Parlby, looking like a distinguished old relic from the Victorian age, by David Ghilchik hangs in the London Sketch Club. His proudest achievement, however, was a portrait of the Duke of Windsor commissioned by the South Wales Borderers after his abdication. This had to be completed from reference books and photos without any sittings. The result was splendid and when last heard of could be found in Lydd in Kent. Most of Ghilchik's other paintings depicted the Thames and the London scene in general. He had joined the London Sketch Club back in 1920 and was a stalwart member until his death in 1974. Ghilchik firmly believed in the life class as a worthwhile venture. After his death Veronica Attfield, his long-time companion, continued to rent the LSC for use by the Ghilchik Life Class which operated on a different night to the London Sketch Club's own Life Class of Tuesday nights.

If David Ghilchick was a member of the ROI, Edward Bishop was a member of the RBA. Bishop was born in Islington in 1902. At the age of fourteen he was forced to leave school to earn a living and became a messenger boy for Stoll Theatres. Whilst working there he was introduced to classical music and saw the Diaghilev ballets at the Colosseum Theatre. This transformed his life: he was mesmerized by the great dancers at that time such as Njinsky, Lopokova, Karsavina and Nemchinova. Bishop, however, had a yearning to become an artist and after spending a year (part-time) at the Central School of Art, he won a scholarship to the Central. During this time he trained under A. S. Hartrick and Noel Rooke. When he left the Central he returned to Stoll Theatres where he designed posters and other publicity material for them under the legendary Leo Dowd, the hunchback designer and brother of J. S. Dowd. In 1929 there was an open competition for an advertising campaign which Bishop won: as a result he was offered a position with Lintas, the advertising agency of Unilever. He became its Art Director and his designs were shown worldwide.

In 1939 he was unfit for active service, having had rheumatic fever as a child, so he worked for the Ministry of Information. He designed propaganda material directed mainly at Japan, but also to encourage the Americans to enter the War. His mother, brother and one sister were killed in the blitz when their house was bombed during an air raid. His own flat in Fetter Lane was also completely destroyed by a bomb whilst he was away one weekend. But his worst experience came when he dived into an air raid shelter near Holborn for cover. The shelter received a direct hit and Edward Bishop was buried alive. He escaped by clambering up a disused lift shaft and was finally rescued, one of only five out of 150 people to survive. The incident left him partially paralysed and very ill, but he convalesced slowly, helped greatly by friends from the Chelsea Arts Club and the London Sketch Club.

From 1941 onwards Edward Bishop exhibited regularly at the Royal Academy and permanent works can now be found in the Nottingham Castle Museum and Sydney Art Gallery in Australia. His paintings, particularly his night paintings of London, show the influence of Vuillard and Bonnard. Bishop was a keen amateur photographer in the 'thirties. He was also a member of the New English Art Club for many years and in 1978 won first prize in the "Spirit of London" exhibition at the Festival Hall. In 1991 he was given just a month to live due to throat cancer but, as his wife Celeste Radloff (a naïve painter whom he married in 1956) said: "That's Edward Bishop!"

Probably the most unlikely member of the London Sketch Club from those war years was Sir Arthur William Tedder (1890-1967) who was knighted in 1942. As Air Officer Commander-in-Chief Middle East from 1941 to 1943 and Air Commander-in-Chief, Mediterranean, 1943 he became the first British airman to hold such an important post when he was appointed Deputy Supreme Commander under General Eisenhower for the Anglo-American Expeditionary Force. Tedder always referred to the London Sketch Club as his "Peter Pan Club". Neither did he shirk his duties, often rolling up his sleeves to help with the washing up after smoker nights. In 1949 Lord Tedder (as he was then) relinquished his position as Chief of Airstaff at his own request in order to facilitate the advancement of younger officers.

Another casualty of those war years was John Hassall's house at 88 Kensington Park Gardens. When a bomb fell on the house next door and demolished it this left 88 unsafe and the Hassalls were forced to evacuate. The bomb had dropped through the neighbours' roof, fallen through the bedrooms and exploded in the drawing-room. John Hassall, who had been asleep upstairs, dashed down his wrecked staircase to see if his wife Constance was all right. Fortunately she had protected herself by crawling underneath the dining-room table and could not help laughing when she saw her husband tumbling down the stairs, pushing his feet through fallen picture frames. She said later, "Mercifully he had slept with his boots on."

John Hassall's eldest son, Ian (1899-1970), who had served with the London Scottish Regiment during the First World War, joined the Navy, but if he had been too young in the First World War he was over age in the Second. Undeterred, he had joined as an ordinary seaman, but retired in 1945 a Lieutenant Commander. Ian Hassall had to suffer the indignity of being portrayed in silhouette on the London Sketch Club walls as a baby, complete with dummy, throughout his life. He had been elected to the Sketch Club on the day of his birth and at the age of two had exhibited a work entitled "Carnk", alongside the likes of Lee Hankey, Sir James Linton, C. Q. M. Orchardson, Hugh Thomson and Terrick Williams. In 1949, after his father's death, Ian Hassall emigrated to Australia where he set up Australia's first open air art gallery at Eltham, near Melbourne. Many artists followed him and Eltham became something of an artists' colony. When he died in 1970 the writer of his obituary commented, "He was like Health coming into the room", with many people from all walks of life attending his funeral.

The London Sketch Club remained open during the Second World War, just as it had during the First. It provided welcome relief for those on active service who came home on leave. However the Club building was leased and the lease needed renewing every five years or so. Fortunately honesty prevailed in those days and huge rental increases were not imminent, as this letter from John Hassall to George Dixon (then Secretary of the Sketch Club) demonstrates:

23 June 1942

Thank you for your topping letter. I hope you'll never have to put your proficiency to the test in the fire fighting line. [George Scholefield Dixon was 52 years old at this time.] It's a jolly good thing to know that you and thousands of other men and women have undertaken the job so wholehearted-ly ... I'm also glad to hear there's five years more of the lease of the Sketch Club, from many points of view. The last time I saw the proposed situation for us to move to in Portland Road, there was a big crowd standing looking at it, and tho' I didn't go down the bit of lane it looked as if it had been bombed — But if 246A had got an extension we'll have more time and more hands to

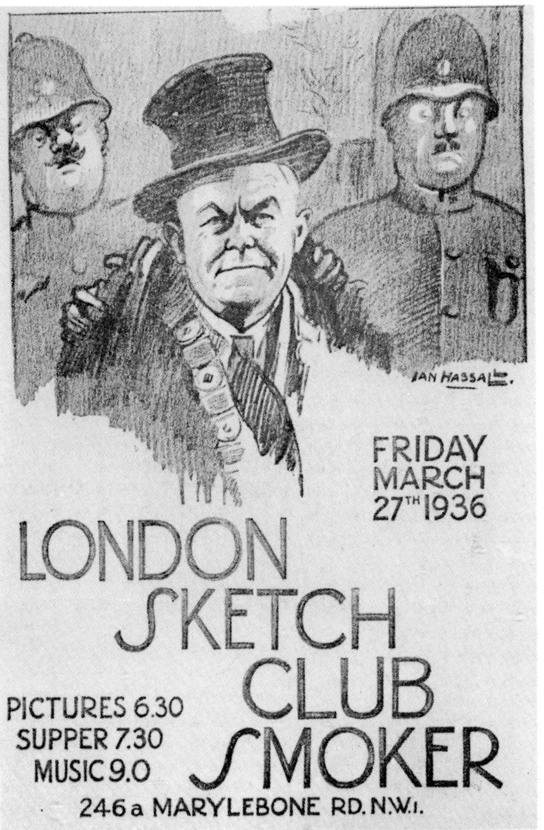

Invitation card by Ian Hassall: a caricature of Fred Buchanan wedged in between two policemen (John Hassall's favourite costume).

(*Below*) Card by Charles E. Pierce, RI (1908-1979). He was born in Edinburgh and educated at George Heriot's School and Edinburgh College of Art. He was Honorary Secretary of the London Sketch Club from 1951 to 1964 and was instrumental in the move from Marylebone to Dilke Street.

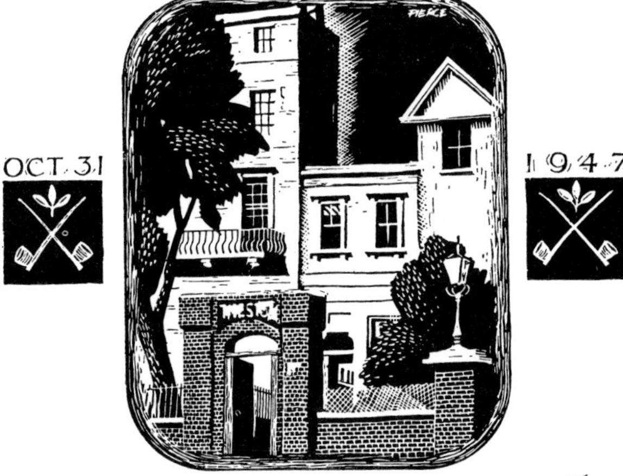

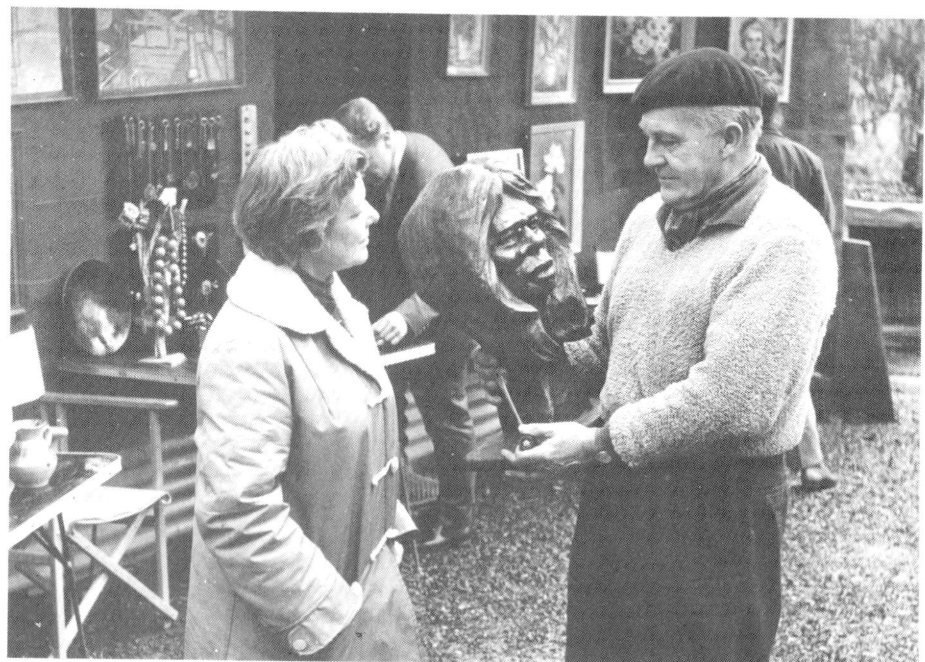

"A true Bohemian all his life", Ian Hassall emigrated to Australia in 1949 and founded the first Australian open air art gallery (many were later to follow). Examples of Hassall's work can be seen in Canberra, and many are in private Australian collections. During his time there he produced mainly landscapes, including some vigorous bush scenes. In the above photograph Ian Hassall is holding an aboriginal head which he carved from wood whilst Joan Hassall is looking on. The picture below shows the open air art gallery.

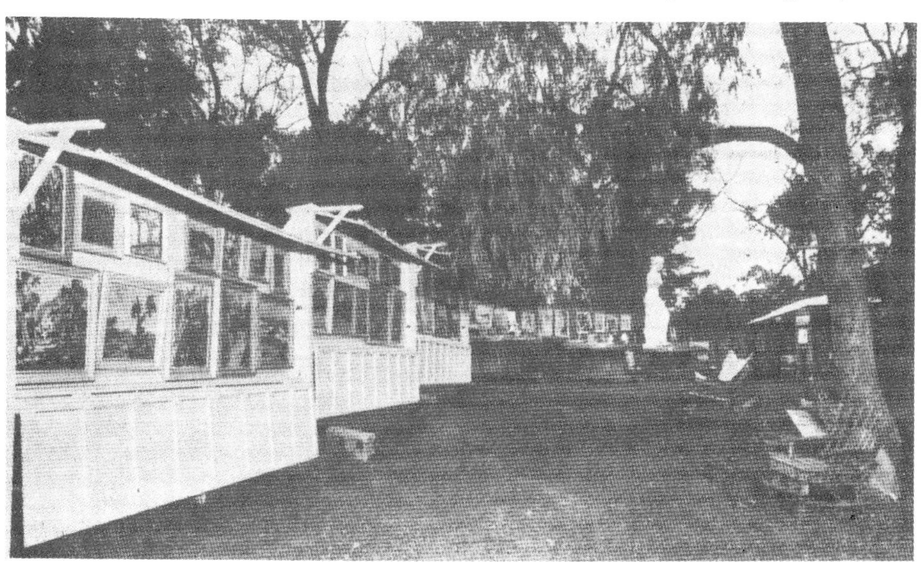

work out the scheme. Besides, in five years everybody will be in a better mood for it. No one can get enthusiastic when work is so scarce and for moving one wants some easily spared time. So if we get five years more it will give us breathing time. And let's hope people won't be messing around in uniforms. I'll let you know when we come back to Town, quite soon I think. All the best ever yours.

John Hassall

The letter was written from an address in Didcot to which the Hassalls had been evacuated. What Hassall does indicate is that even during the War it was possible that the Club might have to move. In fact this did not happen until 1957. Had the Club continued leasing its premises the rent increases of subsequent years would have killed it off completely: there were no vast financial reserves hidden away. In those post-war years the Chelsea Arts Club also faced the dilemma of whether to purchase their own freehold or continue renting. They chose the latter. That decision nearly sunk the Chelsea Arts Club in the 'seventies but the post-war committee had no crystal ball! In this, as in the blitz, the London Sketch Club was fortunate.

A frequent wartime visitor to the Sketch Club, although not a member, was David Langdon, a self-taught cartoonist who first contributed to *Punch* in 1937. During the war he joined the RAF as an AC2 and left the service a squadron leader, having edited the *Royal Air Force Journal* from 1945 to '46. His posters of "Billy Brown of London Town", produced for the London Passenger Transport Board, aimed to help travellers during the blitz. Other London Sketch Club members were doing their bit for the War Effort. Bert Thomas did a series of posters: "Is your journey really necessary?" and "Don't help Hitler by travelling this summer" (the latter was withdrawn in 1944). H. M. Bateman worked for the Ministry of Information and produced a series of propaganda posters entitled "Save Fuel to Make Munitions for Battle" (captioned "The wife who squandered the electricity!"). Arthur Ferrier delighted the troops with his piquant pin-ups in *Blighty*, *Men Only* and *Tit-Bits*.

Arthur Ferrier, whom I have failed to mention yet, achieved the reputation of foremost British magazine illustrator in the 'twenties and 'thirties. Born in Glasgow in 1891 this determined Scot had suffered the same fate as many of his contemporaries: for the first four years of his working life he studied as an analytical chemist at Glasgow Technical College. But his yearning to become an artist took up every spare minute of his time, until the Glasgow *Daily Record* finally employed him as a cartoonist. Ferrier and two colleagues worked in the studio once occupied by Sir John Lavery a quarter of a century previously. In 1919 Ferrier left Glasgow to settle in London and a year later joined the Sketch Club. Although he drew for the *Sunday Pictorial* and *News of the World*, Ferrier was to make his mark in magazines, illustrating most of Britain's popular novelists in the inter-war years.

"Ferrier, like George Whitelaw and Graham Simmonds, completed his early training at D. C. Thomson in Dundee", according to Bert Wilson, yet Ferrier never mentions this. What Ferrier did admit to was being influenced in his youth by the Americans Charles Dana Gibson and Flagg.

Ferrier invented an ideal pin-up, dressed in lace knickers, suspender belt and the rest, for the troops. She gave them something to look forward to back home. Norman Pett followed a similar formula when he created Jane for the *Daily Mirror*.

She first graced their pages back in 1932 in "The Diary of a Bright Young Thing", then achieved a vast following in the 1939-45 years. Jane was the original blonde bimbo, all bosom and no brain, which may account for her enormous popularity.

While these talented draughtsmen were inventing their fantasies a very real Ley Kenyon was having a difficult time of it in Germany. Kenyon, who did not join the Sketch Club until 1972, was a dashing young Flight Lieutenant in 1943. His aircraft was shot down over Belgium, where he was harboured by MI9, an escape organisation operated by the late Airey Neave. He was given civilian clothes and passed as 'a parcel' along the established escape route. Unfortunately he was arrested by the Gestapo near the Spanish frontier and imprisoned at Bayonne before being transferred to Fresnes in Paris. He quite expected to be shot as a spy but when his service record became known he was accepted as a PoW and landed up in Stalag Luft III, scene of the Great Escape of 1944.

Although Kenyon did not himself escape — his name went on the list too late — he designed the escapees' forged documents, and helped build the all important air pump for the tunnel, constructing it from Red Cross parcel cocoa tins and pieces of cloth from uniforms. He also made sketches of the tunnel under construction (these sketches were used for Paul Brickhill's book after the war). Ley Kenyon also sketched other aspects of camp life, in particular theatrical activities featuring his friend Rupert Davies who later achieved fame as Maigret on television. Kenyon managed to record in Stalag Luft III what Ronald Searle recorded on the Burma Railway — a different way of life — and without the camera.

Bennet Ley Kenyon was born in 1913, the son of an undertaker, and grew up in Kenyon's Kensington Funeral Parlour, sketching from an early age. He would often wander around the stable yard sketching the open silk-lined coffins and their occupants (no problem about keeping the models still!). He was educated at Marylebone Grammar School and studied at the Central School of Art and in Paris before joining the RAF in 1940. In 1941 he remustered as an air gunner on Halifax bombers and was commissioned. By 1943 he had been awarded the DFC for his cool direction of evasive tactics which so often assured the safety of aircraft and crew. He flew 45 missions before being shot down.

After the war Kenyon worked briefly as a book illustrator and freelance artist but it was his association with Jacques Cousteau which directed much of his life. He was approached by the Frenchman to represent him in Britain. As a result, Kenyon took a crash course in aqualung diving and became entranced by underwater photography. In 1960 he was summoned to Buckingham Palace to instruct the Duke of Edinburgh in diving and six years later was asked by the Science Museum to mount its first exhibition of deep-sea diving equipment. In the 'seventies he entertained the London Sketch Club with a series of underwater films from all parts of the globe, some of which had been made with Jacques Cousteau. They made a refreshing change from the Sketch Club's otherwise predictable format.

Two London Sketch Club members who endured the treacherous Burma Railway were Fergus Anckorn and Cliff Swann. Neither talked freely about his experiences, though Anckorn once described how both his hands were smashed by the rifle butts of his Japanese guards. Usually Anckorn made light of his ordeal, as in a small anecdote reported in *The Sketch Pad*:

> In one of the prisoner of war camps in which I found myself during the last war, we made sun-dials to tell the time and placed them at the entrance of our

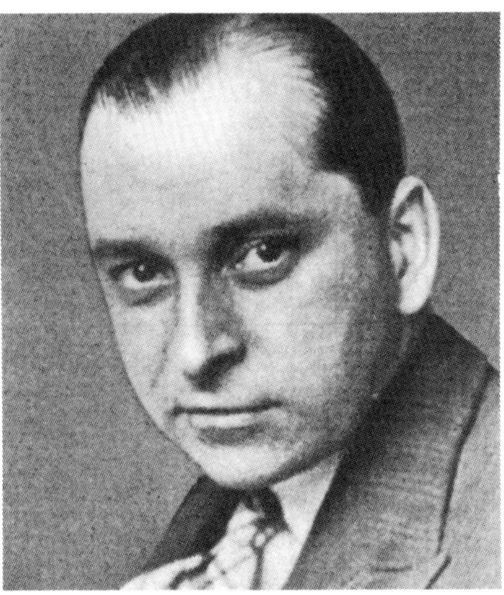

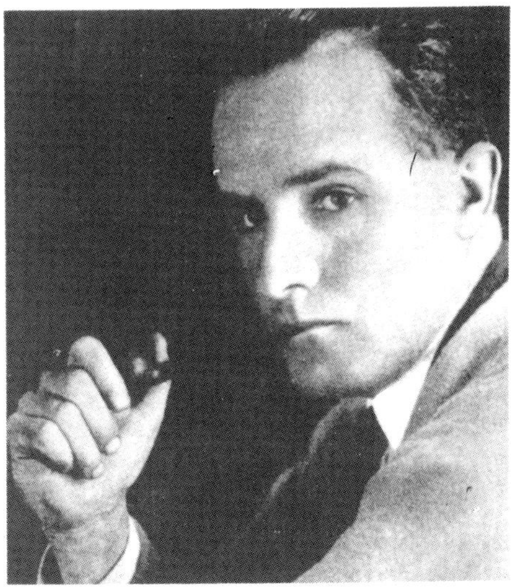

Because of his pin-up girls, the public often imagined Arthur Ferrier to be surrounded by a bevy of beauties. Nothing could have been further from the truth. He would work surrounded by an alsation, a terrier and a marmoset, with the radio for company.

With Bert Thomas and Phil May, Gilbert Wilkinson ranks as one of the century's finest black-and-white artists. As he grew older the brilliance of his early vigorous line left him, but his cartoons still retained a keen sense of humour.

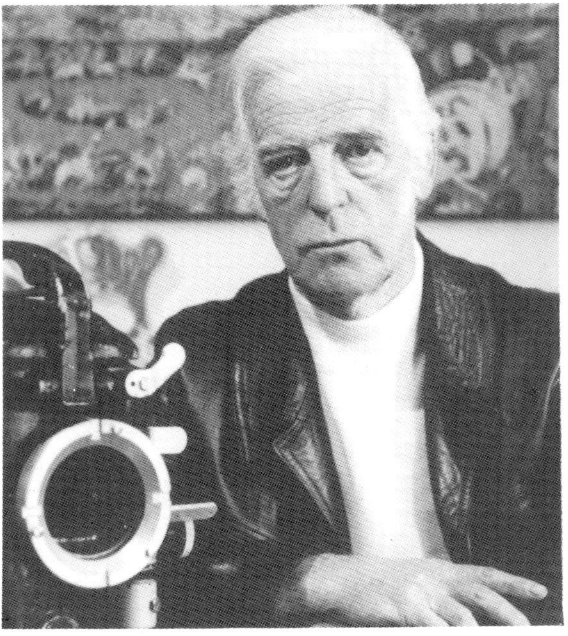

Ley Kenyon, DFC (1913-1990), who died in New Mexico, was probably much better known for his interest in underwater diving than he was as an artist. His publications included the *Pocket Guide to the Undersea World* (1956) and later *Aqualung Diving* (1970), and I also seem to remember a set of tea cards (similar to those old cigarette cards) featuring his underwater scenes. In 1984 Kenyon was invited to act as Art Director for Operation Raleigh which helped young people develop self-confidence and leadership skills. He rarely went anywhere without his sketch book. During the last War he buried his sketches of Stalag III and returned later to retrieve them from the occupied Russian Zone.

At Ley Kenyon's memorial service in Chelsea Old Church, the London Sketch Club was represented by John Seabrook, John Brass, Dennis Gilbert, Maurice Armytage and Peter Sanderson.

huts. Some of these dials consisted of a stick for the gnomon which threw its shadow along the ground on to areas that we had graduated into the hours of the day, others were of the more conventional sun-dial type. Our guards were amazed at the mysterious way we could tell the time from these dials. They tested us from time to time and tried to conceal their amazement when they found that we really could! Of course they would never admit that they did not know the principle involved. Instead they consulted the "time sticks" in a knowledgeable way and hoped that everybody was convinced that they knew how to use them. Eventually the news spread to the "Jap" camp office and the sundials were inspected. Then they ordered us to put them all round the camp at strategic places. They also made us put little atap roofs over them to protect them from the weather! Finally we had to put one up on the wall inside the camp office. After that, if you asked them the time in the office, they would casually glance up at the sun-dial and tell you their idea of the time. Even at night, camp guards could be seen consulting the dials in the darkness with the aid of a hurricane lamp!

Another London Sketch Club member who served in both World Wars was A. Cecil Wade, the calligrapher. Like Ian Hassall, Cecil Wade was too old for active service but still enlisted. James Green, a gallery owner of Forest Hill, served under Colonel Wade and remembered "his meticulous, highly disciplined yet fair attitude". Cecil Wade had trained at the Sunderland School of Art and King Edward School of Art, Newcastle-on-Tyne before coming down to London. He worked mostly as a commercial artist until his retirement in 1972, during which time he lived at 31 River Way, Ewell in Surrey. On his retirement he moved back to Tyne and Wear and took up residence in Gateshead. In 1976 he had a small one-man exhibition at the Gateshead Art Centre. It was Cecil Wade who said, in a letter dated 1976:

> I look upon the London Sketch Club now, as Bransby Williams put it, as "pictures in the fire": past scenes of painting with grand fellows like John Hassall, Sydney Weeks, Edgar Norfield, Norman Lloyd, Irwin Atkinson, Charles Robinson, Charles Bryant, Harry Riley and many others of equal stature. All happy memories and quite impossible to put into writing ...

A. Cecil Wade had contributed a number of articles on the art of lettering to the *Artist* magazine in the 'thirties. It was thanks to his lettering that the front cover of the London Sketch Club membership book looked so smart. During his lifetime he designed thousands of book covers in his effective minimalist style which used the sparsist amount of affectation. A few examples were listed in his *Modern Lettering and Lay-out*, published by Pitmans in 1950. They show the technical precision of a craftsman.

Two deaths to affect the Sketch Club during the war were those of George Parlby and W. Heath Robinson, both in 1944. The pair left a gap which no-one else could fill. Parlby especially had given so much time and effort to the Club. Some of his rituals had bordered on the Masonic. Nevertheless the Club kept going. Presidents during those War years were S. Van Abbé, Norman Lloyd, David Ghilchik, Fred Gardner and F. Donald Blake, RI. Norman Lloyd, ROI was another Australian, born in 1895 in Hamilton. He studied at the Sydney School of Art and on the Continent before settling in England. He was elected to the ROI in 1935 and in the

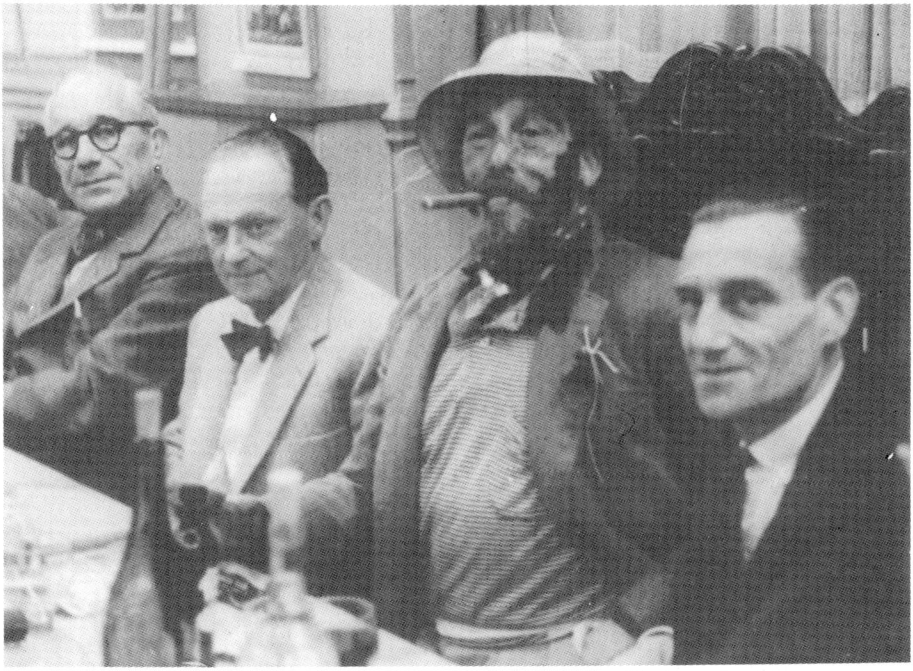

Leslie Sarony, seen here with the bow tie, on the Chairman's right.

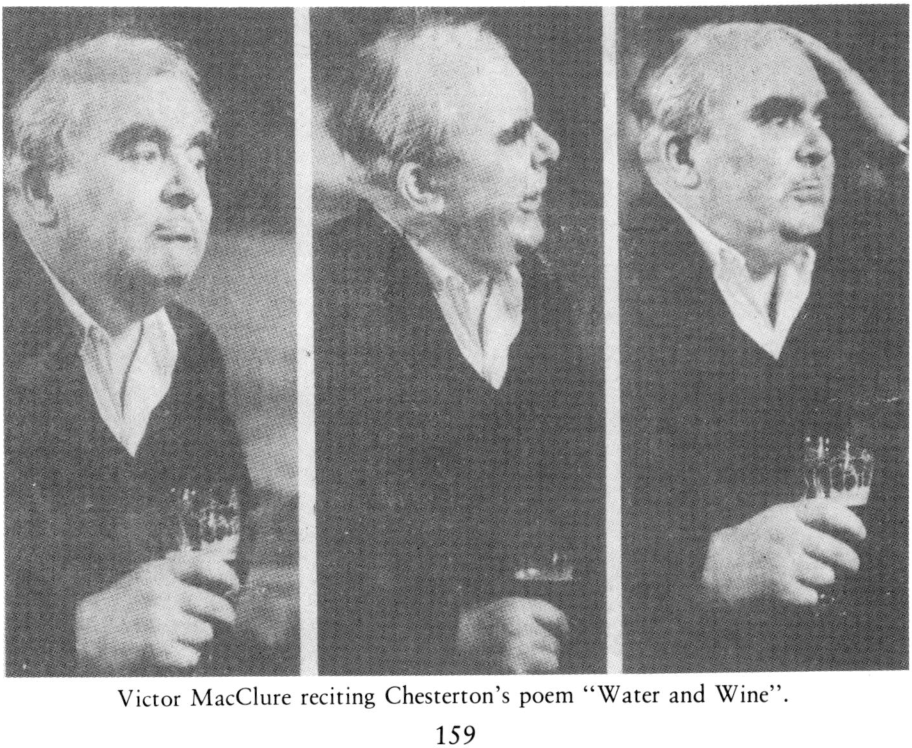

Victor MacClure reciting Chesterton's poem "Water and Wine".

'sixties retired to France, letting his membership of the London Sketch Club lapse. He rekindled his association with the Club in 1984 shortly before his death.

Despite all the difficulties on the Home Front during the war, British morale ended on a high note. The damage Bomber Harris inflicted on Germany far outweighed casualties sustained in England. After Germany finally surrendered on 7 May 1945 Winston Churchill broadcast the news and sent Air Chief Marshal Tedder with Tassigny from France and Zhukov from Russia to ratify the agreement.

Meanwhile London commenced its VE celebrations. Troops returning home were treated like heroes and Britain welcomed peace. Servicemen demobbed in their thousands to return to peacetime occupations whilst the country anticipated a brighter future. Although the London Sketch Club had remained open during those dark war years attendances had been poor. When the war was over smoker nights began to fill up once again. It has often puzzled me how the Sketch Club coped with the problem of food. The Hungry Forties forced housewives to invent oddities such as carrot cake, cornbeef hash and dried egg spectaculars, but how did institutions like the London Sketch Club survive when it was so difficult for the ordinary individual to obtain rations. Perhaps they pooled their coupons or found some other way round the system.

The entertainment at the Sketch Club at this time was of the highest standard. Harry May Hemsley had finally become known as an entertainer in his own right. His radio broadcasts featuring the imaginary family of Horace, Winnie, Elsie and Johnny were extremely popular on *Children's Hour*. The famous phrase, "What did Horace say, Winnie?" will still make people of a certain age smile. One may even be forgiven for thinking that Harry May Hemsley's nursery sketches were the inspiration for Joyce Grenfell's later classroom of children which left us with the catchphrase "George, don't do that ...!".

Harry Hemsley had an undistinguished career as an illustrator: he contributed to *Chums* and was responsible for the caricature of Sketch Club members at their Coronation Dinner in 1902 (page 32). Although he was a capable draughtsman, and would frequently pitch in with a drawing or cartoon for an autographed collection of sketches sometimes presented to a valued member for services to the Club, his metier lay in the world of entertainment. Harry May Hemsley was the son of William Thompson Hemsley, a scenic artist from Swindon who designed stage sets at the turn of the century for some of London's leading theatres, including those for *Quo Vadis, A Midsummer Night's Dream, The Taming of the Shrew* and *The Merry Wives of Windsor*. As a young man Harry Hemsley would tour the music halls both before and after the First World War. Amazingly the old music hall circuit was still in existence in the 'fifties! He joined the London Sketch Club in 1901 and was a prominent member of the Concert Artists' Association and the Savage. He was due to become President of the Sketch Club in 1951 but sadly died in April of that year.

Another member of the Concert Artists' Association who was also a member of the Sketch Club was Clay Thomas. A professional singer all his life, he was meticulous about his dress: stories abound of the flower seller at Oxford Circus "who danced attendance to provide him with seasonal floral adornment". During his long, illustrious career this passionate Welshman sang at the Palladium and Covent Garden, and gave an annual concert at Weston-super-Mare. His favourite song was probably "Leaning" by Sterndale Bennett, which Thomas would deliver in his lusty baritone voice. Many members also remember his "Twins" duet with Harold Goodrich and his version of "Merrie England" which he liked to perform on

WARM GREETINGS

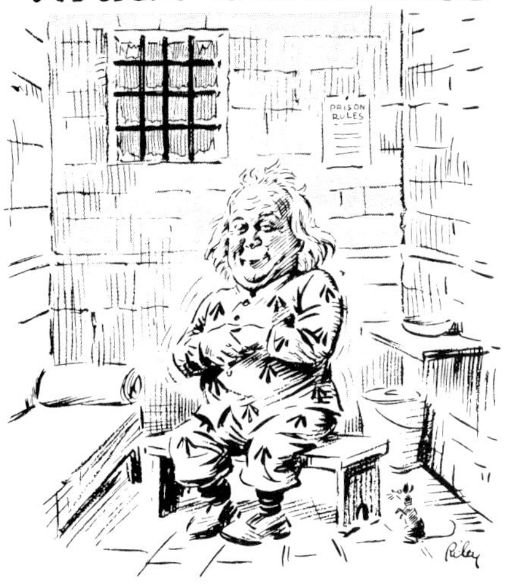

"PLEASE NOTE CHANGE OF ADDRESS"

Harry Brunning
Caricature by Harry Riley, RI.

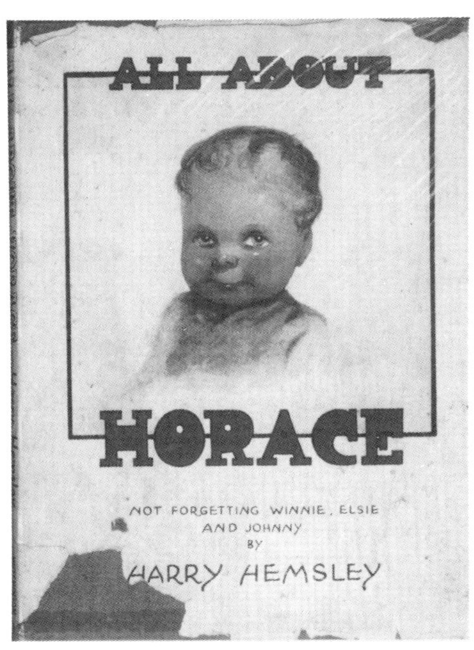

The cover of *Horace* by Harry Hemsley.

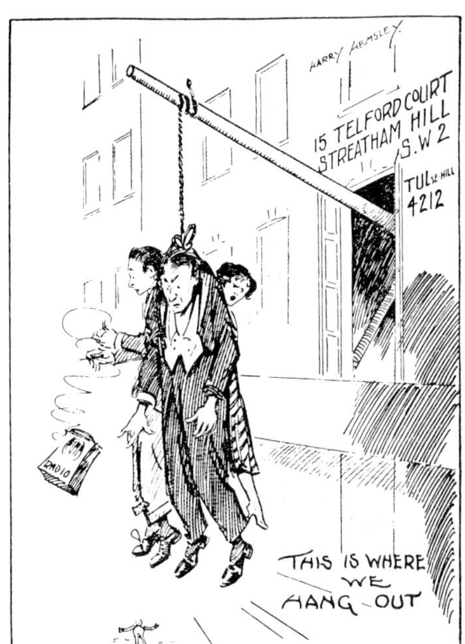

Greeting card by Harry May Hemsley.

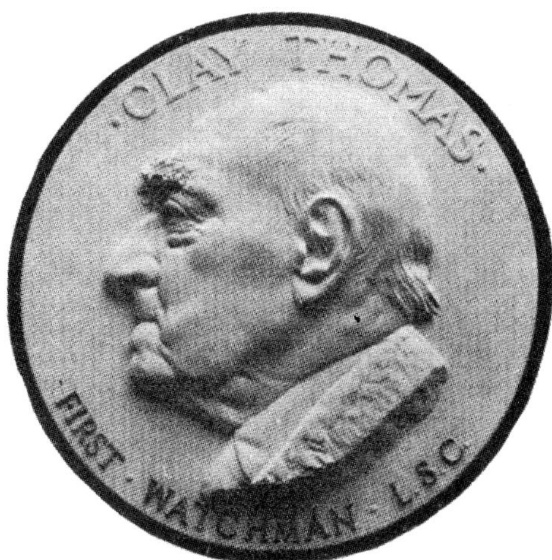

Clay Thomas by Fred Mancini.

Latterly the Buchanans moved to Telford
Court and lived in the flat underneath
the Hemsleys. Occasionally a spider on a
bit of string would descend outside the
window and other pranks to livèn up
city life.

St George's day. However, the song which every London Sketch Club member associates with Clay Thomas is "Watchman, What of the Night?" He was nicknamed First Watchman after this became the Sketch Club's theme tune. For nearly sixty years Clay Thomas brought Friday evening dinners to an end with this catchy dirge and for nearly sixty years Sketch Club members enjoyed it. Clay Thomas was a loyal member of the Club; he even sat as a model for early members. He suffered from the disability of a stutter though this did not affect his singing voice. In memory of Clay Thomas the Club commissioned a plaque by sculptor Fred Mancini to be placed on the bar wall.

Another member who was meticulous about his dress was Leslie Sarony. Always dapper and smartly turned out, Sarony (1897-1985) had already achieved fame as part of "The Two Leslies" when he joined the Club in 1955. Despite the fact that he never wanted to go on stage (his ambition was to be a drummer in the Guards!) he seemed to spend little time off it. Sarony adopted his mother's maiden name: he was the son of artist William Ralston Fry. It was his sister Mabel (who also painted) who first pushed young Leslie on to the stage, where he won £5 for a ragtime competition in Clapham Common. This led to the Shoreditch Hippodrome and The Star in Bermondsey, where he worked for £1.00 a week! During the First World War he joined the London Scottish Regiment and endured terrible conditions in France. As consolation he invented Private Albert Edward·Soddit to entertain the troops. After four years in France he returned to England and his first job as Buttons in Pantomine at the Hammersmith. He was also in the first performance of *Rita, Rita* at the Prince Edward. While staying in digs he composed "Old Peggarty with his Peggarty Leg" one morning over breakfast. On a visit to his music publisher he met Leslie Holmes. This proved a fortuitous meeting: "The two Leslies" were to make records, appear in films and frequently broadcast. Leslie Savony prided himself on being lively on his feet, but not so when it came to women — and Sarony had an eye for the fairer sex. The fortune he amassed soon dwindled and he was forced to look for work at the age of 75! Many London Sketch Club members will remember his renditions, often delivered with banjo accompaniment, on smoker nights.

Another entertainer was the excellent raconteur Victor Mac Clure, also a failed illustrator who went on to become a well-known actor. It was Victor Mac Clure who first had the idea of writing a book on the Sketch Club, but sadly he never put pen to paper.

The other great character actor who joined the Club in 1948 was Henry Oscar, who appeared in a number of films including *Penn of Pennsylvania*, *The Seventh Survivor* and *The Flying Squad*. He also appeared with Robert Newton in *Hatter's Castle*, Michael Denison in *Tilly of Bloomsbury*, and the young Deborah Kerr in *The Day Will Dawn*.

Then there was Harry Brunning, a versatile comedian who played understudy to the great Syd Fields in *Harvey*. When Fields died Harry Brunning stepped into the breach and continued in the play for the rest of its run. Brunning will be remembered as the impersonator of George Robey. When dressed up even his closest friends could not distinguish him from the real Robey. This may explain why Brunning deputised for Robey so often. By the time Brunning joined the Club in 1954, the famous trio of Max Jaffa, Jack Byfield and Reginald Kilbey were very much part of Club life. The famous trio, well-known through radio, were in fact a quartet which included pianist and composer Freddie Curzon. It was Curzon who, with Don Blake,

Edward Swann (1897-1978), artist, tutor, organiser, creative thinker and writer. His love of sketching (in the style of Adrian Hill) was infectious. His publications included *Sketches for Painting Practice, Prelude to Painting Improvement* and *How to Master Oil Painting*, all published by Charles Skilton (the last posthumously).

(*Below*) John Seabrook (born 1913) was invited to join the tutor panel of Galleon Painting Holidays in 1968, becoming Director in 1973. Like Watkins, Seabrook followed a career in banking in the City of London and turned to art late in life. Largely self taught, he has exhibited at the RI and had a one-man show in 1974. He worked tirelessly for the London Sketch Club and is an inveterate sketcher. Many members have been delighted with his renditions of old time music hall songs, especially "Coppernob". His other clubs include the Chelsea Arts Club and Savage.

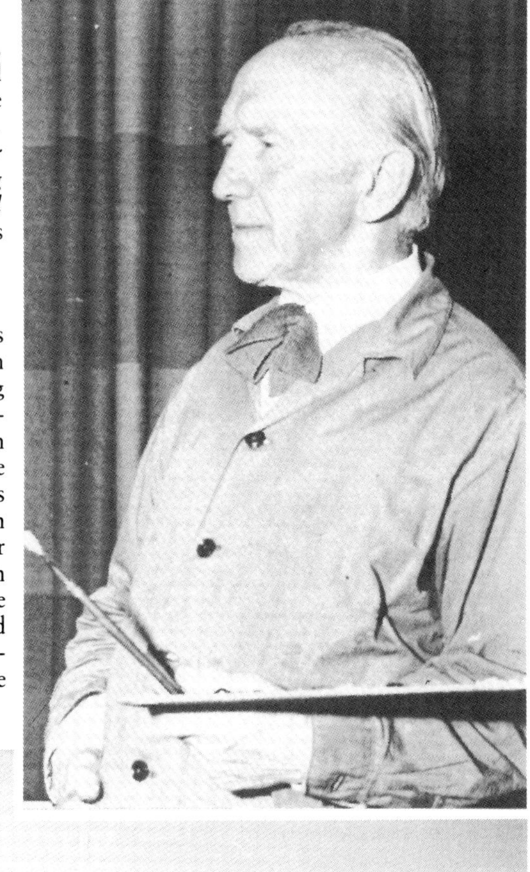

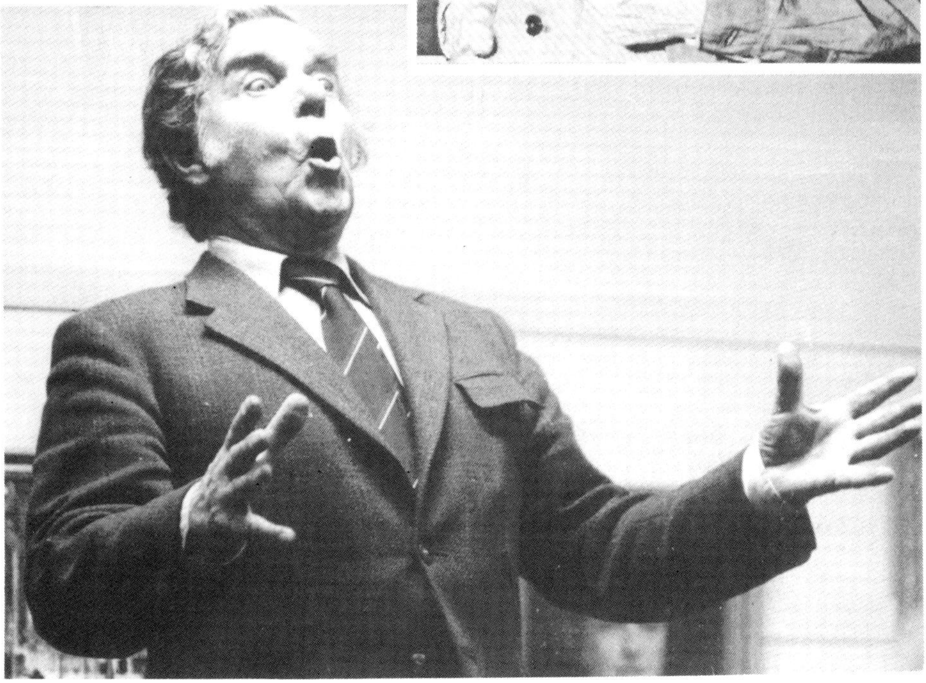

invented an "Anti-Watchman" song. Freddie Curzon joined the Sketch Club just after the War in 1946.

There were also a great number of conjurers and magicians who appeared at the Club, starting with Herbert Collings, alias Koh Ling Soo whose patter in pidgin-English, whilst dressed in Chinese robes, was extremely popular. His wife Hilda Bertram was a pianist and a favourite at the Club's Ladies' Days. Lionel King was an expert with playing cards, showing the sort of dexterity René Bull had demonstrated a quarter of a century earlier. Jimmy Rogers was another conjurer, who produced live doves from every part of his well-tailored suit. Magician and ventriloquist Alan Stainer also composed monologues. He performed at Maskelyne and Devant's House of Mystery as well as producing an annual summer show in Newquay in Cornwall. His wife Maud Davidson was a well-known singer who performed at Ladies' Day concerts. When the couple retired they took on The Old Bell Inn in East Molesey which must have been hard work. Many Sketch Club members went down to East Molesey to sample Stainer's hospitality and Harry Riley painted a picture of the pub for them.

The tradition of magicians appearing at the London Sketch Club has continued up to the present. Over the years firm favourites have included Percy Press (that great old Punch and Judy man), Billy McComb, Harold Taylor, Fergus Anckorn, John Palfreyman and John Wade.

However, the number of magicians is minimal in comparison with the number of singers who have gone through their paces at the Sketch Club. One of the reasons for the host of fine tenors, baritones and basses may have been the provision that Don Blake made for Julian Kimble to teach music in the Club itself from 1945. This was an excellent arrangement. Kimble's pupils included Heddle Nash, Robert Tear and Gwen Catley: as a music teacher his standards were high. His rental brought in a bit of sorely needed cash at a time when the Club was counting every penny and his presence at odd times during the night and day gave the Club a bit of security, it deterring any would be burglar. I nicknamed Kimble the Quasimodo of the Sketch Club because although I never met him I could always feel his presence. After Kimble's death in 1975, some unexplained thefts took place.

Julian Kimble (1888-1975) had himself studied under Gervase Elwes and Victor Beigl, making his debut in Raymond Rose's *Joan of Arc* at Covent Garden before the 1914-18 War. However, he lost his voice as a result of a throat infection contracted during the First World War and subsequently worked as a music critic. When his singing voice returned after a successful second operation in 1942 he became a teacher. Students of his who sang at the London Sketch Club included Harold Goodrich, Joe Beechus and Noel Noble; others included Edward Leer, Frank Sale, April Cantelo and Valerie Masterson.

Although entertainment in those post-war years was excellent, Sketch Club artists were experiencing a bitter blow. Just as the First World War had seen the collapse of the illustrated book so the Second World War saw the collapse of magazine illustration. Photography swept the market. As so often happens in life, when one door closes another opens. Book illustrators who once enjoyed a highly lucrative market had turned to magazines, but where did they go now?

The answer came in the form of painting holidays. As yet unaware that quite so many people had an interest in painting, Edward Swann (1897-1978) took a small group of students for an Easter weekend to Seaview on the Isle of Wight. Initially such painting holidays were organised by the WTA (Workers' Travel Association)

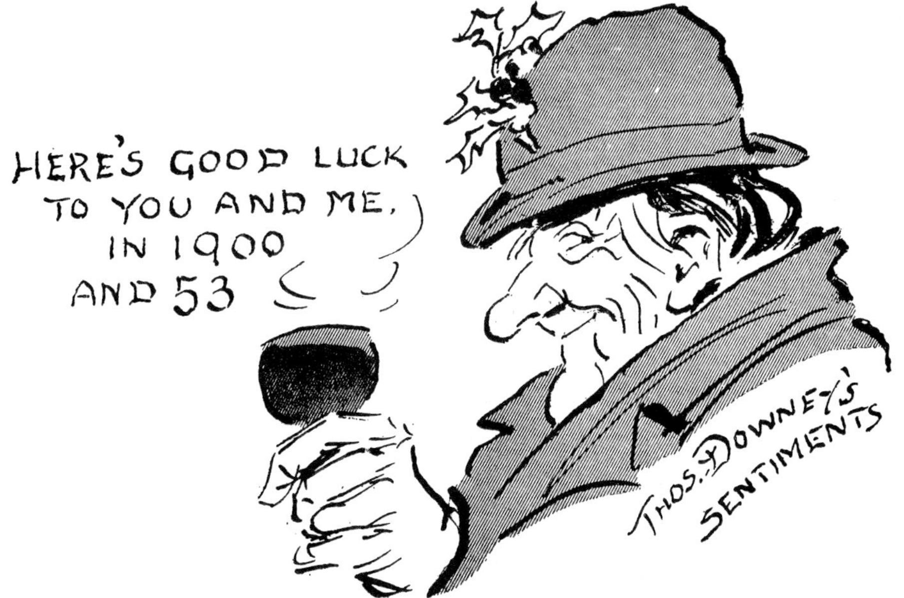

Card sent by Thomas Downey in 1953.

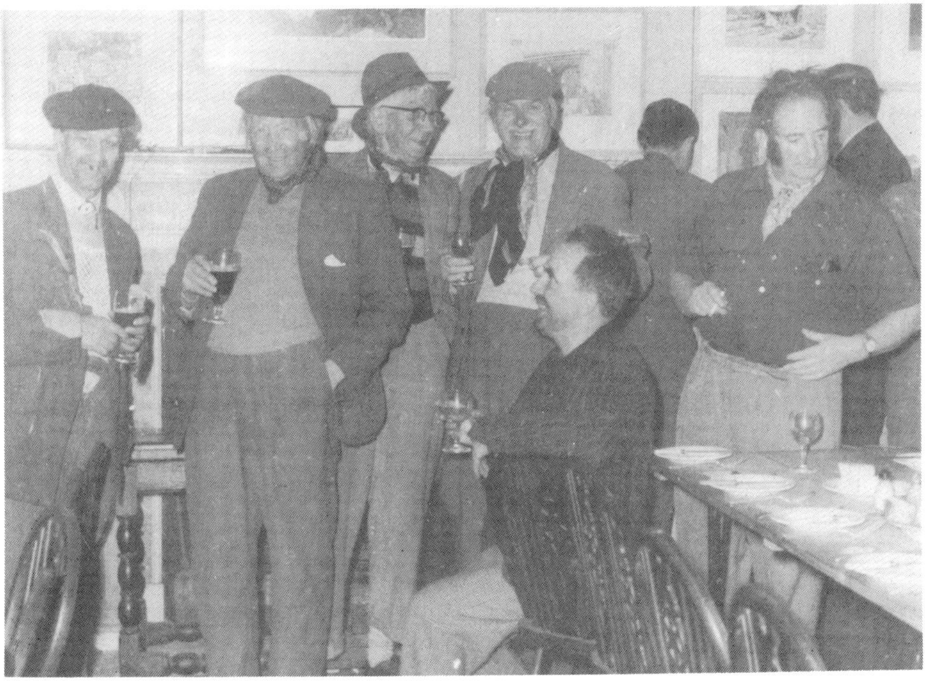

(*Left to right*): Albert Berbank (President 1960), William Watkins (President 1961), Bill Fryer, Kenneth Graham (Presidents 1957), Harry Weatherill (seated, President 1965) and Harold Goodrich (President 1966).

which in 1947 pioneered what were to become known as "special interest holidays". London Sketch Club members had established schools before and at first few people gave much thought to Edward Swann's venture — which probably included Edward Swann himself.

Gradually these painting holidays became more and more popular. The name changed to Galleon Painting Holidays, and London Sketch Club tutors such as David Ghilchik, Harry Riley, Charles Pierce and William Watkins were shipped off to all parts of the globe to advise on their subject and get paid for it. Swann, who was well-known in Fleet Street, gradually built up his business into what must now be one of the largest leisure activities in the country. Swann was a natural organiser and succeeded where many had failed. Born in Stratford in London, he studied at the West Ham School of Art back in 1912. He taught for a time at the Polytechnic School of Architecture and at the Central School of Art before establishing a large commercial studio. However, he had a leaning towards fine art, like many London Sketch Club members, rather than commercial art.

Swann had stumbled upon a society of wealthy amateurs prepared to indulge their hobby. In those post-war years although the country was heavily in debt to the USA there were plenty of takers who saw themselves as potential artists. Between the Wars, artists such as Will Owen and Lawson Wood had tutored for The British and Dominion's School of Drawing in Greycoat Place, London. Frank Sherwin, RI held classes, as did Leonard Richmond, RBA, but Edward Swann found a totally different market. Swann milked the "I would like to go on holiday first and foremost and if I can learn to paint at the same time, all the better" market. It was the Winston Churchill approach of "painting for pleasure", which hitherto had been unacceptable, the very opposite of the Henry Tonks method of teaching. Swann's acute business sense did the Club a lot of good and benefited many members.

One of the students on the early courses was Wee George Wood, who accompanied his tutor Harry Riley on a holiday to Italy. The painting which Wood completed, entitled "Near Capri", was later sold in aid of The Water Rats charity. On one occasion Edward Swann parked his students on a village green. As they were assembling their easels a group of local schoolchildren were passing by. "Look!" said one small boy, "Artists, and there's their keeper!"

It was John Seabrook, a later London Sketch Club member, who took over as the "Gaffer" of Galleon Holidays in 1973 when Edward Swann stepped down due to ill-health. Seabrook continued where Swann had left off and recruited just as many London Sketch Club members to act as tutors, if not more. These included Christopher Stones, Ley Kenyon, D. Walduck, Sydney Foley, Dudley Burnside, Will Raymont and Matt Bruce, RI. By the time Seabrook took over Galleon Holidays, they were rollercoasting from success to success, due largely to personal recommendation. People were learning to paint and enjoying their holidays as well. Today a vast spectrum of outdoor activities is offered to holidaymakers, but I doubt whether anyone could have foreseen such consequences back in 1947.

Swann's drive and energy had been the powerhouse of Galleon for many years and he supplemented his teaching with a list of publications. One of his closest friends was William Watkins (1885-1965) (known in the Sketch Club as Wattie Watkins). The son of Arthur Robinson Watkins, an undistinguished illustrator, he studied at the Portsmouth School of Art, Croydon School of Art and City of London School of Art where his tutor was Herbert Dicksee. Then he went into banking. His first job

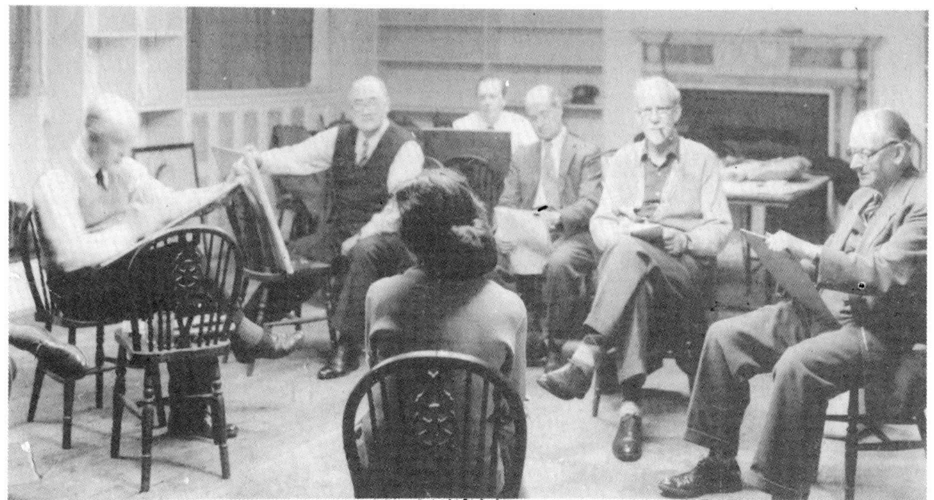

The first sketching meeting held in Dilke Street after the move from Marylebone. Sketchers include Don Blake, RI and Henry Coller. The fine Adam fireplace in the background was to pay for a new roof on the property. When this work was done the old guttering was not replaced and rubbish from the old roof was not cleared away, being left to collect dampness. Subsequently dry rot set in and nearly every brick in the place had to be treated. Overseeing this mammoth task was Clifford Fisher, who also undertook much of the redecoration.

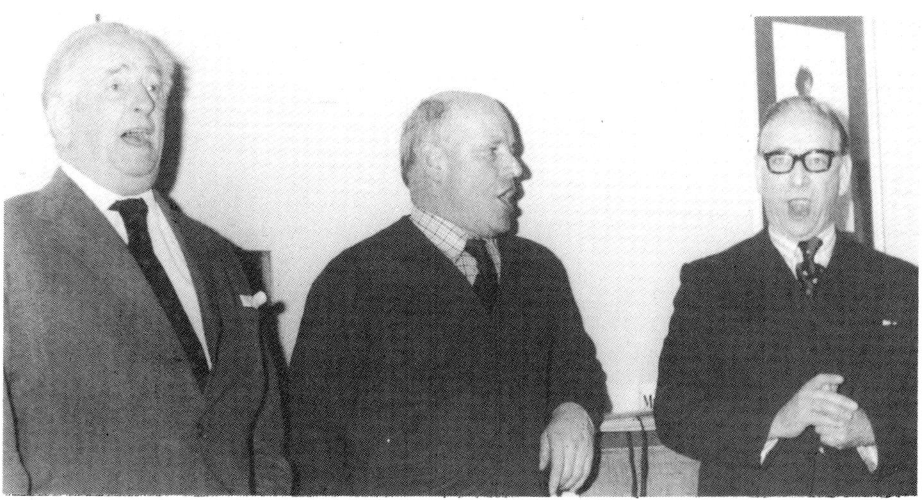

Two of Kimble's students were the singers Harold Goodrich and Joe Beechus, seen here with Edgar Rhys Evans (1913-1984). Harold Goodrich was born in London, the son of a master engraver. He served in the Royal Naval Air Service in the 1914-18 War and in 1919 joined an advertising agency. In 1923 he acquired Chelsea Studios with which many London Sketch Club members had connections, including Harry Riley, Jack Holt, Jerry Laking, George Dixon, Edward Bishop and Harry Winslade. Goodrich (1899-1984) remained with Chelsea Studios until his retirement in 1980, but singing was his great love. He was a member of the Sketch Club for 47 years and organised the entertainment in Dilke Street up to the time of his death. He will long be remembered for his renditions of "Watchman" and "The Bold Gendarmes", together with Sidney Peak.

was with the National Provincial Bank where he remained until 1946. The reason for his safety first attitude may have been his father's failure. Watkins always played safe. Even when he joined the Croydon Art Society, where he made friends such as Jack Merriott and Wilfred Fryer, he still would not give up his steady income for the irregular life of an artist. In 1939 he became a member of the RI but it was not until 1946, when he retired, that he took up painting full-time. After his death in 1965 Galleon Holidays announced an annual award for the best watercolour of the year and called it the Wattie Award.

One of the publications for which Watkins was responsible was a delightful little book entitled *Landscape into Pictures*, based on his Continental travels with Galleon. It was written with Edward Swann in mind and captured the heightened sunlit colours of the Mediterranean. Watkins' paintings were purchased by the Port of London Authority, Croydon Corporation, National Provincial Bank and Accrington Corporation. After his death the Arnham Gallery showed a retrospective of his work.

One of Watkins' close colleagues was George Ayling (1887-1960) who spent much of his life painting along the Thames. He specialised in seascapes and in particular the changing face of the Thames. Born in Kennington, he studied art at Putney, but was forced to serve his apprenticeship in the family business of E. Ayling & Sons, oar and scull specialists, before being allowed to follow his vocation. Works such as "A Link Between Surrey and Middlesex", "Blackfriars Bridge and St Paul's", "In Surrey Docks" and "Escorts into the Docks" all show his love of the sea. He was a member of the Wapping Group of Artists and their President for a number of years. It was Ayling, Watkins, Don Blake and Thorp who formed the backbone of the Wapping Group. Here again the Sketch Club played an important role as an umbrella for a smaller, less fortunate society.

Ayling was a highly disciplined artist, and a man of habit. Prints of his works such as "St Ives" and "A Natural Cornish Harbour" were extremely popular, while paintings such as "Gibraltar" could be found as far afield as the National Gallery of Ceylon. Ayling frequented the same haunts as W. W. Jacobs: Limehouse, Wapping and Gravesend, full of picturesque wharfs and bollards, where barges and coasters landed their cargo. Ayling lived in much the same spirit as W. W. Jacobs' "Bill the Night Watchman", emerging from shadows to view a twinkling sea, but whereas Jacobs was wrapped up in the yarns of his bargees and watermen, Ayling was content with the river itself.

On smoker nights there was a significant change to the Sketch Club format after the war. The Watchman still closed Friday night proceedings but the working sessions which had taken place before the meal had lapsed. Friday nights were given a theme reflecting various elements within the Club and there was a danger that it might become a purely social club. One unusual step to rectify this was the election of William Hutchinson in 1951 as an honorary member. Artist members were rarely given honorary status, and only if their contribution to the Club warranted it.

Sir William Oliphant Hutchinson (1889-1975) was born in Fife in Scotland and educated at Rugby. He trained in Paris, where he studied fencing as well as art, before going to the Edinburgh College of Art. Whilst a student his first portrait of E. A. Walton's daughter was exhibited at the RSA. He married her in 1918, after the end of the war, and they spent their early life together in Chelsea, where he achieved a considerable reputation as a portrait painter. Later he returned to Scotland as Director of the Glasgow School of Art. In 1950 he was elected President

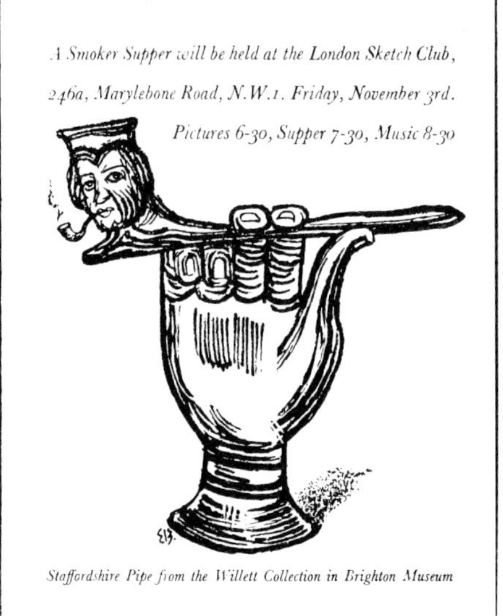

Drawing by Edward Bishop
from the 1950s.

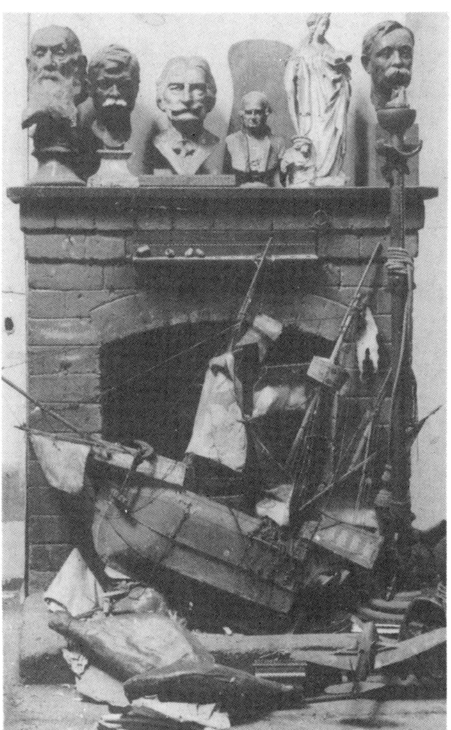

The removal of curios from the Marylebone Club to Dilke Street left one or two items smashed beyond repair. Fortunately the busts survived.

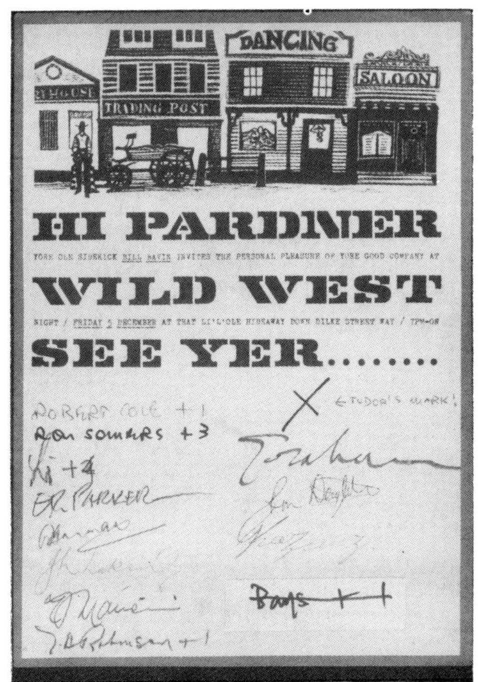

(*Left*) Friday night smokers were given a theme. This poster (probably by Tom Robinson) was for Bill Bavin's Wild West Night in 1969. Bavin, an engaging former insurance/property dealer turned author, was fascinated by the simplistic Wild West culture. He eventually bought a ranch in Tuscon, Arizona where he became a Deputy Sheriff and was proud to ride with the local posse. If many Sketch Club members were inveterate sketchers, Bavin was an inveterate scribbler. His letters, often lengthy and detailed, bore witness to that. He had turned to writing at the age of 38 and was responsible for many racy novels, but probably his most memorable book was *The Strange Death of Freddie Mills*, published by Howard Baker in 1975. Other journalists subsequently championed Bavin's cause and there was a television programme about that tragic episode. Bavin himself met an untimely end when the plane he was flying crashed in 1985 killing both pilot and passenger. Bavin was also a Freeman of the City of London and no mean slouch with a guitar.

of the Royal Scottish Academy. His own most prized paintings were two portraits which hung over his mantlepiece: "Hutchinson" by James Gunn, and "James Gunn" by Hutchinson.

In 1957, when Kenneth Graham was President, the London Sketch Club moved premises. Although it was Charles Pierce, RI who masterminded the plan it must not be forgotten that George Dixon had renegotiated the lease of the old Marylebone Club with such foresight that the Club was left in a strong position. The chosen site was in Dilke Street, Chelsea, an area steeped in artistic history. Whistler, Sargent and Augustus John had all owned or rented studios in nearby Tite Street; Oscar Wilde had lived a few blocks away. Behind Dilke Street was Turner's Reach overlooking the Thames and Rossetti had once lived further down Cheyne Walk. It was an excellent site, if a little difficult to reach by underground or bus. In the 'fifties parking restrictions were of course not as fierce as of late.

The Dilke Street premises were ideal for the Sketch Club and Woolworths made the move possible when they bought the old Marylebone site to incorporate into their new headquarters, Woolworth House. With money in the bank and its own freehold the Club could look forward to a healthy future. However, just as the move from Wells Street to Marylbone had upset one or two members, so the move to Chelsea left some tempers frayed, leading to a few emotional outbursts. One involved Albert Berbank (1896-1960) who, after a heated argument, collapsed and died of a heart attack. Berbank was an etcher-engraver, born in Nottingham. He trained at the Nottingham School of Art, went on to study at St Martins and Westminster, where he came under the influence of Meninsky and Walter Bays, and joined the Society of Graphic Artists in 1920. He was elected President of the London Sketch Club in 1960. After his death it was left to Vice-President Watkins to take over.

At this time the average age of members was older than it should have been. Few youngsters were being groomed to fill vacant places. Harry Lawrence Oakley was sixty-five when he was President of the Club in 1947-48. Born in York, he studied at York, Leeds and the Royal College of Art. During the First World War he served with the Green Howards and subsequently carved out a career as a profilist. He attained the rank of Major and had one full length silhouette of the Prince of Wales (later the Duke of Windsor) cut in France during the 1914-18 War. It now hangs in the National Portrait Gallery. He contributed regularly to *London Opinion, The Graphic* and *The Bystander.*

By the time he was President Oakley he was part of a previous generation. The 'fifties, with its Festival of Britain and new outlook, and the 'sixties with its revolutionary working-class affectation, were very different eras to those in which Oakley had developed. Even Henry Coller's caricatures of past members of the Sketch Club which now lined the bar looked strangely out of date. These drawings, in the style of Joseph Simpson, have a 'forties naivety: the London Sketch Club seemed stuck in that rut. The Club membership seemed to have adopted a *laissez faire* attitude to developments going on around them. They were to experience a rude awakening in the 'seventies and 'eighties.

CHAPTER 11

A Personal View of the 'Seventies

Like so many people who have been invited to the London Sketch Club I found that as soon as you enter its portals you cannot fail to be fascinated by the place. It is like a cocoon preserving its contents in time for future generations to enjoy: the dust that lies on the busts of John Hassall and Odell is there for everyone. Soon after I was invited by the Greek Cypriot born singer George Kazanzi I became Club Secretary. It happened so quickly I was amazed. The job of Secretary in any organisation is odious; in the Sketch Club it was doubly so as no one wanted to take responsibility for anything!

Artists are not noted for practical ability and the only thing for a Secretary to do was act, then take the flak later on, otherwise everything would have come to a full stop. Council meetings which should have provided the answers usually ended in turmoil. When I think back on those meetings, held in the downstairs room of the Club now occupied by PEN, I shudder. Most of the Council was made up of lay members and the only people who made any sense in the 'seventies were Charles Skilton and John Seabrook who could always be relied on to crack a joke just as a heated exchange was brewing. Those Council meetings put me off joining any bureaucratic body ever again!

The advantages the London Sketch Club enjoyed were owning their own freehold premises and holding a small amount of surplus cash in the bank. It was in a healthier position than most London Clubs. On the minus side, Friday evening smoker nights were eating away any surplus cash: they never made a profit; and there was the upkeep of the building. The latter caused a shock when all the tenders came in. Repairs were an ongoing drain on the Club's resources: no sooner had one problem been solved than another reared its ugly head.

The Sketch Club changed my life. If I managed to achieve any good I like to think it has helped the Club continue to move towards its centenary. I took over the job of Hon Sec from Tom Robinson (1903-1982). There was nothing special about Robinson. He was an ordinary commercial artist who had lived through the best times and seen the last of the old agent/artist setup. He was always immaculately turned out: he could have been mistaken for a retired Major or schoolmaster rather than an artist. It was through Tom Robinson that I first visited the Chelsea Arts Club and the Savage (he was a member of all three clubs). He had his critics within the London Sketch Club but I know how many hours he spent washing glasses, serving drinks and generally doing the Club's housekeeping. He must also have spent hours designing posters for smoker evenings (some of which I managed to retrieve, have framed and place in the hallway of the Club).

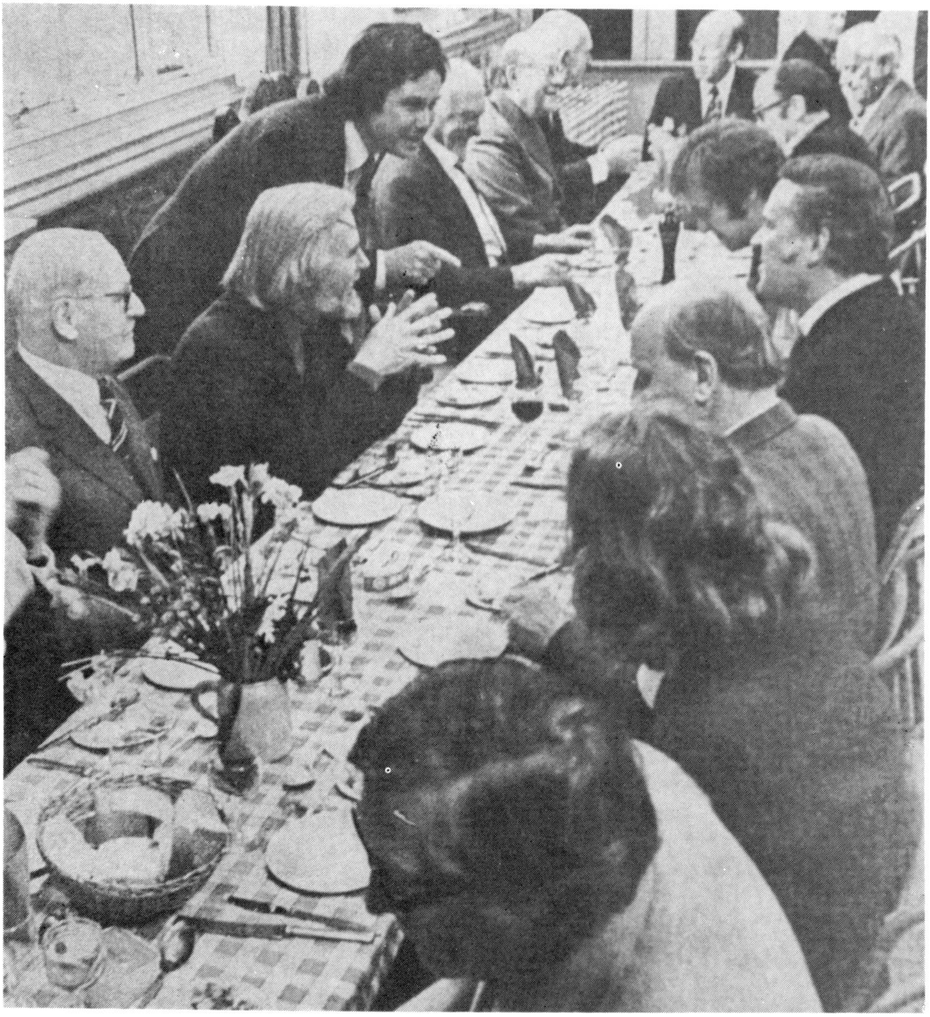

London Sketch Club members and guests. Clockwise round the table are: Dr R. O. Swaine, Frederick Deane RP, David Cuppleditch, Ruskin Spear RA*, Carel Weight RA*, Robert Easton, Dr Alan Joel, David Langdon*, "Jak" (Raymond Jackson)*, "Mac" (Stanley McMurtry)*, Reginald Bosanquet*, Donald Blake RI, Dominic Lambert* and Maurice Litten RO. (*Guests)

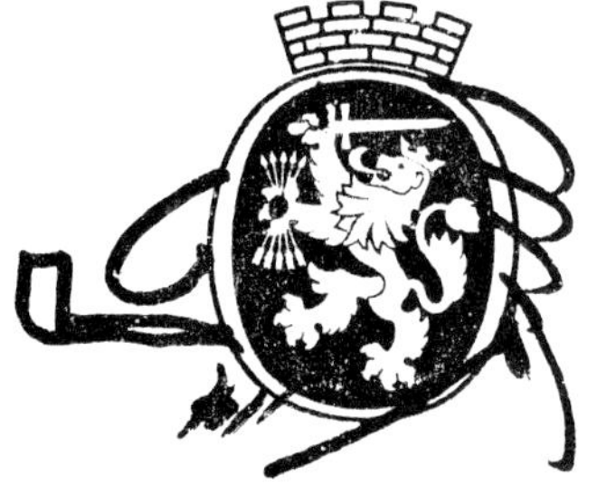

Caricature of Rembrandt Spear by Robert Buhler.

The small coterie that frequented the bar on Tuesday nights (life class night) could be counted on the fingers of one hand. There were Don Blake, Oliver Robinson, Adrian Bury, Tom Robinson and myself. Friday nights (Club smoker nights) were a different matter: the bar was often so packed it was difficult to get served. Among the people who sketched on Tuesday nights were George Chambers, Ley Kenyon, Rudolph Benesh, Tom Espley, Henry Stringer, Bernard Bays, Ken Hardy and, occasionally, Ashton Cannell.

Rudolph Benesh, or Rudy as he was better known, was a regular Tuesday-nighter and loyal member of the Club. He would patiently sit through Sketch Club trials and tribulations without criticism or cynical comment. In outside life he was the same quiet, gentle man. None of us realised he had cancer. When, just after Christmas 1974, he stopped coming to the Club, it was because he was fighting for his life. He recovered from his first operation and went home for a few days, but fell critically ill again. He went back into hospital for a second operation from which he was not to recover.

To the outside world he will be remembered for the "Benesh Movement Notation" used by professional dance companies, as well as in medicine and anthropology. It was his wife who first suggested the dance notation back in 1947. Benesh saw that it could be applied to all forms of human movement and should be expressed in a concise way and written in conjunction with musical notation. Using his training in music and art and with the five-line musical stave as a matrix, he showed positions and movements of the body by marking simple signs depicting exact positions of the limbs on the matrix.

In 1955 Dame Margot Fonteyn demonstrated the notation, and later that year Ninette de Valois adopted it for use in the Royal Ballet and the Royal Ballet School. In 1962 the Institute of Choreology was set up by Benesh and his wife to develop the notation. This was so successful that in 1965 new premises were needed, which were opened the same year. Benesh died, aged 59, on 3 May 1975.

Adrian Bury, RWS was another member of the group, who was often accompanied by Ley Kenyon. If Benesh was uptight and nervous, Adrian Bury was laid back. He had enjoyed a long and illustrious career in journalism and had managed to reach the grand old age of 99 before his death in 1991. His knowledge of watercolour painting was extensive; he wrote about it profusely. In his younger days he had caricatured under the nom de plume "Tell". In 1932 Her Majesty the Queen bought one of his paintings of Midhurst in Kent.

Adrian Bury had been born not far from the Sketch Club's Dilke Street premises, in Edith Grove, Chelsea. His father had been a sculptor and his uncle was Sir Alfred Gilbert of Eros fame. For a time he worked on the *Bystander* before continuing his studies at the Academie Julian in Paris. A friend had pre-warned him of the initiation ceremony there — drinks all round or *payer la goutte*. To quote Bury:

> I told the head student that I would be delighted to *payer la goutte*. Suddenly all the students and the model stopped working and I was frog-marched out of the studio into a nearby café. Within a few moments the place was bedlam and in the general uproar every kind of drink was ordered from chocolate to fine brandy. I was hoisted on to a table and had to make a little speech. In my halting French I said how happy I was, how honoured in fact to be admitted to Julian's, after which they all went back to the studio, the model took up the pose again and they carried on working.

His studies were interrupted by the outbreak of the First World War. Bury was forced to take a job on the *Sunday Pictorial*. During his career in journalism he met and befriended many important artists of the twentieth century, including Pietro Annigoni, Russell Flint, Alfred Munnings and Flora Knight. As a businessman Bury was not a success. He accumulated a fortune on the stock market only to lose every penny in the Wall Street Crash. Towards the end of his life he turned to writing poetry; his numerous titles included *Look Back in Love, The Immortal Ship, In Spite of Time, Just in Time* and *Faith, Love and Beauty*. The last included a poem entitled "The Beech Tree", dedicated to Ley Kenyon. All these books were published by Charles Skilton under an assortment of imprints including Charles Skilton Ltd, The Fortune Press (which was first to publish the works of Dylan Thomas and Philip Larkin), The Mitre Press and Evergreen Books.

Charles Skilton, Hon RWS (a lay member) was the person I knew best from the Sketch Club. We collaborated for many years on all sorts of projects (including the *Sketch Pad*) and although Skilton did not attend the Club as often as he would have liked in the latter part of the 'eighties, due to his lung cancer, he kept in touch with one or two members on a regular basis. If he passed Roehampton he would drop in to see Adrian Bury and perhaps take him a bottle of wine; in the United States he visited Bill Bavin at his ranch in Tuscon, Arizona.

Charles Skilton, who died on 21 January 1990 aged 68, was described in an obituary as the "versatile and engagingly eccentric proprietor of one of the last independent one-man publishing houses". Although he published many worthwhile and informative books such as those on the artists Joseph Crawhall, Russell Flint, Francis Towne, De La Tour, Phil May and Felician Rops, as well as Adrian Bury's autobiography *Just a Moment, Time*, he made his fortune with a series of soft-porn paperbacks under the Luxor Press imprint. Skilton once confessed to having a "miscellaneous mind" which led to an interest in a wide range of subjects. He was, for example, an authority on windmills and watermills (writing a book in the Britain in Pictures series published by William Collins back in the 1940s); he was also responsible for first publishing the Billy Bunter stories in book form after their appearance in *The Magnet*. It would need a further volume to unravel the rest of Skilton's enterprises: from postcards published under the banner of Skilton & Fry (including the most comprehensive selection of aircraft subjects in England), a brief ownership of *Bookdealer* magazine (for the secondhand and antiquarian book trade), to a firm of dry-cleaners in Edinburgh bought as a tax loss, the list was endless and often puzzling. Needless to say, everything got into such a muddle towards the end of his life that I don't think even he understood all the complexities.

When I first knew him he had just acquired Banwell Castle in Avon, a Victorian mock gothic folly which formerly belonged to Simon Wills of the W. D. & H. O. Wills tobacco family. The castle was soon overwhelmed by books — they were stacked everywhere. If only one household in ten in Britain houses a book, Skilton did his best to make up for the other nine. When he eventually sold Banwell Castle he bought Whittingehame House near Edinburgh, once the home of A. J. Balfour, the Prime Minister. Skilton was particularly pleased with the library which was where the famous Balfour Declaration had been signed. I never visited him in Scotland but I am sure he would have had no difficulty in filling those library bookshelves.

Another item which Skilton was proud to possess was an "American desk" (the original name for a roll-top desk, usually made of mahogany) which had once

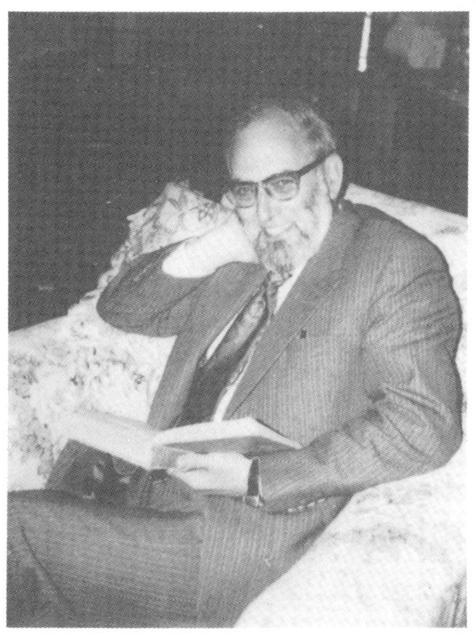

Charles Skilton

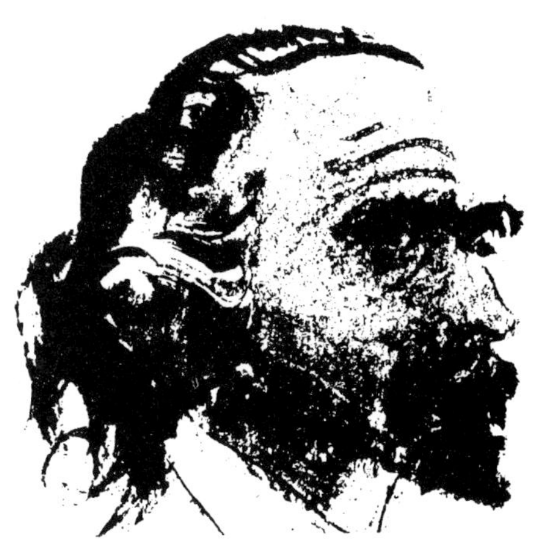

Rudolph Benesh from a caricature
by Bernard Bays.

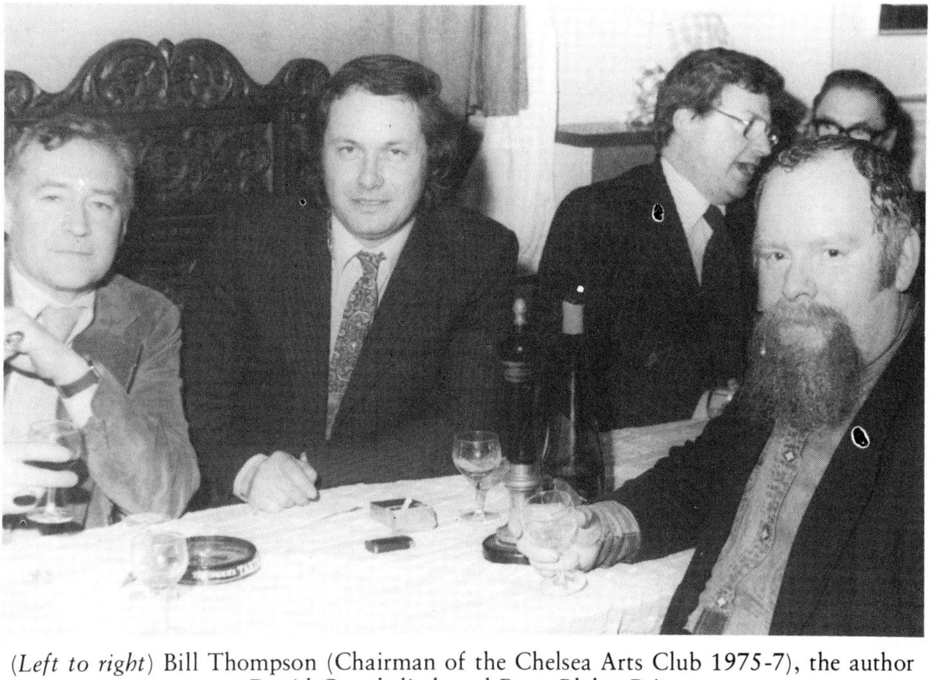

(*Left to right*) Bill Thompson (Chairman of the Chelsea Arts Club 1975-7), the author
David Cuppleditch and Peter Blake, RA.

belonged to that grand old gentleman of the publishing world, Grant Richards. Skilton had bought the desk from Martin Secker of Secker & Warburg. In the good times he employed a chauffeur for his old Rolls-Royce and spent weekends at Oldlands Hall in Sussex (but that was before I knew him). His "mansionette" at Oldlands was bought with the proceeds from the expurgated version of Fanny Hill. His friend Alan Fry (of Charles Skilton & Fry) dubbed it "Fanny Hall".

Charles Skilton was the illegitimate son of Charles Core, a self-employed master builder (and amateur artist) who lived in Dulwich; he was born on 6 March 1921. Brought up by his mother with few special advantages, he won a scholarship to the prestigious Alleyn's College in Dulwich (much later in life he published the school's history). At the age of fourteen he procured a small handpress and some type with which he did odd printing jobs. At sixteen he went to work for Stanley Gibbons before moving to the publishing house George Allen & Unwin, where he assisted the legendary Sir Stanley Unwin. He was so impressed with Unwin that he adopted one or two of his mannerisms which were to stay with him for the rest of his life. Judging from photographs of Unwin, it was not just mannerisms that Skilton picked up from the venerable old sage: he dressed in the same way as Unwin, sported the same beard and glasses, even walked in the same way. By the 'eighties Skilton's homburg, long overcoat and bookbag made him look quaintly old-fashioned.

During the Second World War Skilton was imprisoned for a short time as a conscientious objector, later being released to do compulsory service at a mental hospital. When he left Unwin's to set up his own publishing house he went through some difficult times. In a period of financial stringency he was forced to sell the Bunter rights, which had taken much effort to acquire, to Cassells in the early 'fifties; in 1954 he had to pawn the office typewriter to buy Christmas lunch! This was a decade before he alighted on the idea of publishing steamy paperbacks, which brought in a steady flow of cash for several years. He could have made an even bigger fortune in the 'sixties had he entered the soft porn magazine market then in its infancy. He never abandoned publishing more legitimate and prestigious titles which included the Annual Volume of the Old Water-Colour Society's Club, edited by Adrian Bury. As it said in his obituary, "Skilton was a man of great contradictions". A confirmed bibliophile, he had a deep appreciation of fine printing and book binding. In his lifetime he published well over a thousand titles which was remarkable for a small publishing house.

Skilton was always leaning on me to help in some way or other. Even when I bullied him into taking the chair at the London Sketch Club for a "publishers night" he insisted that I support him with guests. It was 9 January 1976, the middle of winter. I invited Rowland Hilder, Gerald Scarfe and Dennis Castle (an excellent raconteur and good member of the Savage Club). Meanwhile John Seabrook had invited Malcolm Fry (then Secretary of the RWS) and our small coterie sat down to eat. Fortunately Charles had organised a special hor's d'oeuvre because the remainder of the meal, which consisted of ham and pease pudding, was practically inedible.

The entertainment which followed the meal commenced with Robert Easton, who was blessed with a wonderfully deep bass voice; he sang in the style of Paul Robeson (whom he knew well). He was followed by Joe Hannah on the piano (Joanna on the pianna) who always had a cigarette dangling between his lips as he plonked the ivories. Then there was Fergus Anckorn with a selection of magical tricks, and Dennis Castle. It was Castle who stole the show that night. His quick witted humour on the vagaries of cricket was immensely popular — he was a

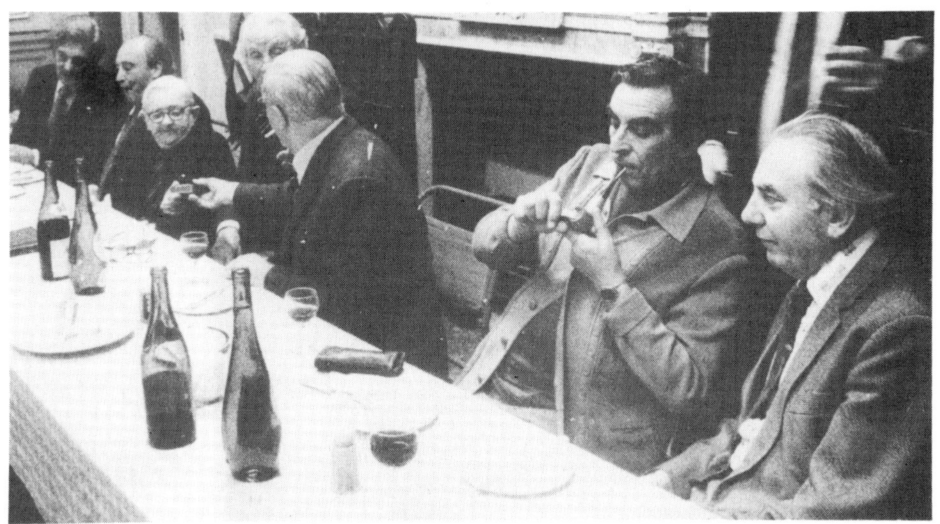

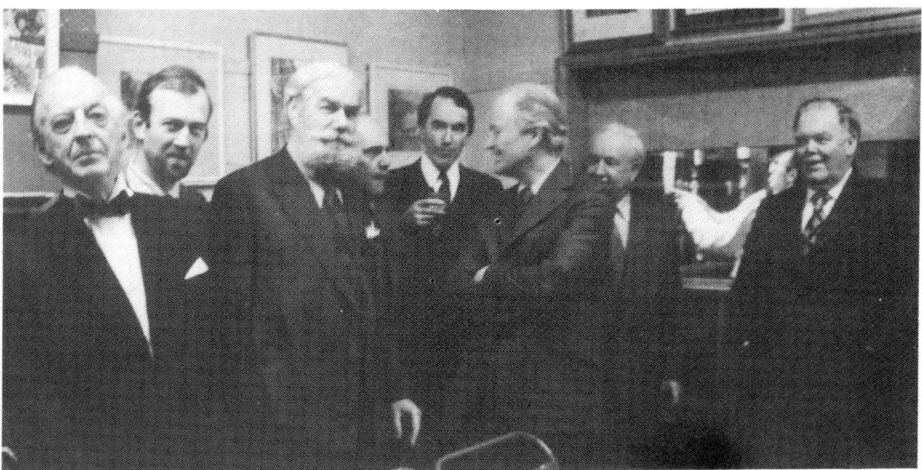

Each Friday night (when the Chairman of the evening was expected to bring along guests) had a theme (such as Cockney Night, Chelsea Arts and Savage Night or Tramps Night). The most popular one I recall was Old Soldiers Night when E. G. ("Egg") Goldring was in the chair. 4 April 1975 was an Old Time Music Hall Night (*above*): that great impressario Gordon Marsh (1893-1982) was in the chair. Marsh had toured with the Roosters Concert Party during the First World War, had been a charleston ballroom champion and arranged for many stars to appear in London cabarets. He was a member of the Concert Artists Association and the Savage in addition to the London Sketch Club. In the picture are, (*left to right*) Billy McComb (magician), John Presino,* Wee Georgie Wood* (music hall star), Gordon Marsh, Dr Dick Swaine, Martin Benson* (actor) and George Crozier (flautist). (*Below*) Dr Donald Page was in the chair for a Doctors night on 6 December 1974. In the picture are (*left to right*) Dr Donald Page, Paul Telling (dentist), Sir John Briscoe,* Dr Lewis Gavin and four other doctors. (*Guests)

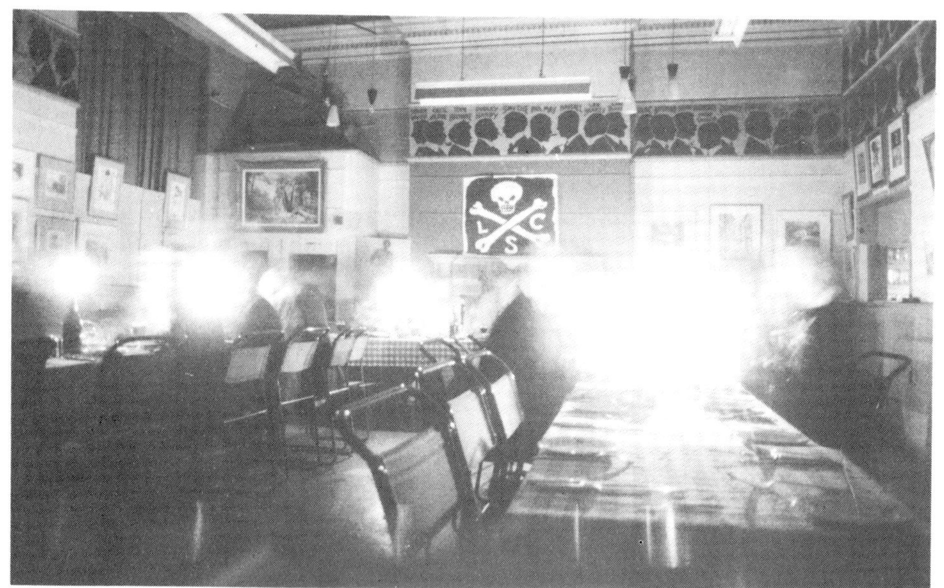

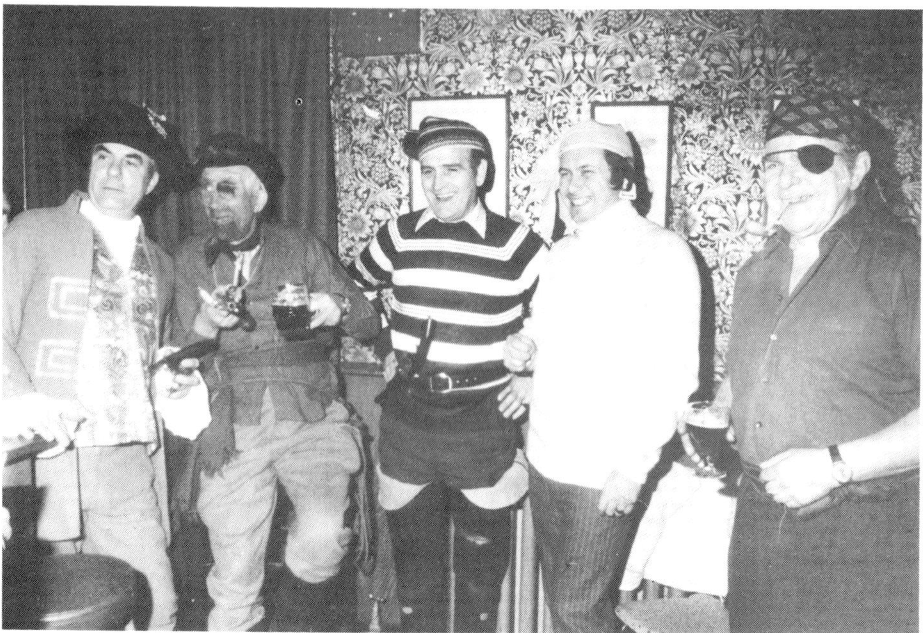

Pirates Night, 28 November 1975, with Ted Snoad in the chair, was a particularly memorable Friday night because there was a power cut in Chelsea due to heavy gales. The studio in candlelight had an atmosphere of intrigue and skullduggery. Michael Noakes the portrait painter was my guest on this occasion: he was horrified at being confronted by this strange assortment of rogues. Pictured below are (*left to right*) Ted Snoad (who eventually became tired of the ''Ah . . . Snead!'' jokes), Freddie Hill, Clifford Swann, the author and John Seabrook.

raconteur in the Gerald Hoffnung mould, with equally superb timing and delivery. There are many social graces I admire but the ability to make an entertaining after dinner speech would be top of the list.

Another of my guests that evening, Rowland Hilder (who died in 1993 aged 87), was never a member of the Sketch Club but he was sympathetic to its aims and achievements. Hilder had spent years propping up the RI (he was its President from 1964 to 1974) and there had always been strong links between the London Sketch Club and the RI. Hilder's background was similar to that of many Sketch Club members: he came up through the ranks of illustration to fine art. It was only in the last few years of his life that he achieved artistic recognition. At the time of Skilton's night in the chair in 1976, he was busily preparing for an exhibition in the States. Hilder's work became well known through the card publishers Royle's who used a wide selection of his views, especially winter scenes (known recently as "Hilder-scapes"!).

There were one or two artists who dabbled with the Sketch Club in the 'seventies. One was Michael Foreman who joined for two or three years. He was well known for his book illustrations. He invited a camera crew to film the inside of the Club for a "possible' *Omnibus* programme. It was the only time a television crew was allowed into the Club: should the videotape (circa 1976) still be available it would be an invaluable memento. No doubt it is buried somewhere in the BBC archives.

Foreman, born in Pakefield, Suffolk, in 1938, has become one of Britain's most prolific book illustrators. His work is distinctive for its sensitivity and curiously luminous effect. He found out by accident that he had purchased Hassall's old School of Art in Stratford Studios. In the 'seventies he divided his time between London and St Ives in Cornwall.

Another member was the "pop" artist Peter Blake who joined the Club in the late 'sixties or early 'seventies. Blake was not a regular attender but was also fascinated by the London Sketch Club. At the time he was teaching at the Royal College of Art while living at the Old Station House in Bath — no mean feat! He was particularly interested in Dudley Hardy's paintings of Bertram Mills' circus: Blake was going through his circus phase. It always struck me as odd that Peter Blake, who spent so much of his life within the art school system, both learning and teaching, should choose popular imagery for his subject matter. Looking at Blake's work as a record of the 'fifties and 'sixties, it is seen to comprise largely of strippers, pop musicians and hulky wrestlers. Was England really like that? Perhaps it was and I just didn't notice.

One of Peter Blake's more memorable commissions from the 'sixties was the cover for the Beatles' Sergeant Pepper album, and I seem to remember some Daimler advertisements. His bravest achievement was to form "The Brotherhood of Ruralists", a daring move unlikely to be commercially successful, but what a wonderful idea! Blake's use of sentimental and popular imagery was part of his quest for definitive subject matter. He faced the same dilemma as his old tutor and mentor Ruskin Spear. Both men used photography in their work, as indeed did Rowland Hilder.

Ruskin Spear came to the London Sketch Club only once. He was more at home in the convivial surroundings of the Chelsea Arts Club, which he treated like a pub. I had the temerity to suggest he be made an Honorary Member of the Sketch Club but my proposal was turned down by the Council. Perhaps it was just as well: when drunk Spear could become belligerent. Over the years Ruskin Spear confided many

A. R. Thomson, RA (1895-1980)
Tommy Thomson was a frequent visitor to
the Sketch Club, often accompanied by his
son, who would help him up the stairs. In
his latter days he relied on a walking stick,
and would scribble down jokes on scraps of
paper: he had withstood the handicap of
being deaf and dumb to become a successful
portrait painter. Born in Bangalore, India,
he went to the Margate School for the deaf,
where the headmaster took much interest in
his painting. He later studied under C.M.Q.
Orchardson at the John Hassall School of
Art and became a mural decorator and
caricaturist. One notable work was a nine-
foot painting of the House of Lords in
session, which contained 170 recognisable
portraits. He became an Associate of the
RA in 1938 and joined the London Sketch
Club in 1969.

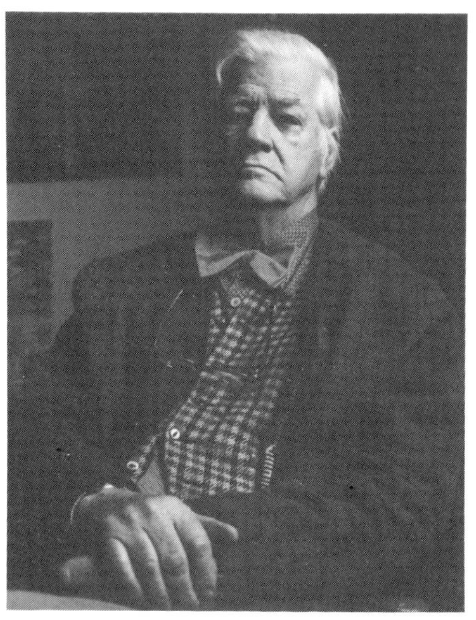

recollections to me but one that he failed to mention was that he used to drink with
Dylan Thomas on a regular basis. Had I known this I would have been much more
wary!

The secret to Ruskin Spear's survival was that he could drink heavily one night
and then go for a few days without a drink at all before imbibing once again. On one
of his drinking bouts in his local he found the juke box particularly loud and
offensive. When his frequent requests to "turn it down" were ignored, he stormed
over to it and kicked it with his artificial leg: his foot went straight through the front
of the machine. Spear was barred from that hostelry but found another a short
distance away.

Ruskin Spear was my special guest in 1975 when, like everyone who joins the
Sketch Club, it was my turn to take the chair. With him he brought Carel Weight,
RA and Robert Buhler, RA who together with Tommy Thomson, RA made a team
of four RAs in the Club that night. It was a tremendously successful evening with
Mac (Stan MacMurtry) and Jak (Raymond Jackson) the cartoonists also present.
There was also a welcome return for David Langdon, and other guests included
Oscar Nemon, the sculptor and Reggie Bosanquet.

For a brief moment I realise just what those old smoker suppers had been like. The
camaraderie was there; the wit was there. Spear caricatured Buhler and Buhler
caricatured Spear on the back of old fag packets. Reggie Bosanquet told a lewd joke,
and the entertainment after the meal was superb. It was the one and only time I
managed to get the whole Club together. Long after Sidney Peak and Harold
Goodrich had sung the "Gendarmes" and "Watchman" (the London Sketch Club
theme tune, which always brought the Friday night evenings to a close), Ruskin
Spear was still tinkling the ivories with a glass of whisky in one hand. I seem to
remember walking through my front door at 5 o'clock in the morning having spent
most of the night trying to see Ruskin Spear home. I have only vague recollections of
that night, despite being in the capable hands of Freddie Deane.

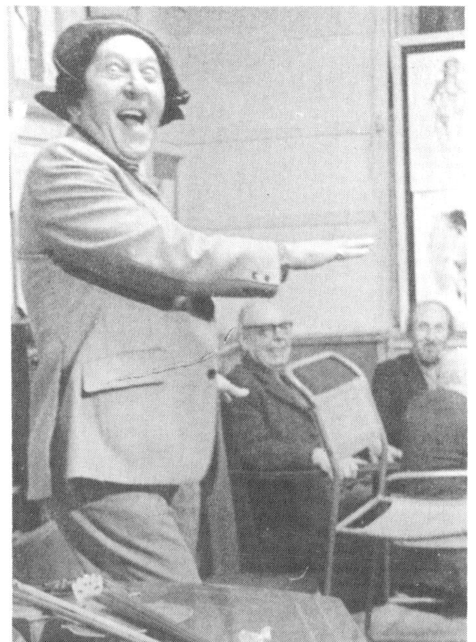

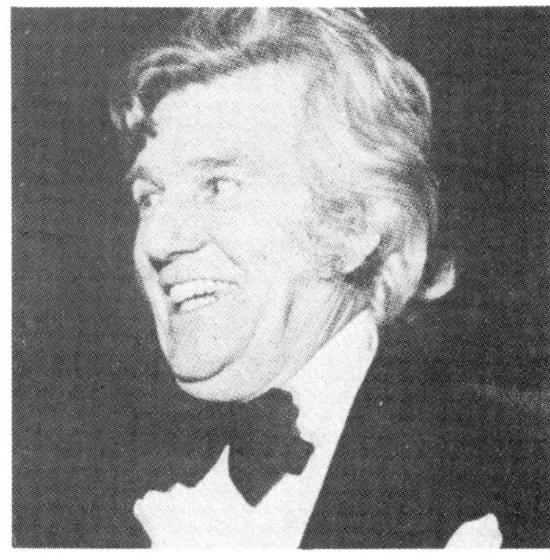

(*Left*) Nick Nissen, a wonderfully talented comedian in the style of Danny Kaye, could also play the violin. In the background are Adrian Bury and Oscar Nemon.

(*Above*) Harold Taylor (1909-1992) the magician was born in Didcot, Berks, where his father was organist. He became interested in magic whilst a Flight Lieutenant in the RAF during the Second World War. His first professional engagement was at the Windmill Theatre; for a time he shared a flat with Tony Hancock. Coming to the Sketch Club as a guest of Harry Riley in the 'fifties, he joined in 1965. He was a member of the Inner Magic Circle, President of the British Ring of the International Brotherhood of Magicians and a Member of the Grand Order of Water Rats.

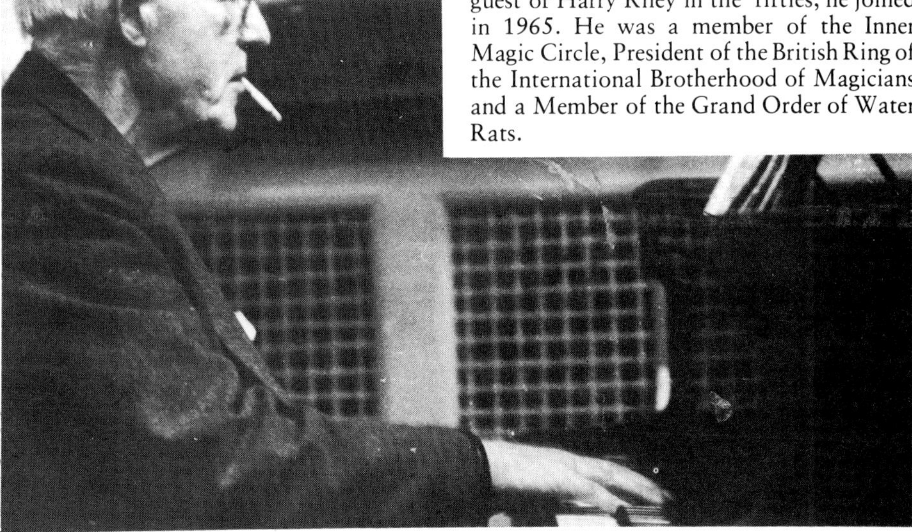

Joe Hannah ("Joanna on the pianna") could sight-read with the proverbial cigarette dangling between his lips.

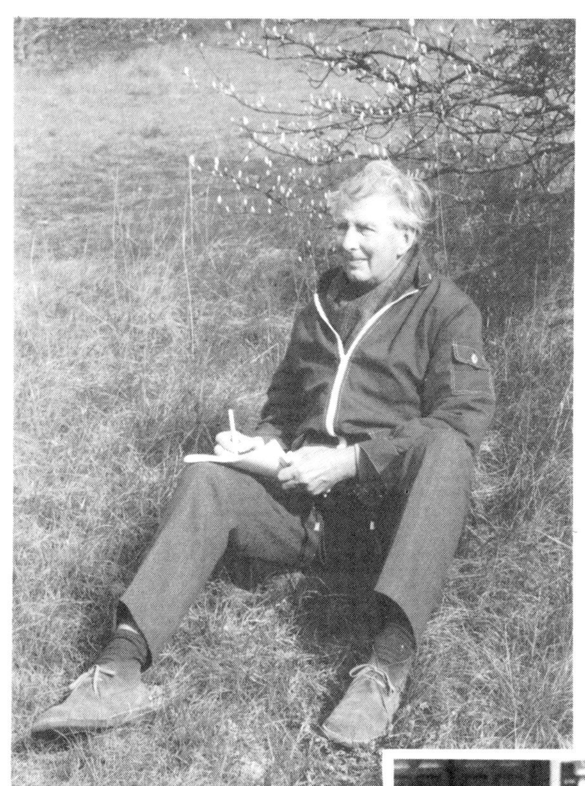

Rowland Hilder (a guest of the Sketch Club) out sketching.

Adrian Bury's real name was Albert Buhler. However he worked and lived under the name of Adrian Bury, RWS. He joined the London Sketch Club in 1967. In the background are Stirling Dick and Bill Clements.

Not long after this the London Sketch Club were invited to entertain the Chelsea Arts Club. In the team were Robert Easton, Joe Beechus, Fergus Anckorn and others, and although the evening was immensely successful it was not the same somehow. Something was missing, and for the life of me I cannot say what the missing ingredient was. The invitation was made by Bill Thompson, then Chairman of the Chelsea Arts Club. He was a Canadian who had married the daughter of Henry Williamson (of *Tarka the Otter* fame). After the experience of being Chairman of the Chelsea Arts Club from 1975 to 1977 he rarely seemed to visit it! If the London Sketch Club had problems, they were miniscule compared to those of the Chelsea Arts Club.

In many respects it was a great thrill to be Secretary of the London Sketch Club. I could pick up the phone and talk to old-timers like Lunt Roberts or Edgar Norfield. But it was a love-hate relationship. Although I enjoyed listening to Lunt Roberts' enthusiasm for golf and Edgar Norfield's love of Cambridge, where he was born, it was an unpaid vocation, yet I seemed to spend more time on the Sketch Club than I did on the job for which I was being paid.

Edgar Norfield, who collaborated for many years with Charles R. Benstead illustrating books such as *Hic, Haec, Hock!, Steady Boys Steady, Alma Mater* and *Mother of Parliaments* had bought Frank Hart's old studio in Lewes. Whilst Daphne Silas, the widow of Ellis Silas, was as charming a person you could hope to meet, she was a wary old bird. I purchased one of Ellis Silas's paintings from her but my salary and indeed my lifestyle could stand only so much.

In this dilemma over finances I thought a public exhibition might do the trick. The Club had not had a public show since 1936 and had relied instead on exhibitions within the Club. A public exhibition might win some sorely needed publicity, *might* even make a profit. I managed to persuade the Council it was a good idea, and, although it did not make a profit, neither did it make a loss!

David Langdon produced the invitation card and Adrian Bury wrote a piece in *The Antique Collector*; Tom Robinson collected pieces of memorabilia from the Club and the exhibition was ably hung by Don Blake. Entitled the London Sketch Club and Friends Exhibition, it included certain artists from outside the Club, notably David Shepherd. Members who supported the exhibition included Walter Lambert, Ashton Cannell, Eric Thorp, Leonard Boden, Derek Mynott and Aubrey Sykes. The exhibition did indeed receive some good publicity but the attendance was poor, set, as it was, in the Mall Galleries. I felt as if I had let the artist members down: many had exhibited on my recommendation but sales were poor. It was a gamble, and not one I should like to repeat.

The two artist members whom I knew best from the London Sketch Club were Walter Lambert (who joined back in 1946) and Eric Thorp. Walter Lambert and his wife Babs lived in a delightful flat on Richmond Hill, near the actor John Mills. The view from their front door overlooking London and the Thames was breathtaking. Lambert had worked as a commercial artist for most of his life, starting way back in 1919 under Tom Purvis. The firm that Lambert joined was the Avenue Press, who also employed another London Sketch Club member, S. T. C. Weeks. In his remembrances Lambert said of Weeks: "He was a very good friend of the Sketch Club and often entertained with conjuring and card tricks and was also a good raconteur. His commercial work covered a wide field and his serious painting was of the Impressionist school — he had a lovely sense of colour and design." The star of the Avenue Press was Frank Brangwyn who produced numerous lithographs and posters during the First World War and into the 'twenties. Lambert's first job was to clean palettes and brushes for Tom Purvis, a stickler for accuracy. He also had to keep Purvis's extensive reference file in order. Purvis was a workaholic who had been influenced by the American J. C. Leyendecker. He was probably the most successful poster artist of the inter-war years and designed War Bond advertisements during the Second World War: these featured a portrait of Purvis's son. Lambert learnt his craft from these two commercial artists and went on to produce posters and advertising showcards of his own. One of Lambert's memorable posters was for a portable gramophone in the 'twenties, produced for His Master's Voice. It was only in later life that Lambert turned to fine art, drawing upon his commercial training and pioneering a use of pastels blended with water-colours or gouache. The effect was stunning and quite individual. He exhibited regularly at the Pastel Society. One day his portraits of the 'fifties and 'sixties which show the influence of Arthur Ferrier will realise their true value in the saleroom.

Eric Thorp, who was just as studious as Lambert, was a marine painter. He lived in a large Victorian semi in Tooting Bec with his wife Margery. A near neighbour of theirs had been another good London Sketch Club member, Oliver Brabbins, who drank himself to an untimely death. Unlike Lambert, who received a regular income from a commercial studio, Thorp lived off irregular sales of his paintings, helped by Margery's renting off part of their huge house to paying guests. He once told me about a painting he had done of the Burtons' yacht moored on the Thames. Either Elizabeth Taylor or Richard Burton enquired of the gallery owner how much the painting cost. "Six!" was the intrepid reply, which gave pause for much thought. The enthusiastic gallery owner blurted out: "At six hundred, it's very reasonably priced!" The Burtons left immediately. "Had it been six thousand I might have stood a chance!" Thorp complained to me.

Eric Thorp (1901-94) was the son of John Thorp, a model maker who helped Bomber Harris in the Second World War by producing replicas of German cities to be used during pilots' briefings. Another example of his work, "Old London before the Great Fire in 1666", is in the British Museum. This eye for detail was passed from father to son. After his education at the City of London School Eric took up painting, claiming modestly that he "was useless at everything else". He trained at the Royal Academy School and was a member of the Langham and the Wapping Group of Artists, and President of the London Sketch Club in 1972.

After two thankless years as Secretary of the London Sketch Club I thought it time to step down. My chirpy replacement was Norman Hemsley, son of Harry May Hemsley. Norman was a quiet, modest man. I feel sure the job he undertook lessened his lifespan considerably. He was naturally shy; the Sketch Club needed someone more forceful to take the reins, though there was nothing very complicated about the day to day running of the Club. I suspect Norman Hemsley took over the job because no-one else would do it.

My own memories include Marlene the cook, a lady of mixed Italian extraction whose standards of hygiene left much to be desired. Admittedly she worked on a limited budget, but in tailoring her expenditure nearly poisoned the entire Club — twice! On the second occasion it was felt, in the interests of self preservation, it was best if Marlene left. Albert the barman came to our rescue, introducing Rosemary, who is still cooking for the Sketch Club some twenty years later. Albert Wallis the barman stayed with the Club some considerable time. He saw the good and the bad sides of the Club but never commented. How he lived off the pittance we paid

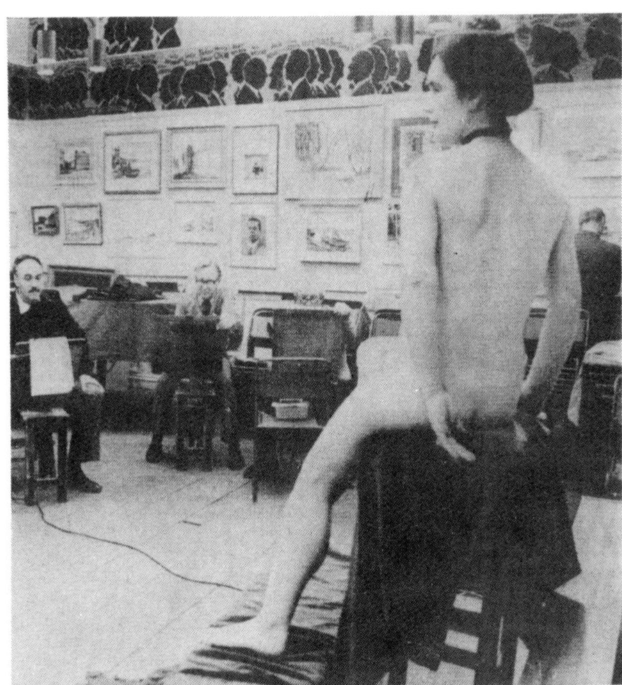

The Tuesday life class.

(*Left*) Yvonne Vinall is the model. Sketching in the background are Ashton Cannell, RSMA (1928-94) and (with specatacles) Ken Hardy. The man standing in the corner with his back to the model is Don Blake, RI.

(*Below*) The sketchers are (*left to right*) Stirling Dick, Ley Kenyon, George Chambers, RI and Michael Egan.

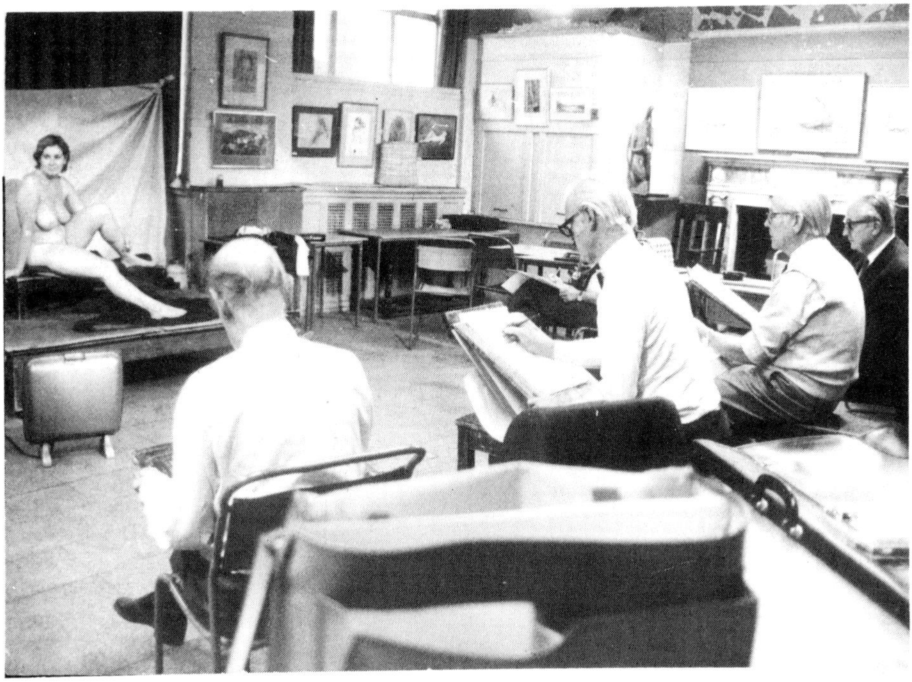

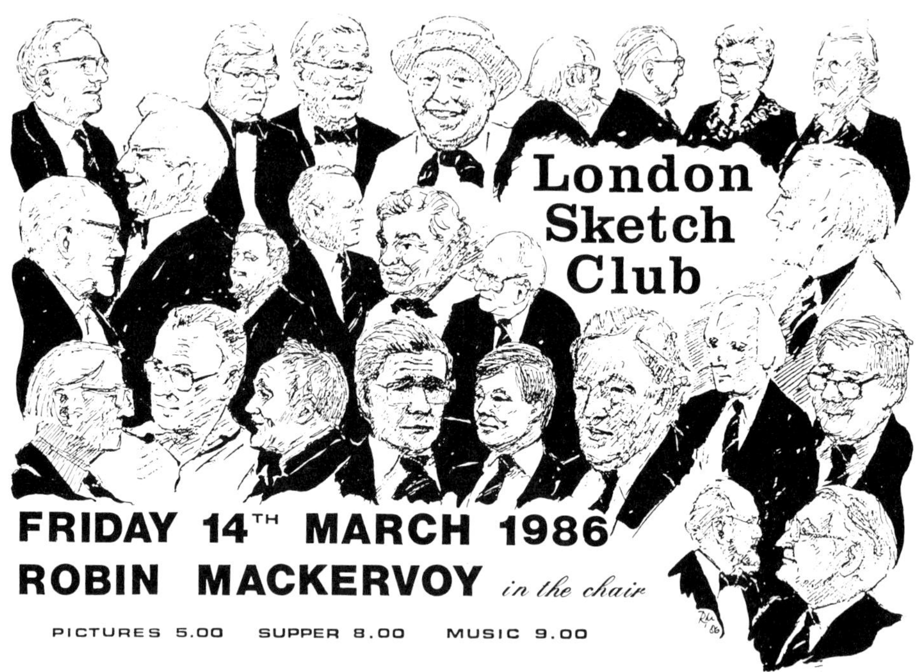

Robin Mackervoy's invitation card captures some members of the London Sketch Club. Easily recognisable are Ley Kenyon, Bernard Bays, Will Raymont, John Seabrook, Fergus Ankorn, Ian Collins and Cliff Swann.

him I will never know, but he remained cheerful; occasionally members would buy him a drink to supplement his meagre nights' earnings.

As in most societies, the work of keeping the London Sketch Club going rests on just one or two pairs of shoulders. In the 'seventies those shoulders belonged to John Seabrook and Don Blake who between them put in a fearful amount of time and effort. The Club was also fortunate to find John Fletcher to succeed Norman Hemsley as Hon Sec; he in turn was succeeded by the very capable Gathorne Butler. These unsung heroes, like many Sketch Club members before them, have given of their time and energy most graciously. To them and to those that follow I can only reiterate the Sketch Club cry "For ...!"

APPENDIX I

1902

LONDON SKETCH CLUB MEMBERSHIP
The Continental Gallery, 157 New Bond Street

President
Dudley Hardy RI

Vice-President
John Hassall RI

Hon Solicitor
W. Sanders Fiske LLB

Hon Treasurer
Walter Fowler RBA

Hon Secretary
René Bull

Hon Auditor
Paul Bevan MA

Bankers
The London City &
Midland Bank,
Richmond

Council
Cecil Aldin RBA
Tom Browne RI RBA
Walter Churcher
George J. Frampton RA
W. Lee-Hankey RI
Giffard H. Lenfestey RBA
Phil May RI
Lance Thackeray RBA
Claude Shepperson RI
Montague Smith

Members
W. Affleck
*Cecil Aldin RBA
J. J. Alsop RBA
A. Ashdowne

Members–*contd*
H. Baker
Lys Baldry
James Barr
K. Bell
E. Warren Bell
R. D. Benn
Paul Bevan
A. W. Binstead
S. Blake
Guy Boothby
H. Bowen
J. P. Brodhurst
H. Bromhead
*Tom Browne RI RBA
René Bull
J. Cahn
R. Canfield
*Walter Churcher
E. P. Edkins Clarke
H. P. Clifford RBA
R. W. Clifton
W. Coggeshall
W. W. Collins RI
A. E. Craven
Edward O. Davey
A. Diosy
Dr Conan Doyle
A. East ARA
A. S. Edward RBA
Lionel Edwards ARCA
E. T. Edwardes
*W. Sanders Fiske LLB
J. A. Fitzgerald
*W. Fowler RBA
G. J. Frampton RA
Innes Fripp
Austin Fryers
A. Granville
E. J. Gregory RA PRI
G. C. Haité RI RBA

Members–*contd*
W. Lee-Hankey RI
Hans Hansen RSW
*Dudley Hardy RI
John Hassall RI
John Dingwall Hassall
C. Van Havermaet
C. Hayes RI
Alfred Hayward
H. M. Hemsley
Cecil J. Hobson RI
Hal Hurst RI
F. Ernest Jackson
F. Hamilton Jackson RBA
Adrian Jones
Champion Jones
Reginald Jones
Nico W. Jungmann
A. Kinsley RI
P. G. Konody
F. Latham
Chas J. Lauder RSW
Arthur Layard
Geffard H. Lenfestey RBA
A. Lillie
A. Linden
Sir James D. Linton RI
A. Loraine
C. Lowe
Ernest H. Macandrew
A. K. Macdonald
Frank H. Mason
J. W. Mathews
Alex J. Mavrogordato
*Phil May RI
Whitworth Mitton
Frankfort Moore
H. E. Nicholls
Frank A. Nott
W. Odell
C. Q. Orchardson RBA

Members–*contd*
L. Owen
E. L. Pattison
H. H. S. Pearse
R. S. S. Baden-Powell
Prof Yorke Powell
Julius M. Price
A. E. Proctor RBA
J. Pryde
Cecil W. Quinnell
W. Raymond
Frank Reynolds
H. K. Rooke RBA
Charles M. Sheldon
F. Newton Shepard
Claude Shepperson RI
S. Smith
Montague Smyth
F. Spenlove-Spenlove RBA
Mel Spur
W. H. Squire
F. Stewart
C. H. Taffs
*Lance Thackeray RBA
Hugh Thomson RI
J. H. Thorpe
Hans Trier RBA
H. H. Vincent
Percy Wadham
Lawrence Walker
Ford Waltham
Frederick Walton
Aaron Watson
Harry Watson
W. Peter Watson RBA
J. Whipple
C. Wilson
Tatton Winter RBA
Lawson Wood
Starr Wood
Murdoch Wright

*The names marked with an asterisk are Founders

APPENDIX II

1926

THE LONDON SKETCH CLUB

246a, Marylebone Road, NW1

President
J. McMath Wilson

Vice-President
Alfred Leete

Hon Vice-Presidents
Lieut-General Sir
R. S. S. Baden-Powell
KCB, KCVO

Joseph Harker
Frank Reynolds RI

Council
Reginald Arkell
L. R. Brightwell
Walter Churcher
Thomas Downey
Harold Earnshaw
John Hassall RI
Alex. Lawson
Alfred Leete
A. J. Mavrogordato
Charles Robinson
Harry Rountree
Montague Smyth ROI

Council–*contd*
G. E. Studdy
Fred Taylor RI
Charles D. Ward ROI
Wilton Williams

Hon Treasurer
A. J. Wilson

Hon Secretary
Edgar L. Pattison

Assistant Hon Secretary
J. McMath Wilson

Secretary
C. V. Sharman

Dance Committee
J. McMath Wilson
Alfred Leete
Charles D. Ward
Roy Hardy
Charles Robinson
Neil MacLaren
Thomas Downey
Wilton Williams
Edgar L. Pattison
(Hon Sec)

APPENDIX III

1968

LONDON SKETCH CLUB MEMBERSHIP
7 Dilke Street, Chelsea SW3 4JE

President
Tom Robinson

Working Members (Town)
Jox de Alberdi ARBS
Bernard Bays
Phillip Bawcombe FRSA
Arnold Beauvais
John Skene Bennett
Denis Berbank
A. Bilibin
F. Donald Blake RI
Leonard Boden ARPS
Marcus Boss
Oliver Brabbins RI
Kenneth Brookes RI
C. J. K. Bulloch
Adrian Bury RWS
H. T. Chevins
William Herbert Choat
William C. Clements
J. B. P. Cole
C. E. Cundy
Harry Dixon ARCA
A. Dobrowolski
F. C. Emberton
R. S. Embleton ROI
Lawrence Farman FRIBA
R. E. Forrest
P. Gascoigne
D. L. Ghilchik ROI
R. Gibbs

Working Members (Town)—*contd*
K. L. Graham NRD, FRSA
H. Greenwood FRIBA
R. Ken Hardy
S. G. Hearn
Edwin Hunter
Fred Johnston
Norman Keene
Walter R. Lambert PS
Frank Leah
Warwick W. Lendon
Maurice Litten RP
Fred Mancini
John M. Merrylees
Derek Mynott RBA
D. A. Neill
N. E. Osborn
E. R. Parker
L. A. D'Arcy Pearce
Charles E. Pierce RI
T. E. Robbins
Lunt Roberts
Tom H. Robinson
Oliver Robinson
Ellis Silas FRSA, RGS
C. H. Smith
Ron V. Somers
K. B. Stack
John Strevens
G. Henry Stringer
Aubrey Sykes RI
W. Szomanski

Working Members (Town)—*contd*
W. Eric Thorp RSMA
R. L. Tumelty
Cecil Wade
C. T. White
R. A. Wilkin
I. D. Wilson
H. R. A. Winslade
T. Dug Wray
G. Wylde

Working Members (Country)
Denis Alford
F. Ball CBE
M. B. Blackshaw ARIBA
R. W. Boorer
D. C. Buckland
Jackson Burton
R. Calloway
M. A. B. Campbell
L. C. Caswell
G. Chambers
R. B. P. Evans
V. R. Furnival
H. F. Holt
Kenneth B. Hunter
M. J. Kerr
Chas A. Munro MBE
A. E. Nobbins
Edgar G. Norfield
Terence Patrick

Working Members (Country)—*contd*
John Pritchard
Basil Reynolds
Gayford Rix
Robert Sharps
Frank Sherwin RI
Geoffrey Squire
M. Tadman
S. Tresilian
Bert Wilson

Lay Members
B. R. Bannister
W. S. Bavin
E. Benfield
Joe Bernstein
Ronald Brush
Robert Cole
P. Cookman-Roberts
Ronald Deighton
Lewis Gavin MD
Harold Goodrich
K. B. Hardy
E. J. Jackson
I. de Keyser
Lewis Laking
Rex Mawby
A. Monk
Charles Skilton Hon RWS
C. J. Songhurst
Michael Stall
C. Stevenson

Honorary Members
Fergus Anckorn
George Anderson
Field Marshal Sir Claude Auchinleck
HRH Prince Baudouin De Ligne
Joe Beechus
Murray Browne
Harry Brunning
Jack Byfield
Lt Col The Earl Cadogan
Fred Curzon
Edward Cutler
Robert Easton
Frank Edwards
Tudor Evans
(Egg) Goldring
L. J. W. Gould
F. Gregory
G. Hancock
Joe Hannah

Honorary Members—*contd*
John Hargreaves
Norman Hemsley
B. C. Hilliam
Stanley Holloway
Sir W. O. Hutchison PPRSA
Major W. J. Jackson
Cecil Johnson
R. Kilby
H. J. Kimbell
John Lewis
Calvin McCord
Leslie Murchie
Noel Noble
Terence O'Donoghue
Henry Oscar
F. G. Parsons
Sidney Peak
J. Pierce
H. J. Pointing

Honorary Members—*contd*
Lewis Powell
Percy Press
Arthur Richards
John Robinson
Thomas Round
Stanley Rubinstein
Leslie Sarony
Gordon Sears
C. V. Sharman
Arthur Sims
Sir John Slessor (Marshal of the RAF)
Robert Sydney
Harold Taylor
Laurie Wilde
Clay Thomas
Robert Wilson
Harry Young
Brett Stevens

APPENDIX IV

August 1993

LONDON SKETCH CLUB MEMBERSHIP
7 Dilke Street, Chelsea SW3 4JE

Life Members
F. Donald Blake FI, RSMA
William Innes PS, UA
Oliver Robinson
John Seabrook

Town Working Members
M. J. R. Armytage
Bernard Bays
Gunter Beetz
Jonathan Berbank
Daniel Broadley
Keith Burtonshaw UA, NP
Gathorne V. Butler MA(Cantab), FBIM
Ashton Cannell FRSA, RSMA
Robert Churchill
Arthur Cotterell UA
Michael D'Aguilar
Paul D'Aguilar
John Patrick Egan
Michael Egan FRIBA
Oliver Elmes
Tom Espley NDD, DFA
Clifford Fisher
John Fletcher
Sydney Roley RSMA, UA, SGA
Brian Gallagher
Philip Gascoine
Denis Gilbert NEAC
Reg A. Graham
Michael G. Gregory
Frederick Hill FRIBA
Deh-Ta Hsiung
Keith Macpherson Hutchinson
Peter Jordan
Alex C. Koolman RP, RBA, PS
Robert Lane FRICS
David Lloyd-Smith
Andrew Lodge
Martin Millard
Bernard Myers
William Newton
David Nicholson
Ken Paine PS
Charles R. Patrickson FABA
John Paul
Roy Pettitt
Arthur James Ranson
John F. Richardson ATD, Dip. Art Hist.
(London), FRSA
Anthony J. Rickards
Adrian Rose
Peter Sanderson, FRIBA, UA, NS
Michael J. Stanger

Town Working Members
–contd
Talim Sunil
Aubrey Sykes PPRI, PPPS
Norval Taylor MB, ChB, MRCP
Paul Telling
James Barrie Temple
W. A. L. Thomas
The Rt. Hon. Baron Thorneycroft
CH, PC, RBA
John Philip Turner
Chris Waddington
D. E. Walduck RAS, SGA. SWLA, FRSA
Bob Warren
Michael John Warren
Ron Whittenbury
Guiliano Mario Zampi

Country & Overseas Working Members
David Addey AADipl, RIBA
Lee Malcolm Andrews
Herbert Choat
David Cuppleditch
William G. Duxbury
Donald Fisher
Sydney Gusman
Geoffrey Humphries
Alojzy Kiziniewicz
Robin Mackervoy
Kenneth Mercer ERD, ATD, DA
Willi Retzler
Angus McNeill Stirling DA
Henry Stringer
Dennis J. Syrett
Angus George Waddington
Jack Widgery
Bert Wilson

Lay Members
John Cooper Brass FRCS
Ian Collins
Alan Fuller FRCS
Lewis D. M. Gavin MD, MRCGP, OStJ
Ronald Paul Gozdeck
Peter Grecian
Kenneth Green
Ken B. Hardy
Douglas Haynes
Nick Hemsley
Alan Joel BSc, BDS(NZ)
Stephen J. Kingshott
James Richard Ley
Peter Lucas CEng, FIMechE, MIGasE
E. Donald Page MD

Lay Members–*contd*
Tony Parkins
Wilfred George Reid
Clifford Swann AMInstMP
Geoffrey Thomas BA
John R. Welsh
Fred H. Wernham

Honorary Members
Fergus Anckorn
Julian Baker
Geoffrey Bowyer
Gerard Bryant
Leonard Chave
David A. Cohen
Michael A. B. Crow
MBBS MRCGP DRCOG
George Crozier
Laurence Cuckney LRAM
Michael S. Dolovitch
Dr Andrew Doughty
T. G. Duggan
Lt-Col E. G. Goldring
Terence Guyatt
Austin W. Hutchison
Stephen Jackson
Maj W. J. Jackson ARCM, MBE
Donald Job
George Kazanzi
Robert Langston
Conrad Leonard
Billy McComb
Keith McDonald
Leslie Murchie FGSM, LRAM, AGSM
Nick Nissen
John V. Palfreyman
Percy Press
Tom Ellis Roberts
Thomas Round
John Rubinstein
Joseph Sentance BA(Cantab),
Mus.B(Dublin), FRCO, FTCL
Bill Shine
H. Charles Smith FRSA, UA
Jack Templeton
Carl Thomas
Evan Ross Thomas
Geoffrey Vince
John Wade
Michael Wakeham
Laurence A. Wilde
George Smith Williams
Robert Wilson
Harry P. Young

APPENDIX V
PAST PRESIDENTS

1898-1902 G. C. Haité RI, RBA
1902-03 Dudley Hardy RI
1903-04 John Hassall RI
1904-05 W. Lee-Hankey
1905-06 Cecil Aldin RBA
1906-07 H. Hughes Stanton
1907-08 Tom Browne RI
1908-09 Walter Fowler RBA
1909-10 Frank Reynolds RI
1910-11 Lance Thackery RBA
1911-12 Chas Dixon RI
1912-13 Montague Smyth ROI
1913-14 Joseph Harker
1914-15 Harry Rountree
1915-16 Walter Churcher
1916-17 A. J. Mavrogordato
1917-19 A. J. Wilson
1919-20 Edgar L. Pattison
1920-21 W. Heath Robinson
1921-22 G. E. Studdy
1922-23 Alexander Lawson
1923-24 Thomas R. Downey
1924-25 J. McMath Wilson
1926-1927 Charles Robinson RI
1927-28 Chas D. Ward ROI
1928-29 L. R. Brightwell
1929-30 Wilton Williams
1930-31 Ellis Silas FRSA FRGS
1931-32 W. H. Barribal
1932-33 S. T. C. Weeks
1933-34 Charles Bryant ROI, RBA, ARBC

1934-35 Harry Riley RI
1935-36 Fred Buchanan
1936-1937 Arnold V. Beauvais
1937-38 George M. Parlby
1938-39 Geo S. Dixon
1939-40 R. J. Lunt Roberts
1940-41 S. Van Abbé ARE, RBA
1941-42 Norman Lloyd ROI, FRSA
1942-43 D. L. Ghilchik ROI
1943-44 Fred Gardner
1944-45 F. Donald Blake RI
1945-46 H. Greenwood FRIBA
1946-47 Eric Parker
1947-48 H. L. Oakley MBE
1948-49 Bertram Prance
1949-50 Victor MacClure
1950-51 William Showell
1951-52 Edward Bishop RBA
1952-53 Kenneth Brookes RI
1953-54 Cecil Wade
1954-55 Charles E. Pierce RI
1955-56 Henry Coller
1956-57 H. R. A. Winslade
1957-58 Kenneth Graham NRD
1958-59 Jackson Burton
1959-60 Warwick W. Lendon
1960-61 A. E. Berbank NRD, FRSA
1961-62 William A. Watkins RI
1962-63 Tom E. Robbins
1963-64 John Merrylees

1964-65 Oliver Robinson
1965-66 Harry Weatherill
1966-67 Harold Goodrich
1967-68 Fred Mancini FRBS, FRSA
1968-69 T. H. Robinson
1969-70 L. D'Arcy Pearce
1970-71 R. Gibbs
1971-72 Bernard Bays
1972-73 W. Eric Thorp RSMA
1973-74 Rex Mawby
1974-75 G. Henry Stringer
1975-76 W. C. Clements
1976-1977 Lawrence Farman FRIBA
1977-78 John Seabrook
1978-79 Edward Snoad
1979-80 F. Donald Blake RI
1980-81 Frederick Hill
1981-82 Will Raymont
1982-83 William Innes
1983-84 Bob Lane
1984-85 Norman Hemsley
1985-86 Cliff Swan
1986-87 Ken Hardy
1987-88 Geoff Thomas
1988-89 Reg A. Graham
1989-90 Robin Mackervoy
1990-91 John Brass
1991-92 Fergus Anckorn
1992-93 Clifford Fisher
1993-94 Peter Sanderson

APPENDIX VI
SELECT BIBLIOGRAPHY

J. A. Hammerton. Humorists of the Pencil. Hurst & Blackett, 1905

L. Lambourne. Caricature. HMSO, 1983

C. Holme. The Royal Institute of Painters in Watercolours. The Studio, 1906

P. Bradshaw. Lines of Laughter. W. H. Allen, 1946

G. Rogers. The Arts Club. Truslove & Hanson, 1920

C. White. The World of the Nursery. Dutton, 1984

S. Dark. Not Such a Bad Life. Eyre & Spottiswoode, 1941

J. B. Booth. Palmy Days. The Richards Press, 1957

J. B. Booth. A Pink 'Un Remembers. T. Werner Laurie, 1937

P. Hodgson. The War Illustrators. Osprey, 1977

N. Bentley & L. Russell. The English Comic Album. Michael Joseph, 1948

D. Hudson. James Pryde. Constable, 1949

J. Thorpe. Happy Days. Gerald Howe, 1933

F. Reynolds. Humorous Drawings for the Press. Methuen, 1947

T. Jeal. Baden-Powell. Hutchinson, 1989

B. Peppin & L. Micklethwaite. Dictionary of British Book Illustrators. John Murray, 1988

C. Beetles. Mabel Lucie Attwell. Pavilion, 1988

D. Cuppleditch. Phil May — The Artist & His Wit. Fortune Press, 1981

D. Cuppleditch. The London Sketch Club. Dilke Press, 1978

The Artist Magazine. The Artist Publishing Co., 1932

The Artist. Artist Publishing, 1897

The Studio. Vols 1908 & 1911

T. Cuneo. The Mouse & His Master. New Cavendish Books, 1977

P. Bradshaw. Brother Savages & Guests. W. H. Allen, 1958

K. Howard. My Motley Life. Ernest Benn, 1927

L. Edwards. Reminiscences of a Sporting Artist. Putnam, 1947

A. Watson. The Savage Club. Fisher Unwin, 1907

H. M. Bateman. By Himself. Collins, 1937

A. Anderson. The Man Who Was H. M. Bateman. Webb & Bower, 1982

R. Heron. Cecil Aldin — The Story of a Sporting Artist. Webb & Bower, 1981

C. White. Edmund Dulac. Studio Vista, 1976

J. Hamilton. William Heath Robinson. Pavilion, 1992

W. Heath Robinson. My Line of Life. Blackie, 1938

P. Bradshaw. Art in Advertising. Press Art School, c.1930

P. Bradshaw. Drawn from Memory. Chapman & Hall. 1943

B. Hillier. Posters. Weidenfeld & Nicolson, 1969

INDEX

Main references are in **bold** type. Illustrations references are given in *italics* after text references. Continuous text references ignore illustration pages, e.g. May, Phil 6-14 (where pp. 7, 10, 13 consist of illustrations).